POLITICAL CHANGE
IN UNDERDEVELOPED COUNTRIES

POLITICAL CHANGE

edited with an original essay by JOHN H. KAUTSKY
Associate Professor of Political Science
Washington University, St. Louis

IN UNDERDEVELOPED COUNTRIES

Nationalism and Communism

JOHN WILEY AND SONS, INC.

New York · London · Sydney

SEVENTH PRINTING, APRIL, 1967

LIBRARY OF CONGRESS CATALOG CARD NUMBER: 62–14650
PRINTED IN THE UNITED STATES OF AMERICA

For Lilli

PREFACE

This book originated in an attempt to summarize and integrate in a brief article some thoughts on the politics of underdeveloped countries that had been developed in my teaching and research on comparative politics. Much to my surprise, this article grew into the essay that now constitutes the first part of the present book. It occurred to me then that it could be far more useful if published in conjunction with a number of outstanding contributions by other authors on the same subjects as my essay—useful both to the undergraduate student and layman in search of a general introduction to the politics of underdeveloped countries and to the advanced student and area specialist in need of some broad integrating hypotheses.

I would like to think that the result, while retaining some of the obvious advantages of books of readings, differs significantly from most works of this kind. Rather than combining bits and pieces of a great number of writings, all probably useful from some point of view, but following quite different approaches, I have here reproduced only twelve articles, but have reproduced these (including their footnotes) without any cuts or changes. Above all, I have sought to attain a high degree of unity throughout the book, so that it can be read in its entirety, rather than serving merely as a source of selections. Unavoidably, this unity had to be bought at the price of excluding many excellent writings, for example certain case studies of politics in particular underdeveloped countries and articles proposing approaches to the study of the politics of underdevelopment. That others were regretfully omitted simply for lack of space needs no emphasis.

The articles included in this book were selected because each of them develops, in its own way, one of the major themes in my essay (and they are arranged roughly in the sequence in which I take up these themes). In this fashion they are all interrelated, and my essay, though written independently, rather than as an introduction to them, serves to tie them together. Of course, the approaches taken by the authors of the twelve articles differ in some respects. Thus, some are inclined to introduce their value judgments into their discussions, while others seek to avoid this as far as possible (as I do in my essay); some make explicit the policy implications of their conclusions, others (like myself) prefer not to do so. But all are chiefly concerned with analysis and the formulation of explanatory hypotheses, and all therefore make a contribution toward a theory of politics in underdeveloped countries. All, furthermore, focus their analyses on the major groups and group conflicts in underdeveloped societies, all look on politics as dynamic and changing, and all seek explanations for the changes.

Merle Kling and George Blanksten are both concerned with the development of theory based on the comparative study of groups. Kling develops a theory of the politics characteristic of some traditional societies, while Blanksten deals with the groups to be found in such societies as well as in those subject to some modernization. James Coleman refines the distinctions among the various movements which have been lumped together under the label "nationalism," and systematically analyzes the factors contributing to and conditioning nationalism in an underdeveloped area.

Edward Shils explores the past, present, and probable future attitudes and role in politics of the intellectuals, the group most responsible for bringing political change to underdeveloped countries, while Harry Benda examines the functioning of this group, and particularly of the "military intelligentsia," as the ruling class in such countries. Mary Matossian explains and illustrates some of the ambiguities in the ideologies developed by intellectuals in underdeveloped countries under the impact of Western influences.

George Lichtblau inquires into the peculiar relationship between intellectuals and organized labor in the process of industrialization; he also alludes to the neo-Maoist strategy. Its adoption by the Communist parties is analyzed and documented by Bernard Morris and Morris Watnick. Neo-Maoism, now somewhat outdated, was important as a transition to the present role of Communism in underdeveloped countries. The development of that new role is traced by Bernard Morris. Joel Carmichael then studies the present "nationalist-Communist symbiosis" in its relation to changes in the Soviet governing élite.

Morris Watnick explains the appeal of Communism to the nationalist intellectuals, and thereby contributes to an understanding of both nationalism and Communism in underdeveloped areas. Finally, Richard Lowenthal, in a review article, investigates the attractions and

the probability of a totalitarianism of intellectuals and specifically of
its Communist form in underdeveloped countries.

I have based this book on the assumption—and hope to substantiate
it—that useful generalizations can be made about politics in underdeveloped countries. Nevertheless, some of the articles included in it
are devoted to particular underdeveloped areas. It has not been my
objective to "cover" each area separately in this book (though, in fact,
each major underdeveloped area is dealt with in at least one article).
Rather, these seemingly more specialized articles were selected, because, like those seeking to generalize about the politics of all underdeveloped countries, they use approaches and develop hypotheses that
can be usefully applied in areas other than those their authors studied.

A volume of this sort need not be "up-to-date" in the sense of cover-
ing the latest events in underdeveloped countries. If the theories and
generalizations suggested here are as good as I hope they are, they
should be able to help account for developments with which their
authors were not yet familiar. Most of the articles are of fairly recent
date and none is more than ten years old. My own essay was completed
in 1960, though some footnote references to subsequently published
writings were added during 1961.

The writer of a sweeping essay like mine cannot hope to acknowledge adequately his debts to those from whom he learned without
writing an intellectual autobiography. I do, however, want to express
my gratitude to three remarkably perceptive students of politics who
have, at various times and in very different ways, helped shape some
of the thoughts I develop here (frequently in a fashion no doubt un-
acceptable to them)—Merle Kling, Morris Watnick, and my late uncle
Benedikt Kautsky.

My colleagues in the Department of Political Science at Washington
University, Merle Kling, Roy C. Macridis, and Robert H. Salisbury,
as well as Professors Rupert Emerson at Harvard, Robert C. Tucker
at Indiana University, and Morris Watnick at Brandeis University, all
read the entire manuscript of my essay. Its present form owes much
to the numerous suggestions I received from them. Each of them
offered me his valuable advice and encouragement. Each of them also
expressed disagreement or doubt regarding some of my interpretations
—as, I suspect, any knowledgeable reader will. That none of them is
responsible for any errors of fact or interpretation in my essay needs
no emphasis.

I am also grateful to many students in several of my courses and seminars who, as a captive but critical audience, helped me clarify my thoughts, and particularly to Arnold Leder, who, as my graduate assistant, did some valuable bibliographical work.

My essay was written during a semester's leave from my teaching duties, which was financed by a grant from the Ford Foundation to the Department of Political Science at Washington University. I am deeply indebted to both the Foundation and my Department for thus facilitating my work. I also thank the Graduate School of Arts and Sciences and the Social Science Institute at Washington University for grants for secretarial services and, above all, Mrs. Dorothy B. Conard, our Departmental Secretary, for her ever cheerfully and efficiently rendered assistance.

I am very grateful to the authors and publishers who have given me their kind permission to reprint their articles.

Last but not least, I am (permanently) in debt to my wife, whose encouragement and patience have been of immense help in this as in all my work, and to whom I dedicate this book.

JOHN H. KAUTSKY

St. Louis, Missouri
February, 1962

THE CONTRIBUTORS

HARRY J. BENDA is Associate Professor of History at Yale University. He was in business in Indonesia between 1939 and 1946 and has taught at the University of New Zealand, Cornell University, and the University of Rochester. Professor Benda is a co-author of *New Era in the Non-Western World*, and the author of *The Crescent and the Rising Sun: Indonesian Islam under the Japanese Occupation, 1942–1945* and of articles on Asian history and politics.

GEORGE I. BLANKSTEN is Professor of Political Science at Northwestern University. He has served as political analyst in the Department of State, and has been a visiting professor at the University of California, Los Angeles, the University of Chicago, and Ohio State University. He has also been Smith-Mundt Exchange Professor at the National University of Mexico. Professor Blanksten has received fellowships, including one from the Social Science Research Council, to do research in Cuba, Ecuador, Argentina, and other Latin American countries, and is the author of *Ecuador: Constitutions and Caudillos, Perón's Argentina*, and numerous articles on Latin American politics. He is a co-author of *Government and Politics in Latin America, Foreign Policy in World Politics*, and *The Politics of the Developing Areas*.

JOEL CARMICHAEL is the editor and translator of Carl Brockelmann's *History of the Islamic Peoples*, of Nikolai Sukhanov's memoirs, *The Russian Revolution, 1917*, and of Theodor Dan's *The Origins of Bolshevism*. He also edited *An Illustrated History of Russia*, and is the author of numerous articles on Soviet and Middle Eastern affairs.

JAMES S. COLEMAN is Professor of Political Science and Director of the African Studies Center at the University of California, Los Angeles. He has done research in West, East, and Central Africa as a Fulbright Scholar and under Rockefeller Foundation and Carnegie Corporation awards. He is a member of the Committee on Comparative Politics of the Social Science Research Council, and of the Board of Directors of the African Studies Association. Professor Coleman is the author of *Togoland, Nigeria: Background to Nationalism,* and numerous articles on politics in Middle Africa. He is co-editor and a co-author of *The Politics of the Developing Areas.*

John H. Kautsky is Associate Professor of Political Science at Washington University, St. Louis. He has also taught at the University of Rochester. He was a research analyst in the Department of State, a Research Associate in the Center for International Studies at the Massachusetts Institute of Technology, and a Research Fellow at the Russian Research Center at Harvard University. Professor Kautsky was the recipient of a Rockefeller Foundation grant, and is the author of *Moscow and the Communist Party of India* and of a number of articles on Marxism and Communism.

Merle Kling is Professor of Political Science at Washington University, St. Louis. He has served as visiting professor at Mexico City College and at the University of Illinois. Professor Kling is the author of *The Soviet Theory of Internationalism, A Mexican Interest Group in Action,* a forthcoming study of the role of unconventional warfare in Castro's rise to power in Cuba, and several articles on Latin American and Soviet politics.

George E. Lichtblau is a labor economist who has held several government positions specializing in international labor affairs. He has also lectured in this field and is the author of a number of articles on trade union internationals, labor, and socialism in underdeveloped countries.

Richard Lowenthal is Professor of International Relations at the Free University in West Berlin. He served for many years as foreign affairs commentator of *The Observer* (London) and has been a contributor on Soviet and Communist politics to numerous journals. He is the co-author of a political biography of Ernst Reuter and of *The Sino-Soviet Dispute,* and is at present at work on a comparative study of totalitarian revolutions.

Mary Kilbourne Matossian is Assistant Professor of History at the College of Education, State University of New York in Buffalo. She was a Research Associate in the Research Program on the History of the Communist Party of the Soviet Union at Columbia University, and was a Research Fellow at the Harvard University Center for Middle Eastern Studies where she did research on Kemalism. Professor Matossian is the author of a forthcoming book on *The Impact of Soviet Policies in Armenia.*

BERNARD S. MORRIS is Adjunct Professor of International Relations in the School of International Service at the American University, and is a political analyst in Washington, D.C. He is the author of numerous articles, which have appeared in professional journals, on international Communist affairs.

EDWARD A. SHILS is Professor of Sociology and Social Thought in the Committee on Social Thought at the University of Chicago, and is a Fellow of King's College, Cambridge. He has also taught at Harvard University and at the Universities of Paris, London, and Manchester. Professor Shils is the translator of works by Max Weber and Karl Mannheim, co-editor of *Toward a General Theory of Action* and *Theories of Society*, and the author of *The Torment of Secrecy: The Background and Consequences of American Security Policies* and of numerous articles in sociology and on the politics of underdevelopment.

MORRIS WATNICK is a Lecturer in Politics at Brandeis University. He has also taught at the University of Washington and has done research and editorial work in the Department of State, the Ford Foundation, and the United States Information Agency and been a Research Fellow in the Russian Research Center at Harvard University. He is the author of several articles on Communism and the translator of a forthcoming American edition of Rudolf Hilferding's *Das Finanzkapital*, and is at present working on a book on Georg Lukacs.

CONTENTS

AN ESSAY IN THE POLITICS OF DEVELOPMENT
by John H. Kautsky

Introduction: The Approach of this Study   3

I. The Politics of Underdevelopment and of Industrialization   13

Social divisions in traditional agrarian societies, 13
Politics in traditional agrarian societies, 18
The impact of industrialization on social divisions and
    politics, 22

II. Nationalism   30

Nationalism in Europe, 30
Nationalism apart from nationality, 32
Nationalism as anti-colonialism, 38
The role of the intellectuals, 44
Unity and diversity in anti-colonial nationalism, 49

III. Communism   57

Pre-revolutionary Russia as an underdeveloped country, 57
Marxism, Leninism, and the Russian Revolution as a nationalist
    movement, 62
Three decades of proletarianism, 70
Neo-Maoism and nationalism, 73
The convergence of Communism and nationalism, 79

IV. Totalitarianism and the Future of Politics in the
Developing Countries   90

The methods of totalitarianism, 90
The totalitarianism of the aristocracy and its allies, 97
The totalitarianism of the intellectuals, 106
Democracy, 113

SELECTED ARTICLES

1. Towards a Theory of Power and Political Instability in Latin America

    Merle Kling   123

2. Political Groups in Latin America

    George I. Blanksten   140

3. Nationalism in Tropical Africa

    James S. Coleman   167

4. The Intellectuals in the Political Development of the New States

    Edward Shils   195

5. Non-Western Intelligentsias as Political Elites

    Harry J. Benda   235

6. Ideologies of Delayed Industrialization: Some Tensions and Ambiguities

    Mary Matossian   252

7. The Politics of Trade Union Leadership in Southern Asia

    George E. Lichtblau   265

8. Current Communist Strategy in Nonindustrialized Countries

    Bernard S. Morris and Morris Watnick   282

9. Recent Shifts in Communist Strategy: India and South-East Asia

    Bernard S. Morris   293

10. The Nationalist-Communist Symbiosis in the Middle East

    Joel Carmichael   304

11. The Appeal of Communism to the Underdeveloped Peoples

    Morris Watnick   316

12. The Points of the Compass

    Richard Lowenthal   335

AN ESSAY IN THE
POLITICS OF DEVELOPMENT

JOHN H. KAUTSKY

Introduction:
THE APPROACH OF THIS STUDY

This study is an essay in the literal sense of that word: it is an attempt and one that may be described more or less charitably as daring, risky, or irresponsible. It is an attempt to develop some very broad generalizations and hypotheses about the politics of societies undergoing the process of change from agrarianism to advanced industrialization.[1] Not only are there all over the world countries with very different cultures that are presently in the midst of this process,

[1] The use of the terms "Western" and "non-Western" to distinguish between industrialized and non-industrialized countries has been avoided in this essay for a number of reasons. It implies that there is a clear dichotomy between two social and political systems where, in fact, there is a continuum whose range is better suggested by the terms "underdeveloped," "developing," and "advanced." It even has certain undesirable static implications, for non-Western countries will always geographically be in the "non-West"—though the clumsy term "Westernization" seeks to overcome these implications. Further, there are countries of "Western" culture that are underdeveloped (i.e., "non-Western"), e.g., Ireland, Spain, Portugal, and the countries of Latin America, and, on the other hand, "non-Western" countries that are industrially advanced, e.g., Japan and also North Korea. Finally, the term "Western" is frequently applied to the Western powers (sometimes including their underdeveloped colonies and allies) to distinguish them from the Soviet-dominated "East"—but the latter includes some of the most highly industrialized countries.

Gabriel A. Almond and James S. Coleman, *The Politics of the Developing Areas* (Princeton, New Jersey: Princeton University Press, 1960), and particularly Coleman's conclusions to this important book, pp. 532–576, summarizing and comparing the principal characteristics of the political systems of underdeveloped countries, are highly relevant to the present essay. So is the excellent general analysis of the process of modernization of underdeveloped countries in Max F. Millikan and Donald L. M. Blackmer, eds., *The Emerging Nations; Their Growth and United States Policy* (Boston and Toronto: Little, Brown and Co., 1961), pp. 1–90. The selected bibliography of this book (pp. 161–168) is extremely useful, particularly in listing works on the economic aspects of modernization, a subject largely ignored in the present essay. Hugh Seton-Watson, *Neither War Nor Peace* (New York: Frederick A. Praeger, 1960), in spite of its title, deals to a considerable extent with the same subjects as this essay. Though quite different in its scope and approach, it reaches some similar conclusions, and furnishes a wealth of highly relevant supporting and illustrative data.

but the now highly industrialized countries passed through it in the past. Therefore, although this essay does not pretend to account for the historical evolution of Western Europe and the United States, because it ignores factors peculiar to these areas in order to focus on the present-day underdeveloped world, it must necessarily operate with very broad categories of analysis.

For example, by the last chapter, we will have found that it is useful to distinguish five types of politics and government—traditional aristocratic authoritarianism, a transitional stage of domination by nationalist intellectuals, totalitarianism of the aristocracy, totalitarianism of the intellectuals, and democracy. To mistake such a typology for an adequate description of any or all existing political systems would clearly be indefensible. There are, in fact, an infinite number of variations, subtypes, and mixed and transitional forms that make it impossible to find any of the five types in pure form. Yet, it is felt, there is virtue in developing these pure types and in analyzing them as if they existed, because only such generalization makes comparison possible, and, in turn, only comparison permits the formulation of further generalizations and hypotheses, i.e., the further development of our understanding of politics.[1]

On the one hand, then, the problem is not to employ too many categories of analysis and not to regard each phenomenon, each system as unique—which would make comparison impossible. On the other hand, if too few categories are used, what may be fruitfully viewed as different phenomena may be artificially forced into a single category, thus blurring some essential characteristics. Thus, one of our main concerns here will be to fit Communism into a larger category, to demonstrate that far from being something unique, it can be regarded as part of the larger movement of nationalism in underdeveloped countries. Similarly, Stalinist totalitarianism emerges as one variant of a

[1] For very general treatments of the differences between the political processes in advanced and in underdeveloped countries and of their significance for the study of comparative politics, see George McT. Kahin, Guy J. Pauker, and Lucian W. Pye, "Comparative Politics of Non-Western Countries," *The American Political Science Review*, XLIX, No. 4 (December 1955), 1022–1041; Gabriel A. Almond, "Comparative Political Systems," *The Journal of Politics*, XVIII, No. 3 (August 1956), 391–409; Dankwart A. Rustow, "New Horizons for Comparative Politics," *World Politics*, IX, No. 4 (July 1957), 530–549; and Lucian W. Pye, "The Non-Western Political Process," *The Journal of Politics*, XX, No. 3 (August 1958), 468–486, and comments on that article by Alfred Diamant, "Is There a Non-Western Political Process?," *The Journal of Politics*, XXI, No. 1 (February 1959), 123–127. See also Almond's introduction to Almond and Coleman, *op. cit.*, pp. 3–64 for an attempt to develop a functional theory of politics to permit comparison of different political systems.

THE APPROACH OF THIS STUDY

more general phenomenon, the totalitarianism of the intellectuals. By thus relating the narrower to the broader phenomenon, it is hoped that a contribution can be made to the understanding of both. On the other hand, the nationalist movements, including Communism, are not put in the same category as Fascist movements, nor is the totalitarianism of the intellectuals, including Stalinism, combined with Fascist totalitarianism in a category simply labeled totalitarianism. To do so would obscure some basic characteristics of both.

Obviously, what we regard as the important similarities and differences depends on our view of what constitute the basic characteristics of a system, i.e., on our conception of politics. Without such a conception to guide our efforts, one category of analysis is as good as another, and the comparative approach is as likely to produce trivial results as it is to bring to light significant interrelationships. In fact, no comparison can proceed without some underlying theory, whether it is made explicit or left implicit, whether, indeed, it is held consciously or unconsciously, and it is the theory that determines what categories of comparative analysis are used. Thus, if party systems are regarded as the crucial element in politics, it is quite reasonable to group Hitler's Germany, Stalin's Russia, and Nkrumah's Ghana in one category and to distinguish these from, say, Horthy's Hungarian Fascism and Sukarno's Indonesian nationalism, since neither of these operated chiefly through a one-party system. If the *Fuehrerprinzip* is regarded as a key element in politics, all the systems just mentioned might go in one category, but Japanese Fascism and the Communism of a number of Eastern European satellites will have to go into quite another one, separate from German Fascism and from Soviet Communism. If ideology is seen as fundamental, Hitlerite and Nasserite nationalism become similar to each other but different from Indian or Nigerian nationalism, which seek to unite people of many different languages, while Soviet Communism and German Social Democracy might go into the same category because of their common professions—significantly watered down in both cases in recent years—of proletarianism and, indeed, of adherence to Marxist principles.

An essay of this type, then, must, in order to make its approach understandable, be preceded by a statement of the theory of politics on which it is based. Ours is an interest group theory of politics, a theory which, stated briefly,[1] sees politics as conflict of interest, as compe-

---

[1] Though interest group theories vary, the single most widely accepted statement of such a theory is probably David Truman, *The Governmental Process* (New York: Alfred A. Knopf, 1951). A very useful initial attempt to analyze the politics of an underdeveloped area by means of group theory and to point out its

tition among people with different interests, generally united in groups defined by an interest, for the limited resources, such as wealth and prestige, available in the governmental arena. If government is the arena of the conflict, those who constitute the government are not impartial umpires, however, but, on the contrary, are themselves the contestants in the conflict or, more probably, the representatives of the conflicting interest groups. This will suffice to explain why this essay focuses on the group or interest (or interest group) content of every movement and political system it considers and seeks to explain their institutional and ideological forms as functionally related to this content.

Two points about the way in which interest group analysis is here employed should perhaps be added, one on the nature and one on the motivation of the groups. It will be immediately obvious that the groups dealt with in this essay are chiefly social classes: the three pre-industrial classes of the aristocracy, the peasantry, and the old middle class and the three industrial classes of the capitalists, the workers, and the new middle class. Is our theory not more Marxian than Bentleyan [1] then, although a key group in our analysis, the intellectuals, and also the new middle class, are not classes by Marxian standards? There is no question that the basic concepts of the theory, which are that politics results from conflicts of interests and that governments represent certain group interests rather than a mythical public interest, were fundamental aspects of Marx's thought, and hence considerably antedate Bentley.[2] The emphasis on dynamics in our analysis, whose principal theme is social and political change, may also be viewed as Marxian, though any good theory of politics must be able to account for the process, or dynamics, of politics.

However, according to Marxian theory, the conflicts that constitute politics are always "basically" class conflicts, the interests represented

significance for comparative study appears in George I. Blanksten, "Political Groups in Latin America," reprinted on pp. 140–166, below.

[1] Arthur F. Bentley, *The Process of Government* (Chicago: University of Chicago Press, 1908) is the work to which modern interest group theory commonly traces its ancestry.

[2] Joseph A. Schumpeter regarded Marx as "the founder of modern political science" for this very reason. "The Communist Manifesto in Sociology and Economics," *The Journal of Political Economy*, LVII, No. 3 (June 1949), 199–212, p. 209. It might well be argued, however, that behind Marx's emphasis on conflict there lurks a notion of the general interest, which would triumph after the class struggle is transcended. James Madison, in No. 10 of *The Federalist*, clearly saw politics as group conflict long before either Marx or Bentley, but also explicitly combined this with a belief in a public interest.

by governments are invariably primarily class interests, and the motor of all political change is the class struggle. These assumptions are not shared by the writer of this essay. We rely heavily on class analysis simply because, in the societies dealt with, classes as such play a significant role in politics. Some of them at least, especially pre-industrial ones like the aristocracy and the peasantry, are often recognized by everyone in the society as separate groups; they are not merely categories imposed on the subject by the observer for purposes of analysis. In the period of industrialization some of the most important conflicts of interest are, in fact, class conflicts. This, incidentally, explains why Marx put such emphasis on the class struggle, for he lived during and analyzed this period, though he mistook it, at least in England, for capitalism close to its highest point of development. But Marx overgeneralized from his observations; class conflict plays no key role in the politics either of agrarian societies or of advanced industrial societies. Most of our essay, however, is devoted to the transitional period between these two stages, where group analysis can hence take the form of class analysis. Finally, class analysis is employed here, because classes are convenient categories for the kind of broad generalizations in which we must necessarily deal. Of course, this does not imply that classes are homogeneous and monolithic and that there are no conflicts within them, or that the leadership of a class always represents the interests of the membership. Whether a class can be regarded as a group is an empirical question. It depends on whether it behaves as a group and whether interests are widely shared among its members. On the matters of concern to us here, it would appear that by these standards classes can validly be regarded as groups, but this assumption is clearly subject to refinement in the light of specific research.

A word should be added on our view of the motivation of the actors in our story. Interest group theory often seems to imply that groups perceive their interests rationally and act accordingly. This essay certainly will suggest that the landowning aristocracy everywhere opposes land reform, that industrial workers everywhere tend to form trade unions. But such suggestions are not necessarily based on the assumption that these groups behave in this fashion because they ought rationally to do so. Rather, our generalizations are based on historical evidence: groups in a certain position have, in fact, behaved in a certain manner, whether their motivation was rational or irrational. What motivates them, whether, indeed, there are the same regularities in their motivations as are observable in their overt behavior, these are questions of obvious importance, but they need not concern us here.

Can an essay that does not even pretend to add significantly to the present store of fairly widely known data yet hope to make even a slight contribution to the development of political science as a science? Those who identify the accumulation of data with science mistake an important part for the whole of the scientific process. Data alone cannot even tell us which data are important or in what relation they stand. Hence they tell us neither how to arrange the data in some meaningful order, so as to make a phenomenon understandable, nor even what further ones we should look for. To lead to at least tentative explanations as well as further research, the gathering of data must be followed by attempts to generalize about them and to sort out regularities of behavior. Only then can we account for the known data by formulating hypotheses, from which sometimes still unknown data can also be deduced. In turn, hypotheses are tested by seeing whether they can account for reality, and they may therefore have to be modified or discarded in the light of newly discovered data. Thus science operates through a union of induction and deduction.[1]

This essay on the politics of developing countries, then, is written on the assumption that not all the pertinent data are now in, but that there are enough of them to make the formulation of generalizations and hypotheses both possible and useful; that to make the available data understandable and to guide the search for more, a theory is needed. The essay is written in the hope that a student not specializing in any underdeveloped area, but generally concerned with comparative politics, can make some contribution to the ultimate emergence of such a theory. Other generalists can subject our generalizations to critical scrutiny, while area specialists can test the hypotheses against their data. Generalizations, and the hypotheses growing out of them explicitly or implicitly, are therefore offered here rather freely. For the sake of simplicity, they are usually stated quite boldly, as if their validity were beyond question. Far from it, they are, in fact, tentative, all subject at best to refinement and at worst to rejection.

It is with the objective of the broadest possible valid generalization in mind that all our interpretations are formulated. No claim is implied that these interpretations are the only possible or correct ones, that they reveal the real nature of the events or developments under discussion. After all, no event, and certainly no complex historical de-

[1] Anatol Rapoport, *Operational Philosophy* (New York: Harper & Brothers, 1953), pp. 47–49. See also David Easton, *The Political System* (New York: Alfred A. Knopf, 1953), particularly pp. 52–63.

velopment, has a single "real nature" of objective validity. The nature of an event is imposed on it by the observer, and he can, depending on his purposes, impose any number of "natures" on it, as long as they are compatible with the objective evidence. Thus, the nationalist movement—the very use of the term involves broad generalization—in underdeveloped countries can variously, but validly, be interpreted, for example, in Latin America as opposition to traditional *caudillismo,* in much of Africa as insistence on "*négritude,*" in Southeast Asia as the effects of Japanese wartime occupation. Certainly the Russian Revolution, which we will regard as another manifestation of this nationalist movement, has commonly been subjected to quite different interpretations. Valid as such interpretations may be, by stressing what is unique and discrete, they make generalization impossible. For our purposes of broad generalization, we prefer to emphasize common characteristics.

Since the only thing underdeveloped countries have in common is their underdevelopment, which is an economic variable, and since this essay is concerned with the impact on politics of industrialization, the interpretation of politics offered here inevitably is an economic one. In fact, non-economic factors, like culture and personality, clearly affect politics importantly (whether they are themselves, "ultimately" and "in the last analysis," the product of economic factors is a question that may be disregarded here as of no practical significance to us). However, if we are to generalize, we are forced to ignore the effects on politics of discrete variables and must concentrate on the effects of the one variable that is general in underdeveloped countries—their economic condition. We can take account of other factors only where they are themselves clearly explicable in economic terms, as when we deal with the effects on politics of the tensions to which peasants are subject upon moving into factories and urban slums or of the personality needs of frustrated intellectuals who have absorbed the values of industrialized societies. In short, in order to point up the effects of industrialization on politics, all variables other than industrialization are being held constant. That this may well affect the validity of our predictions—which, in fact, pretend to be no more than projections of certain trends—is obvious.

One of the most significant factors affecting political change in underdeveloped countries that is not given its due in this essay is the international conflict between the United States and the Soviet Union. It would be tempting and perhaps in some cases not unjustifiable to argue that this conflict affects only the rate but not the nature of political change, that, for example, the Cuban revolution, with its clear involvement in the cold war, follows essentially the same course as the Mexican revolution, which broke out before the Russian Revolution, or that nationalism in Guinea would, at least sooner or later, have developed essentially as it has even if Moscow and French Communists had played no role in it. However, the distinction between the "rate" of change, which is not held "essential," and the "nature" of change, which is, cannot have objective validity. And it would be difficult to maintain that a factor like a major war between the United States and the Soviet Union would not affect the nature of the political development of some underdeveloped countries, as it might, indeed, put an end to such development altogether. It seems hardly necessary, therefore, to repeat that in ignoring such factors we jeopardize the validity of our predictions. Our only justification is our objective—to evolve generalizations about the impact of industrialization on the politics of underdeveloped societies.

Finally, a word on terminology. A necessary prerequisite for the scientific study of any field is the existence of a precise and generally agreed-upon terminology. Only it permits effective communication among students of the field and thus makes possible a cumulative growth of knowledge and understanding. Political scientists are becoming painfully aware that this prerequisite of a precise terminology is almost totally lacking in the area of politics. Some of the most commonly used terms are so ill-defined and devoid of any agreed-upon meaning and so imbued with values in their connotation that they become an obstacle to communication rather than its instrument. The person using such a term can never be certain what it will mean to the person reading or hearing it. Pending a solution to this problem through quantification, which may or may not be practicable, we must nevertheless continue to operate with the present vocabulary of political science.

Like most current discussions of politics in underdeveloped countries, both scholarly and popular, this essay, too, will not try to get along without using such vague terms as "democracy," "nationalism," "Communism," "Fascism" and "totalitarianism." The first of these, in particular, has been applied to such utterly different ideologies and policies, organizations, institutions, and individuals as to have lost all real meaning. We are therefore compelled to resort to a somewhat arbitrary definition of democracy as a political system in which all or most significant groups in the population participate in the political process or, to say the same thing somewhat differently, in which all or most significant interests have access to effective representation in the process of making governmental decisions, i.e., of allocating scarce resources. Such a definition would seem to accord—as it must to be at all widely accepted—with the traditional, conventional concept of democracy, which, though extremely vague, is generally held in the West. At the same time, democracy defined in terms of group or interest participation or representation is related to the substance of politics—the conflict of interest—rather than to the particular institutional arrangements through which the conflict is fought out, such as party systems, elections, representative assemblies, and civil liberties. These may be usefully thought of as more or less reliable symptoms of the existence of democracy rather than factors producing it. Since this definition of democracy is arbitrary, the reader cannot be expected to agree with it; he will, however, have to recall that it, rather than some other definition, is implied whenever the term democracy appears in this essay.

Terms like "Communism," "nationalism," "totalitarianism," and "Fascism" are here defined not arbitrarily but through attempts to analyze the phenomena commonly referred to by these terms. While it is the aim of this essay to throw light on the meaning of some political phenomena rather than on the meaning of some words, it will have accomplished a good deal even if it does only the latter.

I

THE POLITICS OF
UNDERDEVELOPMENT
AND OF
INDUSTRIALIZATION

SOCIAL DIVISIONS IN TRADITIONAL AGRARIAN SOCIETIES

To begin with, it may be useful to limit our discussion of politics to traditional societies in areas with subsistence agriculture, in which neither industry nor a money economy have developed. Such a model will approximate reality more in some underdeveloped countries than in others and will not quite coincide with present-day reality anywhere. It may, however, be assumed to be the starting point of the economic and social changes which virtually all countries are now undergoing.

An analysis of politics requires us to look first at the group divisions of a society. A mere glance at economically very backward countries discloses that the people of most of them are deeply divided along a number of lines. Thus, in many such countries, a variety, sometimes a great variety, of languages is spoken, and the language division is frequently accompanied by more or less deep religious and other cultural divisions. However, such conflicts as exist between immediately adjacent communities, even if these are divided from each other by language or religious lines, are—given the isolation in which most of the population lives—likely to be perceived in purely local terms. Hence they do not give rise to organization and political participation beyond the village or tribal level.

But is there not typically a sharp conflict between the aristocracy and the peasantry in agrarian societies that is of much wider and, indeed, world-wide scope? In fact, politics in such a society does not generally involve a conflict between these two classes. This is true even though or, rather, because they are separated by a vast gulf.

13

Typically, there is a great difference in wealth, but the gulf is by no means bridged where some peasants happen to be rich and some aristocrats poor. For it is also the result of widely different customs and attitudes, sometimes also of differences in language or dialect, themselves the result of quite different ways of life.

The aristocracy is often a warrior caste or is descended from such a caste, originally perhaps a warlike nomadic tribe that conquered the settled and militarily weaker agriculturists in order to exploit them [1]— a hypothesis which would account for the cultural differences between aristocracy and peasantry that often still persist. The aristocracy's main business is intermittent and sometimes almost continuous warfare and government and administration, whether of vast empires or merely large estates with "their" peasants. All are carried on with the goal of maintaining or enlarging the number of peasants and the territory under the aristocracy's control and the degree of their exploitation. The realization of this goal may require no more than military rule and collection of tribute and perhaps some adjudication of disputes—a primitive form of democracy is generally left undisturbed within the peasant village—or may also involve the building and maintenance of roads or systems of irrigation.[2] The administration of religious affairs is also almost always closely tied to that of governmental affairs.

The aristocracy (a term used here sufficiently loosely to include the landed oligarchy of some areas), then, typically consists of the following: the rulers of a territory, whether large or small and whatever their title may be; the armed forces; the bureaucracy, including the judiciary; and the clergy. These may overlap or coincide in different ways, and they may also develop distinct interests of their own and thus come to constitute groups. Where the business of military, governmental, and religious administration requires more people than the aristocracy can or cares to furnish, the lower levels of the armed forces, the bureaucracy, and the clergy are opened up to non-aristocrats, and the aristocracy retains only the higher positions or control of those who occupy them.

Its functions in a traditional agrarian society provide the aristocracy with and require of it a relatively high degree of physical mobility,

---

[1] For an elaboration and some of the sources of this supposition, see my article, "J. A. Schumpeter and Karl Kautsky: Parallel Theories of Imperialism," *Midwest Journal of Political Science*, V, No. 2 (May 1961), 101–128.

[2] For the importance of "hydraulic societies" for the development of "oriental despotism," see Karl A. Wittfogel, *Oriental Despotism* (New Haven: Yale University Press, 1957).

of communication among its members, and of education. In all these respects, the aristocracy differs sharply from the peasantry, and that is so regardless of the specific way in which the former exploits the latter. The aristocracy might (as it does to this day in many under-developed countries, especially in Latin America and the Near East) own virtually all the land, leaving the bulk of the population as dependent peasants, perhaps in some form of serfdom or peonage, but in any case working on land they neither own nor lease. The aristocracy might own big estates, with peasants leasing small parcels of them as tenants or sharecroppers. Peasants might also own their own land, paying tribute to the aristocracy, or being compelled, by force or by their poverty, to work on the large estates as part-time agricultural laborers. Possibly, an aristocracy, as the imperial court and its bureaucracy of scholars in China did, might even own no land at all, leaving it all to be owned by the peasants, either individually or in their village communities, and exploiting them by taking a part of their product in the form of tribute or taxes.

Whatever the system of landownership—and large landownership by the aristocracy in fact prevails throughout much of the underde-veloped world—it remains true that the peasant, simply because he is a peasant in a wholly agrarian traditional society, is generally poor and always ignorant—by the standards not only of industrialized societies but also of his own aristocracy. He is likely to be poor because of his primitive technology, because of population pressure, and because the aristocracy may take from him whatever he produces in excess of his most basic needs. This often means that chronic malnutrition and disease are the fate of a large part of the peasantry. What statistics we have on per capita income and consumption, average dietary level, infant mortality rates, and average life expectancy in agrarian societies all document a material level of life almost incredibly low by the standards of advanced societies.

Even where he is well-fed, however, the peasant is ignorant. He is tied to the soil by the necessities of his work, if not by law, and mobility beyond a very small radius seems to him neither possible nor desirable. Engaged in a subsistence economy, he is dependent on neither imports to nor exports from his small village community. In such a society communications between the village and the outside world are extremely limited, and so, therefore, are the peasant's knowledge of that world and his intellectual horizon. Illiteracy, of course, is general.

Furthermore, in a traditional agrarian economy no capital is accumu-lated and there is hence little change in technology. For centuries

POLITICS IN TRADITIONAL AGRARIAN SOCIETIES

Given the social divisions just outlined, politics in a purely agrarian traditional society cannot consist of conflict among the major social classes. One of these, the aristocracy, is safely and permanently predominant, and the rest of the population, chiefly the peasantry, is in no position to be represented, much less to challenge aristocratic domination. Nevertheless, there is obviously conflict over the control of government and sometimes much governmental instability in economically backward countries. This contest for governmental office is not one among representatives of various interests who seek power in order to favor these interests. Rather, it takes place within the aristocracy, or at least among those who serve its interests. It may be a conflict of individuals within a single aristocratic family, e.g., a royal dynasty, as when, in December 1960, King Saud of Arabia removed his brother from the Premiership and the Imam of Yemen had four of his nephews arrested for plotting against him. Or it may be a conflict between aristocratic families, each with its followers bound to it by the loyalties of the tribe, the clan, or a feudal system.

Frequently, the principal arena of politics is the army, for the armed services constitute virtually the only organized force in wholly agrarian societies. In such countries politics is likely to consist of conflict among cliques of officers for control of the government. As we noted earlier, these officers were at one time generally drawn from the aristocracy and in many countries they still are, but in many cases they may also be non-aristocrats. In becoming officers, however, and particularly in attaining high governmental office, they have no alternative to becoming the political representatives of the aristocracy's interests.[1]

But what is politics, what is the conflict about if the question of which interest shall win does not even arise? The stakes are evidently high, for the conflict can be a very bitter one in which much, even life, is risked. These stakes are the control of governmental offices, not on behalf of the interests of different groups, but for their own sake. Such a conflict, too, is politics, for while the issues do not involve alternative patterns of distribution of scarce resources among major groups, they do involve the distribution among cliques and individuals of what are, in wholly agrarian societies, the exceedingly scarce "resources" of prestige, high social position, and material wealth.

[1] See Theodore Wyckoff, "The Role of the Military in Latin American Politics," *The Western Political Quarterly*, XIII, No. 2 (September 1960), 745–763.

Without the great variety of business enterprises, trade unions, professional societies, churches, and the innumerable voluntary associations and organizations of industrialized societies, positions permitting the exercise of power and influence and the enjoyment of prestige and respect are in very short supply in backward societies.

People of lower class background rarely aspire to the top positions in such a society. Their ability to envisage a changed way of life for themselves is limited, and their acceptance of lower class status is very common. To such talented, ambitious sons of the peasantry and old middle class as may emerge in a rigidly stratified agrarian society, politics (in most cases a career in the armed services or the bureaucracy) is the only road to prestige and high social position, apart from the limited opportunities sometimes provided by the religious hierarchy.

There are not even enough positions providing power and prestige for all aristocrats, however. The younger brothers and sons of landowners and rulers are often more or less excluded from them. Being, unlike the peasantry and old middle class, quite familiar with the privileges such positions can bring, they actively compete for them. This accounts for the nature of politics as a conflict within the aristocracy.

The individual office holder can derive considerable wealth from the control of high governmental office far surpassing his official salary. In the absence of business and industrial activity, such wealth, like prestige and power, is in short supply in backward economies, not only—obviously—among the poor bulk of the population, but also among aristocrats, who cannot all own land or exploit peasants. Corruption among the lower bureaucracy, with which we are not concerned here, is simply necessitated by entirely inadequate salaries. Corruption of high government officials, however, is also such a general phenomenon in backward agrarian societies as to defy explanation by individual character, or, even worse, "national character." Rather, the very nature of politics in such societies would seem to be responsible for it.

Perhaps politicians who do not enjoy the satisfaction of representing the interests and ideals of different major groups, and who, restricted by the interests of the one group they do represent, cannot have the power of making broad policy decisions, must be attracted to their arduous tasks by the prospect of material rewards. Where policy-issues arising from major group conflicts are absent, access to patronage and to more or less honest graft tend to become the only issues in contests for office. Even in Britain, which has since the admission to politics of the industrial middle class often been held up as the model of "clean" politics, corruption was rampant in government as long as only cliques of aristocrats, undivided by major policy differences, were fighting for office. American politics, too, more at some times and levels than at others, tends to substantiate the hypothesis that corruption occurs where major policy issues are absent, even though the absence of such issues is due in this case to causes entirely different from economic backwardness and aristocratic domination.

Room at the top is so limited in agrarian societies, and competition for its occupancy so keen, that there is a high degree of instability in governmental personnel. The frequent misnamed "revolutions" of Latin America have had their counterparts in repeated coups and assassinations of leading government figures in other agrarian areas, such as the Near East and Southeast Asia.[1]

This instability of personnel conceals a high degree of stability of policy. No matter how often the men change and no matter what their individual background, they can govern only if they pursue the same policies—policies that accord with the interests of the aristocracy. Through all changes of regime, therefore, the old social and economic order remains intact, and its continuance is never an issue as long as the society remains free from non-agrarian influences.[2]

This important stability is sometimes further hidden by the tendency of contesting cliques to assume party labels (like Conservatives, Liberals, Radicals, and Socialists) which derive what connotation they have from the experience of industrialized countries and are hence meaningless in an agrarian environment. The same is true of the labels "rightist" and "leftist" which Western observers often insist on attaching to contesting cliques in a futile effort to make their conflicts more understandable to those whose political experience is entirely different.

While political conflicts in purely agrarian societies tend to be of little domestic policy significance with respect to major group conflicts, they may assume considerable importance for international politics. It is not unusual in some areas for a number of industrial

[1] Various methods of capturing power in an underdeveloped area are classified and illustrated by numerous examples by William S. Stokes, "Violence as a Power Factor in Latin American Politics," *The Western Political Quarterly*, V, No. 3 (September 1952), 445–468.

[2] See Merle Kling, "Toward a Theory of Power and Political Instability in Latin America," reprinted on pp. 123–139, below. The important theory presented in this article strongly influenced the preceding paragraphs.

powers, at present especially the United States and the Soviet Union, to lend their support to opposing cliques and try to use them for their own foreign policy goals. In such a situation—one that departs somewhat from our model from which all influences of industry were excluded—these cliques will, in turn, seek to use the foreign industrial countries for their domestic purposes of gaining or holding power, chiefly by securing a maximum of military and perhaps technical aid from them. Much of American and presumably also Soviet arms aid to economically very backward, traditionally ruled countries, like Iran, Afghanistan, and Laos, is in fact not designed to provide the countries against military threats from abroad, but planned to maintain the support of friendly cliques and strengthen them in conflicts with other cliques.

In this fashion, the domestic conflict of personnel in wholly agrarian countries and the international conflict of policy among the major industrial powers can become related, but the relationship is a peculiar one. An alliance between a major industrial power and a clique in the backward country neither is nor can be based on any common purpose, interest, or ideology, because of the utterly different stages of economic development of the two partners. The contesting cliques in the agrarian country, to which "leftism" and "rightism," Communism and democracy, are all equally meaningless, can easily play one industrial power against the other and switch from one foreign ally to the other in a manner totally bewildering to those who take policy labels as used in backward countries seriously. Thus, conflicts like those in 1960 between the "leftist" Lumumba and the "moderate" Kasavubu in the Congo, or between the "leftist" Prince Souphanouvong allied with his half-brother and cousin of the King, the "neutralist" Prince Souvanna Phouma, and the "rightist" General Phoumi Nosavan in Laos are all better understood in terms of tribal or aristocratic clique rivalries than of ideology, though they may come to be of great importance in the international conflict between the United States and the Soviet Union.

All the foregoing shows that government in purely agrarian societies cannot be democratic as we defined that term to denote widespread group participation in politics. An important exception to this statement has to be made with respect to local government. Primitive agricultural communities, like the Russian *mir* until a century ago, the original Swiss cantons, Indian villages, and African or American Indian tribes are frequently governed by some form of direct democracy or an elected leadership. On the "national" level, however, government over inert masses by a small privileged elite, based economically on exploitation of the peasantry and politically on control of the armed forces, has been the rule in agrarian countries throughout history and throughout the world. It prevailed under Egyptian Pharaohs and Chinese emperors, Bourbon kings and Russian Tsars, Indian maharajas and Turkish sultans, Peruvian Incas and Latin American caudillos, until the old agricultural order began to break down.

THE IMPACT OF INDUSTRIALIZATION ON SOCIAL DIVISIONS AND POLITICS

The preceding discussion is essential for an understanding of the present-day politics of underdeveloped countries, even though today no country in the world has not felt the effects of industrialization in one form or another. We must therefore supplement our description of an oversimplified model of a traditional agrarian society by noting briefly and in highly schematic form the effects of the rise of industry on the politics of such a society.

In Western Europe, industrialization created three new classes, initially side by side with the three old classes of the agrarian society—the aristocracy, the old middle class of artisans and traders, and the peasantry. Given the greater fluidity of class lines under industrialism, these new classes are not as clearly separated in fact as the old classes, but for our purposes we may distinguish between the industrial capitalists; the new middle class of white collar workers, professional people, and intellectuals; and the industrial workers. What differentiates all three new classes from the peasant majority of an agrarian society is not only the fact that they have different interests but also that their members can communicate with each other easily, and become aware of these interests, and can organize in their defense. In short, the new classes can participate in politics and offer competition to the hitherto unchallengeable aristocracy for control of the government.

Industry has come to the countries that are or were until recently underdeveloped as an import through colonialism rather than as a native growth. Whether the country is a formal colony or an independent state, its industry is created not by native capitalists but by capital from industrially advanced powers. To begin with, such capital is generally invested in extractive enterprises, such as mines, oil wells, and plantations, established to obtain raw materials for the industrialized countries. The foreign owners of such enterprises constitute a new political force independent of the native aristocracy, but both in independent underdeveloped countries and in colonies, which are generally ruled indirectly through the native aristocracy, the aristocracy shares in one form or another in the profits of the foreign enterprises. A certain community of interest between these two political forces therefore exists. The foreign policy of the country—if it is not, as a colony, deprived of its direction—is likely to be strongly influenced by the foreign owners of its natural resources. In internal politics, the interests of the latter tend towards maintenance of the *status quo* and, particularly, prevention of any expropriation or redistribution of wealth. These interests coincide substantially with the interests of the native aristocracy, whose relation to the rest of the population is not greatly disturbed by the intrusion of this type of industry.

To be sure, the political situation may change, when a group of native industrial capitalists arises, which may or may not happen with the advance of industrialization. Such capitalists, organized in employers' and trade associations, chambers of commerce, and even in individual firms, may wield some influence, which might be directed against the interests of the aristocracy. Thus, where industry produces consumer goods for the domestic market, rather than raw materials for export, it is in the interest of the capitalists to raise the standard of living and buying power of the peasantry, possibly even to advocate land reform. A clash of interests with the landowners then results. Again, industrialists may demand protective tariffs for their infant industries, and landowners may oppose them, since they need to export their agricultural products.

A class of native industrial capitalists appears either relatively late or not at all during the process of industrialization of presently or until recently underdeveloped countries. But a growth of an industrial working class inevitably accompanies the process from its beginning, even while industry is still purely extractive and is entirely foreign-owned. Thus, reversing the historical sequence of developments in the West, a labor movement may become a political force before the native capitalists do. Industrial workers, being in close physical contact with each other, quite naturally organize in defense of their common interests, frequently as soon as industry arises, unless forcibly prevented from doing so. Even in backward Saudi Arabia, the primitive Bedouins employed in the oil refineries soon organized trade unions, though an ineffective regime imposed the death penalty for that crime. While the most immediate conflict of interest of industrial workers is likely to be with their employers over matters of wages, hours and working conditions, the Saudi example illustrates that the very concept of lower class political organization and participation is anathema to and hence opposed by the old aristocracy.

Finally, industrialization creates new groups of white collar workers and intellectuals. The former become numerous only with advanced industrialization, which requires masses of clerks and junior executives, accountants, and sales and advertising specialists, etc. They are not likely to play a major role in the politics of a country passing through the early stages of industrial development. The intellectuals, on the other hand, frequently make their appearance in underdeveloped countries even before industrialization sets in, for they are generally trained in industrialized countries or by their standards. They have everywhere become the key group in the transformation of politics in underdeveloped countries, a role we will discuss more fully in the next chapter. In the meantime, it suffices to state that it is the intellectuals who, more than any other group, are behind the drive for rapid industrialization and modernization in general and that they therefore strike at the very bases of power of the old ruling groups.

If and when the new groups of capitalists, workers, and intellectuals make their appearance as independent actors on the political stage, the very nature of politics is necessarily transformed. As each seeks to have its interests represented in the government, politics ceases to be a conflict for the spoils of office carried on either by aristocrats themselves or by cliques of men who, in their policies, always represent the aristocracy. It becomes a contest among conflicting policies in which even the peasantry and old middle class may here and there participate, in which the aristocracy seeks to save what it can of its predominant social, economic, and political position, and in which each of the new classes attempts to fashion a new society and its political institutions in its own image.[1]

---

[1] For a fascinating attempt to find an index to the change from the old to the new politics in an underdeveloped area, see Merle Kling, "Taxes on the 'External' Sector: An Index of Political Behavior in Latin America?," *Midwest Journal of Political Science*, III, No. 2 (May 1959), 127–150. Many relevant data on Peru, Bolivia, Brazil, Guatemala, and Mexico are to be found in a collection of articles by Richard N. Adams et al., *Social Change in Latin America Today* (New York: Harper & Brothers, 1960). For changes in the Mexican class structure, see also Howard F. Cline, "Mexico: A Matured Latin-American Revolution, 1910–1960," *The Annals of the American Academy of Political and Social Science*, vol. 334 (March 1961), 84–94. How conflicts between old and new social forces resulting from modernization may become intertwined with cultural, linguistic, and religious conflicts is well illustrated in W. Howard Wriggins, "Impediments to Unity in New Nations: The Case of Ceylon," *The American Political Science Review*, LV, No. 2 (June 1961), 313–320. A stimulating attempt to measure in quantitative terms "social mobilization," i.e., the process by which people are moved from traditional to modern ways of life, is made by Karl W. Deutsch, "Social Mobilization and Political Development," *ibid.*, No. 3 (September 1961), 493–514.

Put in the very general terms we have here used, the effects of industrialization on politics appear to be the same in underdeveloped countries of the present as they were in Western Europe during the past century or two (the United States, lacking both aristocracy and peasantry in its background, cannot serve as a relevant model here). In at least one important respect, the ultimate effect is, indeed, the same: industrialization everywhere eventually dooms the predominant economic and social position of the aristocracy and with it the traditional form of aristocratic authoritarianism.[1] However, the process and to some extent the social forces through which this ultimate destruction occurs in underdeveloped countries are generally quite different from those of Western European history.[2]

In Western Europe, the successful opposition to aristocratic rule, then in its absolutist rather than feudal form, came from strata of the old middle classes developing into industrial capitalists. Their opposition was supported to some extent by incipient industrial labor and, in some cases, by peasants who were freed from aristocratic predominance during the conflicts between the old middle class and the aristocracy. In the presently and until recently underdeveloped countries, including Eastern and Southern Europe, the old middle class of artisans and traders never developed sufficient political independence to oppose the aristocracy, as it had in the free cities [3] and strong guilds of Western Europe. Members of the old middle classes in these underdeveloped countries, with few and rare exceptions (as in India), did not accumulate sufficient wealth to develop into industrial capitalists. The only native forms of capital are likely to be in banking

[1] For an interesting theory of the modernization of traditional societies, see Daniel Lerner, *The Passing of Traditional Society* (Glencoe, Ill.: The Free Press, 1958), pp. 43–75. How different types of traditional systems pose different problems for modernization is well shown in David E. Apter, "The Role of Traditionalism in the Political Modernization of Ghana and Uganda," *World Politics*, XIII, No. 1 (October 1960), 45–68.

[2] An excellent introduction to the differences between the political effects economic development had in the West and those it now has in underdeveloped countries, is Harry J. Benda, "Revolution and Nationalism in the Non-Western World," in Warren S. Hunsberger, ed., *New Era in the Non-Western World* (Ithaca, N.Y.: Cornell University Press, 1957), pp. 17–52.

[3] Suggestive contrasts between the development of urban institutions and urban consciousness in advanced and underdeveloped countries are drawn in Bert F. Hoselitz, "Cities in Advanced and Underdeveloped Countries," *Confluence*, IV, No. 3 (October 1955), 321–334. These and related matters are elaborated in three essays on cities in underdeveloped countries by the same author, reprinted in his *Sociological Aspects of Economic Growth* (Glencoe, Ill.: The Free Press, 1960), pp. 159–250.

and commerce, which also existed in Western Europe long before the industrial revolution and which there, too, were not forces opposed to the aristocracy. Industrial capital now comes only as an import, and its foreign owners, as we noted, frequently become allies of the native aristocracy. Thus, in the underdeveloped countries of the present, capitalism is not a principal source of opposition to aristocratic rule, as it was in Western Europe.[1] For reasons we will discuss in the next chapter, its place as the chief foe of the aristocracy and as both the ideological and economic driving force behind industrialization is taken by the intellectuals.

In Western Europe, not only the industrial capitalists but eventually labor, as well, as it grew out of an independent old middle class and sometimes an independent peasantry, could develop strong movements and ideologies of its own, like British trade unionism and French syndicalism. Lacking such a background of independence in the under-developed countries, including Eastern Europe and to some measure even Central Europe, labor tends to come, both ideologically and organizationally, under the leadership of intellectuals.

The movement, led by intellectuals, against the aristocracy and for industrialization has generally taken the form of what is usually called "nationalism" where colonialism has appeared as its most immediate enemy. Where, as notably in Russia, that was not the case, that same movement could also appear in other guises. To analyze the effects of industrialization on the politics of underdeveloped countries, we must therefore now turn to a discussion of the two related phenomena of nationalism and Communism in these countries. These movements inhibit or, at any rate, delay the development of politics into an open conflict among groups with different interests, a development that industrialization favors. Once industrialization has made most of a population organizable and, indeed, organized and capable of par-ticipating in politics, the preconditions of democracy as it was defined earlier are present.[2] But the peculiar form in which industry comes under intellectual leadership to the underdeveloped countries may

---

[1] The differences between the "oriental" and the "bourgeois" revolutions is well summarized by Benedikt Kautsky, "Weltpolitische Tendenzen. Die orien-talische Revolution," *Die Zukunft* (Vienna), No. 10 (October 1951), 258–266, to whom I am indebted for some of the points made here.

[2] See the attempt to analyze the conditions of democracy by Seymour Martin Lipset, "Some Social Requisites of Democracy: Economic Development and Political Legitimacy," *The American Political Science Review*, LIII, No. 1 (March 1959), 69–105, reprinted in rather different form in that author's *Political Man: The Social Bases of Politics* (Garden City, N.Y.: Doubleday & Co., 1960), pp. 45–96. Lipset's attempt to demonstrate, by quantitative methods, a positive correla-

also give rise to totalitarian politics. This type of politics will therefore have to be the subject of much of our last chapter, until we finally return at the end to a discussion of the politics of widespread group participation, of democracy.

Before we proceed to a discussion of nationalism, Communism, and totalitarianism, however, an important point has to be added to this brief analysis of the impact of industrialization on the social divisions and politics of hitherto underdeveloped countries. Much of the foregoing, like references to the growth of a labor movement in the early stages of industrialization but of a substantial stratum of white collar workers only in its later stages, has been based on the experience of industrialization so far. There is some question as to the extent to which this experience will be a valid guide to the future.

Countries now entering upon industrialization do not pass through all the stages of technological development, and of economic, social, and political development, that older industrial countries went through. Rather, industry is likely to arrive in each country in what is, at the time, its most modern form. Thus, when Tsarist Russia began to industrialize at the end of the nineteenth century, its plants were the most advanced in all of Europe, not in spite of, but exactly because of, the late arrival of industry. What was then modern industry required large numbers of manual workers, and this was true until quite recently. Now, however, industry in its most modern form involves automation, and the question arises whether it is this new form of industry with its new social and political consequences, rather than the very different older forms most of us are familiar with, that will be adopted by underdeveloped countries in the future.

Until recently—and perhaps this will be true for some time to come —automation has not been sufficiently developed to play a large role in the industry introduced into underdeveloped countries. Automation may at first appear impractical to those who introduce industry in view of the vast available supply of cheap unskilled labor and the virtual absence of highly skilled technicians and specialists in most underdeveloped countries. These, however, are likely to be obstacles in the short run only. Japan and more recently the Soviet Union demonstrated—and China, India, and some Latin American countries are now demonstrating—that it takes only a few decades to develop adequate numbers of highly trained technicians out of a population consisting largely of illiterate peasants. The problem of

tion between economic development and democracy is expanded to cover all underdeveloped areas by James S. Coleman in Almond and Coleman, *The Politics of the Developing Areas*, pp. 538–544 and 579–581.

accumulating sufficient capital for automated industry may well prove to be far more difficult to overcome.

Underdeveloped countries that begin their industrialization with automated industry will have the same advantage over the now advanced industrial countries that American industry built in the late nineteenth century had over the British industry of the early nineteenth century, or that German industry, rebuilt after World War II, now has over American industry. Perhaps the advantage will be even greater because of the far-reaching difference between traditional machine industry and automated industry. Not only will such countries not be saddled with obsolete industrial plants, which cannot practically and profitably be modernized overnight, but they will not be slowed down by obsolete ideologies that developed with earlier forms of economic organization and change even more slowly than the latter.[1] In underdeveloped countries, such ideologies are held by many of the intellectuals, who absorbed them through contacts with advanced countries, but deep attachment even on their part to these ideologies is often dubious. The great bulk of the population has certainly remained quite untouched by and uncommitted to ideologies like liberalism, socialism, and Communism, which are irrelevant to their traditional agrarian way of life. They are, however—and this is the point made and probably somewhat overstated here—becoming equally irrelevant to industrial societies in this age of automation and eventual abundance, concerned as they are with the questions of the ownership of the means of production and of what to do about poverty-stricken industrial workers. Ownership, being vested in legal fictions like corporations and the state, has effectively disappeared and industrial labor and poverty may ultimately disappear as a result of automation and material abundance.

If this analysis were valid—and it obviously is not wholly valid, for it is based merely on a projection of some trends and ignores some important variables—the ultimate conclusion would be that countries will forge ahead industrially in the future the faster the more backward they now are. "Behold, there are last which shall be first, and there are first which shall be last." One need not accept such a conclusion unreservedly, however, to agree that in dealing with the effects of industrialization on the societies and politics of underdeveloped countries, we cannot operate on the simple assumption that the

[1] On the general problem of the relationship of ideologies and values to economic development, see particularly the first five essays in Ralph Braibanti and Joseph J. Spengler, eds., *Tradition, Values, and Socio-Economic Development* (Durham, N.C.: Duke University Press, 1961).

industrialization, and hence its effects, in the future of these countries will be basically the same as that in the past of the now advanced countries. We cannot, and for our purposes here need not, predict what the social and political consequences of automation will be. We do not have to look so far into the future of underdeveloped countries as to concern ourselves with the effects of general material abundance in a consumption rather than a production oriented society. But neither can we completely ignore the probability that automated industry will produce not a mass labor movement but many groups of specialized personnel with interests distinct from each other but not clearly distinct from those of management. Such an alignment will change the nature of conflict in industrial society, i.e., the nature of politics, and of the forms politics assumes, such as democracy and totalitarianism. These are points on which we will have to touch again in our last chapter.

II

NATIONALISM

NATIONALISM IN EUROPE

Before we can analyze nationalism as the movement through which industrialization comes to the underdeveloped countries, we must deal briefly with the concept of nationalism itself, which, left unexamined, is likely to produce confusion when applied to underdeveloped countries. "Nationalism" is a word constantly used with reference to underdeveloped countries, as if its meaning were entirely clear and to be taken for granted. In fact, the term merely conveys some vague connotations of a striving for "national" independence or "national" unity, which assume what is to be explained, that is, the existence of a "nation" and of "national" consciousness. What meaning the concept of nationalism has is largely derived from European history. If we look for that meaning then, in order to decide to what extent the concept is applicable to underdeveloped countries, we must begin with an examination, as brief and general as possible, of the roots of nationalism as it appeared in Europe.[1]

The rise of a new phenomenon like nationalism can clearly not be explained by the existence of relatively permanent factors like geography, race, religion, or a common culture or tradition, which had existed for centuries without producing nationalism. These factors might inhibit or further its growth, but the original impetus must come from one or more new factors. Such may be found in European history in the growth of commerce and communications and eventually of in-

[1] On nationalism, chiefly of the European variety, see Carleton J. H. Hayes, *Essays on Nationalism* (New York: The Macmillan Co., 1926) and the numerous works of Hans Kohn on the subject, of which his *Nationalism, Its Meaning and History* (Princeton, N.J.: Van Nostrand, 1955) is a convenient brief summary, and also Louis L. Snyder, *The Meaning of Nationalism* (New Brunswick, N.J.: Rutgers University Press, 1954). An original theory of nationality and national sentiment is presented by Karl W. Deutsch, *Nationalism and Social Communication* (New York: John Wiley & Sons, 1953).

dustry, which dissolved the primitive village communities and the narrow provincial boundaries that had limited the lives of most people and which integrated larger areas economically. In this process, many languages and dialects not yet reduced to writing were relatively easily replaced. Fewer languages came to prevail over a much larger geographical area and became firmly fixed by the spread of literacy that accompanies economic development. These major languages then became carriers of cultural elements like literature, certain traditions, and sometimes even religion, and set limits to their spread.

In Western Europe, most notably in France, economic integration in part produced, and was in part produced by, the governmental integration that accompanied the replacement of feudalism by royal absolutism. As commerce and governmental administration affected the lives of more and more people, they had to learn the language of the government, which, in the beginning, was the language of the locality where the government had its seat. Thus, the "King's English" and the language of the Ile de France spread to the point where today only small remnants of Gaelic and Welsh in Britain, of Breton and Basque in France are left, and regional dialects are also disappearing. For two hundred or more years now, the people living under the governments of Britain and, even more, of France, have spoken a single language, a situation then quite novel in history and still quite unusual in much of the world.

With the revolutions of the seventeenth century in Britain and the late eighteenth century in France, broader strata of the population (notably the middle classes) came into a position to influence the government. It became the government of "the people," and the people were defined in terms of their language. Thus, the Bourbon kings had been kings of France, of a territory once inhabited by people speaking various languages or dialects, but Napoleon was emperor of the French, of a people speaking a single language. There now arose the entirely novel identification of the "state," i.e., the government and the territory under its control, and of the "nationality," i.e., the language and culture group, as the "nation." People with a common language regarding a government composed of individuals speaking the same language as "their own" government, or the desire of such people to have such a government, would seem to be an essential element of nationalism as it appeared in Europe.

In Britain and France, the language of the inhabitants had, before the revolutions, been gradually adjusted to the territory ruled by the government so that language and territory became virtually coextensive. Only the broadening of the popular base of government to include non-aristocratic elements, without territorial changes, was sufficient to produce nationalism, the identification of state and nationality. In other sections of Europe, however, notably in parts of the Austro-Hungarian, the Tsarist, and the Turkish Empires, and also in Spain, various languages had become firmly established through the growth of a literature and of literacy before governmental integration had far advanced. Governmental attempts to impose the single language, which had in Western Europe grown naturally under the pressure of changed circumstances, merely tended to arouse resistance and to confirm people in the use of their own languages. Language differences now became politically significant. When in these areas, too, non-aristocratic groups, particularly the urban middle classes and eventually labor (all frequently led by intellectuals), began to demand a voice in government, one inevitable aspect of the demand was that government be carried on in their own language. Only then could they compete effectively in the electoral and parliamentary arenas and be at no disadvantage in their dealings with the courts and the administration, in the armed forces and the universities. Hence democratization in Central and Eastern Europe required not merely changes in the form of government but in the existing territorial units. It resulted eventually in the break-up of the three large multi-national empires that had dominated the area. The same desire to have the territory under a single government coincide with the territory inhabited by people speaking a single language played a part, along with dynastic and other interests, in the unification of Italy and Germany.

NATIONALISM APART FROM NATIONALITY

The concept of nationalism has taken its meaning from the "national" consciousness which began to grow in France with the Revolution, and from the movements that completely changed the map of Central and Eastern Europe during the following century and a half. Nationalism may be defined from this European experience as an ideology and a movement striving to unite all people who speak a single language, and who share the various cultural characteristics transmitted by that language, in a single independent state and in loyalty to a single government conducted in the people's language. A looser and less meaningful connotation of the word nationalism has also been widespread, which would seem to define it merely as the loyalty and emotional attachment of a population, regardless of its language, to an existing government and state. In this sense, one can refer to Soviet, Swiss, Belgian, and American nationalism, though all of these

countries include inhabitants of different language and cultural backgrounds and the languages spoken by at least some of them are also
the languages of other countries.

When we now turn to a consideration of what is generally referred
to as nationalism in the underdeveloped areas, it becomes clear immediately that we are confronted with a phenomenon quite different
from European nationalism. While it might therefore have been pref-
erable to avoid the use of the term with reference to underdeveloped
countries altogether, this would be futile in view of its adoption on
all sides. We can only hope that the use of a single term to designate
the two phenomena will not obscure the differences between them,
that an easy assumption that the "nationalism" of underdeveloped
countries must be like the "nationalism" of Europe will not obstruct
recognition of the quite different forces producing it.

Neither of the two definitions of nationalism we derived from European experience can account for the nationalism of underdeveloped
areas. It seeks to create new independent states and governments
where there were none before. This is clearly a nationalism different
from one that may be defined as loyalty to an already existing state and
government (although, once independent states do exist, this kind
of nationalism may well emerge in underdeveloped countries, too).
However, the nationalism that did create new states in Europe also
proves to be irrelevant for the explanation of nationalism in underdeveloped countries, for in Europe the language or nationality factor
was, as we saw, a key element in its growth. Only the American,
Latin American, and Irish independence movements, for which the
language factor was not responsible, may offer some fruitful parallels
to present-day nationalism in underdeveloped countries. The independence movements in the Western Hemisphere, however, were
directed against colonial powers that were then little more advanced
industrially than their colonies. They differ, therefore, in significant
respects from current anti-colonial nationalism. Ireland, on the other
hand, an agrarian country with a distinct culture, confronted highly
industrialized Britain, and did, indeed, develop a nationalism akin to
that of other underdeveloped countries, though it is located in Western Europe.

Being economically backward, the underdeveloped countries have
not yet been subject (or were not until very recently) to the economic and political integration that created the pressure for the adoption of a single language in large areas of Europe. Nor, as we have
seen, can there be in non-industrialized societies sufficiently widespread participation in politics to provide any large proportion of the

population with the loyalty to "their" government that was essential to the growth of European nationalism. Typically, the more backward a country is economically, the more languages or dialects are spoken in a given area or by a given number of people. There are some striking exceptions to this generalization. Notable are the use of Arabic over a vast area, resulting from conquests which (like the earlier Roman ones) became sufficiently permanent to lead to gradual, voluntary adoption of the language of the conqueror by the conquered, the somewhat similar spread of Spanish and Portuguese in Latin America, and of Russian across northern Asia. Yet, even in these areas, many groups speak languages other than the major ones to this day, and the major ones themselves are frequently subdivided into various dialects.

In most underdeveloped countries, the existence of numerous languages inhibits communication among the population. Thus, the Chinese do not, in effect, speak a single Chinese language, but several mutually incomprehensible dialects.[1] Even more clearly, there is no such thing as a single Indian or Indonesian language. Some ten or twelve major languages and hundreds of minor tongues and local dialects are spoken in India. Some thirty languages are spoken in the Republic of Indonesia, many of them totally unrelated to each other. In territories in which commerce and communications are not even so highly developed as in these three major Asian countries and which have not, like these countries, been united under a single government for centuries, many more languages may be in use. Thus, in Nigeria a population of approximately 34,000,000 speaks roughly 250 different languages, a situation that is not unusual in much of Africa and among the tribes in the interior of Southeast Asia and Latin America. In Australian-ruled Papua and New Guinea, perhaps the most backward area in the world, 1,750,000 natives speak 500 different languages and dialects, no one language being used by more than 50,000 and some by only 300.

In spite of the fact that most underdeveloped countries are inhabited by numerous "nationalities," i.e., language and culture groups, their nationalists have virtually nowhere sought to change the boundaries of their new states to conform to language lines. Apart from boundary changes due to the creation of Pakistan and of Israel, which

[1] The Chinese merely share a single system of writing which, being ideographic, is not bound to any particular language, and is, at any rate, not available to the great bulk of the population. Their intellectuals can communicate in a single language, the Peking dialect of Mandarin Chinese, which serves roughly the same function as Latin in medieval Europe.

were not chiefly motivated by language considerations, and the splitting of Korea and Vietnam into Communist- and non-Communist-governed halves, there have been only two significant boundary changes in the formerly colonial world: the somewhat tenuous linking of Egypt and Syria in the United Arab Republic and the unification of British and Italian Somaliland.[1] In each of these two cases, some, but not all, of the people speaking a single language were brought under a single government. Each of the unions, however, has been talked of as the nucleus of a future larger unification movement based on language. These exceptions apart, it is striking that existing boundaries have remained intact as colony after colony has become independent in recent years and already independent countries, too, have undergone nationalist revolutions. Countries including many language and culture groups, like most African and Asian ones, have not split up and those taking in only part of a single language group, like the Arab ones in the Near East and North Africa, have, with the two exceptions noted, not united. The colonial boundaries which have thus persisted beyond the attainment of political independence, like the boundaries of older independent underdeveloped countries, were in virtually all cases drawn without any regard to language or cultural divisions among the natives. They chiefly reflected the political and economic requirements of the colonial powers, or of earlier conquerors, as in China, Turkey, and Latin America. Whatever it may be, then, nationalism in underdeveloped countries—if it does not aim at changing these boundaries—cannot be a movement seeking to unite all people speaking a particular language under a single independent government.[2]

Only after nationalism has been produced chiefly by other factors, is an attempt sometimes made by Western-trained intellectuals to introduce the language and cultural element into it. The artificial resurrection of the Irish language may be a case in point. So is the

[1] As this essay goes to the printer (October 1961), an army coup in Syria is severing that country's ties with Egypt. On the domestic and international politics of the Somali area, see Leo Silberman, "Change and Conflict in the Horn of Africa," *Foreign Affairs*, XXXVII, No. 4 (July 1959), 649–659.

[2] On the relationship of nationalism to existing colonial boundaries, see Rupert Emerson, "Nationalism and Political Development," *The Journal of Politics*, XXII, No. 1 (February 1960), 3–28, an article offering many insights into the nature of nationalism in underdeveloped countries. See also William Bascom, "Obstacles to Self-Government," *The Annals of the American Academy of Political and Social Science*, vol. 306 (July 1956), 62–70; C. E. Carrington, "Frontiers in Africa," *International Affairs*, XXXVI, No. 4 (October 1960), 424–439; and E. R. Leach, "The Frontiers of 'Burma'," *Comparative Studies in Society and History*, III, No. 1 (October 1960), 49–67.

pan-Arab movement insofar as it is not a mere tool of the nationalist movements of individual Arab states. The continuing failure of Arab unification would seem to indicate that these nationalist movements are in any case a good deal more powerful than pan-Arabism. More significant is the attempt of the Chinese Communist regime, itself a continuation of earlier Kuomintang policy, to impose a single language (that of the Peking region) and a simplified system of writing on all of China, a policy required, and facilitated, by the rapid economic and political integration of that area. Similar in nature, though not in the methods used to attain it, is the goal of the Indian government to spread the use of Hindi to all of India.

Though pursued with more awareness and greater speed, the Chinese and Indian policies (and similar ones in Indonesia) correspond roughly to those of the French kings, who integrated the population of their territory in terms of the language spoken at the seat of government. Just as French absolutism thereby laid the basis for the later language-based nationalism, so such a nationalism may arise in underdeveloped countries if and when most of their population speaks a single language.[1] However, in India there has arisen a countermovement to the policy of language integration demanding that provincial boundaries be redrawn along linguistic lines to provide greater autonomy for the various major language groups. This may roughly correspond to the nationalism of some of the nationalities in the Austro-Hungarian and other multi-language empires of Europe. It remains to be seen whether the central government of India will, like the French kings, succeed in uniting its country around a single language or whether, as in Austria-Hungary, some of the other languages are too firmly established (at least among the literate and particularly the intellectuals) to be easily uprooted, leading India to disintegration.[2]

Even in India and China, as well as in Ireland and the Arab countries, the desire to make all people under one government speak one language (or to give a new autonomous government to those speaking one language) was not among the original motivations underlying the nationalist movement. In most underdeveloped countries no such desire has to this day appeared at all. If the origins of nationalism have

[1] Turkish nationalism under Kemal to some extent assumed this form when the Ottoman Empire was reduced to its Turkish-speaking provinces by its defeat in World War I.

[2] On this problem, see Selig S. Harrison, "The Challenge to Indian Nationalism," *Foreign Affairs*, XXXIV, No. 4 (July 1956), 620–636, and the same author's *India: the Most Dangerous Decades* (Princeton, N.J.: Princeton University Press, 1960).

nothing to do with nationality, i.e., with a common language and culture, nor with loyalty to an existing independent government, for there is none, then what is nationalism?

Nationalism in underdeveloped countries appears to have in common with European nationalism the desire of people to be rid of alien rulers and to have their own government, and it is probably for this reason that it has been labeled nationalism. In fact, the matter is not so simple, even if we leave aside the point, made at greater length earlier, that in underdeveloped countries, until modernization progresses, most people have no desires with reference to the central government at all, and they do not play any active role in politics. Apart from that, the words "alien" and "own" as just used, however, assume what is yet to be proved, that there is a collectivity of people, somehow defined by a common element other than a language, who share "their" nationalism. Why does a community in the South of India regard a prime minister from the North more as their "own" ruler than a viceroy from Britain? Why does one tribe in the Congo think of a government dominated by another tribe as less "alien" than a government of Belgians? In terms of language differences, these questions cannot be answered.

In some underdeveloped countries, notably Moslem ones, a religion and other cultural characteristics shared by all the natives regardless of their language, but different from those of their colonial rulers, may have been a common element around which their nationalism could have grown. But in many underdeveloped countries there are vast religious and cultural differences among the natives who nevertheless produced a single nationalist movement. And not infrequently, such movements are led by Christian natives who share their religion with their colonial rulers, whom they oppose, rather than with the great majority of the natives whom they claim to represent.

A more important element of unity setting the nationalists apart from their colonial rulers may be race, i.e., physical (as distinguished from cultural) characteristics. Some underdeveloped countries are inhabited by people of more than one race, however, and yet, in the Sudan, a European remains more "alien" to an Arab than a Negro, in Bolivia a "North-American" is more alien to a white nationalist than an Indian, in Cuba the "Yanqui" is regarded by nationalists as the enemy of both whites and Negroes. Sometimes certain unity among the natives has been created by Europeans or Americans who set themselves apart by discriminatory practices directed against all natives or "colored" people regardless of their particular race. The racial factor, then, is undoubtedly an important element in an explanation of nationalist unity in some underdeveloped countries, particularly where all natives are of a single non-white race and where it appears as a reaction to racial discrimination by whites. But not everywhere is this the case. There is no clear racial distinction between the European and the native inhabitants of North Africa nor is there between the English and the Irish or between some Americans and some Mexicans or Cubans.

NATIONALISM AS ANTI-COLONIALISM

In the absence of a common language, culture, religion, or race, what is it, then, that provides the focus for the unity among politically conscious elements from all strata of the population that is as characteristic of nationalist movements in underdeveloped countries as of European nationalist movements? Speaking of underdeveloped countries in general, there would seem to be no positive factor at all, but rather the dislike of a common enemy, the colonial power. Since nationalism is based on opposition to the colonial government, it is quite understandable that each colony's nationalist movement should operate within the existing boundaries and should not aim at a change in these boundaries. Thus, Indonesian nationalism is directed at the acquisition of Western New Guinea, because it is ruled by the Netherlands, the former colonial power in Indonesia, but makes no active claims to British-ruled Northern Borneo and Sarawak or Portuguese Timor, even though these are geographically, ethnically, and culturally much closer to Indonesia than Western New Guinea is. That the boundaries of a colony may cut across language and cultural lines is irrelevant; what matters is that they define the very purpose of the movement, anti-colonialism, and a change in them would therefore undermine the power of the movement and its leaders. Hence the general ineffectiveness of unification movements among former colonies, and the opposition by nationalists to movements of secession (as in Indonesia and the Congo), which are regarded as anti-nationalist, i.e., inspired by the colonial power.

However, nationalist movements are not confined to territories that are or were until recently administered by foreign powers as colonies, like India and most of Africa. Quite similar movements have appeared in independent underdeveloped countries like Turkey, China, and Mexico and, more recently, Egypt, Iraq, and Cuba. Unless they are virtually inaccessible, underdeveloped countries almost by necessity stand economically in a colonial relationship to industrial countries, in which the former serve as suppliers of raw materials (often made available by cheap native labor) and sometimes as markets for the

industries of the latter. Anti-colonialism, then, must here be understood as opposition not merely to colonialism narrowly defined but
also to a colonial economic status.

It is opposition to colonialism so defined and to those natives who
benefit from the colonial relationship that constitutes nationalism in
underdeveloped countries.[1] As such, nationalism can unite not only
people of quite different language and cultural background, but also,
interestingly, people of all the major economic and social classes,
even though it is directed against certain economic policies. To be sure,
in underdeveloped countries, as in Europe, many have been opposed
and many indifferent to nationalism. Remarkable unity across social
class lines has nevertheless been attained by nationalism. This is probably even more marked in underdeveloped countries than it was in
Europe, where first the aristocracy and later important strata among the
intellectuals and industrial labor proved to be anti-nationalist. The
social tensions which modernization and industrialization produce
everywhere and which in Europe were necessarily turned inward, resulting in conflicts dividing societies, are, in underdeveloped countries,
largely turned outward. Instead of blaming each other for the difficulties
growing out of modernization, the various social strata all blame the
colonial power, the result being, not internal conflict, but that internal
unity of anti-colonialism which is the basis of nationalism in underdeveloped countries.

This may be illustrated in somewhat more detail by a quick survey
of the effects of colonialism on the six major social strata (three old
and three new, as outlined earlier), and hence of their attitudes
toward nationalism. The peasants are the group in which the greatest
number of those indifferent to nationalism may be found. This is so
both because they form by far the largest of the social strata in underdeveloped countries and because, in their isolation and ignorance, they
tend to be indifferent to politics beyond the local level generally. To
the peasant in an isolated village, depending neither on export to
nor import from the outside world, it may make very little difference
whether a foreigner or a native of the larger territory in which his
village happens to be located occupies the government palace in the

[1] An impressive attempt to generalize about the nature of nationalism in Asia
and Africa, providing both a wealth of data and much thoughtful interpretation,
is Rupert Emerson, *From Empire to Nation* (Cambridge, Mass.: Harvard University Press, 1960). For excellent detailed studies of the bases of nationalism in two
underdeveloped areas, see James S. Coleman, *Nigeria: Background to Nationalism*
(Los Angeles and Berkeley: University of California Press, 1958) and some of the
articles in Walter Z. Laqueur, ed., *The Middle East in Transition* (New York:
Frederick A. Praeger, 1958).

far-off capital. He may, indeed, not even know the difference or even that there is a government and a capital city.

However, such peasant communities unaffected by and indifferent to the outside world are no longer the rule in most underdeveloped countries. Colonialism itself has put an end to their isolation.[1] Through the extension of its influence, the peasant has become integrated into a wider money economy—even in the absence of various kinds of forced labor or of any compulsion to pay taxes in cash rather than in kind. He would want to buy those products of foreign industry which are superior to his own. In order to get the money to pay for them, he has to export his agricultural goods, which he can do effectively only by concentrating on the production of a single product that he can produce most efficiently. This, in turn, makes him more dependent on imports for the other necessities of life, which he himself can no longer produce. The peasant now becomes subject to vast impersonal forces which he can neither understand nor control since they reach far beyond the primitive village community which bounded his horizon for generations. This situation inevitably gives rise to intense frustrations. The peasant comes in contact with the outside world through middle-men and money-lenders who frequently become "big" peasants appropriating the land of their indebted fellows. In any case, they, or tribal or village chiefs who (under colonial laws) appropriate communally owned land as their private property, can easily exploit the peasant in his weak economic and political condition. This becomes a source of resentment. Clearly, much of his frustration and resentment is, or can easily be, directed against the colonial power and its representatives who brought the change from the familiar and, in that sense, secure life of the village to the incomprehensible and insecure life as a small part of a wider economy. Thus while the peasants themselves, because of their apolitical way of life, are very unlikely to initiate any nationalist movement, they can become an important mass base for such a movement led by others, notably by intellectuals.

A second old, i.e., pre-industrial, class is that of the tradesmen and craftsmen of the towns. Wherever industry advances or even where its products become available, this old middle class is threatened. The small shopkeepers cannot successfully meet the competition of large commercial organizations nor the craftsmen that of cheaper and often

---

[1] For an interesting case study of the effects of economic and social changes brought by colonialism but also of the efforts of the colonial power to prepare the natives for self-government, see J. Gus Liebenow, Jr., "Responses to Planned Political Change in a Tanganyika Tribal Group," *The American Political Science Review*, L, No. 2 (June 1956), 442–461.

better mass-produced goods. As they face the end of their way of life and the loss of the relatively high status they enjoyed in the old society, being doomed to descend into the lower classes by forces they can hate but not stop, they are, as a group, likely to become embittered and even desperate. This political mood was one of the important elements contributing to the rise of Fascism in Central Europe in the interwar period and it continues to play a significant role in the politics of some Western countries, especially in France, where its most striking recent manifestation was that of Poujadism.

What led to deep divisions and conflicts in the now more advanced industrialized countries, has, in the underdeveloped countries, contributed to nationalist unity, for the modernization which ultimately dooms the old middle class is brought by colonialism; the large commercial and industrial enterprises which threaten it are usually owned by citizens of the colonial power. The decline of the old middle class, then, which is a general phenomenon accompanying industrialization, feeds anti-colonialist nationalism in the underdeveloped countries. A peculiar type of anti-foreignism—more akin, however, to the Eastern European variety of anti-Semitism than to anti-colonialist nationalism— arises, particularly among the old middle class and also the peasantry, where small business, and often banking, is in the hands of foreigners not from the colonial power, like the Chinese in Southeast Asia, Indians and Arabs in South and East Africa, and Greeks, Syrians, and Lebanese in much of the Near East and Africa.

The third of the old classes, the aristocracy, is also ultimately doomed in its old way of life by advancing industrialization and modernization. However, its political power, virtually unlimited as long as its country was wholly agrarian, may permit the aristocracy to maintain a powerful social and political position long after landownership has ceased to be an important function in the economy. In many European countries it still retains an important foothold in the military and the bureaucracy. In Britain it remains strong even in party and parliamentary politics.

In underdeveloped countries, where the power and prestige of kings and princes, rajahs and sheiks, tribal and village chiefs, big landowners, and the religious functionaries and hierarchies usually allied with them, are still very considerable, the colonial governments have frequently found it less convenient to uproot them and replace them with their own administrators, than to govern the natives through them. Under such arrangements of "indirect rule," some form of which is almost inevitable (especially at the local level), and which have been the way most past empires were formed and administered, the colonial power clearly benefits. However, it must, in turn, protect the aristocracy, and the old order in which its power is rooted, from the native forces desiring modernization (to be discussed shortly), who are themselves a product of colonialism.

Colonialism is thus not only a modernizing influence, but also a conservative force. In some instances, where the modernizing forces among the natives have become strong enough, it may in the end be only the colonial government that maintains the old aristocracy in power. Thus, the princely governments in India could not outlast British rule by more than a few months. Nor does this type of relationship prevail under formal colonial administration alone. In independent underdeveloped countries, too, the aristocracy's position is protected by economic colonialism, as is negatively illustrated by the fate of the large landowners in the Mexican and Cuban revolutions. It is clear that an aristocracy, whose privileged status depends on the continuance of colonialism, cannot be expected to join the anti-colonialist movement. Our understanding of the politics of underdeveloped countries (particularly those like Algeria, the Congo, and some Latin American states, where the battle between nationalism and colonialism still continues), will therefore be greatly improved if the claim of nationalism to represent the interests of "the" people is rejected and it is recognized that some of the most powerful native forces in underdeveloped societies—the aristocracy and the frequently still numerous people whom it can influence—may, in effect, be allies of colonialism and enemies of nationalism.

However, while the conservative side of colonialism preserves the aristocracy, its modernizing aspects threaten its power. Many a formerly absolute ruler now has to accept the "advice" of a colonial official and many a native landowner has had to give up his land to settlers from the colonial power. More generally and more importantly, modernization undermines the traditional society on which the power of the aristocracy rests. The aristocracy and its allies, particularly among the religious officials—the priests and holy men, the monks, mullahs, and medicine men—have almost everywhere fought a rear guard action against modern Western dress and customs, against the type of education and the outlook on life characteristic of industrial societies—just as they did in Europe for some centuries. Those who adopt the perspectives of an industrialized society, which means, above all, those who become familiar with the notion of economic and social change, unheard of in static agrarian societies, are not likely to accept unquestioningly, as generations before them did, the status of an aristocracy based merely on age-old tradition. Yet these perspectives so threatening to the aristocracy are brought to the underdeveloped countries by colonialism (the more so, by and large, the more industrially advanced the colonial power). No wonder that among the aristocracy, too, there may be important forces who join the ranks of the nationalist movement and who, in fact, often lead its traditionalist wing.

The new social groups, which are a product of the growth of commerce and industry, and of the advancement of communications and education that accompany it, in this sense owe their very existence to colonialism. It does not by any means follow, however, that they are more favorably disposed toward it than the older groups from which they were recruited. Thus the industrial workers, like labor everywhere in the early stages of industrialization, form a group with many grievances. The shift to a money, and often a one-crop, economy forced many peasants to go to work in the plantations and mines, and in the factories of the growing cities. At present, these workers are frequently less than a generation removed from their ancestral villages and tribes, where life, although—or because—extremely limited materially and intellectually, provided a high degree of security for the individual. Suddenly torn from the bonds of such a small, highly integrated society and thrown into the anonymity of life in an industrial plant and an urban slum, where not only the physical surroundings, but also many values and behavior patterns, are utterly alien, the worker is bound to be subject to maladjustments, tensions, and frustrations of various kinds.[1]

Furthermore, since the worker is as yet largely defenseless politically and economically, his working and living conditions are likely to be poor, his wages low and hours long, and his wife and children may be compelled to work. The owners of the enterprise and their representatives, whom the worker blames and possibly hates for this situation, are likely to be corporations and citizens of the colonial power. The conflict between labor and capital, then, which in Europe gave rise to radical movements of the left, like anarchism, syndicalism and early socialism, and thus became a prime source of domestic division in the age of industrialization, in underdeveloped countries furnishes more recruits and an important mass base for anti-colonialist nationalism.

Unlike the peasants, who, because of their physical isolation, narrow intellectual horizon, and conservatism, can often be reached and persuaded only with some difficulty by urban intellectuals in search of a mass following, the workers in the cities are relatively easily accessible

[1] On some effects of urbanization, see Lucy P. Mair, "Social Change in Africa," *International Affairs*, XXXVI, No. 4 (October 1960), 447–456.

and organizable and, having been torn from their familiar environment, receptive to ideas advocating radical change. It is therefore not surprising that trade unions, such as they are in underdeveloped countries, have everywhere, under intellectual leadership, tended to become adjuncts of the nationalist movement.[1] This may also be one—though only one—reason for the frequent vague identification of nationalism in underdeveloped countries with "socialism," a term which has by now lost virtually all specific meaning, but retains plenty of emotional overtones.

If labor is anti-colonialist, one might expect the opposite of the native capitalists in commerce and banking, who developed from the old traders and money lenders, and also of the few native industrial capitalists who may have emerged. Undoubtedly, many of them are so closely tied to the colonial economy through their business relations that they favor its continuation. They may therefore become anti-nationalists like some of the aristocracy, to which they may also have social and economic ties. On the other hand, the native capitalists may also suffer from, and hence resent, competition from banking, commercial, and industrial establishments owned by citizens of the "mother" country and located either there or in the colony. They may well feel that the removal of colonialism would enhance their opportunities to expand their own businesses and deal more successfully with their foreign competitors or, indeed, get rid of them altogether. Thus the native capitalists, a group of no great size in any underdeveloped country but of growing political importance in some of them, may also join the nationalist movement for reasons of their own.

THE ROLE OF THE INTELLECTUALS

The third of the new groups produced by modernization are the intellectuals. The peculiar importance of this group in the nationalist movements of underdeveloped countries requires that somewhat more space be devoted to it than to the others. For our purposes, we do not include among the intellectuals the scholars trained along traditional, usually religious (such as Islamic or Confucian) lines in the old society, but, on the other hand, our definition is a much broader one than that usually applied in advanced countries. Like the latter, it

---

[1] See George E. Lichtblau, "The Politics of Trade Union Leadership in Southern Asia," reprinted on pp. 265–281, below. For a useful summary of the sometimes very important role of trade unions in nationalist movements, see George C. Lodge, "Labor's Role in Newly Developing Countries," *Foreign Affairs*, XXXVII, No. 4 (July 1959), 660–671.

embraces persons with advanced standing in the humanities, sciences, and social sciences. However, it also includes all those natives in underdeveloped countries, most likely to be found among the aristocracy and the businessmen, who have, through the contacts afforded by colonialism become aware of the world beyond their own culture area, and have obtained an advanced education appropriate to an industrial country, or who are at present students obtaining such an education.

In some underdeveloped countries, especially those where such an education qualified a native to serve in the administrative service of his government, whether independent, as in Latin America, or colonial, as in India, significant numbers of natives have, for some decades, studied in industrialized countries in Western Europe, and increasingly in the United States and the Soviet Union, and in institutions of higher learning conducted according to European-American standards in their own countries. In other underdeveloped countries, only a handful of natives have been involved. Thus, there were said to be only 16 native college graduates in the entire population of about 13 million in the Belgian Congo when it became independent in 1960.

For our purposes of generalization, an image of the intellectuals will be conveyed which is, no doubt, often far too monolithic. For the study of any particular country or situation, it is subject to revision and refinement. Thus, one might have to draw distinctions and even note conflicts between intellectuals educated at home and those who studied abroad, between civilian and military intellectuals, and between the successive generations of nationalist intellectuals.[1]

The key role of the intellectuals in the politics of underdeveloped countries is largely due to their paradoxical position of being a product of modernization before modernization has reached or become widespread in their own country.[2] In the universities, the intellectuals

[1] For a more complete discussion of the definition of intellectuals in underdeveloped countries, as well as some of the distinctions among intellectuals, see Edward Shils, "The Intellectuals in the Political Development of the New States," reprinted on pp. 195–234, below, and Harry J. Benda, "Non-Western Intelligentsias as Political Elites," reprinted on pp. 235–251, below. See also Edward A. Shils, "The Intellectuals, Public Opinion, and Economic Development," *Economic Development and Cultural Change*, VI, No. 1 (October 1957), 55–62.

[2] The leading role of the intellectuals is excellently stressed in Hugh Seton-Watson, "Twentieth Century Revolutions," *The Political Quarterly*, XXII, No. 3 (July–September 1951), 251–265, an article all the more valuable for relating, as we shall try to do, developments in Russia and Southeastern Europe to those in the present underdeveloped countries. See also Martin L. Kilson, Jr., "Nationalism and Social Classes in British West Africa," *The Journal of Politics*, XX, No. 2 (May 1958), 368–387.

absorb the professional knowledge and skills needed by an industrial civilization; they become students of the humanities and social sciences qualified to teach in universities, and they become lawyers and doctors, administrators and journalists, and increasingly also scientists and engineers. When they return from the universities, whether abroad or not, the intellectuals find, all too often for their taste, that in their old societies their newly acquired skills and knowledge are out of place. Not only is there as yet little need—though it is often rapidly growing—for engineers and scientists where there is little industry, but professors will find few advanced students and lawyers will find few clients in a society still operating largely through simple face-to-face contacts. Although there is plenty of sickness, most patients might prefer the traditional herb-doctor or medicine man to the trained physician and, in any case, could not pay him. Few administrators are needed where the sphere of government activity is still very limited and fewer still where all higher posts are occupied by representatives of a colonial power. Where the bulk of the population is illiterate journalists are confined to writing for their few fellow intellectuals. As a result, intellectuals in underdeveloped countries are frequently unemployed or underemployed, especially since, for all their "industrial" education, they are likely to have retained the aristocratic attitude that manual labor is demeaning and hence will refuse to do other than intellectual work.

During their studies, the intellectuals are likely to acquire more than new knowledge. They also absorb the values of an industrial civilization, above all the notion that continuing material improvement of the life of the mass of the population through continuing technological progress and popular participation in government is both possible and desirable, and they become admirers of the political systems and ideologies embodying these values, whether they be American liberalism, Western European democratic socialism or Soviet Communism. On their return, they discover that these values, too, are inappropriate to the old society. Continuous and cumulative technological progress, which is so typical of an industrial system, is absent from purely agrarian economies. Until industrialization (and changes in agricultural techniques resulting from industrialization) are introduced, a belief in any substantial improvement in the standard of living of the mass of the population is, in fact, unrealistic. At the same time, advocacy, based on such a belief, of ideals of democracy, equality, and social justice, which arose out of an industrial environment, is subversive to the existing order of government by the native aristocracy and the foreign colonial power and is therefore not likely to endear the intellectuals to these powerful forces.

To the extent, then, that a native intellectual has substituted for the values of his traditional society those of an industrial one—a process which need by no means be complete in each case—he becomes an alien, a displaced person, in his own society. What could be more natural for him than to want to change that society to accord with his new needs and values, in short, to industrialize and modernize it? A number of motivations intermingle to produce the intellectuals' drive for rapid modernization. Most obviously, there is their desire for gainful and satisfying employment, for an opportunity to use the knowledge and to practice the skills they have acquired. But beyond this relatively narrow motive, there may be the more or less clear realization that only through industrialization can an eventual end be put to the poverty prevalent in underdeveloped countries, that only rapid industrialization can solve the problem posed by increasing populations, and that only industrialization can produce the "better" society at home which the intellectuals have come to admire abroad.

The peasant's typical response to overpopulation and his consequent hunger for land (if he is sufficiently politically conscious and organizable to respond effectively at all) is the demand for land reform. The intellectuals echo and support that demand, for one thing, because it is in accord with their new ideas of justice and equality. These ideas also make it desirable for them to become the leaders of a mass movement, of "the people." Since most of the people are peasants, they are inclined to seek peasant support, and advocacy of land reform is the most obvious way of mobilizing such support. Intellectuals may favor land reform also because a higher standard of living for the peasantry would create a better market for, and thus further the growth of, native industry. Finally, they press for land reform not because of anything it will do *for* the peasants, but because of what it will do *to* the aristocracy. The latter is the intellectuals' only powerful domestic enemy, and land reform strikes at the very root of its economic and social position.

However, where overpopulation is greatest, as in China, redistribution of land by itself is no longer an adequate solution to the problem, because there is simply not enough arable land to go around. Thus there is underemployment among the peasantry, which in turn tends to depress the wages of labor in the cities. Sooner or later only industrialization can satisfy the "rising expectations" in underdeveloped countries, which are, first and foremost, the expectations of the intellectuals, though they have spread them to the poorer strata accessible to them in the rural and especially in the urban areas. Only through industrialization can the intellectuals hope to realize their various dreams of democracy, equality, and social justice, of liberalism, socialism, or Communism in their own countries.

As the only ones in their societies who can even visualize a new, and, to them, a better order, the intellectuals naturally think of themselves as the leaders of the future society and of the transition to it. Thus a more narrowly political motivation is added to the others underlying their desire for modernization. Modernization serves to undermine and ultimately do away with the leadership of the old aristocratic ruling strata, and replace it with that of the intellectuals. Similarly, industrialization is the only road to the economic independence and military strength that can eventually provide freedom from colonial domination for their "country," that is, their government, which means more power for its new leaders, the intellectuals. Their anti-colonial nationalism thus makes the intellectuals desire industrialization.

It is equally true, however, that it is their desire to industrialize that makes the intellectuals nationalists. They see colonialism as opposed to industrialization, in part because the colonial power does not want industries in the colony to compete with its own industries for the colonial supply of raw materials or for the colonial market, and more generally because, as we have seen, modernization in the colony constitutes a threat to colonialism. Hence colonialism is regarded as an obstacle in the intellectuals' path to modernization as well as in their path to power. This helps explain the apparent paradox of intellectuals in underdeveloped countries who were trained in the West and came to admire it and yet turn against the West in their policies. They do so exactly because they admire it and at the same time see the West as denying them, through colonialism, the opportunity to make their own country more like the West.[1] To the intellectuals in underdeveloped countries nationalism and modernization have become inextricably intertwined as means and ends. Each has become an essential aspect of the other.

In Western Europe, during the process of industrialization, the in-

[1] The intellectuals' ambiguous attitudes are well discussed and documented in Mary Matossian, "Ideologies of Delayed Industrialization: Some Tensions and Ambiguities," reprinted on pp. 252–264, below. Her attempt to generalize about a large number of ideologies of nationalism in underdeveloped countries is most suggestive, though the inclusion of Shintoism, Fascism, and Nazism can, for reasons indicated later in this essay, be accepted only with some reservations. The ambivalence of the nationalist intellectuals toward the West is also noted by Rupert Emerson, "Paradoxes of Asian Nationalism," *The Far Eastern Quarterly*, XIII, No. 2 (February 1954), 131–142.

tellectuals played an important role in developing the ideology of liberalism, but industrialization itself was accomplished by industrial capitalists. In underdeveloped countries, the intellectuals, in effect, play the roles of both groups. A native class of industrial capitalists is virtually or completely absent, and sufficient wealth for the development of industry is not available in private hands—or, if available in the hands of aristocrats, is (for reasons to be indicated later) not likely to be invested in industry. Under these circumstances, the government appears to be the only possible major domestic source of capital, and the intellectuals—if they want to industrialize their country—must wrest control of it from the native aristocracy and the colonial administrators who oppose industrialization. This need to control their government in order to industrialize provides another reason both for the intellectuals' anti-colonialist nationalism and for the appeal of various "socialist" ideas, whether Communist or not, to them. Thus, Nehru and U Nu, Nkrumah and Touré, Castro and many other nationalist intellectuals regard themselves as "socialists."

Through the dominance of the intellectuals in the nationalist movements, which we will have to analyze next, it is their peculiar form of nationalism, which looks at steel mills both as symbols of anti-colonialism and as its instruments, that has become characteristic of nationalism in underdeveloped countries. To borrow some phrases from Marx's prophecies about capitalism, nowhere are the "internal contradictions" of colonialism, its dual nature as a modernizing and a conservative force in the underdeveloped countries,[1] clearer than in its relation to the intellectuals. It produces the intellectuals and yet by its very existence it frustrates them and hence arouses their opposition. In them, it has thus produced "its own gravediggers," it has sown "the seeds of its own destruction."

UNITY AND DIVERSITY IN ANTI-COLONIAL NATIONALISM

That intellectuals should almost invariably emerge as the leaders of the heterogeneous nationalist movements in underdeveloped countries is not difficult to explain. As long as modernization has not set in to any large extent, what native intellectuals there are, are likely to be not merely the leaders of the nationalist movement, but to be *the* movement. Even as, with progressing modernization, members of other

[1] On the effects on nationalism, both before and after the attainment of independence, of this dual character of colonialism, see S. N. Eisenstadt, "Sociological Aspects of Political Development in Underdeveloped Countries," *Economic Development and Cultural Change*, V, No. 4 (July 1957), 289–307.

strata, for reasons indicated for each of them earlier, join the movement, the intellectuals remain dominant. The peasants, the old traders and artisans, and the industrial workers who become nationalists are too poor and downtrodden, too ignorant and limited intellectually, and too used to accepting leadership from above to challenge the intellectuals, though occasionally a few of them may rise into the ranks of the intellectuals themselves. Generally, their nationalism is more likely to be caused by negative resentment induced by their particular grievances than by a positive vision of a new society. The old aristocrats, insofar as they become nationalists at all, are, in a rigidly stratified society, often prevented from leading a mass movement by virtue of their own upper class position. The same may be true of what new businessmen there are, but they are also often handicapped by lack of prestige in societies where money-making does not provide high status.

In some cases, to be sure, members or representatives of the aristocracy have sought to use their power and prestige to lead their societies toward modernization. Yet such attempts can be undertaken only with extreme caution for they place those who make them under pressure from two sides: The more successful the attempts, the more they are resented by most of the aristocracy as a threat, and the more they undermine the position even of the aristocratic modernizers, by strengthening the impatient intellectuals. In Iraq, Nuri es-Said, who, somewhat like the Russian Tsars half a century earlier, had attempted to combine economic development with opposition to land reform and suppression of the intellectuals, was swept out of power and assassinated in the nationalist revolution led by Kassem. Even in Ethiopia, one of the most backward countries in the world, Haile Selassie, an emperor with some ambitions of economic and educational developments for his realm, was, in 1960, threatened with the loss of his throne in a revolt of army officers and students desiring more rapid modernization.[1] In Iran, the Shah has even distributed some of the crown lands, thus trying to attack the problem of land reform without attacking the big landowners on whom he depends. He cannot, at any rate, be simply regarded as the head of the aristocracy, since he is the

[1] Edward C. Jandy, "Ethiopia Today: A Review of Its Changes and Problems," *The Annals of the American Academy of Political and Social Science,* vol. 306 (July 1956), 106–116; Jeanne Contini, "The Winds of Change and the Lion of Judah," *The Reporter,* May 25, 1961, pp. 31–34. For a detailed study of another "modernizing autocracy," the Kingdom of Buganda, see David E. Apter, *The Political Kingdom in Uganda. A Study in Bureaucratic Nationalism* (Princeton, N.J.: Princeton University Press, 1961).

son of Reza Khan, a reforming army officer who played a role in Persia much like that of Kemal in Turkey, though unlike the latter he perpetuated the monarchy by having himself proclaimed Shah.[1] In practice, the lines between modernizing intellectuals and conservative aristocrats are usually, but not always, sharply drawn. In terms of our model, however, we may simply assign aristocrats who become effective modernizers to the ranks of the intellectuals in opposition to the aristocracy.

The intellectuals assume the leadership of nationalist movements, because, unlike the other groups, they have broken out of the rigid class lines of the old society, they have a vision of the future and some ideas, however vague or impractical, of how to attain it, and they are, almost by definition, skilled in the use of the written and spoken word. Furthermore, the intellectuals have the simple advantage over members of other groups of having free time on their hands. Unemployed or underemployed and yet often receiving enough support from their wealthy families to be able to live, they have time to devote to politics, to speaking, reading, writing, to agitating and organizing, and time to spend in jail or in exile and, often soon thereafter, in the government.

In many nationalist movements and especially in newly independent nationalist governments, the armed forces continue to play a key role as the chief source of politicians, just as they did in purely agrarian societies. They do so for the same reasons, viz., that in an underdeveloped society they constitute virtually the only major organized and disciplined force. However, we have to distinguish sharply between the officers of the old army and the new one.[2] The difference often appears as one of generations and also one of rank, ranging the young colonels and majors against the old generals. These old generals, of whom we wrote earlier, were the politicians in some purely agrarian

[1] For a study of the modernization of Iran during the reign of Reza Shah Pahlavi, see Amin Banani, *The Modernization of Iran, 1921–1941* (Stanford, Calif.: Stanford University Press, 1961).

[2] See Edwin Lieuwen, "The Military: A Revolutionary Force," *The Annals of the American Academy of Political and Social Science*, vol. 334 (March 1961), 30–40, and the same author's *Arms and Politics in Latin America* (New York: Frederick A. Praeger, 1960); Majid Khadduri, "The Role of the Military in Middle East Politics," *The American Political Science Review*, XLVII, No. 2 (June 1953), 511–524; Guy J. Pauker, "Southeast Asia as a Problem Area in the Next Decade," *World Politics*, XI, No. 3 (April 1959), 325–345; and the important study by Dankwart A. Rustow, "The Army and the Founding of the Turkish Republic," *World Politics*, XI, No. 4 (July 1959), 513–522. See also Dankwart A. Rustow, *Politics and Westernization in the Near East* (Princeton University, Center of International Studies, 1956), pp. 31–33.

societies, who, in return for the rewards of prestige and graft, governed the country in seemingly endless succession on behalf of the native aristocracy and the foreign colonial power. The new colonels and majors, on the other hand, must be seen as intellectuals. Like the other intellectuals in underdeveloped countries, they have been educated by the standards of industrialized countries, frequently in their military academies. They, too, have absorbed the values of these countries; they, too, want to industrialize their own countries, chiefly, no doubt, to strengthen and to modernize their armed forces—and thereby to add to their own power; they, too, want to modernize to get rid of colonialism and want to get rid of colonialism in order to modernize; they, too, in short, are nationalists. And given their control of the armed forces, they frequently become the dominant force among the intellectuals, who are themselves the dominant force in the nationalist movement. This is most likely to be true in independent underdeveloped countries where leaders of nationalist revolutions like Kemal and Perón, Nasser and Kassem have emerged from national armies. But in some cases colonial armies, too, have trained the intellectual nationalist type of officer. Thus, General Ayub Khan of Pakistan is a product of the British Indian army, General Nasution of the Netherlands Indies Army, and General Abboud of the British-run Sudan Defense Force.

Nationalism may then merely replace one type of military autocracy with another, but the resemblance between the two types is only superficial. Each is led by a man on horseback, but in one case he is only a jockey riding a horse owned by the aristocracy, in the other he leads the race to modernization riding the horse of nationalism. In practice, the distinction is not always so clear, but it is fairly evident that a Perón was not just another Latin American caudillo or a Chiang Kai-shek just another Chinese warlord, that a Kemal was no mere successor to the Sultan nor Nasser to the King of Egypt. The distinction in each case lies in the leader's attitude toward the old ruling forces, the aristocracy at home and the colonial powers abroad. That the leaders just named could not completely overcome these forces and had, to a greater or lesser extent, to compromise with them, does not contradict the point that they were, at least at one time, representatives of the nationalist intellectuals, rather than of the old aristocracy; it merely proves that the transition from the old order of agrarianism to the new order of industrialism, while probably more rapid than in much of Western Europe, comes in the now underdeveloped countries, too, in a process of conflict and hence is not without delays and setbacks.

Since colonialism serves, at one and the same time, a modernizing and a conservative function in the underdeveloped countries and since nationalism in these countries consists of anti-colonialism, it follows, as the two preceding sections demonstrated, that the nationalist movement unites both those who oppose colonialism because they feel that it introduces modernization too rapidly and those who oppose it because in their view it delays and obstructs modernization. Nationalism encompasses both those who want to retain or regain the old order—some of the aristocracy and religious officials and their followers among the peasants and the old middle strata—and those who want to replace that old order as rapidly as possible with a modern industrial one —the native industrialists, if any, the incipient labor movement and, above all, the intellectuals.

The division between traditionalist and modernist nationalists need not always run exactly along these lines.[1] Particularly some intellectuals may sometimes be found on the traditionalist side and are then likely to be its leaders, especially a type of intellectual whom we have ignored here, because he is rather exceptional in underdeveloped countries today. This is the intellectual who is, for one reason or another, so attached to the traditional order in his country that, having become acquainted with the ways and values of industrialized societies, he rejects rather than champions them. Gandhi in India, perhaps Jomo Kenyatta in Kenya, and the historians and writers who have advocated Southern regionalism in the United States may be three widely different examples of intellectuals who oppose colonialism because they oppose industrialization. In Ireland, where the aristocracy—but not the religious hierarchy—was not native but of the colonial power, the intellectuals constituted the main force of traditionalist nationalism. There, rather uniquely, the bulk of the intellectuals seemed to be on the traditionalist side and it, in turn, was the

[1] The distinction between "traditionalists" and "modernists" among nationalists is drawn and refined by James S. Coleman, "Nationalism in Tropical Africa," reprinted on pp. 167–194, below. See also James S. Coleman, "Current Political Movements in Africa," *The Annals of the American Academy of Political and Social Science*, vol. 298 (March 1955), 95–108, and Thomas Hodgkin, *Nationalism in Colonial Africa* (London: Frederick Muller, 1956). The cleavage between traditionalist and modernist nationalists is also the subject of Benjamin Rivlin, "Cultural Conflict in French North Africa," *The Annals of the American Academy of Political and Social Science*, vol. 306 (July 1956), 4–9. The distinction drawn by Ruth Schachter, "Single Party Systems in West Africa," *The American Political Science Review*, LV, No. 2 (June 1961), 294–307, between patron parties and mass parties significantly coincides with that between traditionalist and modernist nationalists.

dominant side of the nationalist movement. Hence in Ireland, the nationalist victory has not been followed by rapid industrialization. Anti-aristocratic yet anti-industrialist views have also been held in Russia in the Narodnik and later the Social Revolutionary parties, and are now held in India in the Socialist Party by intellectuals who look primarily to agriculture for economic development and for the sources of social and political reform; they therefore do not fit clearly into either the traditionalist or the modernist category.

The differences between the traditionalist and the modernist elements of the politically conscious population do not destroy the unity of the nationalist movement. Their common opposition to colonialism obscures the differences and welds them together. A single nationalist movement may claim a Gandhi, whose symbol was the spinning wheel, and a Nehru, who builds steel mills under five-year plans. Jomo Kenyatta, regarded as their leader by the Mau-Mau, who envisaged, at least vaguely, a return to Kikuyu tribalism, is the candidate for prime minister of Tom Mboya, a modern trade-union leader in Kenya. The Moslem Brotherhood and Nasser have both been considered parts of the nationalist movement in Egypt. Thus, nationalism, by uniting various opposed groups against a common enemy, can prevent the tendency of industrialization to produce conflict over alternative policies from coming to the fore.

But what of the future? How long can forces with diametrically opposed objectives remain united? As long—and this may be quite long—as the overriding objective of all these forces is to get rid of the common enemy, who is perceived by each of them as a greater threat than any of the other groups. Their unity is generally embodied in a one-party movement embracing aristocrats and peasants, businessmen and workers, all under intellectual leadership as in the Indian National Congress and the Egyptian Wafd of the interwar period. The first objective of the nationalist movement, around which all the groups can rally, in a country governed directly by a colonial power, is formal independence. But even once this is achieved, or where formal independence existed all along, the nationalist movement finds a basis for existence. Colonialism in its economic form may continue to be preceived as a threat, and it may take much longer to dissolve the economic ties than the political ties with the industrial "mother" country. In fact, some kind of dependence on industrial countries is bound to continue as long as the now "independent" country is underdeveloped, i.e., not industrialized itself, but this need not be on the former colonial power and can be on several industrial countries, perhaps in more than one power bloc, thus providing the government with some room for independent maneuvering.

Once such economic independence, too, has been attained, and colonialism, the common enemy, has, in fact, disappeared, one might expect nationalist unity to break up and domestic group conflict —and with it the possibility of democracy, as defined earlier—to arise. However, the leaders of a powerful one-party mass movement, who necessarily constitute the government of the country, have a vested interest in its continued unity. Its break-up would diminish their power and threaten their hold on the government and perhaps their policies of modernization. The obvious way for them to try to maintain this unity is to emphasize the continued threat of colonialism and, indeed, to manufacture it where it no longer exists, either by creating a false image through their propaganda or by provoking a real threat through their foreign policies. To keep his followers united and to stay in power, a Sukarno *needs* a Dutch "threat" in Western New Guinea; a Nasser *needs* the "menace" of Zionism; [1] a Castro *needs* American "imperialism" in Latin America. At this point, nationalist unity may, instead of breaking up into the disunity of democracy, be turned into the unity of totalitarianism, a possibility to be analyzed later, after we have turned to the subject of Communism in underdeveloped countries.

Meanwhile, it must be added that while the nationalist movement is composed of different groups looking, broadly speaking, in two different directions—backward to the old society and forward to a new one—the power relationship among these various groups does not remain constant. Those who desire modernization are likely to gain strength and gradually to eclipse those who dream of a return to the tribal or highly stratified society of agrarianism. This is so not only because the intellectuals are, for reasons indicated, the leaders of the entire nationalist movement, but above all because modernization itself, as it progresses, strengthens them and their supporters among the native industrialists and the labor movement, while weakening the hold of the old aristocracy on the society and disintegrating the peas-

[1] Curiously, the role of the Jewish settlers in Palestine, in spite of their own ambitions of realizing the goals of European nationalist and socialist ideologies, may itself be interpreted as that of a nationalist movement in an underdeveloped country, led by intellectuals seeking unity among all social strata in pursuit of policies of rapid modernization in opposition to the Arab aristocracy and British colonialism and now in need of the Arab threat to maintain its drive and unity. The historical background for such an interpretation may be found in Noah Lucatz, *Histadruth (The Israeli Labor Movement) as a Nationalist and Socialist Movement, 1882–1948; A Study in Ideology and Political Behavior*, unpublished Ph.D. dissertation in Political Science (Washington University, St. Louis, 1961).

antry and old middle strata.[1] As a result, the nationalism of under-developed areas has more and more become identical with the nationalism of their intellectuals. It may now be defined as the drive of intellectuals for industrialization, industrialization that has to be as rapid as possible and as independent as possible of aid from the former colonial powers. It must be rapid, since the needs of the intellectuals and the needs of their countries, as the intellectuals see them, are felt to be pressing, and it must be independent of aid from the colonial powers, since its motivation is, after all, nationalist; that is, anti-colonialist.

[1] The possibility of the return of the old aristocracy to power through totalitarianism is considered in our last chapter.

III

COMMUNISM

PRE-REVOLUTIONARY RUSSIA
AS AN UNDERDEVELOPED COUNTRY

If the dominant form of present-day nationalism in underdeveloped countries can be defined as the drive of a relatively thin stratum of intellectuals, who absorbed the skills and values of advanced countries, toward rapid modernization in opposition to the aristocracy and independently of the colonial industrial powers, then the Russian Revolution may be viewed as one of the most important manifestations, and certainly the most successful one, of this form of nationalism.[1] This is not to insist that the Russian Revolution can only be understood as a nationalist movement. It can, perhaps with equal validity, also be seen as a proletarian movement, a peasant movement, an atheistic movement, a messianic movement, or an internationalist movement. We merely suggest that an attempt to demonstrate what the nationalist movement in underdeveloped countries has in common with the Russian Revolution may also yield significant hypotheses and may provide some interesting insights into the role and characteristics

[1] This important but widely ignored point, to be developed in this essay, was made very briefly some time ago by Hugh Seton-Watson. "Communism, as developed by Stalin and Mao Tse-tung, is only the most important example of a wider phenomenon, the revolt of the backward peoples, led by a section of their intelligentsia, against the West." "Twentieth Century Revolutions," *The Political Quarterly,* XXII, No. 3 (July–September 1951), 259. See also Hugh Seton-Watson, *From Lenin to Khrushchev: The History of World Communism* (New York: Frederick A. Praeger, 1960), p. 340. Theodor H. von Laue, "Die Revolution von aussen als erste Phase der russischen Revolution 1917," *Jahrbücher für Geschichte Osteuropas* (Munich), IV, No. 2 (1956), 138–158, also places the Russian Revolution in one category with the revolutions in backward countries. While he does not pursue this comparison, he shows by a study of the last decade of the nineteenth century how the impulses for the Revolution came from the West rather than from internal sources.

of both nationalism and Communism, and the relation between the two.

It is only for this purpose that the interpretation of the Russian Revolution and of Communism presented in this chapter is offered.[1] It is developed with the advantage of hindsight, and, to the extent that factors important also in present-day nationalism are elaborated and other factors are de-emphasized, some of the present is even read into the past. If the present did, indeed, exist in the past, this approach is quite justified. Perhaps, in any case, it is almost unavoidable for any interpreter of past events, and it permits him to go beyond the insights of earlier generations. The fact that it was the purpose of some of the participants in the Russian Revolution to introduce proletarian socialism is an important datum for the historian, but the Revolution need not be interpreted solely in this light. It may be equally valid to view it differently in the light of subsequent events, including its own effects. The revolutionaries of 1917 could hardly share our image of the Russian Revolution as a nationalist movement, and we are not implying that they were, consciously or unconsciously, motivated by the same anti-colonialist bias found among the nationalists in under-developed countries today. We merely point out that the actual results of the Russian Revolution were, in many respects, similar to those accomplished and particularly to those desired by nationalists in such countries today. This is especially true of Stalin's "second revolution" of 1927 with its drive for rapid industrialization and its anti-Western overtones.[2]

[1] See G. F. Achminow, *Die Macht im Hintergrund. Totengräber des Kommunismus* (Grenchen/Ulm: Spaten-Verlag, 1950). Along with points of dubious validity, Achminow's analysis of the Russian Revolution, pp. 48–123, contains some important insights. Their relevance to the present chapter may be gathered from two quotations: "The positive goal of modern Communism is not to remove social conflicts or to create a classless society but to overcome the backwardness of the country in question. Communism assumes in the history of some nations the role fulfilled in the advanced countries by early capitalism." (*Ibid.*, pp. 56–57). ". . . this program [of industrialization] opens up almost infinite opportunities for advancement to hundreds of thousands of new people who must administer the factories, enterprises, power stations and everything that goes with them. . . . Not the workers but the propertyless intelligentsia, the future general managers, directors, etc., constitute the social force that—under certain conditions, of course—is induced by its position to profess Communism, to support it and to pave the way for it." *Ibid.*, p. 89.

[2] Achminow, *ibid.*, pp. 122–123, states: "The Soviet system as we know it today crystallized, not during the revolution of 1917, but during the Stalinist 'revolution from above' that was carried out in the period from 1927 to 1933. . . . The Communists of today desire not the Communism of which Marx once dreamt but the one that Stalin made. . . . The Stalinist 'revolution from above' was

The broad generalizations we have so far made about politics in underdeveloped countries do by and large apply to early twentieth century Russia, simply because Russia was then an underdeveloped country. In Russia then as in underdeveloped countries now, the bulk of the population consisted of peasants, poor, ignorant, illiterate, living in the isolation of their village communities, hence unorganizable and without any active role in national politics. In Russia, as in other underdeveloped countries, the people whose interests were taken care of in national politics were the aristocracy, represented by the Tsar and his court, the Orthodox Church, the military, and the bureaucracy. As in other underdeveloped countries, too, there had been for centuries a high degree of instability of personnel at the top of the government, as court intrigues, coups d'état, and assassinations followed one another, masking a high degree of stability in the interests served by the government.

As in other underdeveloped countries, modernization, resulting from contact with Western Europe, brought significant changes to the setting of politics in Russia. As elsewhere, it brought dislocations and discontent to the peasants' villages. Industrialization produced no large class of native capitalists, for the new industry was owned largely by Western capital. It did produce an industrial labor movement, which, as in other underdeveloped countries, was small in relation to the total population and subject to the influence and leadership of intellectuals. However, industry was concentrated in a few localities and was highly advanced for its day, having been organized on a large scale and employing great numbers of manual workers. The labor movement was therefore quite well organized and had a high degree of political consciousness. In view of their poor working conditions and the hostility of Tsarist autocracy, the workers could easily turn revolutionary. The existence of a class-conscious, revolutionary labor movement had some crucial effects in the realm of ideology, for it permitted Russian intellectuals to adopt the proletarian doctrines of Marxism, which had little appeal in other underdeveloped countries until they had been transmuted into Leninism.

Finally and most importantly, the key group in the nationalist movements in underdeveloped countries, the intellectuals, had the key role in the Russian Revolution, too.[1] Even more than in other under-

the revolution of the 'future general managers,' for they profited the most from it. . . ."

[1] See the excellent collection of essays by Richard Pipes, ed., *The Russian Intelligentsia* (New York: Columbia University Press, 1961). In one of these, particularly relevant to our discussion, "The Intelligentsia in Communist China:

developed countries, because of Russia's long history of cultural contact with the West and perhaps because Russians were "European" in race, language, and religion, some of the wealthier families in Russia had given their sons a Western education—either in the West or in Russia—long before industrialization arrived there. The results were the same as in other underdeveloped countries. The intellectuals absorbed values and ideologies, which had grown out of an industrialized environment in the West, such as various types of liberalism and socialism, that made them feel like aliens in their own country. The presence of significant numbers of Jewish intellectuals further contributed to this situation. They felt doubly alien in Russia, not only as intellectuals with Western values, but also as Jews with their distinct culture, subject to discrimination and ghetto-segregation.

To bring Russia into accord with its ideals, the intellectuals had to favor modernization and democratization, which, under Tsarism, meant that they had to be revolutionary. Since Tsarism appeared as the main obstacle to the realization of the intellectuals' goals (and also because of Russia's status as a Great Power in world affairs), the revolution was chiefly anti-aristocratic rather than anti-colonial and anti-foreign in character. It has therefore not commonly been referred to as a nationalist movement. Yet its carriers, the intellectuals, were the same as those of anti-colonial nationalism and so was one of their enemies, the native aristocracy. Also, a significant number of the Russian intellectuals harbored the ambivalent feelings of love and hatred for the West which we found characterizing much of the intelligentsia in present-day underdeveloped countries; they were anti-Western to be free to become more like the West. The Marxists among them, in particular, combined love of Western industrialization with hatred of Western capitalism,[1] and even now the Communists

A Tentative Comparison," Benjamin Schwartz concludes that "the phenomenon of the intelligentsia is a universal concomitant of the confrontation of a 'traditional' society with the modern West." *Ibid.*, p. 176. He also emphasizes "certain overriding differences," between the Russian and the Chinese intelligentsia, however, particularly the "disassociation from nationalistic aspirations" of the former until the rise of Stalin. *Ibid.*, p. 177.

[1] Adam B. Ulam, in his stimulating essay, *The Unfinished Revolution* (New York: Random House, 1960), and in an earlier article, "The Historical Role of Marxism and the Soviet System," *World Politics*, VIII, No. 1 (October 1955), 20–45, argues that the appeal of Marxism in Russia and in all countries going through the early stages of industrialization stems from "its ability to combine anarchism—the most violent protest against industrialism—with an intense cult of technology and a conviction of the historical necessity and blessings of industrialism." *Ibid.*, p. 29.

are anti-American in order "to catch up with and overtake America." [1]

Finally, the Russian intellectuals—or at least those who were ultimately to succeed in the Revolution—shared their chief goal of rapid
industrialization with the intellectuals in underdeveloped countries
today. Lenin indicated this when he defined Communism as "soviet
power plus electrification," but the goal was to be achieved only
under Stalin in his "second revolution," beginning in 1927. Like intellectuals in other underdeveloped countries, Stalin envisaged industrialization as the principal method of ensuring independence from the
West.[2] It is therefore no coincidence that it was mainly under him
that Communism assumed its nationalist form when he, in effect,
substituted the power and security of the Soviet Union for world
revolution as the goal of Communism. As in other underdeveloped
countries, industrialization and nationalism went hand in hand. Industrialization was to enhance the power of the state, and the state
had to be powerful to speed industrialization.[3]

[1] Three decades ago, Stalin expressed this anti-Western Westernism when
he said, addressing a conference of Soviet industrial managers in 1931: "We are
fifty or a hundred years behind the advanced countries. We must make good this
distance in ten years. Either we do it, or they crush us." J. Stalin, "The Tasks
of Business Executives," *Problems of Leninism* (Moscow: Foreign Languages
Publishing House, 1945), p. 356.

[2] Cf. Stalin's statement made at the Fourteenth Party Congress in 1925: "The
conversion of our country from an agrarian into an industrial country able to
produce the machinery it needs by its own efforts—that is the essence, the basis of
our general line," and his own subsequent comment on this statement, showing
the anti-Western rationale behind it: "The industrialization of the country would
ensure its economic independence, strengthen its power of defense and create
the conditions for the victory of Socialism in the U.S.S.R." *History of the Communist Party of the Soviet Union (Bolsheviks). Short Course* (New York: International Publishers, 1939), p. 276.

[3] The nationalist character of the other three Communist revolutions is much
clearer: In China, Yugoslavia, and Vietnam, the Communists appeared, above
all, as nationalists fighting a foreign enemy. As to the nationalist character of
Communism in Eastern Europe, see the fascinating study by R. V. Burks, *The
Dynamics of Communism in Eastern Europe* (Princeton, N.J.: Princeton University Press, 1961), which distinguishes between three types of Communist parties.
The first two, based on Gabriel A. Almond, *The Appeals of Communism* (Princeton, N.J.: Princeton University Press, 1954), are the sectarian or deviational
parties, found in the most advanced Western industrial countries, and the mass
proletarian parties, found in France and Italy. "The third type of party, the
national and anti-Western, flourishes in countries which are poor and backward.
Such a party is comprised mainly of professional people, formally trained or self-
taught, with some large element of Western education or influence. It is so comprised because the intelligentsia is the conductor through which Western influences penetrate non-Western cultures and because this party, to win and hold
power, must provide a ruling class capable of governing in the conditions of that

MARXISM, LENINISM, AND THE RUSSIAN REVOLUTION AS A NATIONALIST MOVEMENT

One of the ideologies produced by Western industrialism that appealed to Russian intellectuals was Marxism. It taught that every social system grows out of the conditions created by the preceding system, that it therefore cannot appear until these conditions are "ripe," but must inevitably appear when that point is reached. Specifically, socialism is said to grow out of the large-scale industry created by capitalism and to be brought about by the industrial proletariat which, as a class encompassing the great majority of the population, is itself a product of capitalism. The socialist revolution, accordingly, presupposes a highly industrialized society, and Marx consequently expected that revolution to break out in the West.

Some intellectuals in Russia, as elsewhere, were attracted by Marx's attempt to develop a science of society and of history and by the Marxist claim to be able to predict, on this basis, mankind's inevitable evolution. To adhere to Marxist teachings and to relate them to the Russian environment, they had to predict that the revolution which would overthrow Tsarism would be "bourgeois" rather than "proletarian" in character, advancing the growth of capitalism and of the proletariat and, in the political arena, of democracy, thus laying the groundwork for the eventual emergence of the next historical stage,

rapid industrialization and cultural metamorphosis which we call Westernization. Such a party is a national party because its basic aim is national power through the development of modern industry." (Burks, *op. cit.*, p. 186.) Burks concludes from his study of eight Eastern European Communist movements, based heavily on interviews and quantitative data, that these movements on the whole "fit the deviant and proletarian types less well than they do the national." *Ibid.*, p. 187. He notes that ". . . in the East European area as a whole it was the more backward provinces . . . which in general developed the stronger Communist movements. . . . This . . . we inferred to be the result of the contrast between conditions in Eastern Europe and those prevailing in the most industrial nations of the West. This contrast achieved its social imprint through students and teachers who had received a Western education, either in schools of the area or abroad, and who found themselves overtrained and perhaps even unemployable in their native environment. From this situation followed the decisive role of what the Russians would call the intelligentsia, the lawyers, teachers, doctors, and other professionals who provided three-fourths of the Communist leadership." *Ibid.*, p. 191. Burks also connects this situation ". . . with the marked tendency of East European Communist parties to industrialize their respective countries under forced draft and to modernize their agriculture; to create, so to speak, a society in which overtrained surplus professionals can find appropriate employment." *Ibid.*, p. 192.

that of socialism. In the area of organization and tactics, the Mensheviks therefore advocated the creation of a mass labor party, on the model of the German Social Democratic Party, to support the bourgeois-capitalist revolution and at the same time seek to advance labor's interests, which were held to lead inevitably to socialism. Although the existence of a relatively strong revolutionary labor movement in Russia lent some substance to the Mensheviks' theory and strategy, they put too much faith in the leading revolutionary role of the bourgeoisie, a class which in fact was not a very powerful independent factor in Russia. When the Revolution did break out in 1917, its leadership was drawn from among the intellectuals, as it is in most modern revolutions, but it also represented merely that group, not the capitalists. The mass following came from the only possible source of a mass following in underdeveloped countries, the peasantry, including soldiers, who were peasants in uniform—though workers, too, played a significant role. The Mensheviks proved ineffective as Western-influenced intellectuals in an underdeveloped country must be if they are faithful to a theory that grew on a foreign soil and is irrelevant to their own environment.

Not all Western-trained intellectuals in underdeveloped countries follow this path. The Sukarnos, Nkrumahs, and Castros, too, made their revolutions inspired by ideals that developed in industrialized countries, but finding them irrelevant in their own countries, have rather quickly adapted their tactics and the governments they established—though generally not their professed ideologies—to conditions prevailing there. In short, the intellectuals who absorb ideologies from industrialized countries generally fall into two categories, with the difference between them probably explicable by differences in personality. Some insist on adhering to the unadulterated, and hence irrelevant, ideology at the expense of gaining power. The others seek power at the expense of the pure ideology. And typically, each accuses the other of treason to the principles of the revolution.

Among the Russian Marxists, too, there was a group, which, in the eyes of most Western Marxists and of the more Westernized Russian Marxists, bought its success by betrayal of the faith, but which, at any rate, was successful. More in the native tradition of the Russian revolutionary intelligentsia than the Westernized Mensheviks, the Bolsheviks were attracted not so much by the "scientific" aspects of Marxism promising the *inevitable* revolution as by its promise of an *early* revolution. But to turn Marx's promise of a workers' revolution in the West into a promise of an intellectual-led revolution in Russia, Marxism had to be transmuted into Leninism. Leninism is an adaptation of Marxism, a product of the industrialized West, to the conditions of an underdeveloped country.[1] But while Lenin—certainly in his practice and to a significant extent also in his theory—carried through that adaptation, he was never sufficiently aware of what he was doing to recognize that the Marxian model of revolution was irrelevant to Russia. He could not see his own revolution as one of intellectuals bent on modernizing an underdeveloped country, that is, by our definition, as a nationalist movement.

Unlike the Mensheviks, Lenin often looked to an alliance of the workers and peasants, rather than the workers and the bourgeoisie, to make the revolution in Russia. This introduction of the peasantry as allies of the workers is in itself a significant modification of Marxism, influenced by a realistic assessment of conditions in underdeveloped Russia. To be sure, in his writings over a period of decades, Lenin is quite inconsistent on the role he expected the peasantry to play in the revolution and, indeed, on the character of that revolution— whether it would be "bourgeois," "proletarian," or "permanent" (i.e., developing without interruption from the bourgeois to the proletarian stage). His inconsistency is explained by tactical considerations as conditions changed, but above all by the fact that these were not the questions that interested Lenin most.

What mattered most to Lenin, and what was therefore the one point on which he remained consistent in virtually all his writings, no matter how he varied on other points, was the role of the intellectuals and hence of the Party in the revolution. Whether bourgeoisie or peasantry were to support the proletariat in the revolution, whatever the character of that revolution, Lenin always insisted that it must be led by the proletariat, which, however, unable to understand its own interests, itself had to be guided by intellectuals, organized as its "vanguard," the Communist Party.[2] It is probably significant that the split among the Russian Marxists into the Menshevik and Bolshevik factions did not occur over the nature of the expected Russian Revolution, that is, the question whether Russian society was basically like that of the West or like that of the underdeveloped world—a question on which

[1] Some of the points made here and in the rest of this chapter were briefly presented by me earlier, with some documentation, in my articles, "From Marx to Mao," *Soviet Survey* (London), No. 16–17 (June–July 1957), 35–40; "Neo-Maoism, Marxism and Leninism," *The New Leader*, XL, No. 50 (December 16, 1957), 12–16; and "From Proletarianism to Nationalism," *Commentary*, XXVIII, No. 1 (July 1959), 86–90.

[2] These points emerge well from an excellent scholarly analysis of Lenin's thought, Alfred G. Meyer, *Leninism* (Cambridge, Mass.: Harvard University Press, 1957).

the Mensheviks were wrong and Lenin never attained clarity. Rather, the break came over the question of organization, where the Mensheviks' advocacy of a mass labor party stood in sharp contrast to the Bolsheviks' insistence on a small, secret, highly centralized and disciplined "shocktroop" of professional revolutionaries, i.e., of intellectuals, a matter on which Lenin was very clear indeed.

This insistence on the leading role of the intellectuals, organized in the Party, and their substitution for Marx's proletariat as the agents of history and the makers of revolution, constitutes the core of Leninism. It is also the essence of Lenin's adaptation of Marxism to underdeveloped countries, where the proletariat is non-existent or small and weak and the intellectuals are the chief group driving for revolution.

Lenin, however, compelled by pressures for orthodoxy engendered perhaps by his personality and certainly by his political situation, concealed the magnitude of this change—and thereby the process of adaptation—from himself and his followers. He did so by claiming that the intellectuals organized in the Party represented the "true" interests of the workers, that they, indeed, embodied that proletarian class-consciousness which Marx had ascribed to the workers, but which Lenin said workers were by themselves unable to attain.[1] From there it is but a step to the claim that the Communist Party is the "true" working class, even where it contains no workers, and where the actual workers are non-Communist—or do not exist. It is in this fashion that Communist theory explains the existence of "proletarian" dictatorship in countries like Mongolia, where there is admittedly no proletariat,[2] and it is in this sense that Communist propaganda everywhere to this day refers to the objectives of the Party as those of "the workers." Lenin himself, however, was still too much of a Marxist to take this step, nor did he need to in view of the existence of a substantial number of real workers in Russia. He always insisted that the Party remain linked to the actual working class and did not regard it as a substitute for that class, though that implication can be and has been drawn from his theory.[3]

[1] His best known statement to this effect is found in V. I. Lenin, *What Is To Be Done?*, in *Selected Works* (12 vols., New York: International Publishers, n.d.), II, 53.

[2] For a discussion in the Soviet Academy of Sciences on the question of whether Mongolia could have a proletarian government without a proletariat, see "On the Character and Attributes of People's Democracy in Countries of the Orient," translated in *Current Digest of the Soviet Press*, IV, No. 20 (June 28, 1952), 5 and 7.

[3] A relatively little known article written by Lenin in 1923, "Our Revolution,"

If Lenin's theory—and practice—on the role of the intellectuals and the Party in bringing about revolution implicitly took account of the

Selected Works, VI, 509–512, illustrates more clearly than most of his writings his view that the revolution itself rather than preceding economic development could create the prerequisites of socialism—industrialization and, with it, an industrial proletariat. It was hence a revolution of intellectuals meant to anticipate the historical development which Marx expected to come only as a result of the growth of industry and a proletariat. The article also shows the extent to which Lenin links his revolution to those in underdeveloped countries as well as his limited ability to distinguish these sharply from the Western revolutions Marx had used as a model. To appreciate these points, one must read the entire short article, but a few quotations will illustrate them:

". . . Russia stands on the borderline between civilised countries and . . . all the Oriental, non-European countries; . . . therefore Russia might and was indeed bound to reveal certain peculiarities, which, while of course following the general line of world development, distinguish her revolution from all previous revolutions in West European countries, and which introduce certain partly novel features in the passage to the countries of the East.

"Infinitely commonplace . . . is the argument . . . that . . . the objective economic premises for socialism do not exist in our country. . . .

"What if the complete hopelessness of the situation, by intensifying tenfold the energies of the workers and peasants, offered us the possibility of proceeding to create the fundamental requisites of civilisation in a way different from that of the West European countries? Has that changed the general line of development of world history? Has that changed the fundamental relations between the basic classes of every state that is being drawn, or has been drawn, into the general course of world history?

"If a definite level of culture is required for the creation of socialism (although nobody can tell what that definite level of culture is), why cannot we begin by achieving the prerequisites for that definite level of culture in a revolutionary way, and *then,* with the help of a workers' and peasants' government and a Soviet system, proceed to overtake the other nations?

"You say that civilisation is necessary for the creation of socialism. Very good. But why could we not have begun by creating such prerequisites of civilisation in our country as the expulsion of the landlords and the expulsion of the Russian capitalists, and then start moving towards socialism? Where, in what books, have you read that such variations of the customary historical order of events are impermissible or impossible?

"Napoleon, one recalls, wrote: *On s'engage et puis on voit.* Rendered freely that means: One must first start a serious engagement and then see what happens. Well, we first started a serious engagement in November (October) 1917, and . . . now there can be no doubt that in the main we have been victorious.

". . . otherwise revolutions could not be made at all. . . . Subsequent revolutions in Eastern countries, which possess vastly more numerous populations and are distinguished by a vastly greater diversity of social conditions, will undoubtedly display even greater peculiarities than the Russian revolution.

"It need hardly be said that a textbook written on Kautskian lines was a useful thing in its day. But it is really time to abandon the idea that this textbook foresaw all the forms of development of subsequent world history. It is time to declare that those who think so are simply fools."

underdeveloped character of Russia in his day, his doctrine of imperialism contains some explicit recognition of the revolutionary potential of underdeveloped societies.[1] Especially after the outbreak of World War I, Lenin was confronted by the fact that the Western European working class was not revolutionary and thus did not behave in accordance with Marx's predictions as Lenin interpreted them. Since his chief concern was revolution rather than, as with the Western Marxists (including Marx), labor's inexorable rise to political power, Lenin needed both to account for this phenomenon within a Marxian framework and to find a new agent of revolution. He did both by the theory that an influential section of the Western proletariat, a labor aristocracy, was being bribed into "social chauvinism" and the defense of capitalism by being permitted to share with the capitalists the super-profits derived from imperialist exploitation of the colonies. Carried to its logical conclusion, this theory implies that all of Western society, including the proletariat, assumes the role of exploiter or capitalist, while all of the colonial society, including its upper classes, become exploited or proletarians. Marx's domestic class struggle is thus replaced by an international conflict between the colonial powers and the colonies. The agent of revolution in the colonial countries is no longer the proletariat but nationalism.

Again, however, Lenin's adherence to Marxism and the presence in Russia of a sizable revolutionary proletariat, prevented him from drawing these conclusions. Lenin regarded his own revolution in Russia not as a nationalist movement in an underdeveloped country but as a proletarian revolution in an imperialist country, though, to be sure, the weakest link in the chain of imperialism. Nor did he give up faith in the re-emergence of the domestic class struggle and ultimate proletarian revolution in either the industrialized or the colonial societies. Being at heart interested in revolution as such, in the overthrow of the existing order, rather than in a specifically laborite, socialist revolution, Lenin, unlike Marx, devoted some attention to the revolutionary potential of nationalism in underdeveloped countries. In order to weaken the Western powers, he even favored Communist support for the "bourgeois-nationalist" movement, though he insisted that the "proletariat," i.e., the Communist Party, must not merge with it.[2] Yet

[1] V. I. Lenin, *Imperialism, the Highest Stage of Capitalism,* in *Selected Works,* V, 3–119. On some of the implications of Lenin's doctrine of imperialism that are highly relevant here, see Meyer's chapter on "The Dialectics of Backwardness," *Leninism,* pp. 257–273.

[2] V. I. Lenin, "Preliminary Draft of Theses on the National and Colonial Questions" (dated June 5, 1920), *Selected Works,* X, 231–238, p. 237.

the fact remains that he looked primarily to the working class in the industrialized West and particularly in Germany for the support which he thought the Russian Revolution needed from abroad.

Most of the contemporaries of the Russian Revolution, whether Communist or not, did not and probably could not see it as a nationalist revolution in an underdeveloped country. Nationalism in the underdeveloped countries was as yet hardly recognized, although the Mexican, Chinese, and Turkish revolutions were all roughly contemporaneous with the Russian one, and the first two had broken out a few years before 1917. At a time when the socialist labor movement in the West was, by both its friends and its enemies, still regarded as the chief agent of a future transformation of society, it is not surprising that the Russian Revolution of 1917 should have been very widely viewed as the first successful revolution by an industrial proletariat intent on introducing socialism rather than as one of the first successful revolutions by intellectuals intent on industrializing a backward country independently of Western capital. Even when what proletarian elements there had been in the early Communist regime, such as the soviets of workers and the trade unions, had been eliminated from power, and when Stalin ceased to rely on the proletariat in the West for the maintenance of the Soviet regime, this image of the nature of the Russian Revolution persisted. It continued even when Stalin's "second revolution" of rapid industrialization made it quite obvious that developments in Russia did not fit the model of revolution Western socialists had developed, which had always pre-supposed a highly industrialized society, but did share some of the principal characteristics of nationalist revolutions in underdeveloped countries.[1]

The Communists themselves, inside and outside the Soviet Union, were too deeply steeped in the Marxist ideology to give up their view of the Revolution, nor could they do so without sacrificing a following attracted by their supposed success in realizing Marx's first goal, the socialist revolution, and by their vistas of a future classless society of peace, justice, and plenty. Conservatives everywhere, on the other hand, could gladly join in describing the Soviet regime as the first socialist one, for by focusing on the suppression and suffering it brought

---

[1] The changes in the nature of Communism that occurred as a result of its adaptation to the requirements of underdevelopment, first in Russia and then in Asia and the other underdeveloped countries, are well delineated in Robert V. Daniels' perceptive introduction, "The Evolution of the Communist Mind," to his *A Documentary History of Communism* (New York: Random House, 1960). He sums them up when he says that "the Western, international, post-industrial, anarchistic, proletarian revolution had become the Eastern, national, industrializing, totalitarian, middle-class-intellectual revolution." *Ibid.*, p. lxi.

to many, they could discredit whatever they chose to call socialist in their own countries, identifying with the Soviet Union anything from the labor movement to river development, from social legislation to racial equality. Western socialists therefore had an interest in stressing the fact that the Russian Revolution had not been proletarian, that the Soviet regime was not socialist as they had traditionally used that term. But so much were they, too, committed to the patterns Marx had derived from Western European history, that they commonly assumed that if the Revolution had not been proletarian it must have been bourgeois. To this day, the debate continues whether the Bolsheviks were the Jacobins or the Bonapartists, whether they pushed the Revolution forward or were in fact counter-revolutionaries. Analogies with earlier revolutions can throw light on some aspects of the Russian Revolution,[1] but they should not be allowed to conceal other aspects pointing to a different interpretation. The old middle class of traders and craftsmen was not a principal driving force in the Russian Revolution any more than it is in the revolutions of underdeveloped countries today. There is, therefore, even less justification for regarding the Russian Revolution as primarily a bourgeois revolution (as that term has been applied to the English and French Revolutions) than for regarding it as a proletarian one. The Russian Revolution, from our point of view, is best interpreted as a revolution of the intellectuals, supported by those parts of the proletariat and the peasantry that were politically conscious or stirred into consciousness by the Revolution. Its goal, or, at any rate, its result, was the destruction of the old aristocratic order of large landownership and bureaucratic and military rule, and the rapid introduction of industry without economic and political dependence on Western capital. We can, in short, classify it as a nationalist revolution in an underdeveloped country, as we defined that term earlier.[2]

The Russian Revolution and the regime it brought to power were

[1] Crane Brinton, *The Anatomy of Revolution* (New York: Vintage Books, 1957), and also Isaac Deutscher, "The French Revolution and the Russian Revolution: Some Suggestive Analogies," *World Politics*, IV, No. 3 (April 1952), 369–381.

[2] Giorgio Borsa, "A Historical Perspective for Western Policy in Asia," *Confluence*, IV, No. 4 (January 1956), 407–420, suggests that future historians may conclude "that world communism, far from exploiting revolutionary tensions in Asia for its own purposes, was but a means by which backward stagnant societies were brought within the orbit of modern civilization." Both in Russia and in China, Communists have failed to achieve what they pretend is their main goal of egalitarianism, but they have achieved "national unity and independence; an agrarian revolution liberating the peasants from oppressive landlordism; capital investment and industrialization." *Ibid.*, p. 418.

no historical accident, as they have so often been called in an effort to explain the appearance of a "socialist" government in an underdeveloped country. Historical accidents are, in fact, generally resorted to as explanations exactly where no adequate explanations of a phenomenon are available. No such explanations of the Russian Revolution and the Communist regime could be available as long as they were sought through the exclusive application of Western European models, including the Marxian one. Perhaps we can help replace accident by regularity and mystery by understanding, which is, after all, the function of science, by fitting the Russian Revolution into the broad historical pattern of the nationalist revolutions in underdeveloped countries.

THREE DECADES OF PROLETARIANISM

For at least thirty years after the Russian Revolution, the Communists suffered from their inability to make as complete a break with Marxism in their thought as they had in their actions. Far from maintaining the "unity of theory and practice" to which they professed to adhere, they could not, in their theory and propaganda, as they did in their practice, entirely replace the party of the proletariat with the party of the intellectuals, the class struggle and the revolution of the proletariat with the nationalist movement and the industrialization of the underdeveloped countries. Had they been able to see themselves for what they were, in fact, more and more becoming, the Communists could have presented themselves to their fellow intellectuals in other underdeveloped countries as the first ones to succeed in attaining their common goal—rapid industrialization and elimination of the aristocracy and Western domination. Instead, they thought of themselves as the vanguard of an industrial proletariat and, therefore, of their revolution as an example to the West. The result was that they fell between two stools. In the West, where there was a proletariat, the appeal of Communism failed because its real achievement was irrelevant in already highly industrialized countries. In the underdeveloped countries, where its achievements were highly relevant, its appeal failed because it obscured that relevance by insisting on the proletarian and hence Western nature of Communism. For this reason Communist propaganda could do little or nothing to overcome Communism's general lack of progress before World War II.[1]

[1] Cf. Harry J. Benda's virtually identical view: "For many years, well into the 1930's and perhaps beyond, Communist progress in Southeast Asia—and for that matter in Asia generally—was seriously hampered by the Marxist blinkers through

Not only in the Soviet Union and in the West, but also in the under-developed countries themselves, Communist parties, for three decades after the Revolution, kept insisting that they were parties of the proletariat. They did this even though they followed two sharply different strategies during this period, each resulting primarily from Soviet reactions to conditions in Europe, particularly in Germany.

The "left" strategy was, with some interludes in the early and middle 1920's,[1] in effect until the mid-thirties. It originated in Lenin's hope for Communist revolutions in Central and Western Europe. This hope, to be realized, required first of all the destruction of the hold of social democracy on the majority of European labor. Though it was, in fact, discarded a long time ago, the "left" strategy is still widely thought to embody Communism's objectives, for it was this strategy that regarded capitalism as the main enemy and the socialist revolution as the therefore immediate goal. Since all other parties were considered capitalist or allied with capitalism, the Communists' approach to all of them, but particularly to the socialists, was that of the "united front from below," an attempt to win over their proletarian, and also poor peasant and petty-bourgeois, followers and to discredit their leadership.

The "right" strategy had its heyday from the mid-thirties until a few years after World War II, interrupted only by a brief return to the "left" during the period of the Hitler-Stalin pact (August 1939–June

which the Russian leaders looked at world events. In spite of the success of their own revolution in an economically 'backward' country, Soviet leaders for a long time continued to expect a proletarian revolution in the West rather than Asian revolutions, to which they assigned at most a secondary significance. They were slow to grasp the nature of the revolutionary situation because of their dialectical misorientation.

"In this serious misreading of the course of events, the Soviets—not unlike the non-Communist nationalist leaders in Southeast Asia—showed their Western intellectual heritage, of which Marxism is after all only one, though the most radical offshoot. As long as the Communists adhered to this heritage, they failed miserably in the East. The inglorious collapse of Communism in China in 1927, for example, can almost certainly be largely attributed to this close reading of Marxist scriptures, which are actually quite irrelevant to Asian developments. No less striking are the failures of Communism to gain a substantial foothold in India and Japan until almost the end of the Second World War." Harry J. Benda, "Communism in Southeast Asia," *The Yale Review*, XLV, No. 3 (Spring 1956), 417–429.

[1] See Jane Degras, "United Front Tactics in the Comintern 1921–1928," David Footman, ed., *International Communism*, St. Antony's Papers, No. 9 (Carbondale, Ill.: Southern Illinois University Press, 1960), pp. 9–22. See also Paul Katona, "Right and Left—A Brief Survey," *Problems of Communism*, X, No. 2 (March–April 1961), 13–17.

1941). It stemmed from the Soviet Union's desire for cooperation with the Western powers and for collaboration between Communist and other parties against the threat of Fascism. Fascism, therefore, was now the main enemy, and the establishment and defense of democracy of the "bourgeois" variety became the Communists' main preoccupation. Not being anti-capitalist, this "right" strategy called for "top-alliances" of the Communist parties with anti-Fascist parties—which the "left" strategy had denounced—through agreements with their leadership; for a "united front from above" with socialist parties; for a "popular front" which would also include "bourgeois" parties of the left; and finally, during the War, for a "national front" which would encompass even parties of the right as long as they were opposed to the Fascist enemies of the Soviet Union.

Both "left" and "right" strategies, in spite of their European origins, were faithfully followed by Communist parties throughout the world, regardless of the fact that, in underdeveloped countries, the industrial proletariat, which the Communists claimed to represent, was either non-existent or extremely weak. This proved particularly disastrous to Communist success under the "left" strategy, which emphasized "proletarian" policies and the early coming of the proletarian revolution and obliged Communist parties to attack all other parties and movements, including the nationalist ones, which, in some cases, had a substantial following. Adoption of the "right" strategy at least permitted Communist parties in underdeveloped countries to escape from this position of hopeless isolation and futility. They now entered into alliances with, or even joined, existing "bourgeois-nationalist" movements, for the nationalists' enemies—aristocratic rule and colonialism (which the Communists called "feudalism" and "imperialism")—were assumed to be also the Communists' principal enemies, corresponding to Fascism in the West; "national liberation" and a "bourgeois-democratic" revolution were now regarded as the proper goals. But even under this "right" strategy, the Communists maintained their identity as a party which claimed to represent the proletariat, and secondarily also the poor peasantry and petty-bourgeoisie, and collaborated with "bourgeois" groups only for limited and short-run purposes.

The Communists' stubborn insistence on appearing as the representatives of a largely non-existent class fighting battles against virtually non-existent capitalists was, no doubt, an important factor in their amazing failure to make headway even in those underdeveloped countries where the growth of a nationalist movement indicated the existence of a very real revolutionary potential. Thus, in India, where the nationalist Congress had 500,000 members by 1936, the Communist Party, during 1934, after 15 years of organizing efforts, increased its membership from 20 to 150! By 1939, the Congress passed the 5 million mark, while the Communist Party had a mere 5000 members by 1942.[1] Only in China, of all the underdeveloped countries, did the Communists make some significant advances before World War II and there they did so to the extent that they broke with the general "proletarian" pattern of Communism, when their failure in the cities forced them to adopt Mao Tse-tung's strategy of reliance on the peasantry.[2]

NEO-MAOISM AND NATIONALISM

The cold war between the United States and the Soviet Union compelled international Communism to develop a new strategy, which was destined finally to bring the policies and propaganda of Communist parties throughout the world, and particularly in its underdeveloped parts, into line with the modernizing nationalist role which Communism had played in the Soviet Union. It was a strategy which, in short, turned Communism from a professedly proletarian into a frankly nationalist movement. This new strategy was first developed by Mao Tse-tung during World War II in his battle against the Japanese. It is for this reason that I have called it the neo-Maoist strategy, but it was adopted by Moscow and the Communist parties, in response to Soviet foreign policy needs, beginning about 1947.[3]

[1] Gene D. Overstreet and Marshall Windmiller, *Communism in India* (Berkeley and Los Angeles: University of California Press, 1959), pp. 155, 172, 357.

[2] See Benjamin I. Schwartz, *Chinese Communism and the Rise of Mao* (Cambridge, Mass.: Harvard University Press, 1952).

[3] I defined the nature of the neo-Maoist strategy, illustrated its appeal by numerous quotations, and traced and documented in some detail its adoption in Moscow and then by the Indian Communists in my book, *Moscow and the Communist Party of India* (New York: John Wiley & Sons, 1956). See also my article, "The New Strategy of International Communism," *The American Political Science Review*, XLIX, No. 2 (June 1955), 478–486, and especially Bernard S. Morris and Morris Watnick, "Current Communist Strategy in Nonindustrialized Countries," reprinted on pp. 282–292, below, and also Robert J. Alexander, "Brazil's CP: A Case Study in Latin-American Communism," *Problems of Communism*, IV, No. 5 (September–October 1955), 17–26. The subject is brought up to date by Hugh Seton-Watson, "The Role of the 'National Bourgeoisie' in Afro-Asian Independence Movement: Theory and Practice in Soviet Strategy," a paper delivered at the Third International Conference of Sovietologists, September 18–25, 1960, in Tokyo, and reproduced by the Evaluation and Analysis Department, Radio Free Europe (Munich), September 19, 1960. See also W. Z. Laqueur, "Towards National Democracy: Soviet Doctrine and the New Countries," *Survey* (London), No. 37 (July–September 1961), 3–11.

Once involved in the cold war, the Soviet Union had to mobilize all possible forces, regardless of their class character, against American foreign policy objectives. Yet at the same time, most of the parties that had been the Communists' wartime and immediate postwar "national front" allies, such as the socialist and Catholic movements in Western Europe, were now pro-American, making continued collaboration impossible. In 1947, Zhdanov, at the founding meeting of the Cominform, divided the entire world into two "camps," one led by the United States and one by the Soviet Union.[1] Viewed through the black-and-white spectacles of this doctrine, even most of the nationalist movements in underdeveloped countries appeared to the Communists as mere stooges of "American imperialism." There was no doubt, then, that the "right" strategy of cooperation with non-Communist parties had to be abandoned with the onset of the cold war. For the next two years there was uncertainty in Moscow as to whether it should be replaced by the old "left" or the new neo-Maoist strategy, while the various Communist parties pursued either one or the other. But by 1949 it had become clear that the "left" strategy unnecessarily limited Communist parties' support to the "exploited" classes in each country and concentrated their fire on local capitalists, rather than on the Soviet Union's enemy, the United States.

The neo-Maoist strategy was an attempt to appeal to all classes at a time when an alliance with most major parties, including most nationalist movements, was impossible. Under it, the Communists' main enemy was identified as neither capitalism nor Fascism, but as "imperialism," a term that has become virtually synonymous with the United States in the Communist vocabulary. Whether the opposition to foreign imperialism and its alleged native allies, such as the nationalists, was to be peaceful or violent was a matter of flexible tactics rather than world-wide strategy, but it was always to be based on what the Chinese Communists have called the bloc of four classes. That bloc consisted of the proletariat, the peasantry, the petty-bourgeoisie (which is the rather inappropriate Marxist-Western term the Communists apply to what we have designated as the old middle class, and to some extent also to the intellectuals), and, most notably, the anti-imperialist capitalists. That this latter group may, in fact, hardly exist in underdeveloped countries does not reduce the importance of its explicit inclusion by the Communists in the neo-Maoist front, for it is at this point that the wholly novel character of their new strategy becomes apparent.

[1] A. Zhdanov, "The International Situation," *For a Lasting Peace, for a People's Democracy!* (Journal of the Cominform), November 10, 1947, pp. 2–4.

Neo-Maoism did not differ much from the old "right" strategy in establishing a broad front of the four classes (to which have since been added aristocratic elements). But since the former party-allies were not available any more, the Communist appeal to all these groups now had be to directed "from below." This meant that the Communist party now had to claim to represent the true interests not only of the "exploited" classes, as it had always done, but also of their "exploiters." For the first time, Communist parties could transcend the limits imposed on them by their former "proletarianism"; they freed themselves from the proletarian myth after being prisoners to it for thirty years.

What Lenin had merely implied, as he took account of the realities of Russian underdevelopment and of the anti-colonialist movement, was now realized in neo-Maoism. This was true of the implication in Lenin's doctrine of imperialism that the colonial powers, including their working classes, were the main enemy of all classes in the colonies and that the latter would and should unite against the former. It was also true of Lenin's identification of the intellectual leadership of the Communist party with the "true" proletariat. Once this identification was accepted, the Party could use any class to attain its objectives, and its objectives would, by definition, be proletarian.[1] Lenin had still insisted on a link between the Party and the actual proletariat, though in his practice he also relied very heavily on the peasantry. Under neo-Maoism all classes, including the capitalists, became acceptable as tools of the Party. The Leninist doctrines of imperialism and of intellectual leadership, then, contained in embryonic form (or were at any rate quite compatible with) the abandonment of the class struggle and of the socialist revolution, Marxian doctrines which Communist parties in underdeveloped countries have by now fairly openly given up. Russia was too close to Western Europe, not only geographically and culturally but also in her economic development, and Lenin was too close to Marx for these implications to become apparent either to him or to most of his generation. The logic of the changes he introduced into original Marxism in transplanting it to the underdeveloped soil of his native land has become fully clear only with its further transplantation to countries even more backward industrially than was Russia at the turn of the century.[2]

[1] See Morris Watnick, "Continuity and Innovation in Chinese Communism," *World Politics,* VI, No. 1 (October 1953), 84–105, pp. 92–97.

[2] On the growth of an "Eastern orientation" in the Soviet view of world revolutionary development, from Lenin's day to the present, see Robert C. Tucker, "Russia, the West, and World Order," *World Politics,* XII, No. 1 (October 1959),

The relative success of Communism in the postwar period as compared to the prewar era has been due to a number of factors in addition to its adoption of the neo-Maoist strategy. Thus, colonialism was weakened both by the war itself and by changes that had taken place in the colonies as well as in the colonial powers. Communism's prestige and power had grown as a result of the Soviet Union's victory in the war and its occupation of Eastern Europe and North Korea, and of the role Communist parties played in the anti-German and anti-Japanese resistance movements. Perhaps most important, the achievements of Soviet industrialization have been far more dramatic and obvious recently than they were before World War II. Neo-Maoism, however, made it possible for the Communists to exploit fully the attractiveness of these achievements to underdeveloped countries.

With a strategy openly appealing to, in their own often-used phrase, "all classes," [1] the Communists in underdeveloped countries were no longer tied to a non-existent or very weak proletarian base or obliged to attack the native capitalists, if any, or, for that matter, any other native groups except those closely connected with "imperialist" interests. They could thus seek support from any group to whom their anti-colonialist program appealed.[2] The main domestic plank of this

1-23. See also Roy C. Macridis, "Stalinism and the Pattern of Colonial Revolt," *The Western Political Quarterly*, VII, No. 1 (March 1954), 23–35.

[1] In the single most important directive issued jointly by Moscow and Peking to the Asian Communist parties to adopt neo-Maoism, the first point reads: "The working class must unite with all other classes, parties, groups, organizations and individuals who are willing to oppose the oppression of imperialism and its lackeys, to form a broad nationwide united front and ready to wage a resolute struggle against imperialism and its lackeys." "Speech by Liu Shao-chi at the Conference of Trade Unions of Asia and Oceania," *For a Lasting Peace, for a People's Democracy!*, December 30, 1949, p. 2. For additional quotations and comment, see Milton Sacks, "The Strategy of Communism in Southeast Asia," *Pacific Affairs*, XXIII, No. 3 (September 1950), 231–236, and Kautsky, *Moscow and the Communist Party of India*, pp. 95 ff. A more recent authoritative international Communist pronouncement similarly declares: "The urgent tasks of national rebirth facing the countries that have shaken off the colonial yoke cannot be effectively accomplished unless a determined struggle is waged against imperialism and the remnants of feudalism by all the patriotic forces of the nations united in a single national-democratic front. . . . In the liberation struggle . . . a big role can be played by the national patriotic forces, by all elements of the nation prepared to fight for national independence, against imperialism." "Declaration of Representatives of the Eighty-one Communist Parties, Meeting in Moscow, November-December, 1960," Dan N. Jacobs, ed., *The New Communist Manifesto and Related Documents* (Evanston, Ill.: Row, Peterson & Co., 1961) pp. 31, 32.

[2] This program, with its striking absence of proletarianism and anti-capitalism, is well summarized in the "Declaration . . . of the Eighty-one Communist Par-

program was the promise of rapid modernization and industrialization on the Soviet and Chinese Communist model. For the first time, the appeal of the Soviet Union having achieved the goals of intellectuals in underdeveloped countries—elimination of aristocratic rule and quick industrialization without dependence on Western capital— could be fully brought home to these intellectuals. In industrialized countries, it is difficult to appreciate the power of this appeal and the depth and urgency of the intellectuals' concern with the problem of modernization. To them the appeal is hardly weakened by knowledge of the sacrifices which the Communist path to modernization imposed on millions in the Soviet Union and China. In countries where mass starvation was a common occurrence and millions are still undernourished, sick, and illiterate, and where there is no tradition of individualism and civil liberties, such sacrifices do not weigh very heavily as against the hope of future improvements. Nor do the intellectuals expect to bear these sacrifices themselves; what makes the Soviet and Chinese example so attractive is also the fact that it put intellectuals in control, with seemingly untold opportunities to gain power and prestige.[1]

ties . . .": "The national democratic tasks on the basis of which the progressive forces of the nation can and do unite in the countries which have won their freedom, are: the consolidation of political independence, the carrying out of agrarian reforms in the interest of the peasantry, elimination of the survivals of feudalism, the uprooting of imperialist economic domination, the restriction of foreign monopolies and their expulsion from the national economy, the creation and development of a national industry, improvement of the living standard, the democratization of social life, the pursuance of an independent and peaceful foreign policy, and the development of economic and cultural cooperation with the socialist and other friendly countries." *Ibid.*, p. 32.

[1] On the Communist appeal to the intellectuals in underdeveloped countries, see Morris Watnick, "The Appeal of Communism to the Underdeveloped Peoples," reprinted on pp. 316–334, below, an important article that anticipates some of the points made in this essay on the nature of nationalism in underdeveloped countries. For another interesting approach to the Communist appeal to intellectuals, see Eduard Heimann, "Marxism and Underdeveloped Countries," *Social Research,* XIX (September 1952), 322–345. See also Joel Carmichael, "The Nationalist-Communist Symbiosis in the Middle East," reprinted on pp. 304–315, below; Eugene Staley, *The Future of Underdeveloped Countries* (New York: Harper and Brothers, 1954), pp. 174–178; Sidney Hook, "Grim Report: Asia in Transition," *The New York Times Magazine,* April 5, 1959, pp. 11, 104, 106, 108; and, for an excellent review article, G. L. Arnold, "Communism and the Intelligentsia in Backward Areas: Some Recent Literature," *Problems of Communism,* IV, No. 5 (September–October 1955), 13–17. Justus van der Kroef, "Marxism in Southeast Asia," *Current History,* XXVII, No. 159 (November 1954), 289–297, also contains some relevant points.

In fact, Russia in 1917 was not, like many underdeveloped countries today, overpopulated, nor did her industrialization really proceed without Western aid: it began with the foreign capital accumulated under Tsarism and continued with the support of Western credits, machinery, and technicians until the end of World War II, after which the industrial plant and specialists of the newly conquered European satellites were heavily relied upon for some time. But all this is little understood in underdeveloped countries and does not seem to reduce significantly the relevance of the Soviet—and not at all that of the Chinese—example to the intellectuals in these countries.[1] The fact remains that the Communist revolutions in Russia and in China, like their own nationalist movements, confronted the problems of backwardness at home and weakness and dependence in international affairs, and that they have already in large measure attained the goals which to the intellectuals in most underdeveloped countries are still chiefly unfulfilled aspirations. This is an appeal that the Western societies, which have been industrialized and powerful so much longer, and have acquired their industry and their power under such different circumstances, inherently have difficulty in matching.

If, as we saw earlier, nationalists in underdeveloped countries are intellectuals appealing to all strata of the population in their drive for industrialization and against colonialism, and Communists in underdeveloped countries are, as we have now seen, intellectuals appealing to all strata of the population in their drive for industrialization and against colonialism, then Communists are nationalists.[2] This conclusion sums up the vital change that the neo-Maoist strategy brought to

[1] The relevance to underdeveloped countries of the Soviet model, particularly in the area of economic policy, is examined by Alec Nove, "The Soviet Model and Under-developed Countries," *International Affairs*, XXXVII, No. 1 (January 1961), 29–38, and by Oleg Hoeffding, "The Soviet Union: Model for Asia?—State Planning and Forced Industrialization," *Problems of Communism*, VIII, No. 6 (November–December 1959), 38–46. See also Alex Inkeles, "The Soviet Union: Model for Asia?—The Social System," *ibid.*, pp. 30–38.

[2] "As the Chinese experience illustrates, Asian communism is not based on a class-struggle strategy or appeal; it is primarily a movement of belligerent nationalism." Robert Vincent Daniels, "The Chinese Revolution in Russian Perspective," *World Politics*, XIII, No. 2 (January 1961), 210–230, p. 229. On the relation between nationalism and Communism in an area where, because of its backwardness, proletarianism is particularly irrelevant, see Walter Z. Laqueur, *Communism and Nationalism in the Middle East* (New York: Frederick A. Praeger, 1956), and also some of the articles in Laqueur, ed., *The Middle East in Transition.* See also Victor Alba, "Communism and Nationalism in Latin America," *Problems of Communism*, VII, No. 5 (September–October 1958), 24–31; and David T. Cattell, "Communism and the African Negro," *Problems of Communism*, VIII, No. 5 (September–October 1959), 35–41.

international Communism, beginning in the late 1940's. To be sure, since complete and sudden breaks in ideological development are impossible, the Communists still conceal this change from themselves and from others by their continued habit of seeking doctrinal support for their practice in quotations from Marx and Engels and by their continuing affinity for the vocabulary of the nineteenth-century Western socialist movement. But though words lag behind action or, to use Marxist terminology, the ideological superstructure is transformed more slowly than the material base, even in Communist propaganda and theoretical writings, the "people's masses" and "all peace-loving people"—and, most broadly, simply "the peoples"—are more and more replacing the "proletariat" and the "working class," fighting now not the "class struggle" for "class interests" and for the "socialist revolution," but in the "national interest" for "national independence."

In slowing the complete identification of Communism with nationalism, the remnants of a proletarian vocabulary have been less important than the fact that neo-Maoism was originally developed as a strategy of opposition to the major nationalist movements in underdeveloped countries which appeared to the Communists to be tools of the "imperialists," rather than genuinely anti-colonialist. In the period of the adoption of the neo-Maoist strategy, it was only in exceptional cases, such as those of the regimes of Arbenz in Guatemala, Mossadeq of Iran, and the Nationalist Party in Indonesia, that Moscow considered a nationalist government sufficiently pro-Soviet and anti-American to have the local Communist parties support rather than oppose the non-Communist nationalists.

THE CONVERGENCE OF COMMUNISM AND NATIONALISM

With the adoption of neo-Maoism, Communist parties had been turned into nationalist parties with respect to their ideology and policies, but they and the Soviet Union were still opposed to the older nationalist movements in underdeveloped countries. In the early 1950's, however, even before Stalin's death, a change in Soviet and subsequently in Communist party policy became apparent.

The realization evidently grew among Soviet policy makers that their anti-American objectives could be served at least as well by the non-Communist nationalist movements and governments as by the Communist parties in underdeveloped countries. This had become true not so much as a result of changes in the policies of these non-Communist nationalist movements as of the gradual ripening of changes in Communism itself. Communist goals had now become limited to those that can be effectively served by nationalism—chiefly the elimination of American political, military, economic, and cultural influence wherever possible.

Soviet reliance on non-Communist nationalists to help carry out Soviet objectives would have been quite impossible when the Communists still thought of themselves as champions of the lower classes, and of their goal as a social revolution. Then the nationalist movements were contemptuously referred to as "bourgeois-nationalist." A generation after the Revolution, the dream of world-wide social revolution, which had conditioned even some short-run policies of Lenin and Trotsky and probably affected the long-run calculations of Stalin, had receded so far into the background as not to influence Soviet policy any longer. Statements by Soviet leaders that world Communism is their ultimate goal are of the same significance as similar statements with regard to world-wide justice and liberty made by other government leaders. They are no doubt believed by those who make them and they serve as important symbols to mobilize the loyalties and exertions of their followers, but they cannot account for any particular foreign policy decision.

This change of Soviet objectives from proletarianism to nationalism, from world revolution to the expansion of Soviet power—which, at the present time, is more or less synonymous with the reduction of American power—is to be explained in terms of changes in Soviet society and leadership. Immediately after the Revolution, that leadership consisted of "professional revolutionaries," men who had spent most of their lives dreaming and plotting revolution, philosophers, journalists, and agitators, who could make passionate appeals because they were passionately moved by what they considered injustice and misery. These men did not change their outlook after they came to power. They continued to consider themselves revolutionaries and champions of the underprivileged and looked on the country which they now controlled as the base for further advances of the revolution. But as that base was consolidated through industrialization, its society has, inevitably, changed. A new bureaucratic and managerial leadership has emerged to whom the Revolution is not something yet to be made or even completed, but something in the past, on which its own power is based, and that hence should be preserved. They are conservatives, for they wish to preserve the *status quo* in their own society. To be sure, as is true of any regime established by revolution, the symbols of the *status quo* are those of the Revolution, but this must not conceal the fact that the new leaders can maximize their power not, as their predecessors did for most of their lives, by overthrowing the government of their country, but by strengthening it.[1] They share many of the concerns of managerial and bureaucratic elites in other industrialized countries[2] and, being at the top of their own society, they have little understanding or sympathy for the underprivileged in other societies. As they seek to strengthen their power position through their foreign policies, they are, therefore, not bound, either by conviction or by any affinity of interests, to rely on the lower classes in other countries for support. Rather, they can appeal to any strata that may, for whatever reasons, be opposed to the policy objectives of the United States.

Once world Communism had, in effect, been dropped as a Soviet policy objective and replaced by the much more realistic one of expansion of the power of the Soviet Union and of those who govern it, Khrushchev could recognize the existence of a third, neutralist, "camp" in addition to Zhdanov's two.[3] In an evolution not entirely dissimilar from that of American foreign policy, which also at one time tended to regard neutralism as "immoral," Moscow came to accept and even to see advantages to itself in the existence of governments that were, if not pro-Soviet in their policies, at any rate frequently anti-American. During the 1950's, the Soviet Union acted more and more as the champion of the neutralist countries and supplied some of their regimes

[1] Robert C. Tucker concludes his analysis of the 1961 Soviet Communist Party program, "The CPSU Draft Program: A Credo of Conservatism," *Problems of Communism*, X, No. 5 (September–October 1961), 1–4, with this statement: "Despite the impression of radicalism created by its use of revolutionary phraseology, the new Communist Manifesto is, in its underlying significance, a credo of Soviet conservatism. It is the political expression of a ruling and possessing class which wants to project an image of a Soviet Russia on the march—and towards full communism at that—but which, in actuality, is concerned most of all with the preservation, without radical change, of the existing institutional structure and its associated pattern of power, policy, and privilege."

[2] See the interesting work by Clark Kerr, John T. Dunlap, Frederick H. Harbison, and Charles A. Myers, *Industrialism and Industrial Man: The Problems of Labor and Management in Economic Growth* (Cambridge, Mass.: Harvard University Press, 1960), which, in discussing "the inevitable structuring of the managers and the managed in the course of industrialization" (pp. 7–8), concludes that ". . . the similarities of enterprise management in all advanced industrializing societies are far greater than their differences." (p. 164).

[3] At the 20th Party Congress of 1956, he hailed the emergence of "a vast peace zone," "of a group of peace-loving European and Asian states which have proclaimed nonparticipation in blocs as a principle of their foreign policy." N. S. Khrushchev, "Report of the Central Committee of the Communist Party of the Soviet Union to the 20th Party Congress," February 14, 1956, in Leo Gruliow, ed., *Current Soviet Policies—II: The Documentary Record of the 20th Communist Party Congress and Its Aftermath* (New York: Frederick A. Praeger, 1957), p. 33.

with increasingly significant amounts of economic and technical aid, all, of course, in an attempt to swing these governments to its side. Its side, however, could no longer be defined as that of Communism, if by Communism we mean either an ideology or a social system, whether of Marx, of Lenin, or even of the present-day Soviet Union. Rather, its side is now simply that of the Soviet Union in the international power conflict, in which the neutralist governments can lend support to the Soviet Union by denying to the United States and its allies military bases, raw materials, markets, and diplomatic support, and by extending similar advantages to the Soviet Union.

Soviet backing of neutralist regimes, therefore, is generally in no way dependent on the adoption by such regimes of policies favorable to the lower classes, such as land reform or support for trade unions, or even of policies favorable to the local Communist parties. Many nationalist movements do, for reasons of their own which we have discussed, pursue such policies, but regardless of that fact, there is today hardly a nationalist movement left anywhere, either in the government or in the opposition, with which Soviet foreign policy-makers do not consider cooperation to be possible and profitable. Some of the few underdeveloped countries that are still so backward as to have virtually no movement of nationalist intellectuals—Ethiopia, Yemen, Afghanistan, and Nepal—are among the chief beneficiaries of Soviet foreign aid, again regardless of the fact that their governments are what traditional Communists would have considered the most reactionary regimes in the world today.

The change in Soviet foreign policy deeply affected the role of the Communist parties in underdeveloped countries.[1] As the nationalist movements and governments changed, in the Soviet view, from stooges of Western imperialism to peace-loving defenders of national independence, Moscow expected the Communist parties to give up their opposition, which they had, with very few exceptions, maintained in the late 1940's. At first, they were directed to support the foreign policies of the nationalists wherever these were anti-American in their implications. Soon, however, as the Soviet Union found the nationalist regimes of some underdeveloped countries useful for its now more limited purposes, Communist parties were pushed to give

[1] The changes in their strategy are clearly outlined against the background of the earlier neo-Maoist strategy by Bernard S. Morris, "Recent Shifts in Communist Strategy: India and South-East Asia," reprinted on pp. 293–303, below. See also Bernard S. Morris, "Continuity of Communist Strategic Doctrine Since the Twentieth Party Congress," *The Annals of the American Academy of Political and Social Science*, vol. 317 (May 1958), 130–137.

up their opposition to their governments' domestic policies as well. Particularly, as Soviet economic assistance to some underdeveloped countries expanded, the Communist parties were expected to support government policies in the area of economic development, a key issue in the politics of underdeveloped countries.

In countries where the Communists' appeal depends largely on discontent and particularly on the disillusionment that almost inevitably follows independence among some strata of the population, especially among some intellectuals, giving up their opposition role was likely to cost the Communists some strength, which might or might not be compensated for by increased prestige resulting from their association with the nationalist government. Some Communists in underdeveloped countries have certainly been most reluctant to praise the very movements and leaders that they had for so many years been denouncing as the representatives of capitalism and, when that was no longer regarded as a proper enemy, of imperialism. The Communist Party of India, for instance, has followed Moscow's lead only slowly all through the 1950's, has been badly split during all this time over just how much support to lend to the Nehru government, and has sought to maintain its opposition to the Congress wherever this has been at all compatible with Moscow's directives, first in a shrinking area of foreign policy, then in a similarly shrinking area of domestic policy, and most recently still on some issues of local and regional government.[1]

Whether Soviet policies happen to strengthen or weaken Communist parties is probably of relatively little concern to the policy-makers in Moscow. Their main interest lies in strengthening their ties with the nationalist movements and governments of underdeveloped countries, which are generally far more powerful than the Communist parties, and can hence be far more useful for the accomplishment of Soviet foreign policy objectives. The Communist parties are now only one tool, and generally one of decreasing importance, available to the Soviet government for influencing policy in underdeveloped countries. With the growing political and economic strength of the Soviet Union and the change in the character of its leadership, diplomatic pressures, economic aid, technical advice, and perhaps even cultural ex-

[1] Kautsky, *Moscow and the Communist Party of India*, pp. 129–130, 133–134, 173–175; Marshall Windmiller, "Indian Communism and the New Soviet Line," *Pacific Affairs*, XXIX, No. 4 (December 1956), 347–366; Overstreet and Windmiller, *Communism in India*, pp. 304–323; and Gene D. Overstreet, "Soviet and Communist Policy in India," *The Journal of Politics*, XX, No. 1 (February 1958), 187–202, pp. 199–200.

change programs are becoming the more important weapons of Soviet foreign policy. Khrushchev's visits to India and steel mills erected there by Soviet engineers are likely to be more significant in establishing Soviet influence in India than anything the Communist Party of India can do.[1] Similar efforts in Afghanistan could create a strong Soviet foothold there even in the absence of any Communist party. And in no case do such Soviet efforts have anything to do with the advancement of Communism if that term refers to a revolutionary social movement and ideology.

By 1956, Moscow began to hint that the Communist parties should take a further and even more startling step along their line of development from proletarianism to nationalism. It was now suggested that underdeveloped countries could evolve along "socialist" lines under the leadership of their bourgeoisie and that the Communist parties were to follow that leadership.[2] To Marx and even to Lenin such a view would have been utter nonsense—after all, it implies that the leadership in the class struggle be turned over to the enemy in that struggle —but, as we have seen, the class struggle has long been abandoned by the Communists, and if the term "socialism" is now devoid of any domestic-policy significance and merely means a government influenced or even dominated by the Soviet Union, the new view does make sense.

Of course, the Communist parties cannot be expected to take kindly to the suggestion that they subordinate themselves to the non-Communist nationalist movements and give up the raison d'être they have always claimed, i.e., that they are the only ones capable of leading society to socialism (whatever that term may mean). However, Communist parties in non-Communist countries have historically almost never been in any position to resist Moscow's desires for long. More

[1] For a summary of current Soviet attempts to influence Indian policy, see ibid., pp. 194–199.

[2] See, for example, the quotation, ibid., p. 193, from D. Degtiar, "Development of the National Economy of India," Kommunist (Moscow), March 1956, and the quotation in Overstreet and Windmiller, Communism in India, p. 326, from Modeste Rubinstein, "A Non-Capitalist Path for Underdeveloped Countries," New Times (Moscow), July–August 1956. Further references to more recent such Soviet statements, particularly with respect to Cuba (which is said to move toward socialism under the leadership of the petty bourgeoisie) and Africa (where leadership is to be left to the bourgeoisie) may be found in David T. Cattell, "Changes and Variations in Soviet Policies toward the Underdeveloped Areas," a paper presented to the annual meeting of the American Political Science Association, St. Louis, Mo., September 6–9, 1961, which discusses current Communist party and Soviet policy toward the nationalist movements in a manner extremely relevant to the analysis presented in this essay.

important than their opposition to the new view are the objections of the Chinese Communists. It would appear that, since about 1957, Peking would have preferred to revert to the neo-Maoist policy of "revolutionary" opposition—peaceful or violent—by a Communist-led front drawing followers from all social classes to the non-Communist nationalist movements and governments. Since the Communist parties in underdeveloped countries may also prefer an opposition role, it is not surprising that some of them have sided with the Chinese Communists in their controversies with the Soviet Communists. To be sure, the Chinese Communists have themselves not been entirely consistent on this issue; where non-Communist nationalist movements have been militantly "anti-imperialist," like the Algerian and Cuban ones, they have, if anything, been more eager than Moscow to support them.[1]

The split between Moscow and Peking over whether to support non-Communist nationalism and subordinate and possibly even sacrifice the Communist parties to it, or to support a rival Communist-led nationalist movement against non-Communist nationalism is part of the larger controversy over peaceful "co-existence" with the "capitalist" world, which had, by 1960, come out into the open.[2] It may be patched up again, but is likely to persist beneath the surface for some time, because it results not from different interpretations of the Marxist and Leninist classics, but from the different stages of economic development prevailing in the two countries at the present time, the different types of leadership corresponding to each, and their different needs and views of the world.

The Chinese economy is not yet developed to the point of inspiring the Chinese Communists with confidence like that of the Soviet Communists in their ability to defeat the United States through economic competition and through economic aid to the so-called uncommitted underdeveloped countries. Moreover, the views of the two Communist party elites as to what constitutes defeating the United States probably differ. Chinese society has not yet undergone the changes

[1] The issues dividing the Soviet and Chinese Communists on the strategy to be followed in underdeveloped countries are well summarized and documented in Donald S. Zagoria, "Sino-Soviet Friction in Underdeveloped Areas," *Problems of Communism*, X, No. 2 (March–April 1961), 1–13. See also Thomas Perry Thornton, "Peking, Moscow, and the Underdeveloped Areas," *World Politics*, XIII, No. 4 (July 1961), 491–504.

[2] The controversy is analyzed by Richard Lowenthal and documented by a large collection of Soviet and Chinese statements in G. F. Hudson, Richard Lowenthal and Roderick MacFarquhar, *The Sino-Soviet Dispute* (New York: Frederick A. Praeger, 1961).

which, in Soviet society, produced the new leadership with its new attitudes that we have just mentioned. In China, the professional revolutionaries and agitators, rather than the managers and bureaucrats, are still in control. Such men are more likely to think of their mission in terms of social revolution and, in view of their specific background, of prolonged civil war, than in terms of diplomatic and economic conflict. "Revolution," however, as their early adoption of neo-Maoism indicates, does not mean to them class struggle or championship of lower class interests, but industrialization under the leadership of intellectuals, by totalitarian methods.[1]

The present Soviet policy of subordinating the Communist parties to the leadership of the nationalist movements in underdeveloped countries points, if carried to its logical conclusion, to the total abandonment of Communist parties as tools of Soviet foreign policy in favor of Soviet cooperation with the nationalists. In fact, such organizational liquidation, to follow the ideological one, is not likely to be carried out. To be sure, where the Communist party is weak and the nationalist movement is powerful and can serve Soviet ends, the Communists may be virtually, though perhaps only temporarily, abandoned and sacrificed by Moscow. Thus, the Egyptian Communist leadership was in jail, evidently with Khrushchev's approval, during the period of greatest friendship between Nasser and Moscow.[2] However, where

[1] "Chinese communism has not fought anything resembling a class war. It has become instead a movement to discipline and regenerate the nation as a whole. The Chinese Communists . . . profess to lead 'the people' against 'the lackeys of imperialism,' whose status is defined not by their social standing but by their political attitude toward the Communist regime. . . . The real nature of the Communist movement must be understood on quite another basis than Marxism and the class struggle. This is particularly true of China. The equation of revolution and the class struggle is a Communist illusion." Robert Vincent Daniels, "The Chinese Revolution in Russian Perspective," World Politics, XIII, No. 2 (January 1961), 218.

[2] See the statement by an Iraqi Communist that "an anti-government conspiracy would be a crime in any Arab state struggling against imperialism, even if Communism were persecuted," quoted from the Polish paper Zycie Warszawy of February 17, 1959, by Donald S. Zagoria, "Sino-Soviet Friction in Underdeveloped Areas," Problems of Communism, X, No. 2 (March–April 1961), 9. Even when Khrushchev, in his speech to the Twenty-first Party Congress, defended the Egyptian Communists against Nasser's attacks, he made it clear that first things come first: "We do not conceal that we and some leaders of the UAR have different views in the ideological field, but in questions of struggle against imperialism . . . our positions coincide. . . . Differences in ideological views must not hinder the development of friendly relations between our countries and the cause of the common struggle against imperialism." N. S. Khrushchev, "On the Middle East," in Alvin Z. Rubinstein, ed., The Foreign Policy of the Soviet Union (New York: Random House, 1960), p. 401.

Communist parties are fairly strong, as is the case in India and Indonesia and even more in Iraq and Cuba, they retain some usefulness to Moscow as instruments through which pressure can be brought on the nationalist movements to remain anti-American or become more so. Most Communist parties in underdeveloped countries thus have been assigned the rather unenviable function of making their domestic rival more, and themselves less, indispensable to the Soviet Union.

Organizationally, then, Communists retain their identity, and in terms of formal party membership it is still possible to distinguish between Communist and non-Communist nationalists. But in their policies, the Communist intellectuals, driving for industrialization and independence, and the non-Communist intellectuals, driving for industrialization and independence, have become virtually indistinguishable. The frequently asked question whether leaders like Touré in Guinea and Lumumba and Gizenga in the Congo and, above all, Castro in Cuba are "genuine" nationalists or "really" Communists is hence meaningless; such nationalists have come to be like Communists because Communists have come to be like them. The identification of Communism with nationalism has gone farthest in Cuba where a non-Communist nationalist revolution in the short time of about two years turned the country into a self-proclaimed "socialist" one, following the present Communist party line—all without the Cuban Communist party, which had existed for years before the Cuban revolution, coming to power in the process, and with individual Communist leaders occupying top positions only in its later stages.

It is true that nationalist movements have advocated or pursued some policies of nationalization of industry, of land reform, and generally of a redistribution of wealth to favor the poor, policies which are popularly associated with Communism and which may, indeed, be quite similar to those pursued by the Bolsheviks after their Revolution in Russia. If nationalists act in this fashion, it can be accounted for by their nationalism alone, however, and without reference to Communism. For nationalism in underdeveloped countries is, as we have seen, a movement directed against political and economic domination from abroad by colonialism and against domestic political and economic domination by the native aristocracy. Nor is it surprising that it may adopt policies similar to those of the Russian Revolution if we consider that Revolution itself as a nationalist movement in an underdeveloped country.

Individual nationalist intellectuals in underdeveloped countries have, to be sure, been influenced by Leninist thought, which, as we saw, adapts Marxism to the needs of such people.[1] In this sense, they may indeed be called Communists, but in this sense the Communists in Russia and in the Communist parties are not Communists any more. When nationalists today are expropriating and redistributing property, they may be influenced by Marx or Lenin, but they are not likely to be acting at the behest of Khrushchev and of local Communist parties. These domestic aspects of nationalism—the "class struggle"— are precisely the ones in which the Communists are least interested. To them, nationalism is chiefly useful as anti-Americanism, and hence changes in the property system matter to them only if the property involved happens to be American-owned, as was often the case in Cuba. On this point it is instructive to compare the non-Communist party member Castro's policies of far-reaching nationalization and land reform with the official Communist Party government in the Indian state of Kerala. The latter, the only Soviet-influenced Communist government to come to power since the present Communist attitude has matured, was far less radical on land reform than the Cuban government and no more so than the non-Communist Indian state governments. It took steps to attract private Indian capital to the state and did not even carry out its campaign promises to nationalize foreign-owned enterprises.[2]

Being largely interested in the foreign policy aspects of nationalism, the Communists, even more than the non-Communist nationalists, seek to maintain domestic unity cutting across all class lines. Since non-Communist nationalists may threaten this unity with their policies of expropriation of landed, and sometimes of industrial and commercial proprietors, the Communists may be found to oppose such policies, as they apparently did in Iraq after Kassem's seizure of power. To the extent that they are ideologically distinguishable from the other nationalists at all, then, the Communists are likely to be found on the "right" and the others on the "left" on matters of domestic policy—that area of policy where the terms "right" and "left" have traditionally been used.

If Communism is defined not as some ideology of the past, whether Marx's or Lenin's, but as whatever movement abroad Moscow backs, then Communism has become more and more identical with nation-

---

[1] According to Adam B. Ulam, *The Unfinished Revolution*, every society undergoing industrialization passes through a "Marxist" stage, even if there is no Soviet or Communist influence whatever, because of Marxism's peculiar appeal to such societies. Cf. footnote 1, p. 60.

[2] Overstreet, "Soviet and Communist Policy in India," *The Journal of Politics*, XX, No. 1 (February 1958), 200–202.

alism in underdeveloped countries. It did not invent that nationalism any more than it had earlier invented proletarianism, but it is using it with vastly more success. Nothing said here implies that this nationalism can be used only by Communism. Its demands for rapid modernization and independence can perhaps also be met by the West, conceivably even better met. But it must be realized that in the past the Western powers have, by and large, been widely regarded as the enemies of independence and often also of modernization in the underdeveloped countries. The Soviet Union, on the other hand, can claim never to have been colonialist and to have granted equality with the Russians to the subject peoples of the Tsarist empire. Soviet expansion both in Asia and in Eastern Europe has everywhere been accompanied by rapid industrialization and modernization. To the underdeveloped countries and particularly to their intellectuals, it is therefore anything but a relevant example of colonialism, no matter how much suffering and suppression it may have brought to many. Finally, the Soviet Union can claim a background similar to that of the underdeveloped countries and shares the enmity of many of their intellectual leaders towards the West, a situation of which the Communists have, if only in recent years, taken advantage by converting themselves into nationalists.

IV

TOTALITARIANISM
AND THE
FUTURE OF POLITICS
IN THE
DEVELOPING COUNTRIES

THE METHODS OF TOTALITARIANISM

What of the future of politics in countries moving from underdevelopment to industrialization? Clearly, any prediction for a particular country would have to be based on an analysis of the specific forces operating in it, including many beyond the scope of our generalizations. These generalizations will, at best, make it possible to sketch out the broad alternative courses open to countries now entering on the process of industrialization. The conclusions reached in this chapter are therefore offered less as speculation, and much less as prediction, than as an attempt to trace, in highly schematic form, some tendencies of possible development inherent in various political systems.

The rise of nationalism and Communism in underdeveloped countries suggests the possible development of what is commonly referred to as totalitarianism. Like "democracy," "nationalism," and "Communism," the term "totalitarianism" has been applied so loosely as to become virtually useless in communicating any specific meaning. Before it can be employed in a discussion of the future of politics in underdeveloped countries, the concept of totalitarianism must therefore be somewhat sharpened.[1] As we did in the cases of nationalism and

[1] See Hannah Arendt, *The Origins of Totalitarianism* (New York: Harcourt, Brace & Co., 1951) and Carl J. Friedrich and Zbigniew Brzezinski, *Totalitarian Dictatorship and Autocracy* (Cambridge, Mass.: Harvard University Press, 1956). See also Carl J. Friedrich, ed., *Totalitarianism* (Cambridge, Mass.: Harvard University Press, 1954), and Richard Lowenthal, "Totalitarianism Reconsidered," *Commentary*, XXIX, No. 6 (June 1960), 504–512.

Communism, we must attempt to accomplish this not by setting up an arbitrary definition, but by analyzing the role and characteristics of what is commonly called totalitarianism.

Whatever other system may be properly described as totalitarian, there seems to be general agreement that Fascism and Stalinism constitute the prototype of totalitarianism. Since these two systems differed widely with respect to the groups in control of each and their ideologies and policy goals, we cannot define totalitarianism in terms of these factors. Rather, we define it merely as a set of methods used, under certain circumstances, by a group or several groups in control of a government in order to retain that control. Governments can, therefore, be more or less totalitarian, depending on the extent to which and the success with which these methods are applied. To gain an understanding of totalitarianism, we will first try to analyze the methods of totalitarianism and to explain them by reference to the circumstances that give rise to them, leaving for later a discussion of the groups that have, in fact, come to employ these methods and of the likelihood of their future employment in the underdeveloped countries.

Totalitarianism is a relatively new historical phenomenon, almost entirely one of the twentieth century. Its rise, like that of nationalism, can therefore not be sufficiently accounted for in terms of relatively permanent factors like the supposed peculiar properties of German "national character" or the Russian "soul," the authoritarian structure of the German family or Russian swaddling patterns. Factors such as these might contribute to the success of totalitarianism, but its origins must be sought in some new situation. That new situation resulted from industrialization. Not only does industrialization produce the technical instruments required by totalitarianism, chiefly the modern military weapons and means of communications; it alone can create the need and desire of certain groups for the use of totalitarian methods.[1]

The old authoritarian rulers in pre-industrial societies, as we described them at the beginning of this essay—the Pharaohs and emperors, kings and tsars, khans and rajahs, sultans and caudillos—had no need for totalitarianism. It would have been quite senseless and unthinkable for them to subject the mass of their population to terror and propaganda, when that mass consisted of peasants living in ignorance and isolation, hence unorganized and unorganizable. Peasant revolts were relatively rare and, because of their isolation and lack of organization, were almost invariably easily crushed by a regime in

[1] I am indebted for some of the points made in the following paragraphs to Benedikt Kautsky, preface to the Austrian edition of 1948, *Teufel und Verdammte* (Vienna: Wiener Volksbuchhandlung, 1961), pp. 14–22.

control of the armed forces. The bulk of the population, then, because of its very way of life, constituted no threat to the established regime in pre-industrial societies.

At the same time, the power of the old authoritarian regime was relatively independent of the mass of the population. A total stoppage of production throughout the society, which might cause such a regime to collapse, was unimaginable, both because peasants must continue to produce for their own sake and, even if they could destroy the surplus usually collected by the regime, because they could not organize on any large scale. The regime was not dependent on any one or any few villages that might take joint action, however, because each village community constituted an independent unit of production, so that while production stopped in a few, it would continue undisturbed in all the other villages.

In a pre-industrial society, there would therefore have been no point in trying to terrorize or persuade the bulk of the population. Only where, as a result of growing commerce, urban strata gained some significance (as in the ancient Mediterranean world and under the absolute monarchies of Western Europe), could rulers feel so threatened by these strata or be so dependent on them that they would resort to the use of terror and propaganda against them. But such terror and propaganda would affect only a small proportion of the population and hence would not be "total"—except where virtually the entire population was urban, as in some Greek city states ruled by tyrants, or in Calvin's Geneva.[1]

The advance of industrialization vastly expands the urban strata of the population and even, gradually, draws the formerly inert rural strata into politics. The rise of different organized groups conscious of their different interests and of their collective strength is bound to produce conflict, to tend toward "democratization," as we defined that term. In such a situation, any authoritarian regime, no matter what group it represents, is likely to be attacked, weakened, and ultimately threatened in its survival. Among the groups produced, or vastly augmented, by industrialization, labor and intellectuals have in the past generally been the most menacing to authoritarian government. Once labor constitutes a large proportion of the population, its very demand for participation in the governmental decision-making process becomes an attack on both the theory and practice of any authoritarianism. Intellectuals, though few in number as compared to labor, can help

[1] Cf. Barrington Moore, Jr., "Totalitarian Elements in Pre-Industrial Societies," *Political Power and Social Theory* (Cambridge, Mass.: Harvard University Press, 1958), pp. 30–88.

undermine the ideological foundations of authoritarianism, whether they engage in political pamphleteering and journalism, in writing novels and poetry, or in pursuit of the social and even natural sciences.

Not only does industrialization create groups that threaten an authoritarian regime, but it also makes the regime more dependent on these very groups—and hence makes their threat all the greater. An industrial society is a vastly more complex and more highly integrated mechanism than an agricultural one. If its government is not to succumb to domestic and perhaps also foreign pressures, it must be able to rely on the reasonably smooth functioning of this mechanism. But that can be disturbed by the non-cooperation of a relatively few people at any one of a great number of key points of the industrial economy. In this context, too, industrial workers and intellectuals are significant.

If, in the future, industry should come to a now underdeveloped country immediately in a highly automated form, there would be no large group of manual workers, much less a large labor movement, to threaten any regime. Intellectuals might be discontented and opposed to the government, but their suppression would not require totalitarian methods, since they constitute only a fraction of any population. As automated industrialization became widespread they would disappear as a group. Many would be absorbed in the growing number of managerial and technical positions created by automated industry, while others would become politicians, i.e., representatives of the many interests characterizing an advanced industrial society. Most important, in such a society there would probably be no group, as we shall see later, to try to exercise authoritarian rule. In such a situation, totalitarianism as we have known it is difficult to imagine.

If we disregard the possibility of automated industry, however, and confine ourselves to the traditional forms of industrialization, we may regard totalitarianism as a way of having one's cake and eating it, too—of having industrialization and yet retaining or establishing authoritarian government. Ordinarily, industrialization is accompanied by the growth of political parties, trade unions, and many other types of voluntary associations representing the interests of their membership. Totalitarianism grows out of the attempt to make the maintenance or even the acceleration of industrialization compatible with the prevention of the growth of such organizations, or their suppression where they have already grown.

The most obvious means, for an authoritarian regime, of prevention or suppression, is that of terror. While executions and tortures, imprisonment and forced labor affect only a fraction of the population directly, the terror is nevertheless total, because it generates fear and distrust throughout the society. Enough is known of what goes on in prisons and concentration camps to instill fear in everyone, for the reasons for the arrest of any individual are left so vague, and the circumstances of his disappearance are often so mysterious, that no one can feel safe in his own innocence. Under the pressure of this ubiquitous fear, no one can be relied upon not to denounce his fellows. Therefore any large-scale conspiracy or organization directed against the regime—except possibly one originated by a group within the regime, like the army—becomes virtually impossible. Terror thus serves to break up the natural units of an industrial society—the parties, trade unions, professional and trade associations, clubs and churches, and even the family—as potential centers of resistance, to atomize society, and so to confront the isolated individual, without any intermediary, with the all-powerful government.

Such an atomized society, composed of individuals feeling lost and frustrated and subject to severe tensions, would, to be sure, contain no threat to the regime, but neither would it serve as a very useful tool for the purposes of such a regime under conditions of industrialization, which require the cooperation of large numbers of people. Therefore, once the old associations with their different values, serving the interests of their different memberships, have been broken up, the regime provides new organizations to compensate the members for their loss. These are likely to have the same names, procedures, and symbols as the old ones, in order to maintain the loyalty of the membership, but in fact they differ radically from the old ones in two respects.

First, membership is no longer voluntary but, more or less officially, compulsory. All workers must now join unions, all professional people and artists must join their respective professional associations, all children must join the youth organizations. Rival organizations appealing to the same type of membership, such as opposing trade union federations, different sports or youth clubs, and, above all, rival political parties are no longer permitted. Total terror is joined by total regimentation, regimentation in organizations encompassing all members of the society. The new organizations, all run by the regime, thus become organs of supervision. The more of his life the individual spends in these organizations, the less of a threat he poses to the regime. Hence the emphasis under totalitarian regimes on organized mass activities, such as meetings, lectures, parades, hikes, sports, singing, which can occupy a large part of the individual's "free" time.

Second, all the new organizations profess the same ideology—the ideology of the regime. No matter how divergent the interests of their various memberships, all organizations serve primarily the interests of the regime. Thus, the individual member is led to believe that his own special interests, which he considers represented by his organization, coincide with the interests of the regime. The party and the ideology of the regime become the party and the ideology of both workers and managers, of peasants and professional men, of different nationality groups, and of different religious groups; the widely appealing notion of the general interest is triumphant under totalitarianism. In this fashion, the new organizations are not only organs of regimentation and supervision but also instruments of persuasion.

The attempt at total manufacturing and control of opinion, positively through propaganda and negatively through censorship, is, in addition to total terror and total regimentation, the third major characteristic of totalitarianism. The goal is, again, to turn the population from a potential threat to the regime into its pliant tool. The insecure, powerless individual is to be satisfied by having himself and his interests associated with, and indeed submerged in, a large and powerful community. The community may be defined by the existing state, by a nationality and culture group (that may be mislabeled a "race"), by the prevailing economic system, by the ideology of the regime, or by several of these. If nationalism is defined simply as intense loyalty to a state and its existing institutions, then nationalism can be regarded as an essential ingredient of totalitarianism. It must be noted, however, that nationalism so defined is different from both the language-based nationalism of Europe and the anti-colonial nationalism of the underdeveloped countries which we discussed earlier. To be sure, if a totalitarian country happens to be inhabited by people of a single language and culture, as Fascist Italy and Nazi Germany were, but the Soviet Union is not, its totalitarian nationalism may build on the earlier "language nationalism" and appear as merely an extreme form of it.

The nationalism of totalitarianism does have an important similarity to the nationalism of underdeveloped countries. That similarity is its emphasis on an outside enemy. For totalitarian propaganda aims to create unity behind the regime, not only by encouraging loyalty and positive identification, but also by inculcating hatred and fear of some common enemy. This enemy must always be an outsider, so that the unity of the society is not disrupted, although what is in fact a part of the society may by the regime be arbitrarily declared outsiders, as were the Jews in Nazi Germany. To have one's outsider inside has a peculiar advantage: it permits the venting of hostility by physical abuse, which is far more convenient, and cheaper and safer, than war. One of the principal functions of the outside enemy is to become the focus of the frustrations and hostilities of the various groups in the population, which might otherwise be directed against the regime or against other groups, thereby producing domestic conflict and weakening the regime. Thus the Jews in Germany were to be hated by workers as grasping capitalists, and by capitalists as radical labor agitators; by small manufacturers as big businessmen, and by shopkeepers as owners of department stores; by the peasants as exploiting bankers, and by lawyers and physicians as lawyers and physicians in unfair competition. They were blamed for inflation and deflation, for pacifism and war mongering, for being anti-Christian and for having created Christianity. If all the various groups in the society with their conflicting interests can hate the common outside enemy and blame him for their various troubles, they can all unite among themselves.

At the same time, the regime identifies all its real and imagined enemies with the outside enemy. The enemy of each individual and group in the population is then the enemy of the regime, and the regime becomes the protector of each individual and group. Thus, to the Nazis the Western Allies and the Soviet Union were all tools of international Jewry, and non-Jewish anti-Nazis within Germany were regarded as stooges of the same vast international conspiracy. To Stalin, all unfriendly foreign powers were capitalist—or, more recently, imperialist—and all domestic opponents, including old Bolsheviks, were foreign spies, wreckers, and saboteurs. For most Fascist countries, international Communism and occasionally (as in the cases of Italy and Japan) also Western imperialism have served as the outside enemy.

All failures of the regime are blamed on the outside enemy, implying that the regime, of itself, can do no wrong. And all domestic opposition is identified with the outside enemy, implying (by a definitional trick) that there is complete domestic unity behind the regime—since anyone opposing the regime is, by definition, no longer a good member of the society but an agent, subjectively or objectively, of the outside enemy. This outside enemy is always pictured as morally inferior to one's own society—be it by reason of his race, nationality, ideology, or form of government and society. His ultimate defeat is therefore assured. This compensates the individual in a totalitarian society for his weakness and lack of power by making him feel strong and superior. At the same time, the outside enemy is described as powerful and cunning, a constant threat not only to the regime, but to every individual and everything he cherishes, requiring his continuous exertions on behalf of the regime's objectives. A state of permanent physical and emotional mobilization is thus created, by maintaining a continuous crisis atmosphere.

The outside enemy is, then, essential to a totalitarian regime. Every such regime must claim that its country is encircled or its people denied living space. It must therefore carry on aggressive foreign relations, at least on the verbal level—but in foreign policy, words themselves come much closer to being policy than they do in the domestic arena. Thus, the assertion that there is an outside enemy may become a self-fulfilling one, encirclement may turn from phantasy into fact. When the outside enemy has become real, he is even more useful in creating unity at home and solidifying support for the regime. Confronted with what may now be a real threat, the regime can only respond by increased aggressiveness. Hostility, tension, cold war, and often war thus characterize the relations of totalitarian powers with their neighbors. This situation contributes to the general militarization of life under totalitarianism, which is in turn related to its major characteristics: to total terror, under which each individual and group is confronted with the overwhelming armed forces of the regime; to total regimentation and organization, under which a large part of the population is in some kind of uniform and subject to military discipline; and to total propaganda and censorship, which maintain a permanent state of mobilization.

THE TOTALITARIANISM OF THE ARISTOCRACY
AND ITS ALLIES

Although Mussolini probably learned from Lenin, Hitler from Mussolini and Stalin, and Franco clearly from Mussolini and Hitler, the striking similarities between the totalitarian features of their various regimes cannot be accounted for by international copying. They must be considered as similar responses to similar conditions, conditions which arise when authoritarianism seeks to establish or maintain itself in a society either already industrialized or in the process of industrialization. Since the underdeveloped countries are today undergoing this process of industrialization, the possibility of a totalitarian path would seem to exist for them, provided there are groups who can successfully maintain or impose an authoritarian regime in the face of industrialization. To discuss the prospects for totalitarianism, then, we must focus on such possible ruling groups.

Even in the advanced industrialized countries of the West (leaving the United States out of consideration, because it was never under aristocratic rule), the industrial capitalists, contrary to the Marxian thesis, never controlled political power by themselves. They generally —perhaps least in Britain—had to leave it to, or share it with, the old aristocracy until the lower classes had become strong enough to compete effectively with both of them. In the underdeveloped countries, where there is no substantial native industrial capitalist class, and where most industry is owned either by foreign capital or by the government, the capitalists are certainly neither actually nor potentially a ruling class. Labor, the industrial middle strata of white collar and lower professional workers, and ultimately even what may remain of the peasantry, can participate in politics on their own, rather than under the leadership and as pawns of other groups, only when industrialization has progressed quite far. Until then there are only two possible native ruling elites in underdeveloped countries, both of which we dealt with earlier: the old aristocracy and the new intellectuals. To investigate, first, the possibility of a totalitarianism of the aristocracy in underdeveloped countries, we must analyze the reactions to industrialization open to the aristocracy, and particularly the totalitarian reaction it did in fact resort to in some of the more advanced countries.

When the old aristocracy is faced with industrialization, it can react in a number of ways. In view of the fact that industrialization will sooner or later deprive the aristocracy of its power, one might think that its most reasonable reaction would be to try to prevent the growth of industry in its country. Even if it were rational enough to make such an attempt, it would probably fail, however. In a colony, the native aristocracy is in no position to prohibit the introduction of industry by the colonial power or its citizens. In an independent underdeveloped country, the aristocracy, having in the past ruled only over peasants and craftsmen, is not so organized as to be able to prevent foreigners or its own subjects from establishing industrial enterprises. In addition, the aristocracy's own interest may make its opposition to industrialization impossible. In an entirely non-industrialized country, the aristocracy may be safe from the menace of internal revolution, but it may be all the more threatened from without. For over a century now, industrial superiority has been a key element of military superiority, and no regime wanting to avoid military defeats, and perhaps to make conquests of its own, has been able to afford resistance to the introduction of modern techniques of mass production and means of transportation. The Tsarist regime was taught that lesson by its defeat in the Crimean War. Faced with the unpleasant choice of preventing industrialization and thereby risking early military destruction at the hands of foreign enemies, and of accepting industrialization and thereby risking destruction in the long run by domestic enemies, an aristocratic regime is likely to take the latter alternative.

The opposite to resisting industrialization would be for an aristocracy to embrace it so wholeheartedly as to liquidate itself. This, too, is a possible but not very probable reaction. It would, of course, mean suicide by the aristocracy as a class, but by no means of aristocrats individually. Rather, the most probable way in which they would cease to be aristocrats would be by investing their wealth in industry, and thus becoming capitalists. To some extent this is what has happened to the British aristocracy, but the merger of the two upper classes in Britain has been at least as much due to capitalists being accepted into the aristocracy and adopting its mode of life as to aristocrats becoming capitalists. Elsewhere this latter process is likely to prove even more difficult, since going into "trade" generally involves loss of status for a stratum extremely conscious of, and dependent on, its status. The capitalist virtues of saving and investment are alien to the aristocracy and appear contemptible to it. As a class living by exploitation of the peasantry and the soil, investing no part of their product in the expansion or improvement of the process of production, the aristocracy is inclined not to save but to waste freely and spend generously, not toward investment but toward conspicuous consumption. It regards generosity and waste, rather than accumulation and investment of wealth, as symbols of prestige.

A third possible reaction by the aristocracy to industrialization is, of course, to yield power in one way or another to the new groups coming to the fore. It may yield gradually and gracefully; in Britain it has done this so successfully as to retain at present probably relatively more power than in any other advanced country, though it came under attack there much sooner. Or the aristocracy may resist concessions to the bitter end and may, as in Russia, be utterly wiped out as a result. Or it may be driven out of some positions of power and yet retain a more or less important foothold in others, typically in the military, and at least some branches of the bureaucracy (such as the foreign and colonial service), as in France. A loss of some degree of power to the new groups is the most probable fate of the aristocracy in the underdeveloped countries. Such a loss has by now occurred in most of them. Whether the loss has already become irreparable cannot be stated generally, for there is yet a fourth alternative reaction to industrialization available to the aristocracy.

That reaction is the totalitarian attempt to keep the new groups created by industrialization out of power by means of total terror, total regimentation and organization, and the total manufacture and control of opinion. The human and material apparatus required for such an effort is so vast and complex that an aristocracy ruling in a backward society is not capable of it. Only after industrialization has progressed to some extent do the techniques and means required by totalitarianism, such as the media of mass communication, become available. Similarly, only industrialization provides the modern weapons, which give the government unquestioned military superiority over its subjects and thus rule out successful urban uprisings against it. Such insurrections were always possible while oppositional groups (if any) could own and operate the same kinds of weapons as the army.

Equally important, only industrialization creates the allies which the aristocracy needs in order to operate the huge totalitarian system of terror, organization, and propaganda. Where the aristocracy has, in fact, resorted to totalitarian methods, two groups in particular have contributed significant support to its efforts to fight, or prevent the rise of, a political system in which the new urban groups, like labor and the intellectuals, have their interests represented.

One of these allies of the aristocracy has been the group of big capitalists, people generally non-existent in underdeveloped countries but important in more advanced countries, not only because of their wealth and role in the economy but also because their ideological influence reaches far beyond their own relatively small numbers, especially into the new middle class of managerial, professional, and white collar personnel. Themselves a product of industrialization, the capitalists have, as we noted, generally failed to become the sole ruling class in industrialized countries. After more or less prolonged and more or less unsuccessful efforts at gaining political predominance, they were generally driven, by fear of a rising movement of labor and intellectuals, into an accommodation with their erstwhile enemies, the aristocracy: government was largely left to the aristocracy, in return for a free hand for the capitalists to develop and control industry. Such an accommodation was clearly reached in Bismarckian Germany, but broadly similar developments may be found in the history of most industrialized countries with a background of aristocratic rule, for example in Japan and even in Britain, where the aristocratic element was relatively weak and the capitalist one relatively strong. In any case, once the alliance of the big capitalists with the aristocracy has been formed and the capitalists have a stake in the preservation of the old order, they have been likely to join the aristocracy also in its efforts, if such were made, at controlling by totalitarian methods the enemies they have in commom (though they have feared them for somewhat different reasons): industrial labor and some of the intellectuals.

A second group that has been able to make common cause with the aristocracy in opposing democracy has been the old middle class of small artisans, shopkeepers, and traders. While not a product of industrialization itself, its resentments are, and its role as an ally of the aristocracy is hence dependent on some degree of industrialization. Unable to compete with big factories and stores and to meet the demands of organized labor, it may be placed in a desperate economic position; also, at least equally important in a class-conscious society, its social status may be jeopardized when it is forced to join the ranks of labor. In this situation, the old middle class may well associate itself with the aristocracy, which is also fighting to maintain the old society, with its old order of rank and privilege, in the face of the rising industrial forces. Under pressures somewhat similar to those on the old middle class, many peasants, too, may join this common front. Even industrial workers, if they are ideologically still close to the old middle class, and particularly if they are unemployed and hence resentful and desperate, or if they are alienated from democratic forms because their demands were not satisfied through them, and intellectuals and white collar workers, if they are ideologically tied to the aristocracy, may all furnish allies and tools of the totalitarianism of the old ruling groups.

This movement of the despairing old middle class, with some of its following also recruited from the peasantry and labor, its leadership often drawn from the intellectuals, and its typical ideology made up of anti-trade unionism, anti-capitalism, and sometimes anti-clericalism, is Fascism.[1] So-called Fascist *regimes,* however, have nowhere represented solely the Fascist *movement.* For an understanding of these regimes, it is unfortunate that they should have come to be known as Fascist—a term we, too, will use loosely to characterize the totalitarianism of the aristocracy and its allies. Such regimes are named after only one component in the alliance on which they are based, and the name obscures the role of the equally essential aristocratic component. Fascist *movements* have come to power only with the support of non-Fascist elements, namely big capitalists and the aristocracy with its strongholds in the military and in the bureaucracy, and frequently with its allies in the higher clergy. The aristocracy and the big capitalists, on the other hand, have been able to set up a totalitarian regime only with the aid of a Fascist movement, because only it could furnish

[1] S. M. Lipset in his *Political Man,* pp. 131–176, argues persuasively that Fascism is a middle rather than an upper class movement. He demonstrates this well in the cases of Nazism in Germany and Austria and Poujadism in France and draws some parallels to populism and McCarthyism in the United States.

the mass following required to operate the vast apparatus of totalitarianism.

That, typically, each side to the alliance of Fascists and conservatives (aristocrats and capitalists) expected merely to use the other for its own purposes, only demonstrates their dependence on each other, as well as the fact that they shared a common enemy, the forces pressing for democratization. On the other hand, that the alliance was made of disparate elements was clearly shown by conflicts among them, like those between the Fascist Falange and the conservative monarchists in Spain, the split between Mussolini's Italian Social Republic and the conservative elements who made peace with the Allies in 1943 (a split continuing to the present in the division between the Monarchist and the neo-Fascist parties in Italy), and the conspiracy of aristocratic army and big industrial elements to kill Hitler and take over the German government in 1944.

The relative strength of the various elements in the alliance may vary. Roughly, the less industrialized the country, the stronger the aristocracy and the weaker both the capitalists and the Fascists. Since the aristocracy is a key element both in Fascist regimes and in the traditional authoritarian governments typical of agrarian societies, intermediate forms between these two are possible. In a country still largely agricultural, where "Fascism" may come to power as a reaction to a relatively weak movement of workers and intellectuals, it will be based largely on the landed aristocracy and will not be too different from traditional aristocratic regimes, since the bulk of the population it confronts, being composed of peasants, will not require suppression. The Horthy regime in Hungary and the Pilsudsky regime in Poland during the interwar period illustrate such "Fascism" in which the Fascist element is relatively unimportant.

In Austria, the Dolfuss-Schuschnigg regime of 1934–38 had strong ties to the clerical-monarchist tradition of the old aristocratic Austria, as much of the country was rural. The regime contained strong Fascist elements as well, however, as a result of the advanced industrialization of Vienna and some other areas: it represented not only the aristocracy, but also the capitalists, old middle class, and large parts of the peasantry. It was also characterized by a one-party system, terror, and government propaganda and censorship, as Fascist regimes are, but traditional aristocratic ones are not. Similarly, Franco stands somewhere midway between the traditional Latin American caudillo and the modern Fascist dictator, relying on the one hand on the aristocratic forces of the landowners, the army, and the Church, but on the other hand also on capitalists and elements from the old and new middle classes and intellectuals, as represented in the Falange. His regime may well be more Fascist, i.e., totalitarian, in relation to the intellectuals of Madrid, the workers of Catalonia, and the miners of Asturias, and more traditional-authoritarian towards the peasants of Castile and Andalusia.

On the one hand, then, the totalitarianism of the aristocracy and its allies cannot develop directly out of the old agrarian society and the old aristocratic political order. It emerges both as a result of and a reaction to some industrialization and consequent democratization or the threat of democratization. The technical means of suppression and propaganda, as well as the necessary allies of the aristocracy, are created only by industrialization and so, indeed, are the enemies who challenge the aristocracy's predominance and cause it to resort to totalitarian methods.

On the other hand, our analysis indicates that Fascist totalitarianism is a product of some degree of underdevelopment and is not likely to appear in advanced industrialized countries, because for it to develop the aristocracy must have retained some positions of strength. Wherever Fascist regimes have come to power—in the Germany, Japan, Italy, Austria, Poland, and Hungary of the interwar period, to some extent under the Vichy regime in France, and in Spain and Portugal to the present—the landed aristocracy, entrenched in its power positions in the armed forces, the bureaucracy, and frequently the church, has played a key role in it. If the United States, Britain and her advanced dominions, the Scandinavian and the Low Countries, and Switzerland may be ruled out as potentially Fascist countries, it is because of the absence in their societies of an aristocracy that has successfully withstood the political challenges of capitalists, old and new middle classes, intellectuals and labor.

As long as there is a powerful aristocracy in an industrialized environment, the possibility of Fascism exists, and it is then compatible with varying degrees of industrialization. By and large, the more industrialization, the more the aristocracy recedes in the Fascist regime and its allies become preponderant, and also the more terror, regimentation, and propaganda—the more total the totalitarianism—since there are more people to be suppressed, organized, and persuaded, and more means available to do the job.

The most advanced industrialized country to come under Fascist rule was Germany. It has often been cited as an exception to our generalization that Fascism is a phenomenon of some backwardness. It was, indeed, an exceptional case of Fascism, just as it has been exceptional for an aristocracy to remain very powerful, as it had in Germany, in the face of advanced industrialization. For that very reason, Germany was the exception that proved the rule, the rule of the key role of the aristocracy in Fascist regimes (though not in Fascist movements). The success of Nazism would have been unimaginable without the powerful Junkers and their control of the army and the bureaucracy; without the alliance between them and the capitalists in heavy industry concluded in the days of Bismarck on the basis of mutually profitable policies of protective tariffs, armaments, and colonialism; and without the pervasive influence of the aristocratic ideology of authoritarianism and violence on the old and new middle classes and some of the intellectuals in Germany. The top posts of the Nazi regime were largely occupied by Fascist middle class elements, but both the big capitalists in heavy industry and the aristocracy, chiefly in the army, continued to play crucial roles in it. Once in power, Nazism became the most total form of Fascist totalitarianism exactly because of the advanced stage of German industrialization, but for that reason it was also, in its very "perfection," an atypical instance of the totalitarianism of the aristocracy and its allies.

What are the chances of the now underdeveloped countries coming under the rule of Fascist regimes? The foregoing has shown that the traditional aristocratic regimes of wholly agrarian societies cannot directly transform themselves into either democratic or totalitarian regimes, because these are, in one way or another, the result of some industrialization. Industrialization on any large scale, however, is generally brought to the underdeveloped countries by the intellectuals and in its early stages tends to establish the intellectuals in power. As such countries begin to emerge from their first stage of underdevelopment, therefore, they almost invariably go through a second stage of leadership by nationalist intellectuals.

A Fascist regime could thus appear in an underdeveloped country only as a possible third stage. As such, it could establish itself only if the old aristocracy had managed to retain a good deal of its power throughout the second stage of rule by nationalist intellectuals. During that stage, however, both the political power and the prestige of the aristocracy seem to be severely weakened in many underdeveloped countries under the impact of modernization. The degree to which this is the case may vary widely from country to country, depending in part on the strength of the aristocracy's position in the original pre-industrial society and on the role it played in the nationalist movement.

Fascist regimes, however, are in any case an unlikely prospect in the now underdeveloped countries, because the aristocracy cannot count on the allies which in Europe supported it in establishing totalitarian regimes. The big industrialists are non-existent or far weaker in coun-tries being industrialized under the auspices of intellectuals and of governments dominated by them. The old middle class, too, is often weaker and, lacking a background of some political independence, is unlikely to form a movement like the Fascist one. Also, for some time at any rate, its resentments against the effects of industrialization may be deflected by nationalism from any domestic victims to the colonial power, a situation which, as we noted earlier, can prevail long after a country has attained political and even economic independence. Since the aristocracy often is, or was, the ally of the colonial power, it cannot easily use that power as the outside enemy, against whom other groups could be united under aristocratic leadership.

Not only capitalists and the old middle class are usually unavailable as powerful allies of the aristocracy in underdeveloped countries now being industrialized. There is also, generally, no significant stratum of intellectuals ideologically close to the aristocracy, as there was, for example, in Germany, France, and Japan. And labor and the new middle class are under intellectual rather than aristocratic leadership. Only among the most backward peasantry can the aristocracy hope to find a substantial following, but, being politically powerless, the peas-antry is of little help in establishing a totalitarian regime.

As we shall see in the following sections, regimes other than Fascist ones may, and are indeed more likely to, succeed the government of nationalist intellectuals. As to the probability that they, in turn, will be succeeded by a Fascist regime—in what would be, roughly, a fourth stage of development—only this much has to be said here: If the forces on which a Fascist regime has to rest are probably too weak to establish such a regime immediately after the nationalist intellec-tuals' rule, they are even less likely to have sufficient strength when a further intervening stage, with further industrial development, has weakened them still more.

Though improbable, the development of a totalitarianism of the aristocracy and its allies is not unimaginable in some particular under-developed countries. We may therefore ask ourselves how Fascism would evolve if it did come and may seek the answer in the experience of past Fascist regimes. Since the totalitarianism of the aristocracy and its allies is in its main goals a conservative system, or indeed a reaction-ary one, seeking to protect or restore the status and privileges of ex-isting classes, and since it is not particularly interested in furthering or accelerating industrialization, it has, like the traditional aristocratic authoritarianism of wholly agrarian societies, no inherent evolutionary tendencies. Also, as in agrarian societies, though for the very different reasons we described, there is little possibility of domestic revolution as long as the regime is effectively totalitarian as we defined that term.

If the Fascist country is only a minor power, like Portugal, its most probable fate is stagnation. Its economic, social, and political system remains unaltered, until change is introduced by some impulse from the outside world. If, however, the country is sufficiently strong to attack its neighbors, a Fascist regime is very likely to be involved in war. This is so because of the aggressive tendencies of any totalitarian system resulting from the role played by the "outside enemy" in all of them. It is even more likely in the case of totalitarian regimes of the aristocracy, because its background as a warrior caste that considers war—and also robbery and hunting—its proper occupation,[1] produces an ideology glorifying war and the military way of life. Such an ideology is typically associated with Fascist regimes and makes them even more warlike than other totalitarian ones. Historically, virtually all Fascist regimes have found their end in war.

Since Fascism does not profoundly change the social structure, any kind of political system that preceded Fascism, or indeed another Fascist regime, is imaginable as its successor.

THE TOTALITARIANISM OF THE INTELLECTUALS

In almost all underdeveloped countries there has by now been enough modernization—and enough demand for more modernization—to produce the nationalist movement led by intellectuals. For a totalitarianism of the aristocracy and its allies to succeed that movement, a change in ruling elites would be required. If the intellectuals themselves were to erect a totalitarian regime, however, only a more or less gradual change in their methods of government, but no change in the ruling elite, would be involved. The development of a totalitarianism of the intellectuals seems therefore much more probable than one of the aristocracy and its allies in the now underdeveloped countries.

While the intellectuals are in the van of the nationalist efforts to bring modernization and independence to their countries, they are able to create considerable unity, behind their leadership, among all politically conscious elements. But the very success of their efforts threatens this unity. Growing industrialism develops more elements capable of participation in politics, with more diverse interests, and

---

[1] This aspect of the aristocracy is well discussed in Joseph A. Schumpeter, "The Sociology of Imperialism," in *Imperialism and Social Classes* (New York: Meridian Books, 1955), an essay providing important insights into the background of the aristocracy as a ruling class.

the common enemy, colonialism, which held the movement together, fades into the background. Organized groups—of the old landed aristocracy, of new industrial capitalists (if such have developed), of industrial labor, and eventually of white collar workers and even of peasants—may challenge the sole rule of the intellectuals and demand representation of their interests in the government. If they are able to obtain it, there will then emerge the situation we defined as democracy, on which we will touch in the next section.

When industrialization and independence spell the end of unity behind the intellectual elite, however, the latter cannot always be forced to yield a share of its power to other groups. Rather, the intellectuals may, in order to maintain their power, impose totalitarianism on the society.[1] They do this, in part, like the aristocracy when it applies totalitarian methods as a reaction to industrialization, in an effort to maintain authoritarianism in the face of the democratic pressures produced by industrialization. But—and here they are likely to differ from an aristocracy establishing a Fascist regime—the intellectuals also resort to totalitarianism because it enables them to accelerate industrialization, which, as we saw, is one of the principal goals of the nationalist intelligentsia in underdeveloped countries. Industrialization of an underdeveloped society inevitably requires sacrifices on the part of many of its members. Those who want to speed the process, and are deeply convinced that they represent the "true" interests of all, or the inevitable course of history, are easily tempted to substitute the more overt means of totalitarianism for slower, economic forms of compulsion—to accumulate capital resources in the face of pressure for increased production of consumer goods, to force peasants to go into factories and subject them to harsh industrial discipline, and to force the remaining peasants to produce and deliver food for the growing urban population.

Like the aristocrats, the intellectuals need allies to operate the vast apparatus of totalitarianism. We saw earlier that nationalism in underdeveloped countries can receive support from all strata of the population. This has also been true where the role of the nationalist movement has been played by Communism. Its allies can be drawn from the ranks of industrial labor, attracted by the leftist phraseology of a "proletarian" program; they can, and in both Russia and China did,

[1] Why such a development is probable is excellently summarized by Zbigniew Brzezinski, "The Politics of Underdevelopment," *World Politics,* IX, No. 1 (October 1956), 55–75. The appeals of a totalitarian solution to the intellectuals are also evaluated by Richard Lowenthal, "The Points of the Compass," reprinted on pp. 335–347, below.

chiefly come from the peasantry, attracted by promises of land reform;[1] and they can even be sought, as under neo-Maoism, among all groups of the population, including the capitalists, by appeals to their hatred of the common enemy of imperialism. Once the totalitarianism of intellectuals has succeeded in establishing a fairly advanced industrial system, it has, in the process, also created a new basis of support for itself in a vast new bureaucratic and managerial elite. However, in that process, it has also changed its own character, a matter to be noted at the end of this section.

In Russia, where the equivalent of the nationalist movement of intellectuals came to power in the Communist revolution, Lenin's regime was not yet a full-fledged totalitarian one. Given the relatively advanced character of the country by the time of the Revolution, the regime's terror, its organizations, its propaganda and censorship were rather widespread. Still, they were directed at relatively limited strata of the population, as had been those of the Tsarist regime, and for the same reason, viz., that Russia was still largely an agrarian country.

Unlike the Tsarist regime, however, the Communist regime was one of intellectuals aiming at rapid industrialization. When Stalin took steps to achieve that goal, he also had to convert his regime into a totalitarian one, both in order to carry through industrialization under forced draft and in order to render harmless any opposition groups which industrialization would tend to create. It was only under Stalinism that the elements of totalitarianism inherent in Leninism developed fully, that terror, regimentation, and propaganda and censorship came to be total, i.e., to affect the entire society.[2] In China, on the

[1] The ability of the Communists to exploit the peasants', as well as the intellectuals', discontent is emphasized by Harry J. Benda, "Communism in Southeast Asia," *The Yale Review*, XLV, No. 3 (Spring 1956), 417–429.

[2] That Lenin's system was completely revolutionized by Stalin and supplanted by a totalitarian system is heavily emphasized by Robert C. Tucker, "The Politics of Soviet De-Stalinization," *World Politics*, IX, No. 4 (July 1957), 550–578, pp. 555–563. However, he regards Stalinism chiefly as "a product of Stalin" and his pathological personality, and does not relate it to industrialization. Alex Inkeles, "The Soviet Union: Model for Asia?—The Social System," *Problems of Communism*, VIII, No. 6 (November–December 1959), 30–38, also see two "quite distinct and markedly discontinuous" major phases of Soviet development. The first one put an end to capitalism and autocracy, but left the old social structure relatively intact and free. The second one began with rapid industrialization and collectivization of the farms and was causally linked with totalitarianism. "Moveover, since the full industrialization of the USSR developed largely out of the policies of the second phase, it is the latter model which is likely to be the more compelling in its attraction for Asian leaders, even though the model offered by the earlier phase

other hand, the Communist regime became totalitarian immediately, because industrialization had been planned and undertaken from the beginning.

Communist regimes are but one form of the more general category of the totalitarianism of the intellectuals, designed to introduce or accelerate industrialization as well as to suppress its political consequences.[1] The seeds of totalitarianism, which were inherent in Leninism and bore fruit in Stalinism, are also present in the nationalist regimes of intellectuals in many underdeveloped countries. In their twin drives for independence and industrialization, which we subsumed under the label of nationalism, the intellectuals have everywhere demanded unity of the whole society behind their own leadership. This demand has frequently found expression in the organization of single-party regimes, and in emphasis on the single outside enemy (imperialism), which all groups in the population are to blame for their diverse difficulties. These are important elements of totalitarianism in the nationalist regimes. Such elements may develop further, as the unity of their nationalism begins to disintegrate. The intellectuals in power may then seek to substitute for it the artificial unity of totalitarianism by turning their single party into an instrument of total terror, total regimentation, and total propaganda and censorship.

Sun Yat-sen in China—his Kuomintang was reorganized along Leninist lines with the assistance of a Bolshevik adviser—and Kemal in Turkey, Vargas in Brazil, Perón in Argentina and Castro in Cuba,[2]

of Soviet development might appear to have much greater real relevance for the majority of Asian countries." *Ibid.*, p. 33. R. V. Daniels states: "If the Communist embodiment of Marxism has today a special relevance for the countries of the East and their aspirations to national power and modern economic standards, this is due to the refashioning of communism that Stalin accomplished in the early years of his power in Russia—above all, at the time of the First Five-Year-Plan." Robert Vincent Daniels, "The Chinese Revolution in Russian Perspective," *World Politics*, XIII, No. 2 (January 1961), 228–229.

[1] For another, highly suggestive attempt to compare Communist and nationalist single-party systems, which, however, treats them along with Fascism as "three species of a single political genus," rather than as phenomena significantly distinct from Fascism, see Robert C. Tucker, "Towards a Comparative Politics of Movement-Regimes," *The American Political Science Review*, LV, No. 2 (June 1961), 281–289.

[2] Theodore Draper, "Castro's Cuba: A Revolution Betrayed?", *Encounter*, XVI, No. 3 (March 1961), 6–23, though largely polemical in nature, contains some valuable analysis and data. Thus, Draper shows that of the 18 Cuban cabinet members in 1960, "every one attended a university (some in the United States), came from upper- or middle-class homes, and became or aspired to become a

Nasser in Egypt, Kassem in Iraq, Ayub Khan in Pakistan, and Sukarno in Indonesia, Bourguiba in Tunisia and Nkrumah in Ghana, are all nationalist leaders who have taken at least some steps in the direction of totalitarianism. Their ideologies vary and none of them is a Communist party member, but, seen in our framework, they differ from Stalin and Mao Tse-tung chiefly in that their industrialization has not progressed as far and as fast as that of Russia and China and their totalitarianism hence has not become as total. Insofar as their regimes did develop along totalitarian lines, they, along with Communist regimes, fit into the general category of the totalitarianism of the intellectuals.[1] On the other hand, they do not fit into the category of the totaliarianism of the aristocracy and its allies. Some of the leaders just mentioned have been called Fascists, and Perón and Nasser have, indeed, themselves displayed their sympathy for Fascism, for instance, by giving refuge to prominent Nazi leaders. Nevertheless, if Fascism is to be more than a term of political abuse, it must be defined in terms of its group content, and this can be done best by focusing on its relation to the two upper classes, the aristocracy and the capitalists. No Fascist regime, properly defined and distinguished from the Fascist movement, which is only one of its components, breaks up or even threatens to break up the big estates of the aristocracy, as both Nasser and Perón did. Nor does a Fascist regime rely on urban labor for much of its support or favor that group in its policies, as both Vargas and Perón did. Fascists, once in power with their allies, may appeal to many desires of the lower classes, but never to their desire for equality. They may wear black shirts or brown shirts, but they are never shirtless (descamisados).

If underdeveloped countries come under totalitarian regimes of intellectuals, how will such regimes evolve? Trying to answer this question, we can refer to the experience of such regimes of the past, notably of the Soviet one, and to the tendencies inherent in the totalitarianism of the intellectuals. For, unlike the totalitarianism of the aristocracy, that of the intellectuals contains dynamic forces

professional or intellectual" (p. 20). On the relationship between Marxism, Communism, and nationalism in underdeveloped countries, he reaches conclusions quite similar to ours.

[1] Robert C. North, with the collaboration of Ithiel de Sola Pool, in *Kuomintang and Chinese Communist Elites* (Stanford, Calif.: Stanford University Press, 1952), ch. iv, demonstrates by the use of quantified biographical data the far-reaching common social characteristics of the Kuomintang and Chinese Communist leaderships, most significantly that in both "the majority were alienated intellectuals, men and women whose Western educations isolated them from the main currents of Chinese society" (p. 46).

bound to modify its character in time. To be sure, like any totalitarian system, it can, as long as it operates effectively, prevent domestic revolution by those it suppresses. But its chief goal is rapid modernization, and the more successfully that goal is approached, the more the social basis of the regime itself is changed.

The rate of economic, social, and political change can vary and this has important consequences. In Turkey, the Kemalist regime was never a far-reaching totalitarian one, and the peasants, with a background of independence very different from Russian peasants', were never effectively regimented. Industrialization proceeded so slowly as to permit traditionalist and religious forces, leaning on the support of the peasantry, to regain a good deal of political power under Menderes. This situation produced what appears to be a second Kemalist revolution under General Gursel to renew the drive for modernization.[1] Indeed, the Turkish example is but the most recent one of a "second wave" of a nationalist revolution where the initial wave did not succeed in carrying out its objectives of modernization, and where traditionalist forces retained or regained positions of power. The Cárdenas regime in Mexico and the Communist regime in China may be viewed as two, to be sure very different, such "second waves" of nationalism. Both came, like the Turkish one, in countries where the first revolution had taken place several decades earlier and had not led to the establishment of effective totalitarian controls. One may conclude that such "second waves" of nationalism may yet, in the next few decades, appear in other underdeveloped countries, for example, possibly in Pakistan or Indonesia.[2] They may, in turn, result in the establishment of a totalitarian regime of intellectuals, as happened in China, or of the kind of balance of forces that emerged in Mexico, which we will consider next under the heading of democracy.

But there may be no occasion for a "second wave." The nationalist intellectuals, once firmly established in power, may proceed to introduce large-scale industrialization very rapidly and, with it, totalitarianism. That, at any rate, was the case in Russia (though one could conceivably regard the Stalinist revolution of 1927 itself as a "second wave" following the emergence of the NEP-men and Kulaks in the preceding years) and is now the case in China. Under totalitarian controls, the peasants, who must be compelled to feed the growing

[1] On Turkish politics, see Kemal Karpat, *Turkey's Politics* (Princeton, N.J.: Princeton University Press, 1959). See also Daniel Lerner and Richard D. Robinson, "Swords and Ploughshares: The Turkish Army as a Modernizing Force," *World Politics*, XIII, No. 1 (October 1960), 19–44.

[2] Or in Syria, now that she has broken away from Nasser's nationalist-ruled Egypt.

urban population, and the workers, who must operate the growing industrial plant, can continue to be excluded from participation in politics. But the vast bureaucracies of the single party and its many organizations, of the government, of the armed services and police and, above all, of the managers and technicians in industry in fact inevitably assume more and more decision-making authority. For a while, the nationalist revolutionary intellectuals who established the totalitarian system may succeed in dominating them by playing one bureaucracy against another, as Stalin did, but after a generation or so the new elites of conservative bureaucrats and managers are likely to be able to assert their power. Once several such elites with diverse interests, comprising a large and growing part of the population, can effectively influence government policy (a point the Soviet Union —but not yet China—seems to be approaching now), the system no longer quite fits our definition of totalitarianism.[1] Totalitarianism is, after all, a matter of degree, and it is pointless to argue about exactly where it begins and where it ends. Certainly, as long as large classes of people, especially the peasants, are still excluded from active participation in the political process, we cannot call the Soviet system democratic, by our definition of that term, either.

As industrialization proceeds, with the ever more rapid technological changes peculiar to it, the very groups still subjected to totalitarian controls will lose importance. The peasantry tends to be reduced, both in relative and absolute numbers, by urbanization, and is replaced by managers and technicians as modern technology is introduced into agriculture. Industrial labor also becomes less important. Once mechanization reaches a certain point, particularly when automation is introduced, the growth of industry is accompanied no longer by a corresponding growth but rather by a decline in the number of industrial workers. Their place is increasingly taken by service employees, white collar workers, and a multiplicity of scientific, professional, and technical specialists. These groups, with their divisions and varying interests, unlike a united labor movement, pose no threat to a

[1] A mass of data indicating the emergence, under the impact of industrialization, of individual values in the Soviet Union quite similar to those in other advanced industrial countries, including that of a consumer ethic, may be found in a study of fundamental importance, Alex Inkeles and Raymond A. Bauer, *The Soviet Citizen, Daily Life in a Totalitarian Society* (Cambridge, Mass.: Harvard University Press, 1959). Extremely relevant, too, on the uniformities in the industrialization process with respect to managers and workers is Clark Kerr *et al.*, *Industrialism and Industrial Man*, cited in footnote 2, p. 81. See also the discussion "Toward a 'Communist Welfare State'?" by Alec Nove and several commentators in *Problems of Communism*, IX, No. 1 (January–February 1960), 1–22.

totalitarian regime; on the contrary, they may identify their interests with those of the various bureaucratic and managerial elites now in control. Hence a progressively decreasing proportion of the population needs to be subjected to the pressures of totalitarianism, and the smaller it becomes the less need there is for any totalitarian controls. In this fashion, the industrialization sponsored by the totalitarianism of the intellectuals may yet, in the future, convert that system into one in which most of the groups of the new society have access to representation in the governmental decision-making process, a system approximating democracy.

DEMOCRACY

The rule of nationalist intellectuals, which now prevails in most underdeveloped countries, is not likely to be followed by a totalitarianism of the aristocracy, i.e., by Fascist regimes as Europe has known them. It may well turn into a totalitarianism of the intellectuals, but it need not do so everywhere. It may also be succeeded by democracy.[1] Democracy develops when the intellectuals controlling the government are compelled to share their power with other groups, ultimately with all major groups—a process in which the intellectuals themselves lose their identity as a distinct group and become the representatives and often the leaders of the other groups. These other groups include the old aristocracy—or what is left of it after some land reform—and its allies in the higher clergy; new native capitalists, if any emerged during the early stages of industrialization; organized labor,[2] almost invariably led by intellectuals; perhaps some of the old

[1] Edward Shils, in "Political Development in the New States," *Comparative Studies in Society and History*, II, No. 3 (April 1960), 265–292, and No. 4 (July 1960), 379–411, discusses the "determinants of political development" in the new states of Asia and Africa and then sets up five models of possible political development in these states, viz., (1) political democracy, (2) tutelary democracy, (3) modernizing oligarchy, (4) totalitarian oligarchy, and (5) traditional oligarchy. He considers approximations to the third and fourth models to be the most likely to arise in fact. The first of Shils' models corresponds roughly to what we call democracy in this essay, the second, third, and fourth to rule by intellectuals with no, some, and highly developed totalitarian features, respectively, and the fifth to rule by the traditional aristocracy.

[2] For an interesting case study of the emergence of a trade union federation into an independent role in the post-independence politics of an underdeveloped country, which split the nationalist and, indeed, the labor movements, see Douglas E. Ashford, "Labor Politics in a New Nation," *The Western Political Quarterly*, XIII, No. 2 (June 1960), 312–331, on the Moroccan labor movement in the period from 1955 to 1959.

middle class of craftsmen and traders now organized in self-defense against the inroads of industrialization; and, as industrialization proceeds, a new urban middle class of professional and white collar workers; [1] and finally even such sections of the peasantry as become politically conscious through improved communications among themselves and with the cities.

The growth of democracy, then, frequently involves not only the emergence of new groups created by industrialization—labor, the new middle class, and perhaps capitalists—which we discussed in our first chapter, but also the temporary resurgence of some of the traditionalist forces. This resurgence remains a possibility if the intellectuals, during their dominance, were unable to industrialize their country rapidly and to retain their power by totalitarian methods until the traditionalist forces were gravely weakened or eliminated. We mentioned a resurgence of these forces in Turkey; it is imaginable in the future of other countries, and accounts in part for the downfall of Perón in Argentina.

Democracy can prevail if the various old and new forces with their diverse interests balance each other sufficiently to prevent one or a few of them from becoming predominant and eliminating the others from open participation in the arena of politics. According to our conception of it, democracy, then, is not, any more than totalitarianism, instituted because it appears desirable to one or several groups. Rather, it is a form that the political process assumes under certain circumstances, viz., the condition of balance. Where that condition is not present, democracy will not emerge, even if it is considered highly desirable by many individuals or groups. Where it is present, democracy will emerge even if no one desires it. Once the balance, on which democracy is based, has been established, each of the forces that contributes to it may be expected to seek to upset it in order to increase its own power and reduce that of its opponents. Only where such efforts have long proved futile, and democracy has thus been maintained, has its preservation itself become a value accepted and upheld by some groups and, in a relatively few countries, by all major groups in the society.

In developing countries, then, where a balance of forces producing democracy has emerged, there is little doubt that some groups, particularly the aristocracy and the intellectuals, will hope and perhaps try to upset it. The question is merely whether any of them can succeed

[1] See John J. Johnson, *Political Change in Latin America: The Emergence of the Middle Sectors* (Stanford, Calif.: Stanford University Press, 1958).

in eliminating democracy. For the aristocracy, a return to the old, traditional order of aristocratic authoritarianism is by now impossible. That old order was based on the inability of the bulk of the population to participate in politics, a condition which no longer prevails after some industrialization and consequent democratization have taken place. The aristocracy can return to power only by totalitarian methods. We have seen, however, that all its possible allies—capitalists, old middle class, peasants, and intellectuals ideologically close to the aristocracy—are politically weak or even non-existent in underdeveloped countries now and will, in the future, probably not develop much strength that they would want to put at the disposal of the aristocracy. Indeed, the aristocracy itself, weakened by modernization under the nationalist intellectuals, is not likely, after a period of democratization and more advanced industrialization, to rally sufficient strength to attempt the establishment of totalitarianism. Still, one cannot be sure of this in all cases, for the outcome depends on the depth of the inroads modernization has made in an underdeveloped society. The possibility of a development in the direction of a totalitarianism of the aristocracy cannot be ruled out entirely. In some of the underdeveloped countries now evolving along democratic lines, there have been some movements looking toward re-establishment of aristocratic rule, with possible Fascist-totalitarian overtones. Generally, they are not likely to succeed and, as a rule, their success becomes less likely the more industrialized the country and the more firmly established its democratic system.

Where democracy has not been effective for long, but the balance of power favors the traditionalist forces so that modernization is being slowed, the intellectuals may become sufficiently impatient to try to re-establish their own sole rule through a "second-wave" nationalist revolution. To maintain themselves in power after a period of some democracy, they may now have to resort to totalitarian methods—which they may be the more inclined to do as they failed to industrialize rapidly and to eliminate the traditionalist forces when they were in power the first time. Once democracy is well entrenched and industrialization fairly far advanced, however, the establishment of a totalitarianism of intellectuals becomes improbable. The energies of the intellectuals are now increasingly absorbed by the industrial economy and in the service of the various groups created by such an economy. Indeed, intellectuals—if we define that term as broadly as we have to include all persons with a higher education appropriate to an industrialized society, i.e., not only thinkers and writers, but lawyers and physicians, scientists and engineers, administrators and military officers —can be said to constitute a distinct group with common interests chiefly during the period of industrial development; they are non-existent before and they tend to merge with other groups with advanced industrialization. Historically, no well-established democratic and industrially advanced country has come under a totalitarianism of intellectuals. The one possible exception, Czechoslovakia, is to be accounted for largely in terms of foreign pressure rather than domestic developments.

In a number of the now developing countries, the power relations among the various groups have been such as to create the conditions of democracy, a situation in which most of the major groups in the population participate in politics. The change from the rule of nationalist intellectuals to democracy may come about suddenly or gradually. In Argentina, where Perón sought to perpetuate nationalist-intellectual rule through the suppression of groups opposed to him, but had not succeeded in establishing a thorough-going totalitarian system to eliminate or at least to suppress them, democracy, with its system of balance among old and new forces, came through the overthrow of Perón. In other countries, like Mexico or India, for example, the groups who compete with the intellectuals and eventually absorb them, and whose continued competition with each other constitutes democracy, grew so gradually as neither to challenge the intellectual nationalist rulers to suppress them nor to have to overthrow the regime of the latter. In form, too, the democracies among the developing countries differ. They may, like Uruguay, Chile, and the Philippines,[1] operate through the two or more parties we have come to associate with democracy in advanced countries. But just as a two-party system does not fit our definition of democracy if, as the eighteenth-century British one, it does not represent many of the major interests in the country, so a one-party system is, by our standards, democratic if, as in many states and local government units of the United States, most of the major interests are represented in the single party. This is the case in the single parties of Mexico[2] and of India—though in India a multi-party system

---

[1] The role of one group in Philippine politics in a recent period is analyzed in Frances Lucille Starner, *Magsaysay and the Philippine Peasantry. The Agrarian Impact on Philippine Politics, 1953–1956* (Berkeley and Los Angeles: University of California Press, 1961).

[2] Philip B. Taylor, Jr., "The Mexican Elections of 1958: Affirmation of Authoritarianism?," *The Western Political Quarterly*, XIII, No. 3 (September 1960), 722–744, sees the PRI as an arena for changing conflicting forces. See also L. Vincent Padgett, "Mexico's One-Party System: A Re-Evaluation," *The American Political Science Review*, LI, No. 4 (December 1957), 995–1008; and Martin C. Needler, "The Political Development of Mexico," *The American Political Science Review*, LV, No. 2 (June 1961), 308–312. That the PRI no longer integrates all the power-

may now be developing,[1] and most major groups may well receive representation in other countries with a single dominant nationalist party, like most African countries,[2] and eventually perhaps even in countries with a single dominant Communist party. It would seem probable that new groups entering the arena of politics may find it easier and more profitable to operate within the single party, thus broadening the party's base of representation, than to start rival parties.

If a democratic system will probably not be replaced by a totalitarian one of the aristocracy or of the intellectuals, and cannot revert to the traditional authoritarianism of an agrarian society, it will remain democratic. That, however, according to our definition, means merely that all the major groups will continue to be represented in politics. It does not mean that the groups—and hence the nature of politics—will remain the same. A discussion of the changes in politics under conditions of advanced industrialization is beyond the scope of this essay. We may merely suggest that with the development of the industrial economy, the problem of poverty and the distribution of wealth ultimately cease to be burning issues.[3] Politics no doubt continues to be the conflict over "who gets what," but the "what" is less and less the difference between life and death or even between a comfortable and a miserable life. Consequently the broad interest groups that fought the major conflicts during the period of industrial

ful interests in Mexico and excludes major business groups is shown by Merle Kling's case study, *A Mexican Interest Group in Action* (Englewood Cliffs, N.J.: Prentice-Hall, 1961), particularly p. 65. For a thorough study of Mexican politics, see Robert E. Scott, *Mexican Government in Transition* (Urbana: University of Illinois Press, 1959). For the earlier stages of a Latin-American intellectual-led nationalist movement, see Robert J. Alexander, *The Bolivian National Revolution* (New Brunswick, N.J.: Rutgers University Press, 1958), and Richard W. Patch, "Bolivia: The Restrained Revolution," *The Annals of the American Academy of Political and Social Science,* vol. 334 (March 1961), 123–132.

[1] Myron Weiner, *Party Politics in India. The Development of a Multi-Party System* (Princeton, N.J.: Princeton University Press, 1957).

[2] See Ruth Schachter, "Single-Party Systems in West Africa," *The American Political Science Review,* LV, No. 2 (June 1961), 294–307. An outstanding analysis of the conditions of change from the traditional tribal order to a modern democratic one in a one-party African country is David E. Apter, *The Gold Coast in Transition* (Princeton, N.J.: Princeton University Press, 1955). For a rather different view of the same country, see also Henry L. Bretton, "Current Political Thought and Practice in Ghana," *The American Political Science Review,* LII, No. 1 (March 1958), 46–63. For an excellent study of the evolution of another single-party nationalist movement in the post-independence period, see Douglas E. Ashford, *Political Change in Morocco* (Princeton, N.J.: Princeton University Press, 1961).

[3] On the problems of such a society and of adjusting to it, see Kenneth Galbraith, *The Affluent Society* (Boston: Houghton Mifflin Co., 1958).

development break up more and more into distinct minor groups with distinct interests that differ from each other in only relatively minor fashion. If workers no longer have to fight for power and prosperity as workers, if businessmen no longer have to oppose them as businessmen, the miner and the carpenter, the banker and the textile manufacturer each come to be concerned chiefly with the interests peculiar to his special occupation rather than those of his class. Classes cease to be politically relevant groups because they no longer hold significant interests in common. This development is reinforced by technological changes, such as automation, which tend to replace great numbers of relatively undifferentiated unskilled and semi-skilled workers with highly specialized and differentiated technicians. At the same time as interests proliferate, the differences between the groups shrink in scope, for all are agreed on the desirability of continuing the existing political and governmental order. It is the end of class-consciousness and ideology,[1] of movements and revolutions. The end of poverty as a mass phenomenon, something totally new in history, gives rise to a totally new type of politics, which, far more than before, will involve conflict over scarce resources other than economic ones.

Britain is now entering this stage of politics, which, to the remaining intellectuals, who yearn for the excitement of the struggles for equality and social justice of the past, appears as a period of dull politics, quite different from what they had imagined the political concomitant of economic abundance and social equality to be. America has to some extent anticipated the new politics throughout her history, not so much because of her economic abundance—for that was only relative to other countries and for a long time did not abolish poverty—but because, in the absence of a feudal background with its rigid class divisions,[2] social conflicts have not split the society along sharply drawn class lines. As in more and more countries the traditional agrarian society fades into a more distant past and the remnants of the old aristocracy, its ideology, and its power die out, and as finally even the class lines which modern industrialism added to those of the traditional society become blurred—if, indeed, it ever added clear lines—American society becomes less and less exceptional. Parallels from American history cannot throw much light on the evolution of underdeveloped

[1] For some relevant essays on this subject, see Daniel Bell, *The End of Ideology. On the Exhaustion of Political Ideas in the Fifties* (Glencoe, Ill.: The Free Press, 1960).

[2] On the effects of this absence on American political ideology, see Louis Hartz, *The Liberal Tradition in America* (New York: Harcourt, Brace & Co., 1955).

countries. The American present and future, however, may yet become relevant for an understanding of societies becoming far advanced industrially. When they reach that stage, the politics of policy issues, introduced by early industrialization, may again be replaced by the politics of personnel. But those contending for office will represent, not a thin aristocratic stratum ruling over a vast mass of poverty-stricken peasants, but the huge middle class of the affluent society.

SELECTED
ARTICLES

1

TOWARDS A THEORY OF
POWER AND POLITICAL
INSTABILITY
IN LATIN AMERICA

Merle Kling

I

"One may consider science," James B. Conant has observed, "as an attempt . . . to lower the degree of empiricism or to extend the range of theory. . . . Almost all significant work of scientists today, I believe, comes under the heading of attempts to reduce the degree of empiricism."[1]

Despite the conception of science and theory prevalent in the natural sciences and reflected in the formulation of Conant, the discipline of political science has yet to reject decisively the notion of theory as an aggregation of metaphysical speculations unrelated to experience and practice. Academically, in fact, the field of political theory, within the discipline of political science, traditionally has defined its role as recording, with varied degrees of interpretation, the history of metaphysical speculations in the area of politics and the state.[2] But "theorizing, even about politics," as Lasswell and Kaplan correctly assert, "is not to be confused with metaphysical speculation in terms of abstrac-

Reprinted, by permission, from *The Western Political Quarterly*, IX, No. 1 (March 1956), 21–35.

[1] James B. Conant, *Science and Common Sense* (New Haven: Yale University Press, 1951), pp. 58–59. "Only by the introduction of a theoretical element can the degree of empiricism be reduced." James B. Conant, *Modern Science and Modern Man* (New York: Columbia University Press, 1952), p. 28.

[2] For a systematic expression of dissatisfaction with the contemporary state of theory in American political science, particularly its "decline into historicism," see David Easton, *The Political System: An Inquiry Into the State of Political Science* (New York: Knopf, 1953).

tions hopelessly removed from empirical observation and control."[3]

Within a scientific framework, consequently, a theory of power and instability in Latin America must attempt to discharge at least four functions. (1) An adequate theory must serve "to reduce the degree of empiricism"; that is, it must place in a broad and meaningful context the apparently disconnected manifestations of instability in Latin America. (2) It must offer generalizations regarding the exercise of power and the prevalence of instability in Latin America which are compatible with the available evidence. (3) It must offer a guide and provide a framework for relevant research. A scientific theory neither anticipates every future event nor solves every practical problem. A theory with scientific pretensions, however, does provide directions for the investigation and solution of subsequent problems. (4) A theory of Latin American instability, if it is to endure, must not be rooted in relatively static elements in the Latin American environment; it must take account of dynamic forces which are subject to change. For example, a "theory" which "explains" instability in Latin America on the basis of the "hot blood" of the "Spanish temperament" is vulnerable on at least two grounds: the biological laboratory cannot sustain the assumption of peculiar heat in the blood of persons of Spanish descent; and the ultimate development of political stability in Latin America can be rationalized only by the projection of fantastic concepts of biological mutation.[4] Similarly, a "theory" of Latin American instability rooted in geographical factors is not reconcilable with probable changes of a significant order; for the Andes mountains are not likely to lose important elevation and the Amazon River is not likely to contract in length appreciably in the relevant future. By ignoring the dynamic aspects of Latin American society, however, such a "theory" postulates major geographical transformations if political stability

[3] Harold D. Lasswell and Abraham Kaplan, *Power and Society: A Framework For Political Inquiry* (New Haven: Yale University Press, 1950), p. x.

[4] Reflecting a "racist" emphasis, William Lytle Schurz—two years before the *coup d'état* which brought Perón's group to power in Argentina—wrote: "Conditions in Argentina are unusually favorable to the development of political democracy. It is peopled by a predominantly white race. It is free from the dead weight of a heavy Indian population, the too mercurial influence of the Negro, and the disturbing leaven of mixed peoples, who move in an uncertain world between the fixed status of the pure bloods." *Latin America: A Descriptive Survey* (New York: Dutton, 1941), p. 140. In a new and revised edition (1949), Schurz, while retaining his descriptive comments on the "races" of Argentina, rephrases his opening conclusion in a more cautious vocabulary: "Basic conditions in Argentina would appear to be unusually favorable to the development of political democracy." P. 135.

is achieved.[5] To attribute political instability in Latin America, finally, to "history" and the heterogeneous cultures of Spaniards and Indians buries any viable theory in an inextricable maze of historical and cultural determinism. This arbitarily excludes the possibility of rapid developments in the direction of political stability.

A theory of power and political instability in Latin America, therefore, is not a substitute for empirical research. But, while subject to verification by experience, the theory must reach beyond the scope of analysis of isolated and superficially haphazard political episodes; and the theory should provide a guide for fruitful and detailed investigations.

II

Political instability in Latin America is distinguished by three characteristics: (1) it is chronic; (2) it frequently is accompanied by limited violence; (3) it produces no basic shifts in economic, social or political policies.

Political instability in a Latin American country cannot be evaluated as a temporary deviation in a pattern of peaceful rotation in office. In many Latin American republics, despite prescriptions of written constitutions, an abrupt change of governmental personnel through violence is a regular and recurrent phenomenon. In Honduras, "from 1824 to 1950, a period of 126 years, the executive office changed hands 116 times."[6] "During the nine-year interval ending in 1940, Ecuador had no less than fourteen presidents, [and had] four of them during the single month which ended on September 17, 1947. Instability is likewise dramatized on the cabinet level: twenty-seven different ministers occupying eight cabinet posts between May 29, 1944, and August 23, 1947. Twelve foreign ministers attempted to administer Ecuadoran foreign policy in the two-month period between August and October 1933."[7] And the observations of a member of a United Nations mission to Bolivia in 1951 would not be inapplicable in substance to many

[5] ". . . policy consists of decisions about the future. The scientist who wishes to contribute to such decisions therefore focuses his research on problems which bear upon the relevant future. . . ." Ernest R. Hilgard and Daniel Lerner, "The Person: Subject and Object of Science and Policy," in Daniel Lerner and Harold D. Lasswell, The Policy Sciences: Recent Developments in Scope and Method (Stanford: Stanford University Press, 1951), pp. 42–43.

[6] William S. Stokes, Honduras: An Area Study in Government (Madison: University of Wisconsin Press, 1950), p. 181.

[7] George I. Blanksten, Ecuador: Constitutions and Caudillos (Berkeley: University of California Press, 1951), p. 32.

Latin American states: "In the past ten years, Bolivia has had nine major revolutions. None of its Presidents has served out his constitutional term of office during the last twenty-five years. There have been eighteen Ministers of Labor in four years; eight Ministers of Finance in eighteen months." [8]

Reflecting the persistence of political instability since World War II, governing personnel, including presidents, have been displaced by "irregular" methods on at least the following occasions:

October 1945. Venezuela	June 1950. Peru
October 1945. Brazil	May 1951. Bolivia
January 1946. Haiti	May 1951. Panama
July 1946. Bolivia	March 1952. Cuba
January 1947. Paraguay	April 1952. Bolivia
May 1947. Nicaragua	December 1952. Venezuela
August 1947. Ecuador	June 1953. Colombia
September 1947. Ecuador	May 1954. Paraguay
March 1948. Costa Rica	July 1954. Guatemala
June 1948. Paraguay	August 1954. Brazil
October 1948. Peru	December 1954. Honduras
November 1948. Venezuela	January 1955. Panama
December 1948. El Salvador	September 1955. Argentina
January 1949. Paraguay	November 1955. Argentina
November 1949. Panama	November 1955. Brazil
May 1950. Haiti	

Occupancy of key governmental positions, consequently, has been secured at least 31 times in disregard of formal procedures since the Second World War. Nor does the above list take into account the numerous "unsuccessful" plots, suppressed uprisings, arrests, deportations, declarations of state of siege, boycotts, riots and fraudulent "elections" which have punctuated Latin American politics in the last decade.[9] And the list, of course, does not include references to political irregularities in non-sovereign areas such as British Guiana.

Revolts, uprisings and *coups d'état,* moreover, constitute incomplete evidence of the range of political instability in Latin America. For obscured by data of these kinds is the presence of "concealed" instability. The protracted tenure of a Vargas in Brazil (1930–1945), of an Ubico in Guatemala (1930–1944), the single candidate (*candidato único*) "elections" of Paraguay, Honduras, the Dominican Republic, Nicaragua and Colombia, the abortive "elections" of 1952 in Venezuela

[8] Albert Lepawsky, "The Bolivian Operation," *International Conciliation,* No. 479 (March, 1952), 106.

[9] Evidence of recent political instability, particularly for the year 1952, is summarized in a pamphlet by Miguel Jorrín, *Political Instability in Latin America* (Albuquerque: University of New Mexico, 1953).

are not to be construed, of course, as symptomatic of political stability. For these also constitute instances in which governmental authority has been retained by the exercise of force in disregard of formal requirements. *Continuismo,* prolonged office-holding by a strong *caudillo,* in its essence represents the reverse side of the shield of political instability. *Continuismo* signifies not the absence of political instability, but the effective suppression of potential and incipient rebellions by competing *caudillos. Continuismo,* in fact, may be regarded as perpetuation in office by means of a series of successful *anticipatory* revolts.

Unlike cabinet instability in France, political instability in the Latin American states is neither sanctioned by the written constitution nor dictated by the rigidity of domestic party alignments. Latin American instability, in contrast with the French version, occurs in an environment of amorphous political parties and involves the limited employment of violence. It is not the withdrawal of votes by a doctrinaire bloc of deputies which precipitates the collapse of a Latin American regime; rather, it is the personal military following of an opportunistic *caudillo* which impresses a Latin American president with the timeliness of seeking asylum in a foreign embassy. The pervasiveness of violence justifies the conclusion of Stokes: "Violence seems to be institutionalized in the organization, maintenance, and changing of governments in Latin America." [10]

Although violence provides a continuing strand in the fabric of Latin American politics, revolution, in the sense of a fundamental transformation of society, "is rare in Latin America, and even mass participation in violence is only occasionally found." [11] A leader may be assassinated or exiled, a new junta may assume the posts of political authority, but control of the economic bases of power is not shifted and the hierarchy of social classes is not affected; in short, there is no restructuring of society. The label "palace revolution," as defined by Lasswell and Kaplan, can be appropriately applied to the pattern of political change in

[10] William S. Stokes, "Violence as a Power Factor in Latin-American Politics," *Western Political Quarterly,* V (1952), 445. "One of the most typical aspects of Latin American life is the tendency to settle political issues by force. Government by revolution might almost be said to be the rule. Since the turn of the present century the governments of the nations to the south have been overthrown by revolt seventy-six times—an average of nearly four successful uprisings per country. No one knows how many unsuccessful rebellions have occurred during these years because no one has ever taken the trouble to count them, but they certainly run into the hundreds." Austin F. Macdonald, *Latin American Politics and Government* (2d ed.; New York: Crowell, 1954), pp. 11–12.

[11] Stokes, *op. cit.,* p. 461.

Latin America; for political instability in Latin America, like a palace revolution, involves "a change in governors contrary to the political formula but retaining it." Again violence in Latin America, in conformity with the characteristics of a palace revolution, produces a "change in government without corresponding changes in governmental policy." [12] General Gustavo Rojas Pinilla may be a party to a successful revolt in Colombia, and General Zenón Noriega may be a party to an unsuccessful revolt in Peru; but the basic economic, social and political policies of Colombia and Peru are not altered by either the successful or the unsuccessful general. Violence is virtually always present; fundamental change is virtually always absent.

III

"In the general course of human nature," wrote Alexander Hamilton in *The Federalist* (No. 79), "a power over a man's subsistence amounts to a power over his will." And research in Latin American studies suggests that the distinguishing characteristics of the Latin American economy, despite the influence exerted by the Church and other institutions, are of primary importance in determining conditions for the retention and transfer of power.

Traditionally, ownership of land has been regarded as a major economic base for the exercise of power in Latin America. Despite the continued dependence today of more than two-thirds of the Latin American population on agriculture as a chief source of income, the system of land tenure operates to prevent the widespread diffusion of economic power. Concentration of land ownership in the hands of a tiny minority—whether symbolized by the *latifundio, hacienda, estancia, fazenda,* or *finca*—represents the prevailing, as well as historic, agrarian pattern of Latin America. "In many countries in Latin America," concludes a recent analysis by the United Nations Department of Economic Affairs, "the main feature of the agrarian structure is the high degree of inequality in land ownership." [13]

Although they can be introduced only with qualifications as to reliability, statistical estimates offer striking evidence of the narrow agrarian base of power. In Chile, whereas 43.4 per cent of all land holdings are under five hectares, they account for only 0.5 per cent

[12] Lasswell and Kaplan, *op. cit.*, p. 270. For striking evidence of the equanimity with which economically dominant groups view rivalries among military cliques in El Salvador, see *New York Times*, February 6, 1955, p. 12.

[13] United Nations, Department of Economic Affairs, *Progress in Land Reform* (New York, 1954), p. 37.

of the farm area; large holdings (1000 hectares and over), on the other hand, constitute only 1.4 per cent of all holdings, but they incorporate 68.2 per cent of the farm area. Acknowledging that "the agrarian structure of Chile is characterized in the main by an abundance of very small holdings and a large concentration of large estates in the hands of a small number of proprietors," the government of Chile, in reply to a United Nations questionnaire, emphasized the difficulty of modifying the pattern of land ownership:

Owing to the economic and political structure of the country, land reform in Chile is difficult to carry out. Landholders who would be affected by any action of an economic, political, administrative, legal or social nature will vigorously oppose its implementation, and their political and economic influence is very powerful.[14]

In Brazil, 1.5 per cent of all land holdings account for 48.4 per cent of the farm area.[15] According to the 1950 census of Bolivia, 4.5 per cent of the rural landowners possess 70 per cent of the private landed property.[16] In the province of Pichincha in Ecuador, 1.5 per cent of all holdings incorporate 65.3 per cent of the farm area, and the government reports that "Ecuador has not developed a policy of land reform." [17] In Cuba, 1.4 per cent of all holdings comprise 47 per cent of the farm area.[18] Even in Mexico, where the government claims that about 23 per cent of the total area in holdings was distributed to *éjido* farmers between 1916 and 1940, in lands not under the *éjido* system 0.8 per cent of all holdings constitute 79.5 per cent of the farm area.[19] And patterns of highly concentrated landownership persist in Argentina, Peru, and Venezuela.

This monopolization of agrarian wealth injects an element of rigidity

[14] *Ibid.*, pp. 42–43.

[15] *Ibid.*, p. 41.

[16] *Ibid.*, p. 40. In Bolivia, "the most usual model, surviving with little change from colonial times, is the large estate with absentee owner and cultivated by native labour." Harold Osborne, *Bolivia: A Land Divided* (London: Royal Institute of International Affairs, 1954), p. 111.

[17] United Nations, Department of Economic Affairs, *op. cit.*, pp. 43–44. "An Ecuadorian economist recently called attention to the fact that, according to the register on real-estate tax paid in the greater part of the Sierra between 1943–8, 486 landowners, i.e., less than 2 per cent of the persons subject to the tax, owned three-quarters of the land, while the remaining quarter was distributed among over 23,000 small owners. Many properties were no larger than one-tenth of an acre, while others extended over more than 15,000 acres." Lilo Lanke, *Ecuador, Country of Contrasts* (London: Royal Institute of International Affairs, 1954), p. 118.

[18] United Nations, Department of Economic Affairs, *op. cit.*, p. 46.

[19] *Ibid.*, p. 39.

into the power relations of Latin American groups; for the effect of the land tenure system is to establish relatively fixed economic boundaries between the landowners and the peon, since "the relationships growing out of the large estates have matured into deep inflexibility." [20] Indeed, the authors of a very carefully documented study of Latin America have concluded: "Monopolization of land has been and still is both the source and the technique of political power in Latin America." [21]

Yet it is possible to exaggerate the independence, the freedom from restraint, of the landowner in Latin American society. Viewed solely in terms of domestic Latin American patterns of land tenure, the landowner appears almost to personify the classical definition of sovereignty. He seems to possess virtually absolute power. But an analysis of the nature of agricultural production reveals important inhibitions on the discretionary power of the landowner, and he fails to qualify as an economic sovereign. For as a producer of crops peculiarly dependent on foreign markets, in an agrarian economy characterized by monoculture, the landowner finds his economic base of independence subject to severe limitations. When 50 per cent to 60 per cent of Brazilian exports consists of coffee,[22] when normally 80 per cent of the total value of exports of El Salvador consists of coffee,[23] when "coffee cultivation . . . contributes more than 70 per cent of total exports and is the basic cash crop on which nearly everything else depends" in Guatemala (according to a Mission sponsored by the International Bank for Reconstruction and Development),[24] when coffee represents 73.2 per cent of the value of all exports in Colombia for 1953,[25] when coffee is the predominant export of the Central American Republics (representing 56.4 per cent of all exports in 1953) [26]—when the Western Hemisphere produces about 85 per cent of the world's exportable

[20] Simon G. Hanson, *Economic Development in Latin America* (Washington: Inter-American Affairs Press, 1951), p. 67.

[21] George Soule, David Efron, and Norman T. Ness, *Latin America in the Future World* (New York: Farrar and Rinehart, 1945), p. 63.

[22] United Nations, Department of Economic Affairs, *Economic Survey of Latin America 1953* (New York, 1954), p. 54; Pan American Union, Division of Economic Research, *Economic Developments in Brazil 1949–50* (Washington, D.C., 1950), p. 37.

[23] United States, Department of Commerce, *Foreign Commerce Yearbook 1949* (Washington, 1951), p. 402.

[24] International Bank for Reconstruction and Development, *The Economic Development of Guatemala* (Washington, D.C., 1951), p. 24.

[25] United Nations, Department of Economic Affairs, *Economic Survey of Latin America 1953* (New York, 1954), p. 56.

[26] *Ibid.*, p. 64.

coffee and the United States consumes 65 per cent to 75 per cent of all the coffee shipped [27]—the domestic proprietors of coffee plantations cannot be immune to the pressures (regardless of the indirection, diplomacy and circumspection with which they may be exerted) that emanate from their principal export market. When over half of the total value of exports of the Dominican Republic [28] and about three-fourths of the total value of Cuban exports [29] consist of sugar, the domestic owner of sugar plantations cannot be indifferent to the influence of international markets. "Sugar," reported an Economic and Technical Mission organized by the International Bank for Reconstruction and Development, "is not only Cuba's principal source of livelihood. It dominates the economy—and the outlook of the people—in various ways. Sugar plays an even greater part in the exports of Cuba today than it did in the past." [30] Hence the fundamentally colonial and monocultural nature of the Latin American economies, as evidenced by the role of coffee and sugar exports, constricts the economic base even of the apparently omnipotent landowner. [31]

The main characteristics of the ownership of mineral wealth and the conduct of the mining industries in Latin America further accentuate the colonial nature of the economies and add to the obstacles in the path of discovering native, local command over decisive economic elements of power. Foreign ownership of mineral resources and foreign utilization of mineral products imply that an important economic base of power in Latin America is not indigenously controlled. Thus over 90 per cent of Chilean copper is regularly produced by United States-owned enterprises; of 351,000 tons of copper mined in 1953, in excess of 325,000 tons were produced by large mining companies financed by United States capital. [32] The United States-owned Cerro de Pasco

[27] *Americas*, II (January, 1950), 2.

[28] Pan American Union, *Foreign Commerce of Dominican Republic 1941–1947* (Washington, D.C., June 1950), p. 17.

[29] United Nations, Department of Economic Affairs, *Economic Survey of Latin America 1953* (New York, 1954), p. 57.

[30] International Bank for Reconstruction and Development, *Report on Cuba* (Washington, D.C., 1951), p. 7. In 1954, the United States absorbed 60.1 per cent of Cuban sugar exports. United Nations, Department of Economic and Social Affairs, *Economic Survey of Latin America 1954* (New York, 1955), p. 59.

[31] In certain conspicuous instances, of course, the landowner is not a native of a Latin American state. The United Fruit Company, for example, is reported to own about 3,000,000 acres, mainly in Colombia, Costa Rica, Cuba, the Dominican Republic, Ecuador, Guatemala, Honduras and Panama. *New York Times*, July 4, 1954, p. 4E.

[32] United Nations, Department of Economic Affairs, *Economic Survey of Latin America 1953* (New York, 1954), p. 185.

Corporation of Peru accounts for about two-thirds of the Peruvian copper output.[33] In the case of Bolivia, despite the nationalization of the
principal tin mines, the virtually complete reliance on exports of the
mining industry as a source of indispensable foreign exchange perpetuates a political climate which is subject to foreign pressures. For
"the products of the mining industry account for some 98 per cent of
the country's total exports. And tin concentrates account for some
75 per cent of the total mineral exports." Consequently, "the financial
position of Bolivia is always peculiarly sensitive to—is indeed danger-
ously dependent upon—fluctuations of price and demand in the world
markets for non-ferrous metals." [34] Control of petroleum production in
Latin America resides almost exclusively in the hands of foreign-
owned corporations. A United States company produces more than 70
per cent of Peru's crude petroleum; in Venezuela, which accounts for
almost 80 per cent of the crude petroleum output of Latin America, a
subsidiary of a United States company ranks as the largest oil company
in the country.[35]

Venezuela and its oil industry perhaps may be cited as a case study
in the predominant role of foreign capital with respect to the control
of the mineral bases of power in Latin America. Petroleum, which is
exploited almost exclusively by foreign-owned companies, operating
under government concession, occupies a crucial position in Venezuelan exports.[36] In one fashion or another, more than 60 per cent
of the revenue of the Treasury in Venezuela is contributed by the oil
companies; during the budget year 1949–1950, about one-third of the
total budget receipts consisted of petroleum *royalties* alone.[37] Unlike
other mineral industries, moreover, petroleum has continued to attract
new capital investment from the United States. Since 74 per cent of
United States private direct-investment in the period following the
Second World War (1947–1949) was channeled to the petroleum industry, a considerable share has been invested in Venezuela as a country

[33] *Ibid.,* p. 187. The Cerro de Pasco Corporation "accounted for 84 per cent
of the copper, 36 per cent of the gold, and 55 per cent of the silver produced
in Peru between 1906 and 1938." Division of Economic Research, Pan American
Union, *The Peruvian Economy* (Washington, D.C., 1950), p. 104.

[34] Osborne, *op. cit.,* p. 107.

[35] United Nations, Department of Economic Affairs, *Economic Survey of
Latin America 1953* (New York, 1954), pp. 233–238.

[36] *Ibid.,* p. 62; United States Tariff Commission, *Mining and Manufacturing
Industries in Venezuela* (Washington, 1945), p. 47.

[37] United Nations, Department of Economic Affairs, *Public Finance Surveys:
Venezuela* (New York, January 1951), p. 47.

with exploitable petroleum resources.[38] Clearly the foreign-owned oil companies constitute factors which cannot be ignored in the power structure of Venezuela. But a precise description of the manner in which power is exercised by the petroleum industry cannot be documented. It would be valuable, for purposes of a study of power, to have accessible a public record of the specific reactions of the oil companies to the seizure of governmental authority by a revolutionary junta led by Rómulo Betancourt in 1945. It would be valuable, for purposes of a study of power, to have available an accurate record of the policies and decisions of the oil companies in so far as they affected the deposition of President Rómulo Gallegos and his supporters, including Betancourt, in 1948. But details of this type are unavailable not only to academic investigators of power in Latin America; they elude public detection and identification in most systems of power. The obscure nature of certain details, however, cannot serve to justify the rejection of an inference that a correlation exists between the economic dominance of the oil companies and the pattern of political behavior in Venezuela. While the exact techniques of the exercise of power are not easily demonstrated, obviously a substantial economic base of power in Venezuela is controlled by economic institutions beyond the geographical boundaries of the country. The control of mineral wealth, consequently, within the framework of colonial economies, introduces an external element of restraint on the exercise of power by domestic forces and movements within Latin America.

Industrialization would appear to represent a significant challenge to the economic forces of colonialism in Latin America. Undoubtedly a successful program of industrialization could alter radically the distribution of power in the Latin American area. Tangible fragments of evidence, in fact, suggest that the present level of industrialization has stimulated modifications in the established patterns of economic power. Consumer goods industries, particularly textiles, have expanded rapidly. Reflecting the influence of domestic manufacturing interests, Latin American governments have been anxious to maintain protective tariff policies. With industrialization, labor organizations have evolved and have made it possible for new leaders, drawing upon fresh sources of support, to compete for the possession of power. The well-publicized role of Lombardo Toledano in Mexican politics, the prolix constitutional and statutory provisions for social security, the turbulent strikes in some of the Latin American states, the ostentatious,

[38] Gordon Gray, *Report to the President on Foreign Economic Policies* (Washington, November 10, 1950), pp. 61, 121.

if demagogic, manifestations of solicitude for labor on the part of Juan Domingo Perón, testify to the enhanced prestige of labor and labor unions in a society experiencing the initial tensions and strains of industrialization in the twentieth century.

But the position of manufacturing as an economic base of power in Latin America can be overstated. Hitherto a level of industrialization has not been achieved which would make possible the displacement of the conventional economic bases of power. By United States standards, the Latin American consumer continues to absorb only a small amount of manufactured goods. The Latin American countries continue to be dependent on imports for many items utilized in manufacturing, as well as for much of their machinery, transportation facilities, and factory equipment. And "the most significant economic trend in 1953," according to the Secretariat of the Economic Commission for Latin America, "was, without doubt, the clear indication of a slackening in the rate of industrialization. . . . As a consequence, the industrial share of the gross product in 1953 was only 25.6 per cent, no greater than in 1945." The fact, moreover, that the industrial labor force, compared with total manpower, has not increased since 1950 constitutes evidence of a "fundamental decline in industrialization" in Latin America.[39] A decline of 21 per cent in total Latin American imports of capital goods in 1953, in relation to 1952, also emphasizes the limited potentialities of industrialization in the immediate future.[40]

Notwithstanding the somewhat spectacular construction of the Volta Redonda steel plant in Brazil and the opening of the earthquake-proof Huachipato steel works in Chile, heavy industries remain in an embryonic stage of evolution. By 1954, for example, Brazilian industry produced only 1,100,000 tons of steel ingots annually, and total Chilean production of steel ingots in 1954 amounted to 320,000 tons.[41] "Such industrialization as exists," Gordon concludes with ample evidence, "is either an undernourished image of the Great Society or else a highly specialized form, such as in mining, which exists by grace of foreign ownership and foreign markets." [42]

[39] United Nations, Department of Economic Affairs, *Economic Survey of Latin America 1953* (New York, 1954), pp. 10–11.

[40] *Ibid.*, p. 68.

[41] United Nations, Department of Economic and Social Affairs, *Economic Survey of Latin America 1954* (New York, 1955), p. 96. For data regarding the share of manufacturing in Latin American national incomes, see: George Wythe, *Industry in Latin America* (2d ed.; New York: Columbia University Press, 1949), p. 13; and the United Nations, Secretariat of the Economic Commission for Latin America, *Economic Survey of Latin America 1948* (New York, 1949), p. 2.

[42] Wendell C. Gordon, *The Economy of Latin America* (New York: Columbia University Press, 1950), p. 20.

From the point of view of locating the economic sites of power, the current program of industrialization in Latin America presents an apparent paradox. The desire for industrialization evidently originates with leaders who seek to transfer economic bases of power from foreign to domestic jurisdiction; and the economic nationalism which normally has accompanied the drive for industrialization would seem to substantiate this assumption. But the financial techniques utilized have not hastened the transfer of power, based on control of industry, to native groups in Latin America. For, lacking huge reservoirs of local capital to finance heavy industry, unwilling (and perhaps unable) to compel modifications in the investment practices of landowners, the Latin Americans, in their attempt to move toward the goal of industrialization, once again have sought foreign capital. Prominent among the suppliers of new capital to Latin America has been the Export-Import Bank of Washington. Every sovereign state in Latin America except Guatemala has received funds from this Bank. By 1954, the Export-Import Bank, which supplied more than half of the investment capital required by the Volta Redonda and Huachipato steel plants,[43] had authorized credits of $2,152,023,000 to the Latin American countries.[44] In addition, half of the states in the Latin American region have received loans from the International Bank for Reconstruction and Development. By 1954 this specialized agency of the United Nations had authorized loans of $426,000,000 to Latin American countries.[45] Since voting power in the International Bank for Reconstruction and Development is based on the proportion of capital subscribed by each

[43] *New York Times*, November 26, 1950.

[44] Export-Import Bank of Washington, *Seventeenth Semiannual Report to Congress for the Period July–December 1953*, p. 22.

At least one member of the Chilean Senate has argued that President Gabriel Gonzalez Videla was forced to revise his internal policies in order to qualify for an Export-Import Bank loan designed to encourage industrialization. Salvadore Ocampo, "You Have Invaded My Country," *New Republic*, CXVII (December 1, 1947), 10–12. Also see Roger S. Abbott, "The Role of Contemporary Political Parties in Chile," *American Political Science Review*, XLV (1951), 454, 457.

[45] United Nations, Department of Economic and Social Affairs, *Foreign Capital in Latin America* (New York, 1955), p. 13. ". . . one of the most noteworthy developments in the field of foreign investment during 1954 was the marked increase in the loan activity of the International Bank for Reconstruction and Development and of the Export-Import Bank. After authorizing development-type credits to Latin America to a value of 90 million and 57 million dollars in 1953 and in the first half of 1954, respectively, they approved total credits for 196 million dollars during the second half of the year and over 100 millions in the first quarter of 1955." United Nations, Department of Economic and Social Affairs, *Economic Survey of Latin America 1954* (New York, 1955), p. 51.

member, the United States speaks with a dominant voice in the affairs of the Bank.

Potentially, then, industrialization may prove of large consequence in creating new economic bases of power in Latin America. At some future date, it may modify drastically the position of the conventional economic bases of power. But industrialization on such a scale as yet has failed to materialize. Promise, hope, and aspiration must be distinguished from performance and accomplishment. Accordingly, at the present time, industrialization in Latin America, realistically appraised, is taking place within the context of an environment which in its economic content remains basically colonial.[46]

IV

An analysis of the distinguishing characteristics of the economic bases of power in Latin America suggests that the conventional economic sources of power constitute relatively static elements of power. Since ownership of land or mines does not pass readily from the hands of one group to another, control of conventional bases of power cannot be secured by the ambitious mestizo, mulatto or Indian without a major social upheaval. The system of land tenure dooms to frustration ambitious individuals in search of a new agrarian base of power. Foreign exploitation of mineral resources effectively blocks the possibilities of shifts in the possession of mineral bases of power. And at its current pace of development, industrialization has failed to expand into a broad, substantial base of power.

But while the conventional economic bases of power, landownership and control of mineral resources, represent essentially economic constants in the contemporary equation of power in Latin America, government and the army—often indistinguishable in Latin American society—represent notable variables. For in Latin America, government does not merely constitute the stakes of a struggle among rival economic interests; in Latin America, government itself is a unique base of economic power which, unlike the conventional economic bases of power, is subject to fluctuations in possession. Whereas direct profits from oil fields or copper mines may not be within the grasp of the Latin American, the legal sovereignty of the Latin American states demands that the governmental personnel who serve as intermediaries

[46] Fourteen Latin American states are classified as "underdeveloped" and none as "highly developed" by Eugene Staley, *The Future of Underdeveloped Countries: Political Implications of Economic Development* (New: Harper, 1954), pp. 16–17.

between the foreign-owned company and the domestic concession shall
be of native origin. Thus the discrepancy between the political independence and the economic colonialism of the Latin American
states permits government, in the power system of Latin America, to
occupy an unusual position as a shifting base of economic power. With
the number of lucrative governmental and army posts necessarily limited, the competition understandably is keen. As political office provides a uniquely dynamic opportunity to acquire an economic base of
power, however, sufficiently large segments of the population are prepared to take the ultimate risk, the risk of life, in a revolt, in a *coup
d' état*, to perpetuate a characteristic feature of Latin American politics
—chronic political instability. In the distinctive power structure of
Latin America, government serves as a special transformer through
which pass the currents of economic ambition.

The pattern of political instability, significantly, has not evolved as a
challenge to the conventional economic bases of power, for irregular
shifts in control of government take place without disturbing the established economic bases of power. Although widespread industrialization, accompanied by an intensification of economic nationalism,
could alter the existing pattern of power, although an extensive program of land reform could not help but affect the distribution of
power, seizure of government by a new *caudillo*, on the contrary, does
not provoke profound social and economic repercussions in Latin
America. Thus chronic political instability serves as an avenue of socio-
economic mobility, but it does not pose a genuine danger to the control
of the conventional economic bases of power. When a "revolutionary"
junta replaced Federico Chaves as President of Paraguay in May
1954 with Tómas Romero Pereira and subsequently, in July, arranged
for the election of General Alfredo Stroessner without opposition, the
pattern was a familiar one: the cast of political characters was shuffled,
and the colonial economy of Paraguay remained intact. Indeed, such
events can be evaluated adequately only in terms of the French aph-
orism, "Plus ça change, plus c'ést la mème chose."

The interpretation of power and political instability in Latin America
developed by this study may be summarized in a series of generalized
propositions. A decisive correlation exists between the control of the
economic bases of power and the real exercise of political power in
Latin America. Control of the conventional economic bases of power
remains relatively static. Because of the colonial nature of the Latin
American economies, an exceptional economic premium attaches to
control of the apparatus of government as a dynamic base of power.
Whereas the conventional bases of power effectively restrict mobility

in economic status, control of government provides an unusually dynamic route to wealth and power. Thus the contrast between the stable character of the conventional economic bases of power and the shifting, unconventional position of government provokes intense and violent competition for control of government as a means of acquiring and expanding a base of wealth and power. In the vocabulary of mathematics, *chronic political instability is a function of the contradiction between the realities of a colonial economy and the political requirements of legal sovereignty among the Latin American states.*

V

Significant implications for both public policy and research appear inherent in the interpretation of Latin American politics here formulated. In the field of public policy, this interpretation implies that it is not possible for the United States to have powerful allies in Latin America so long as present economic patterns persist. Contemporary economic patterns of colonialism are conducive to the maintenance of reliable *diplomatic* allies for the United States in Latin America; and the *diplomatic* reliability of the Latin American states is faithfully registered, on many issues, in the voting records of the General Assembly of the United Nations. But the same economic conditions which ensure diplomatic reliability weaken the *power* position of the Latin American states. For, as Hans Morgenthau recognizes in the second (and not the first) edition of his *Politics among Nations*, the quality of government itself is a factor of power in international politics.[47] Hence economic colonialism promotes political instability, which detracts from the power of reliable diplomatic allies of the United States; but, while the achievement of political stability would augment the power of the Latin American states, the elimination of a status of economic colonialism may diminish the diplomatic reliability of their governments! And the dilemma thus brought to the surface by the interpretation of Latin American politics offered in this study has never been publicly acknowledged by the United States Department of State.

For research, the implications of this interpretation of Latin American politics are rather obvious. If political studies of the Latin American area are to rest on more than superficial foundations, they can rest neither on formal analyses of constitutions nor on the diplomatic exchanges between the United States and various Latin American countries. Nor, in the light of this interpretation, can a study nourish the

[47] Hans J. Morgenthau, *Politics among Nations* (New York: Knopf, 1954), p. viii.

illusion that it has penetrated to the realities of Latin American politics when it has applied the label "dictator" to a particular holder of governmental office in Latin America. The Latin American *caudillo*, according to the implications of the interpretation presented here, operates within a narrowly-circumscribed range of power, since he may not tamper with the traditional economic bases of power. Serious attempts to analyze the nature of politics in Latin America, therefore, must seek to identify the ambits of political maneuverability within which power may be exercised by those who occupy posts of governmental authority in sovereign states with colonial economies. The successful conclusion of such attempts should result in a new awareness of the limitations on the nature of the power actually exercised by presidents and junta members in the politically unstable environment of Latin America.

2

POLITICAL GROUPS
IN LATIN AMERICA

GEORGE I. BLANKSTEN

I feel it is necessary to begin with an attempt to define the term "political group" as used in this paper: it is a system of patterned or regular interaction among a number of individuals. The interaction is sufficiently patterned to permit the system to be viewed as a unit, and the action of the unit is directed toward some phase of the operation of government. Every political group has an interest. This is simply the central and continuing type of activity that gives the group its property as a system or a unit. Interest, then, is consistent with the observed pattern of interaction, and not contrary to it. "The interest and the group are the same phenomenon observed from slightly different positions, and an 'interest group' is a tautological expression. The interest is not a thing that exists apart from the activity or that controls activity."[1]

Let me add a few points regarding the relationship between the political group and its member individuals. If the group be regarded as the pattern of interaction among its members, then it follows that the group has an existence apart from that of the individuals associated with it. So a political group may have a history or a career of its own, distinguishable from those of the individuals participating in the interaction. Further, at any given time a single individual may take

Reprinted from *The American Political Science Review*, LIII, No. 1 (March 1959), 106–127, by permission of The American Political Science Association. This paper was delivered at the 1958 Annual Meeting of The American Political Science Association, St. Louis, Missouri, September, 1958. Some of the material presented was developed in connection with the author's work with the SSRC Committee on Comparative Politics, to which he expresses his indebtedness.

[1] Charles B. Hagan, "The Group in a Political Science," in Roland A. Young (ed.), *Approaches to the Study of Politics* (Evanston: Northwestern University Press, 1958), pp. 38–51, particularly pp. 44–46.

part in more groups than one; a person with such "overlapping memberships" may pursue different and, in some cases, contradictory interests.[2] Finally, the size of a group is not material here. No issue is raised by queries as to how large or small a political group may be. It is defined by the pattern of interaction, and not by the number of individuals contributing to it.

I

Two propositions about political groups should be obvious. First, the number of such groups functioning in a given political system is likely to be quite large. Second, a wide variety of types of groups exists, suggesting the feasibility of some system of classification. Several bases for classification are, of course, possible; let me advance one scheme here. Political groups may be regarded as (1) institutional, (2) associational, and (3) non-associational. Each of these categories, as used in the context of research in Latin American politics, calls for some discussion.

(1) *Institutional* groups are formally constituted agencies, or segments of them, with established roles in a political system, roles usually recognized and generally accepted. It is useful to distinguish between two broad types of such institutional groups. One is the species which is formally and ostensibly assigned authoritative political functions—such as rule-making, rule-application, and rule-adjudication—and which performs them. In other words, formally established government is itself composed of a number of groups whose role it is to carry out political functions, and so some political groups can be studied in the examination of formal agencies of government. If to nothing else, American political scientists have been conventionally trained to direct their attention to such structures. Let me therefore pass by this category, pausing only to remark that, while we are still with the old familiar subject-matter of conventional political science—the formal structures of government—the group emphasis does imply a difference in the *manner* in which these agencies are studied. I plan to return to this proposition at a later point.

The second type of institutional political group needs to be examined more closely. This is the group which, while associated with a formal institution, performs a political function differing markedly from the established or ostensible role of the institution. The study of political groups of this type in Latin America is of high importance, and

2 See David B. Truman, *The Governmental Process* (New York, 1951), *passim,* especially ch. 2.

deserves priority among political inquiries in the area. Let me mention a few such institutional groups of this type in Latin America—not an exhaustive list, but rather a relatively small sample illustrative of one type of political organization to which the serious attention of research scholars is urgently invited.

The Roman Catholic Church is one of the major political groups of this sort in Latin America. Historically, Church and State were united in the Spanish tradition. This was true throughout the colonial period; indeed, the movement for separation of Church and State is, in a sense, a relatively recent development in the area. In most of the countries, the Church pursues political objectives, and in some of them its functions resemble those of a political party. Some Latin American political parties are essentially Church parties, as for example the Conservative parties of Colombia and Ecuador. Consider this statement by the Conservative Party of Ecuador of its *political* program: "Man is essentially a religious being and religion, consequently, is a natural phenomenon. . . . The end of man is God, whom he should serve and adore in order to enjoy after death the beatified possession of divinity. . . . The purpose of the state is to facilitate religious action so that its subjects will not lack the necessities of the spirit and will be able to obtain in the next life the happiness which can never be achieved in this." [3] The power of the Church as a political group varies, of course, from country to country. It is perhaps strongest in Ecuador and weakest in Mexico, but there is no Latin American state in which the Church is not to be counted as a major political group.[4] It has, of course, been studied from several points of view, but published assessments of it in this capacity are rare.

Similarly, there are very few studies of the armed forces, particularly the armies, of Latin America as political groups. This is a curious indictment of political scientists interested in the area, since militarism has long been recognized as a fundamental characteristic of Latin American politics. "The last step in a military career is the presidency of the republic" [5] is a well-known and frequently practiced precept in the area. Rather than the defense of the community, the basic functions of the Latin American military lie in domestic politics. Everywhere high-ranking army officers are important politicians; every-

[3] Jacinto Jijón y Caamaño, *Política Conservadora* (Riobamba: La Buena Prensa del Chimborazo, 1934), Vol. 1, pp. 26, 32.

[4] See J. Lloyd Mecham, *Church and State in Latin America* (Chapel Hill: University of North Carolina Press, 1934).

[5] Quoted in George I. Blanksten, *Ecuador: Constitutions and Caudillos* (Berkeley, 1951), p. 36.

where the military influence provides a species of backdrop for politics. Generally this is more true of the armies than of the other armed services, although in a few of the countries—notably Argentina [6] and Paraguay—the navies also operate as significant political groups. Political studies of the Latin American armed services are sorely needed. Topics especially requiring investigation include the process of political clique-formation among military and naval officers, and the relationship between militarism and the class system. Certain military ranks— e.g., major and lieutenant-colonel—appear to be of peculiarly critical political significance.

Few studies, again, have been made of bureaucracy in Latin America, and consequently little can be said of the roles of public workers as political groups. In some of the countries government work, like other types of occupations, is organized on the basis of part-time jobs. Moreover, few of the republics have developed effective merit systems of civil service, and a spoils system is generally characteristic of the area. These considerations suggest patterns of action differing from those to be found in Western Europe or the United States. Latin American government workers no doubt may be regarded as political groups. However, the current state of research on this problem does not permit evaluation at this time of their full significance.

(2) Let me now turn to the *associational*, or second major category of, political groups. These are consciously organized associations which lie outside the formal structure of government and which nevertheless include the performance of political functions among their stated objectives. Generally speaking, associational groups carry out less authoritative functions than the institutional organizations. That is to say, this second category tends to concentrate its activity on such matters as political recruitment, interest articulation, interest aggregation, and—in some cases—political communication, rather than on more authoritative political functions such as rule-making, rule-application, and rule-adjudication.

Two chief types of associational groups may be distinguished. The differences are roughly similar to those, familiar to students of politics in the United States, between political parties and pressure groups. However, the distinction sought here is not quite the same as that. In the United States and in many of the countries of Western Europe, "political parties tend to be free of ideological rigidity, and are aggregative, that is, seek to form the largest possible interest group coali-

<hr>

[6] See Blanksten, *Perón's Argentina* (Chicago, 1953), pp. 314–316; and Arthur P. Whitaker, *Argentine Upheaval* (New York, 1956), *passim*.

tions by offering acceptable choices of political personnel and public policy." [7] On the other hand, pressure groups in those same so-called "Western" systems "articulate political demands in the society, seek support for these demands among other groups by advocacy and bargaining, and attempt to transform these demands into authoritative public policy by influencing the choice of political personnel, and the various processes of public policy making and enforcement." [8] In many Latin American countries, particularly in those with the more underdeveloped economies—and, no doubt, in most of the so-called "non-Western" political systems—the dividing line does not fall in quite the same place. Political parties tend to be more non-aggregative than aggregative, and some of the functions of the other associational groups include activities usually restricted to political parties in the United States and in some of the Western European systems.

Despite the fact that political parties have long been included among the accepted concerns of political scientists, it remains a curious circumstance that very little research has been done on these organizations in Latin America. Indeed, only one political party in the area has been the object of a full-blown monographic study. [9] "The field is one which needs a vast amount of spade work of a primary sort and on top of that additional synthesis in order to put the raw materials in proper arrangement and perspective," Russell H. Fitzgibbon has said. "I commend the field of Latin-American political parties to a whole generation of prospective graduate students in political science." [10]

Not only the party systems, but also the parties themselves, are of various types in Latin America. Let me once again, therefore, undertake the task of classification. Although the existing literature of political science contains a number of fairly elaborate attempts at categorization, nothing more complicated is necessary for the present purpose than a simple dichotomy separating one-party systems from competitive party systems. Both types are to be found in Latin America.

The one-party system, of course, is the situation in which a single political party holds an effective monopoly of public power and con-

[7] Gabriel A. Almond, "A Comparative Study of Interest Groups and the Political Process" (unpublished paper, Committee on Comparative Politics, Social Science Research Council, 1957), p. 20. See also Sigmund Neumann, *Modern Political Parties* (Chicago, 1956).

[8] Almond, *op. cit.*, pp. 19–20.

[9] Harry Kantor, *The Ideology and Program of the Peruvian Aprista Movement* (Berkeley, 1953).

[10] Russell H. Fitzgibbon, "The Party Potpourri in Latin America," *The Western Political Quarterly*, Vol. 10 (March, 1957), pp. 21–22.

trols access to government office. In some one-party systems, this may be provided for by law, other political parties being considered illegal or subversive; in another type of one-party system, other parties may exist legally but—for reasons largely unrelated to legal questions or government coercion—find themselves unable to challenge effectively the dominant party's hold on the system.

Thus conceived, two varieties of dominant parties hold power in the one-party systems of Latin America. One may be dubbed the "dictatorial" party. Where it exists, an official attempt is made to obscure the distinction between the party in power and the government of the country, and so to render opposition to the party virtually synonymous with treason against the state. By definition, then, the party in power being the only legal party, any others are not merely in opposition but in rebellion, open or covert. The best current Latin American illustration of this type of party is to be found in the Dominican Republic. Such a system has also operated in Venezuela. Paraguay's arrangement is a borderline case—other parties than the *Colorado* are theoretically legal, but the price of participating in them is often imprisonment or exile.

The other type of group holding power in a one-party system may be designated as the "dominant non-dictatorial" party. In this case, one party holds a monopoly of political power in the sense that it is victorious in virtually all elections, but other parties are legal and do exist. This is somewhat similar to the stereotype—but I beg you not to hold me responsible for its validity—of the "Solid South" or of northern rural areas in the United States. The leading Latin American case is in Mexico, where the Party of Revolutionary Institutions (PRI [11]) is without a serious rival. Other Mexican parties exist legally, but they exercise virtually no authority in government.[12] Uruguay's system may also be included here, if we agree with Fitzgibbon that it cannot be regarded as a two-party affair.[13] Further, it has been noted that the situation in Paraguay's case is borderline—if one Paraguayan foot is in the "dictatorial" party camp, the other is with the "dominant nondictatorial" party.

Competitive party systems exist where two or more parties, none of

[11] After the initial letters of *Partido Revolucionario Institucional.*
[12] See L. Vincent Padgett, "Mexico's One-Party System: A Re-evaluation," *The American Political Science Review,* Vol. 41 (December, 1957), p. 995; Frank R. Brandenburg, "Mexico: An Experiment in One-Party Democracy" (Ph.D. thesis, University of Pennsylvania, 1955); and Robert E. Scott, *Mexican Government in Transition* (Urbana: University of Illinois Press, 1959), particularly pp. 145–196.
[13] See below, note 15.

them a dominant or "official" organization, contend among themselves. In general, there are two classes of competitive systems, multi-party and two-party arrangements.

A multi-party system contains three or more major political parties, normally making it impossible for any one of them to command a majority of the seats in a representative assembly. Politics in these systems frequently operates through coalitions or blocs involving two or more parties, and these understandings are designed to produce working majorities. Latin America's best illustration of a multi-party system is to be found in Chile, where there are at least six major political parties, none of which controls a legislative majority.[14] Multi-party arrangements also exist in Argentina, Bolivia, Brazil, Costa Rica, Cuba, Guatemala, Panama, and Peru.

Two-party systems contain two major political parties sufficiently matched in strength to permit their alternation in power. "Third" or "minor" parties are legal in these systems, but are rarely serious rivals at the polls of the two major parties. Thus conceived, two-party systems are rare in Latin America; indeed, they are rare outside the English-speaking world. The best Latin American illustration is to be found in Colombia, where the Conservative and Liberal Parties, roughly evenly matched, have historically alternated in power. Uruguay also has two major political parties—the Colorados and the Blancos—but there is some question as to whether this is a clear case of a two-party system. Fitzgibbon, for example, believes that, since the Colorados have been victorious in almost all national elections, it cannot be said that Uruguay's is a true two-party arrangement.[15]

Most of the major parties in the competitive systems of Latin America are what might be called traditional political parties. In general, they have two major characteristics. First, the issues which concern them have historically troubled Latin Americans as long-range political problems of their respective countries. Primarily, these issues have been the questions of land tenure and the temporal role of the Roman Catholic Church. Second, the traditional parties draw their membership, in terms of the class systems of Latin America, primarily from the upper classes; the other classes—often involving majorities of national populations—virtually are excluded from direct participation in these parties. The traditional parties may be roughly branded as conservative or liberal. Conservative parties generally defend the interests of the

---

[14] See John Reese Stevenson, *The Chilean Popular Front* (Philadelphia: University of Pennsylvania Press, 1942).

[15] Fitzgibbon, *op. cit.*, p. 18; see also his *Uruguay: Portrait of a Democracy* (New Brunswick: Rutgers University Press, 1954), especially pp. 137–152.

large landowners and advocate an expanded temporal role for the
Church, sometimes including union of Church and State. Conservative
parties have been in power in most of the countries of Latin America
during most of the years of their respective national histories. Representative conservative parties include the Conservative Party of Argentina, the Conservatives of Colombia, the Conservative Party of
Ecuador, the *Blanco* Party of Uruguay, and COPEI of Venezuela.
Liberal parties, on the other hand, have generally advocated some
kind of land reform, separation of Church and State, and a general
reduction in the temporal influence of the Church. Representative
liberal parties are the Radical Party of Argentina, the Radicals of
Chile, the Liberals of Colombia, the Radical-Liberal Party of Ecuador,
and the *Colorados* of Uruguay.

The parties which participate in the competitive systems of Latin
America may be classed as pragmatic, ideological, and particularistic.
Pragmatic parties are those which make no major ideological or philosophical demands upon their membership. Such parties are far more
interested in commanding the votes than the minds of their followers,
who may enter or leave the pragmatic groups without benefit of the
trauma of ideological, philosophical, or religious conversion on such
occasions.

Pragmatic parties may be broadly or narrowly based, depending on
how large a sector of the politically articulate population the group
appeals to. Perhaps Latin America's best illustrations of the broad-
based pragmatic party are the Argentine Radical Party (UCR [16]) and
the Chilean Radical Party. The UCR has endeavored with some
success to appeal for the electoral support of organized labor, commercial and industrial interests, associations of university students, and
professional and intellectual organizations. Indeed, under the leadership of Arturo Frondizi in the presidential election of 1958, the UCR,
which had bitterly fought the Perón dictatorship (1946–1955), successfully campaigned for the votes of those who had formerly supported
Perón! In Chile, the Radical Party has joined together university students, labor organizations, teachers' associations, and the smaller commercial and industrial interests.

Narrow-based pragmatic parties are more numerous in the area.
In general, these are of two types—personalistic and *ad hoc* parties.
Personalistic parties are an outgrowth of *personalismo*, a long-standing
ingredient of Latin American politics. *Personalismo* may be defined
as the tendency to follow or oppose a political leader on personality

[16] After the initial letters of *Unión Cívica Radical* (Radical Civic Union).

rather than ideological grounds, through personal, individual, and family motivations rather than because of an impersonal political idea or program. This historic attribute of the politics of the area has been noted by many students of Latin America. Pierson and Gil, for example, point to "the high value placed on the individual and personal leadership," promoting "a disposition to vote for the man rather than the party or the platform."[17] Another student has said: "From earliest days the Latin Americans . . . have always been more interested in their public men than in their public policies. They have tended to follow colorful leaders, to the subordination of issues. . . . A picturesque demagogue is virtually assured a large following."[18]

Latin Americans like to say—and this exaggerates the situation—that "Every 'ism' is a somebody-ism." Personalist parties are "Somebody-ist" groups organized in support of the political ambitions of strong personal leaders. Paraguay has its *Franquista* Party, composed of the followers of General Rafael Franco;[19] Brazil had a *Querimista*[20] party; Ecuador a *Velasquista* organization, made up of the followers of Dr. José María Velasco Ibarra; and Uruguay a *Batllista* "faction," founded by the nineteenth-century statesman, José Batlle y Ordóñez. There is some evidence that personalist parties are currently declining in number and influence in Latin America.

Finally, there are *ad hoc* parties. These are fluid organizations created for the purpose of achieving short-range political objectives and disappearing when these ends have been accomplished or defeated. These parties are particularly important in the politics of Bolivia, Ecuador, and Paraguay. "In these times," a Bolivian wrote in 1942, "nothing is simpler than to found a political party. To form a political party only three people and one object are necessary: a president, a vice president, a secretary, and a rubber stamp. The party can get along even without the vice president and the secretary. . . . There have been cases in which the existence of only the rubber stamp has been sufficient."[21] Parties of this type are especially important in times of political instability and so-called revolution, times not infrequent in a number of the countries of Latin America.

[17] William W. Pierson and Federico G. Gil, *Governments of Latin America* (New York, 1957), p. 31.

[18] Austin F. Macdonald, *Latin American Politics and Government* (New York, 2d ed. 1954), p. 2.

[19] Not connected with Spain's Generalissimo Francisco Franco.

[20] Literally, "we wantist," a popular abbreviation of "We want Vargas."

[21] Luis Terán Gómez, *Los Partidos Políticos y su Acción Democrática* (La Paz: Editorial La Paz, 1942), pp. 60–61.

Ideological parties are also to be counted among the actors in the competitive party systems of the area. Communist parties, for example, exist throughout the Americas. The most important Communist organizations are in Argentina; Bolivia, where the party has long been known as the Leftist Revolutionary Party (PIR [22]); Brazil; Chile; Cuba; Guatemala; and Mexico, where the group is called the Popular Party. Although the Mexican party system is not a competitive one, the Mexican Communists are nevertheless worth mentioning here. Despite indications that the party is small and weak from the standpoint of its influence upon domestic politics in Mexico, the Communist organization in that country does perform a noteworthy international function in serving as a point of liaison, and as an informational clearing-house, between European Communists and those of Central America and the Caribbean islands. Meetings of the Communist leaders of the smaller countries of Middle America are occasionally held in Mexico. [23]

Socialist parties also exist in virtually all of the countries of Latin America. The membership of these parties is generally dominated by middle-class intellectuals with a strong interest in Marxism. Despite their avowed interest in the problems of the working classes, the Socialists of Latin America have, in fact, developed little genuine influence with the masses. In country after country, the Socialists "have become increasingly doctrinaire, academic, and intellectualized." [24] Ray Josephs once remarked that "the Socialist weakness lies in addiction to theory and philosophy and what we might call their lack of practical, sound common sense." [25] It need hardly be added that Socialists have never been in power for any appreciable length of time in any country of Latin America.

A number of Church-oriented parties are to be found in the area, and these too may be regarded as largely ideological parties. The best current illustrations are the Conservative parties of Colombia and Ecuador. Heavily Catholic in doctrinal orientation, Church parties have participated in most of the competitive systems of Latin America during the past century. Not since the regime of Gabriel García Moreno in Ecuador (1859–1875) has a Church group been the dominant party in a one-party system. In that case, religious intolerance was revived, only practicing Catholics were permitted to be citizens

---

[22] After the initial letters of *Partido Izquierdista Revolucionario*.

[23] See Robert J. Alexander, *Communism in Latin America* (New Brunswick: Rutgers University Press, 1957).

[24] Fitzgibbon, "The Party Potpourri in Latin America," *op. cit.*, p. 13.

[25] Ray Josephs, *Argentine Diary* (New York: Random House, 1944), p. xxxiii.

of the country—then called the "Republic of the Sacred Heart"—and government was heavily authoritarian in character.[26]

Nationalist groups also may be counted among the ideological parties of Latin America. The typical Latin American nationalist party is narrow-based, addressing a concerted appeal to a small sector of the society in which it operates. Indeed, it is not unusual to find a given country in the area with two or more small nationalist parties functioning in rivalry relationships with each other. While anti-clerical nationalists are not unheard of—one such group once effectively employed "We are Ecuadorans, not Romans!" as its slogan—the nationalist parties more frequently embrace the Church, demand religious intolerance, oppose secularization, and attempt to eradicate foreign influence in their countries. Often such parties are active centers of anti-Semitism. In recent times the most important nationalist parties of Latin America —all of them narrow-based rather than comprehensive—have operated in Argentina, Bolivia, Paraguay, and Venezuela.

The area also has its share of Fascist parties. For many of these, "Fascist-like" or "quasi-Fascist" would probably be better designations, since they generally combine selected elements of Fascist ideology with enough indigenous Latin American ingredients to render the organizations difficult to equate with European Fascist parties. During World War II, most of them pressed pro-Axis foreign policy objectives in Latin America. Representative parties of this type are the *Peronista* Party of Argentina, the Nationalist Revolutionary Movement (MNR [27]) of Bolivia, the Integralist Party of Brazil, the *Nacista* Party of Chile, and the National Sinarquist Union of Mexico.

Also occupying a significant place on the roster of the area's ideological parties are the agrarian-populistic group. In Latin America, these have come to be called *Aprista* parties. They have two distinguishing characteristics. First, they seek far-reaching social and economic change, usually including radical land reform and the integration of the lower classes into the political process. Indeed, there is a greater percentage of lower-class adherents in the membership of *Aprista* groups than in any other type of Latin American party. Second, *Aprismo* is indigenous to the area. Such international connections as the movement has—and they are not many—are entirely within Latin America. The chief prototype of this class of political party is the celebrated *Aprista* Party or APRA of Peru. Other *Aprista* parties include *Acción Democrática* of Venezuela, the *Auténtico Party*

[26] See Richard Pattee, *Gabriel García Moreno y el Ecuador de su Tiempo* (Mexico City: Editorial Jus, 1944), *passim.*

[27] After the initial letters of *Movimiento Nacionalista Revolucionario.*

of Cuba, the National Liberation Party of Costa Rica, and, in a sense, Mexico's PRI.[28]

Particularistic parties have on occasion appeared in the competitive systems of Latin America, although there is no clear illustration of the type operating in the area today. Such organizations, concerned in a separatist fashion with selected ethnic groups or regions and including some form of secession among statements of political objectives, have from time to time filled major roles in the Americas. Indeed, this is one of the reasons why what were once only eight Spanish colonies are now as many as eighteen independent states. In the historic past, particularist parties have been led by such personalities as General José Antonio Páez, who directed the secession of Venezuela from Gran Colombia; General Juan José Flores, who presided over the separation of Ecuador from the same entity; and Dr. Amador, prominent in the detachment of the isthmus of Panama from Colombia. Particularistic parties were also active in the reduction of the former Central American Confederation to its present five separate heirs. So far as the contemporary scene is concerned, although no major particularistic parties are functioning in the area, there are significant evidences of the presence of some of the ingredients of which such groups may be fashioned. In Brazil, for example, the two states of São Paulo and Minas Gerais, which had stubbornly opposed the regimes of President Getulio Vargas (1930–1945; 1951–1954), have fallen into a political collaboration against other sections of the country which approximates particularism. Again, in the countries where regionalism is a major political force—such as Peru, Ecuador, and Bolivia—there is a tendency for political parties to become regionally based. The record of the past and the current scene combine to suggest that it might not be unreasonable to expect the reappearance of such organizations in the area from time to time in the future.

I attempted earlier to distinguish between two chief types of associational political groups, offering parties as the first of them. I turn now to the second type, roughly resembling what are called pressure groups in the United States. In Latin America these organizations perform some of the functions usually restricted in the "North American" system to political parties. Without presenting an exhaustive list, I shall mention a number of them to illustrate their functions in the political systems of Latin America.

Associations of landowners, in one form or another, exist in all countries of the area. In view of the significant role of the land in the

[28] See Kantor, *ibid.*; and Robert J. Alexander, "The Latin-American *Aprista* Parties," *Political Quarterly*, Vol. 20 (1949), pp. 236–247.

economy of Latin America and the predominance of feudal-like systems of land tenure, these groups are of high importance. In Argentina, for example, fewer than two thousand families' landholdings constitute a combined area greater than England, Belgium and the Netherlands put together; and statistics produced by some of the American republics indicate that approximately three-fourths of their respective land surfaces are owned by about two per cent of their respective populations. Landowning groups wield political as well as economic power. The best-known landowners' association in the area is the Argentine Jockey Club; similar organizations operate in most of the other states.

Foreign companies function as political groups in some of the countries. In northern Latin America—particularly in the Caribbean area—United States corporations are prominent among these groups. Excellent illustrations can be found in the United Fruit Company as it operates in a number of the states of Central America, and in the influence of a number of oil companies in Venezuelan politics. In southern South America—Argentina, Uruguay, Paraguay, and Chile—British firms function in a similar fashion.

Labor organizations, though still small, are of growing importance as Latin American groups. The role of these organizations is expanding as industrialization begins to take hold in the area. From the standpoint of their functions as political groups, the most important labor organizations in the area are Argentina's CGT,[29] Chile's CTCH,[30] Cuba's CTC,[31] and Mexico's CTM.[32] Organized labor in Latin America is, in general, quite politically articulate, and its support has long been sought by Socialist parties.

Student associations are vigorously active groups in all of the countries involved. Hear this account of student life in the area: "The . . . university, traditionally, is a miniature battleground of national politics. Students strike, riot, and stage political demonstrations on the slightest provocation."[33] Politics "becomes a passion that invades and confuses everything. I myself remember many postponed examinations; many study hours disturbed; countless meetings, discussions,

[29] After the initial letters of *Confederación General del Trabajo* (General Confederation of Labor).

[30] *Confederación de Trabajadores Chilenos* (Confederation of Chilean Workers).

[31] *Confederación del Trabajo Cubano* (Confederation of Cuban Labor).

[32] *Confederación de Trabajadores Mexicanos* (Confederation of Mexican Workers).

[33] Ysabel F. Rennie, *The Argentine Republic* (New York: The Macmillan Company, 1945), p. 212.

strikes—a whole year lost in them—elections that ended with gun-fire. . . . " [34] As political groups, student associations are far more significant in Latin America than in the United States.

Professional associations should also be counted among the active groups of the area. Lawyers' associations are perhaps the oldest of these. With the growing economic development of Latin America, associations of engineers, still small, are of rising importance. Business groups are also small in the area. However, these may be expected to grow in significance as industrialization and economic development continue.

Veterans' associations, important in the United States, are of little significance as Latin American political groups, except in Bolivia and Paraguay. In both countries, organizations of veterans of the Chaco War (1928–1935) have become major pressure groups. In Bolivia, such a group served as the nucleus for the MNR party. In the absence of systematic studies, however, any explanatory statement at this point can be little more than conjecture. My guess—and it is only that—is that in most of Latin America such influence as veterans' groups might have had has been more than engulfed by the groups representing the armed services. International wars producing veterans are, after all, rare in contemporary Latin America; on the other hand, militarism and the military are ever-present.

(3) Finally, some discussion of the *non-associational* category of political groups is in order. These are not formally or consciously organized. Indeed, they may be regarded more as latent or potential than as currently functioning political groups, for the non-associational variety is far less structured than the institutional and associational types. In Latin America, non-associational interests tend to coalesce around such symbols as class, status, ethnic groups, kinship and lineage, and regionalism.

The class systems are fairly rigid in most of the countries of the area. Classes, of course, are not formally or consciously organized groups; yet significant political interests arise from them. With some variations from country to country in Latin America, the typical class system is composed of three levels. The highest class is usually referred to as the creoles or "whites"; the middle group is known as the *mestizos* or, in some countries, *cholos*; and, in the countries with large Indian populations, these have constituted the lowest class. Scholars who have examined these classes in Latin America have devoted more attention

[34] Luis Guillermo Piazza, "There'll Always Be a Córdoba," *Americas* (January, 1950), p. 27.

to the creoles, and to the Indians, than they have to the *mestizos* or *cholos*.

The highest class—creoles or "whites"—are the most politically articulate of the three, and in most of the countries of the area their interests—the preservation of the systems of land tenure, the control of the Church and of the high military ranks, and the maintenance of a European rather than an indigenous cultural orientation—are the best-protected and espoused. Where commercialization and industrialization have taken hold, new interests are created, primarily among the "whites." In some of the countries, this has a divisive effect upon "white" interests, for landownership is sometimes held to be threatened by commercialization and industrialization. Conscious of themselves as the ruling group in most of the countries of the area, the "whites" share an interest in the avoidance of true revolution and, in general, oppose political reforms believed to imperil their dominant position.

Less is known about the *mestizo* or *cholo*. A detribalized Indian but not yet a "white," the *mestizo* accounts for over 30% of the populations of some of the countries. He is not politically articulate, and rarely organizes. He is interested in working his way into the "white" group and, usually, in severing his ties with the Indians. The *mestizo* is frequently employed as an artisan or a tradesman. In some of the countries of the area, the *mestizo* is an important source of the labor supply. As a class, the *mestizos* no doubt have interests. But given the paucity of available data, little more can be said here regarding their non-associational interests without risking the hazards of a major excursion into the realm of speculation.

About the Indian, entire libraries have been written. Indian communities and villages are tightly organized, and the Indians feel strong loyalties to them, but the Indian class as a whole is not organized in any of the Latin American countries. In general, the Indians resist incursion upon their way of life by the "whites." They desire, as they frequently put it, to be left alone. They seek decentralized, loosely organized, or inefficiently administered government, so that the number of "white" government officials entering their communities bearing rules and regulations from the national capital will be held to a minimum. Having normally a deep love for their villages and communities, they strongly resist resettlement programs involving relocation of the lower classes. Typically, the Indian does not own much, if any, land. Many writers have argued that in Latin America the Indian problem is basically a land problem, and have urged land reform programs which would deliver holdings to Indian ownership.[35] The Indians, however, have rarely expressed this sentiment themselves, and have been slow to respond to land redistribution programs. Being quite inarticulate politically, they rarely communicate their desires to the "white" officials of the governments which rule them.

Interests also arise from the concept of status, especially within the "white" groups. In colonial times the upper class was acrimoniously divided within itself, with the creoles—persons born in the colonies—pitted against the *peninsulares*—born in Europe—who enjoyed higher status. Indeed, this intra-class struggle was one of the factors giving alignment to some of the fighting during the wars of independence. Since then, the *peninsulares* have dropped from the Latin American class structure, but the concept of the "old families" or "good families" remains. These—when they can establish themselves as such—enjoy considerable prestige within the ruling class. Although the "whites" are at least as racially mixed as any other group in Latin American society, the "old families" are constantly engaged in heraldic research designed to demonstrate their unmixed Spanish descent. To be accepted as an "old" or "good" family is to be the aristocracy of the aristocracy. Families which have achieved this enviable position have a strong interest in preserving those elements of the system—particularly the older patterns of land tenure—that lend security to the prestige system, and in making it difficult for "new" families to become "old" and share the higher status.

Again, in view of the paucity of research on the *mestizo* or *cholo* group, little can be said here of the prestige patterns within that class. In general, however, the *mestizos* strive to become "whites."

Status is at least as important among the Indians as it is among the "whites." A significant difference, however, should be noted. Whereas those who acquire high prestige among the "whites" enjoy it on a national—and, in some cases, international—basis, status among the Indians has meaning only on a local village or community level. As in the case of the "whites," status among the Indians rests on ascriptive more than achievement considerations. Village elders, and their rela-

[35] See, for example, José Carlos Mariátegui, *Siete Ensayos de Interpretación de la Realidad Peruana* (Lima: Editorial Librería Peruana, 1934); W. Stanley Rycroft (ed.), *Indians of the High Andes* (New York, Committee on Cooperation in Latin America, 1946); Eyler N. Simpson, *The Ejido: Mexico's Way Out* (Chapel Hill: University of North Carolina Press, 1937); Moisés Sáenz, *Sobre el Indo Ecuatoriano* (Mexico City: Secretaría de Educación Pública, 1933); Sáenz, *The Peruvian Indian* (Washington: Strategic Index of the Americas, 1944); and Sáenz, *The Indian: Citizen of America* (Washington: Pan American Union, 1946).

tives, enjoy prestige, as do witch doctors and medicine men. To hold high status in the Indian community is to exercise some power—frequently of government—within it, and those who have this prestige are interested in preserving it and preventing its adulteration through too-easy access of other Indians to the status positions.[36]

Non-associational interests also arise among some ethnic groups in Latin America. For example, Negroes—numerous in the Caribbean island republics, and in some parts of Brazil—have developed strong interests though they emerge on an unorganized basis. So, too, have a number of the European immigrant groups, notably the Italians, Germans, Spaniards, and Jews. The European immigrant groups are normally more articulate than many of the indigenous groups, particularly the Indians and *mestizos,* and generally have developed interests, usually directed toward the preservation of their social and economic positions in society.

Patterns of kinships and lineage also produce systems of non-associational interest in Latin America. This is especially true among the "whites" and Indians; the *mestizos* again, for the time being at least, stand as an unknown quantity. Among the "whites," reference has already been made to the "old" or "good" families. High values are assigned to belonging to them, or if that is impossible, to being somehow related or connected to them. The extensive use made of, and the exaggerated importance given to, the famous letters of introduction among the "whites" have frequently reached the proportions of a joke. A letter of introduction from a well-known member of an established "good family" is, in many of the countries, indispensable to the candidate seeking employment or some other favor from government. "The municipal department had become a perfect teeming house of *recomendados*—persons for whom jobs had been found whether jobs were to be had or not," an observer has said of local politics among the "whites." "In the old days of the Deliberative Council, it used to be a standing joke that business offices could be wall-papered with the letters of introduction given to job applicants."[37] Although this particular reference is to local government, the practice is general.

Three generalizations can safely be made regarding the role of kinship and lineage among the Indians of Latin America. First, as a determiner of interest, it is even more basic in this class than among the "whites." Next, in many Indian groups, kinship and lineage are more centrally and directly related to politics and government than

[36] See Aníbal Buitrón and John Collier, *The Awakening Valley* (Chicago: University of Chicago Press, 1950).

[37] Ray Josephs, *op. cit.,* p. 26.

is true of the upper classes. Finally, in contrast to the situation among the "whites," this is important among the Indians on the local—village and community—level to the almost total exclusion of other levels of politics. Unfortunately, these are virtually the only generalizations on the subject that can be made with assurance. Practices in this field vary widely among the indigenous peoples of the area, for two major reasons. First, it is in many senses unrealistic to lump all of the Indian groups together and treat them as a unit. These people have differing cultures, languages, and social, economic, and political systems. Secondly, the extent to which "white" practices have penetrated Indian systems varies considerably, not only from country to country but also within many of the countries. Kinship and lineage functioned as a major determinant of political station and interest in the overwhelming majority of the indigenous Indian systems of Latin America. In some areas, where these systems have been relatively little interfered with by the "whites," this is still true. Indeed, instances exist in which Indian systems of village government continue to function undisturbed despite the fact that the "whites" have promulgated written constitutions providing for very different patterns of local government.[38] But there are cases—often in other regions of the same countries—where acculturation has taken the form of Indian responses to "white" influences which have fundamentally altered, or even obliterated, the indigenous practices. A number of monographic studies of such cases in specific Indian communities have been published. Short of reporting these detailed findings, there is little alternative to stressing the importance of kinship and lineage and emphasizing that, as a rule, Indian groups are markedly less politically articulate than the upper class. Thus, this type of interest, while often more crucial in the lower classes, typically receives far less of a hearing when emanating from the Indians than from the "whites."

Non-associational interests also arise on regional bases. Regionalism is characteristically a major feature of the pattern of Latin American politics. It stems not only from the role of regional loyalties in Spanish culture, but also from the historic difficulty of transportation and communication across the mountains and through the jungles of Latin America. Living in a species of isolation from each other, the regions of Latin America have developed their own sets of interests. In Peru

[38] See, for example, Manning Nash, "Relaciones Políticas en Guatemala," in Jorge Luis Arriola (ed.), *Integración Social en Guatemala* (Guatemala City: Seminario de Integración Social, 1956), pp. 137–156; and K. H. Silvert, *A Study in Government: Guatemala,* Part I (New Orleans: Middle American Research Institute: Tulane University, 1954), *passim,* especially pp. 62 ff.

and Ecuador, for example, the regions known in each country as the
"Coast" (located west of the Andes Mountains) are receptive to
secularization and commercialization, fostering commercial and industrial interests; whereas, in both countries, the "Sierra" (lying between
the eastern and western cordilleras of the Andes), less secularized,
cultivates the interests of the landowners and the Church. In both
countries, the sometimes bitter conflict of interests between these
regions is a major element of the national political patterns. In Argentina, to cite another illustration, the interests of the landowners and
the Church in the "interior" have historically been pitted against those
of the secularized and far more commercialized metropolitan region
of Greater Buenos Aires. A second major aspect of the regional base
of non-associational interests arises from the process of urbanization. A
number of the Latin American countries have had to cope with the
problem of *la cabeza de Goliat* (Goliath's head): a giant metropolitan
center (usually the capital city) rests on the dwarflike body of the
rest of the country. In some cases, as much as half the national population lives in the one large city. The secular, commercial, and sometimes industrial interests of the metropolis are in chronic conflict with
those of the religious and quasi-feudal "interior." In Latin America, the
major illustrations of this pattern are to be found in Argentina, Cuba,
and Uruguay.

II

My concluding task is to attempt to show that this sort of group analysis has some merit and may stimulate some productive new depar-
tures for political scientists interested in the field of comparative politics. Let me first enter two disclaimers: novelty is no guarantee of
merit, and an interest in political groups is not new among American
political scientists. Nevertheless, previous expressions of that interest
have not, in general, included two elements significant here. One of
these is the application of group analysis to foreign political systems,
and the other is its use in comparative studies. Notwithstanding the
regrettable tendency within our profession to regard "foreign governments," "comparative government," and "comparative politics" as synonymous terms, the study of political groups in foreign systems and in
comparative analysis are two separate and distinct matters. Let me,
then, turn my attention to the first of them. The bulk of the work—
particularly the earlier work—done by "North American" political
scientists in Latin America has generally involved, in one way or

another, the description of formal structures of governments. It has often taken the form of translating the written constitutions of the various countries and abstracting or summarizing these legal provisions. This type of research has its uses, for some familiarity with constitutional forms is, if not necessary, at least helpful, in the analysis of other political problems. But while there are always new Latin American constitutions to be translated and summarized—and I will even concede that there is room, in the off years when no new constitutions are promulgated in the area, for the improvement of the translations and summaries of the older texts—this type of activity reaches the point of diminishing returns. Indeed, I will argue that we long ago arrived there.

It is, in short, necessary to work with more than the formal structures in Latin America. Again, this is not a new point. For some years Latin Americanists have been looking to non-constitutional materials. Seduced by the anthropologists, many of us have experimented with cultural approaches. We have become enamored of political styles arising from alien cultures. We have examined the class systems and made much of the "whites" while we neglected the *mestizos* in order to carry the torch for the downtrodden Indians, until it took a Moisés Sáenz to tell us that "in order to be fair to the Indian, it is not necessary to stick feathers in our hair or wield a war club." [39]

There are considerable advantages in examining political groups in Latin America as alternative non-constitutional materials. Beginning with the most unstructured considerations, I might start by pointing out that this is a major area of our ignorance in Latin American politics. We know virtually nothing about the area's political groups, and there is some virtue in our beginning to acquire that knowledge for its own sake.

On a little more structured level, it can also be said that research on political groups would help us to understand problems which have long concerned us in Latin American politics. Take the Argentine case as an example. I choose Argentina because it has long been regarded as one of the more important of the countries of the area and because much research has been done there; more articles and books have been published by "North American" scholars about that country than about most other Latin American states. On June 4, 1943, the Argentine government was overthrown in one of the area's most significant so-called "revolutions" of recent times. Who or what was directly responsible for the revolution? A political group: a clique of army officers

[39] Sáenz, *The Indian: Citizen of America*, p. 1.

known as GOU [40] or "colonels' clique." What was the GOU? Where did it come from? How did it operate? Nothing in all our research—none of the product of our long-standing interest in Argentina, nothing in all our scholarly articles and books—could suggest answers to such questions. So far as the existing political science was concerned, the Perón revolution came from nowhere.

If we agree that the Perón coup was one of the more significant political developments of our time in one of the most important countries in the area, how did it happen that the GOU took the area specialists by surprise? How does it happen that we have let militarism and the process of military clique-formation, one of the more basic characteristics of Latin American politics, go unstudied? Why is our ignorance so inclusive that it covers not only the military but most of the other political groups in Latin America? If it is argued that this is an unfair challenge, that as political scientists we have been trained to examine institutions rather than the amorphic entities embraced by the unfamiliar jargon of associational and non-associational groups, I reply that the GOU was an institutional group, part and parcel of the formal structure of government, and nothing so exotic as associational or non-associational.

How many more translations and summaries of Argentina's Constitution of 1853, as remarkable as that celebrated document may be, can we afford to make before we undertake the analysis of the political groups of that and other Latin American countries? Or, to put the question in another way, which route to the mainsprings of the area's politics is more fruitful for the scholar—to wait for GOU after mysterious GOU to ambush him, or to seize the initiative in seeking out these groups, tracking them even to associational and non-associational sources? No doubt this has policy implications as well, but they are not my concern at the moment. My point has been the relatively simple one that the study of political groups in Latin America would not only close considerable gaps in our knowledge of the area but also improve significantly our understanding of its politics.

This is among the less structured of the merits of the study of groups. To move to the arena of comparative analysis is to enter a more sophisticated level. Before taking that step, let me reiterate the high importance of the distinction between comparative politics and the study of foreign governments. In comparative analysis, as I understand it, an attempt is made, through precise study of two or more

[40] These initials conveniently and interchangeably stood for *Grupo de Oficiales Unidos* (United Officers' group), and *¡Gobierno! ¡Orden! ¡Unidad!* (Government! Order! Unity!), the group's slogan.

objects, to isolate and identify their similarities and differences. The techniques of comparative study may be, of course, of varying degrees of complexity. I have heard it claimed for some of the more complex modes of comparative analysis that through them similarities and differences may be not only isolated and identified but also explained. I am not myself convinced that the comparative method alone can do the explanatory job. Isolation, definition, and identification of properties can be handled in this way, but the task of explanation seems to require that the comparative method, where used, be assisted or supplemented by additional modes of analysis.

One of the constantly recurring problems in the comparative study of politics is the circumstance that in this field we generally deal with the so-called "macro" materials—that is, with large units or universes such as entire countries or political systems. In doing this, so far as precision is concerned, we are at a decided disadvantage in comparison with the scholar engaged in a "micro" analysis of a small unit which lends itself more readily to precise study. No doubt, this is one reason why much of what is called "comparative government" consists of roughly parallel descriptions of two or more "macro" systems, without benefit of comparative analysis. It is not easy—and some may think it impossible—to handle two or more national systems in a fashion permitting them to be compared precisely. Countries, cultures, even systems of government, appear in many ways to be unique as large universes. Argentines behave differently from Cubans; even the task of comparing the Mexican congress with the Chilean national legislature presents formidable pitfalls.

One solution to this "macro" problem might involve a conceptualization permitting the abstracting of precisely defined components common to two or more large universes, components which could then be subjected to comparative analysis with some promise of precision. Political groups are among the forms such components might take. So it might be claimed for the introduction of political groups into comparative analysis that it has the advantage of furnishing a method of abstraction rendering political systems more precisely comparable, thereby making comparative analysis more manageable. Indeed, it could be argued that this method creates the possibility of comparative studies of large units which would be intrinsically incomparable in the absence of some such abstractive device.

Another potentially significant contribution of the group emphasis to comparative politics lies in the examination of structures in terms of their political functions. Structural-functional analysis holds some promise of advancing comparative studies. Consider a relatively simple variation of it. If we were to devise a list of the functions performed in all political systems, such as political recruitment, communication, interest-articulation, interest-aggregation, rule-making, rule-application, and rule-adjudication, the group focus might serve to locate the structures performing each of these functions in the systems being compared. These structures, which are groups, might then be analyzed for their political functions.

Suppose, for example, a comparative analysis of the political systems of Chile, Mexico, and Paraguay. The national legislatures of these three countries are given similar names—"Congress" in Chile and Mexico, and "Chamber of Representatives" in Paraguay—by the constitutions, which contain a few additional similar stipulations about the legislatures. But the bases for comparative analysis end here. If, on the other hand, we seek the groups which perform the political functions common to the three systems, we might well be on more significant ground. For example, I suspect that much of the rule-making function is indeed performed in the Congress in Chile, but in the PRI, the dominant non-dictatorial party in Mexico, and by a military clique within the Asunción garrison in Paraguay. If that is so, a comparative analysis of the Chilean Congress, the Mexican PRI, and the Paraguayan military should give us a far more significant result, and a deeper insight into the three political systems, than a comparison of the three national legislatures. Thus, the second branch of my case for the use of political groups in comparative analysis is the argument that it would not only give us greater precision but would also permit us to direct that accuracy to more important propositions about the actual functioning of political systems.

Further, the group emphasis may be expected to make a major contribution in a field of rapidly growing concern in comparative politics, the problems of underdeveloped areas. "Underdevelopment" or "underdevelopedness" has been chiefly an economic concept related primarily to technology. The proposition central to this concept can be demonstrated in comparing two models of economic systems, one "advanced" or "developed," and the other underdeveloped. In the "advanced" model, a given input into the productive process (capital, raw materials, man-hours of labor, etc.) is subjected to a given technology, from which a measurable production emerges. In the underdeveloped model, the same input may go into the productive process, but is subjected to a less efficient technology, and so results in a measurably lower level of production characterized by low standards of living. Owing largely to technological problems affecting the state of their pro'ductive arts, the underdeveloped areas present us with a challenge.

These underdeveloped areas, of course, include much of Latin America. A major key to the problem lies in technological change, to raise the levels of production, and so the standards of living, in the underdeveloped areas. A number of public programs based on this solution are currently in operation. A modest sector of the foreign aid programs of the United States—variously known from administration to administration as technical assistance, "Point Four," and technical cooperation—has as its objective the stimulation of technological change in the underdeveloped areas. The technical assistance programs of the United Nations are similarly conceived. All of the Latin American countries participate in the foreign aid programs of the United States; some of these countries are also involved in United Nations technical assistance. Partly on account of these programs, technological change and economic development should be counted among the more significant movements afoot in contemporary Latin America. In some of the countries—witness Brazil and Mexico—the rapidity of this change is little short of spectacular.

Thus far the economist has done the work for us. But the political scientist interested in Latin America—or any other underdeveloped area—cannot much longer neglect the major analytical task awaiting him there. It is widely assumed that there is some interplay between levels of economic development, on the one hand, and political systems on the other. It is believed that the politics of, say, Bolivia, Haiti, and Paraguay are integrally tied to their underdeveloped economies, and that, as these change, so must their political systems. Again we have policy implications: many of the foreign aid programs of both the United States and the United Nations are based on the assumption that political change goes hand in hand with economic development, but others, in the name of prudence, take recipient institutions as they find them.

Yet all this is still in the realm of belief, of assumption, and even of faith. Apart from the rival slogans of private enterprise and socialism, we have not even the beginnings of a theory of the relations between economic levels and political systems. When the political scientist undertakes, as he must, the search for this theory, he will no doubt have recourse to comparative analysis. I do not claim foreknowledge of the direction this theory will take, but I think it reasonable to expect that again we will be dealing with political groups. I say this because I see one road to the remarriage of economics and politics for this purpose through the theory of interests. Economic development, technological change, and trends toward industrialization imply changes in employment patterns; these alter the distribution of interests. Interest theory is closely allied to group theory; indeed, they may be the same. I suggested early in this paper that every political group has an interest, which could be regarded as the central or continuing type of activity giving the group its property as a system or unit.[41] If such a formulation comes to underlie our understanding of the relationship between economic development and political change, the comparative analysis of groups might then unlock new doors not only to Latin American but also to other underdeveloped areas which, after all, embrace most of the people of the world.

These other areas bring me to the fourth element in my case for the comparative analysis of political groups, the problem of inter-area comparison. Specialists on an area like Latin America are in some danger of becoming the victims of inertia and other forces restricting them to that area alone. It is a danger because it is a form of imprisonment. We should not devote our careers to learning more about Latin America for the sole purpose of learning more about Latin America. Science seeks to generalize, and the more we can apply to other areas what we learn in Latin America, the greater the likely contribution to comparative politics and to political science as a whole.

Substantial obstacles make the practice of this preachment difficult. It is not easy to learn new languages or to develop, in working with the nuances of strange cultures, the skills that we have cultivated, and at some sacrifice, in Latin America. Yet sooner or later we should be prepared to do this. As political scientists in the confines of a single area, we do serious harm to ourselves as well as to our discipline. Actually, there are grounds for optimism on this score. In the last few years, scholars working in other foreign areas have made noteworthy progress toward inter-area comparison. But its difficulties are hard and real. This is another point at which we might make substantial strides through the comparative analysis of political groups. The formula here may be similar to what I have suggested above with respect to the "macro" problem of comparing large universes. In principle I see no serious methodological difference between applying this as between two or more countries in the same area, and as between two or more systems in different areas. If it is feasible to compare the Chilean Congress, the Mexican PRI, and the Paraguayan military, the theoretical task is not substantially different in comparing, say, the *Apristas* with *Mau-Mau* or the GOU with the Young Turks. My point is not

41 See above, p. 140, note 1.

merely that this can be done, but rather that, sooner or later, it must be done.

Further, we should realize that while in loosening our areal shackles in order to work in the underdeveloped areas at large we enter a wider field, this bigger, better, more comfortable, and more significant realm is still an intellectual prison. We will not be fully free until we can compare *all* political systems, inside and outside of the underdeveloped areas. It is in this light that we should view the recent work of the SSRC's Committee on Comparative Politics, which has proposed the curious dichotomy distinguishing "Western" from "non-Western" political systems. We can quarrel with this terminology—for my own part, I am not happy with it, particularly as it applies to Latin America—but to concentrate our attention on the terms is to miss the larger point. Some political systems are significantly more urbanized, secularized, commercialized, integrated and receptive to technological change than others, and we should be able to compare these extremes, whether we call them "western" and "non-Western" or something else. Essentially, this would bring us back to the examination of political structures in terms of their functions. Where these political functions are performed in a "Western" (*i.e.*, secularized, integrated, etc.) fashion in one system and in a "non-Western" (*i.e.*, traditional, unintegrated, etc.) manner in another, we can study these systems by examining structures (*e.g.*, political groups) exercising the functions. Once again, then, we find ourselves with the comparative analysis of political groups.

A final problem remains. This is the question of the extent to which comparative analysis is necessary to the development of general theory. There are those who argue that the comparative method can be—some even say ought to be—bypassed in the development of general theory. But to the extent that comparative analysis has a role to play in the achievement of this objective, we have the final component of my case for the comparative study of political groups. Two aspects of it need mention. First, this would give added point to our re-examination of the work of Bentley, Truman, and Latham. If comparative analysis of political groups is necessary to arrive at a general theory of groups, this is one element that has been missing from the existing literature on the study of groups and the basic justification for dusting off a book published in 1908 to say something new about it. In the second place, if comparative study is necessary to arrive at a general theory of politics, the comparative analysis of political groups carries still deeper significance. In the current stage in the development of political science it has become increasingly clear that the field of comparative government or comparative politics is not paying its own way in the discipline. If the field is to hold its own, it must contribute to political science as a whole; that is, comparative study must take part in the search for a general theory of politics. This is the fundamental element in the case—it may well be that, in the long run, this is the *entire* case—for the comparative analysis of political groups.

This may seem too ambitious an argument for the study of political groups in Latin America. Let me say in conclusion, however, that basically I have made only three claims in its defense. The first is that it would close important gaps in our knowledge of Latin America and thereby lead us to greater understanding of the mainsprings of its politics. In the second place, it would give a sharper edge to comparative political analysis, and so contribute to an improvement of the quality of research in the field of comparative politics by encouraging more meaningful comparisons of the Latin American systems with each other, and with "Western" and "non-Western" systems in other areas. Finally, the types of inquiry I have suggested here would stimulate a more significant contribution from the field of comparative politics to political science as a discipline. If this is indeed too ambitious a case, I hope to learn of a formula whereby the student of foreign politics may shrink from this ambition and at the same time enjoy a respectable role as a useful political scientist.

3

NATIONALISM
IN TROPICAL AFRICA

James S. Coleman

Postwar uprisings and nationalist assertions in Tropical Africa—that part of the continent south of the Sahara and north of the Union—have directed increased attention towards the nature and implications of the awakening of the African to political consciousness. Among scholars this neglected area has long been the preserve of the scientific linguist or of the social anthropologist; only recently have American sociologists, economists, and political scientists developed an active interest in its problems.[1] As a consequence, apart from certain efforts by anthropologists to popularize their findings and insights we have been obliged to rely primarily upon the somewhat contradictory accounts of colonial governments seeking to explain imperial connections, or of African nationalists determined to achieve self-government and the good life of which national self-determination has become the symbol.[2] Thus, we have been placed in the uncomfortable position of having to formulate opinions and policy and to render judgments without sufficient knowledge, or, what could be worse, on the basis of evalu-

Reprinted from *The American Political Science Review*, XLVIII, No. 2 (June 1954), 404–426, by permission of The American Political Science Association. This article was adapted from a paper discussed at the Conference on Problems of Area Research in Contemporary Africa, held at Princeton University, October 14–16, 1953, sponsored jointly by the National Research Council and the Social Science Research Council under a grant from the Carnegie Corporation.

[1] Two notable prewar exceptions were Professor Raymond Leslie Buell and Dr. Ralph J. Bunche.

[2] As an excellent example of the application of the insights of anthropology to the problems of political development in this area, see William R. Bascom, "West and Central Africa," in *Most of the World*, ed. Ralph Linton (New York, 1949), pp. 331–405. For a historian's appraisal, see Vernon McKay, "Nationalism in British West Africa," *Foreign Policy Reports*, Vol. 24, pp. 2–11 (March 15, 1948).

ations provided by participants in the nationalist struggle. There is, therefore, a very real need for independent and objective research regarding the character and probable course of African nationalist development.

I. WHAT IS AFRICAN NATIONALISM?

Not the least burdensome of our tasks is the problem of correlating or distinguishing between the generally accepted political concepts elaborated with specific reference to developments in the Western World (i.e., state, nation, nationality, nationalism) and the conceptual tools developed by the Africanists. The latter have tended to feel that the traditional concepts and methods of the political scientist are unserviceable in the study of the political structure and life of pre-literate societies.[3] Yet notwithstanding the importance of the lineage, clan, or tribe; the role of the diviner, the chief, or the age-grade society; or the wide variations in the organization of power within such societies, the concept and the institution of the modern nation-state, towards the creation of which African nationalism tends to be directed, is distinctly Western in its form and content. It is as exotic to Africa as Professor Toynbee has suggested that it is to the rest of the non-European world.[4] Nevertheless, just as the Indian National Congress

[3] *African Political Systems,* eds. M. Fortes and E. E. Evans-Pritchard (New York, 1940), pp. 4 ff. Insofar as *traditional* concepts and methods are concerned, ethnocentrism has been freely confessed by political scientists in recent self-criticism. See David Easton, *The Political System* (New York, 1953), pp. 33 ff.; also Report of the Inter-University Summer Seminar on Comparative Politics, Social Science Research Council, *The American Political Science Review,* Vol. 47, pp. 641–57, at pp. 642–43 (Sept., 1953). Amongst the modernists in political science one finds the argument that the political scientist should not be rejected too readily since he has developed skills and acquired insights that might well shed new light on the political process and pattern of government of pre-literate societies after the anthropologist has exhausted his resources. Another argument, rather different, is that such societies might profitably be regarded as microcosms in which the political scientist can discern with greater clarity the essentials of government that might be obscured in the more complex Western systems. A final argument might be found in the recent psychocultural studies, especially in terms of their implications for policy formulation. See Ithiel de Sola Pool, "Who Gets Power and Why," *World Politics,* Vol. 2, pp. 120–34 (Oct., 1949).

[4] Arnold Toynbee, *The World and the West* (New York, 1953), pp. 71 ff. It is difficult to accept without qualification Professor Toynbee's argument that the "national state" was a "spontaneous native growth" in Europe. One could argue that the centrally-minded, nation-building elites of emergent Asia and Africa are but the present-day counterparts of the centralizing monarchs of early modern Europe.

has largely created an Indian nation, so African nationalists are endeavoring to mould new nations in Africa (e.g., "Ghana," "Nigeria," and "Kamerun").

On the level of abstraction at which the political scientist is accustomed to roam, a nation is not a loose catch-all term denoting a larger grouping of tribes (e.g., Zulus, Basutos, Mende, Buganda, or Hausa); rather it is a post-tribal, post-feudal terminal *community* which has emerged from the shattering forces of disintegration that characterize modernity. This does not mean that the Hausa peoples of Northern Nigeria cannot become a nation, nor does it mean that the "national" consciousness of the ordinary Hausaman must reach the level of intensity of the average Frenchman before there is a nation. It does suggest, however, that there must be a much greater awareness of a closeness of contact with "national" compatriots as well as with the "national" government.[5] This closeness of contact on the horizontal and vertical levels has been a distinctly Western phenomenon, for the obvious reason that it is the result of modern technology.

Not only is a political scientist quite precise in his use of the concept "nation," but in poaching on the insights of the Africanists he also finds it difficult to place under the cover of "nationalism" all forms of past and present discontent and organizational development in Africa. Thus, it is believed useful at the outset to distinguish the following:

A. TRADITIONALIST MOVEMENTS

1. Spontaneous movements of resistance to the initial European occupation or post-pacification revolts against the imposition of new institutions, or new forms of coercion, referred to herein as "primary resistance."

2. Nativistic, mahdistic, or messianic mass movements—usually of a magico-religious character—which are psychological or emotional outlets for tensions produced by the confusions, frustrations, or socioeconomic inequalities of alien rule, referred to herein as "nativism."[6]

[5] Royal Institute of International Affairs, *Nationalism* (London, 1939), pp. 1–7; Karl W. Deutsch, *Nationalism and Social Communication* (New York, 1953), pp. 1–14.

[6] Nativism is here used in its broad and universal sense, as defined by the late Professor Ralph Linton: "Any conscious, organized attempt on the part of a society's members to revive or perpetuate selected aspects of its culture." See his "Nativistic Movements," *American Anthropologist*, Vol. 45, pp. 230–40, at p. 230 (April–June, 1943). The concept thus includes traditionalist movements in either the European or non-European world. This point is stressed because of the understandable sensitivity of many educated Africans to the root word "native," which

B. SYNCRETISTIC MOVEMENTS

1. Separatist religious groups, which have seceded and declared their independence from white European churches either because of the desire for religious independence or because the white clerics were intolerant regarding certain African customs; hereafter referred to as "religious separatism." [7]

2. Kinship associations, organized and led by the Western-educated and urbanized "sons abroad" for the purposes of preserving a sense of identity with the kinfolk in the bush and "brothers" in the impersonal urban center, as well as of providing vehicles for pumping modernity—including the ideas and sentiment of nationalism—into the rural areas. [8]

3. Tribal associations, organized and led by Western-educated elements—usually in collaboration with some traditionalists—who desire to resurrect, or to create for the first time, a tribal sentiment ("tribalism"), for the purpose of establishing large-scale political units, the boundaries of which will be dertermined by tribal affiliation (i.e., those who accept the *assumption* of common blood and kinship) and the forms of government by a syncretism of tribal and Western institutions. [9]

C. MODERNIST MOVEMENTS

1. Economic-interest groups (labor unions, cooperative societies, professional and middle-class associations) organized and led by Western-educated elements for the purpose of advancing the material

as a result of the colonial experience tends to carry with it the connotation of inferiority. See also A. LeGrip, "Aspects Actuels de L'Islam en A.O.F.," *L'Afrique et l'Asie*, pp. 6–20 (No. 24, 1953); Katesa Schlosser, *Propheten in Afrika* (Albert Limbach Verlag, 1949).

[7] Daniel Thwaite, *The Seething African Pot* (London, 1926), pp. 1–70; George Shepperson, "Ethiopianism and African Nationalism," *Phylon*, Vol. 14, pp. 9–18 (1st Quarter, 1953); Hilda Kuper, "The Swazi Reaction to Missions," *African Studies*, Vol. 5, pp. 177–88 (Sept., 1946); Jomo Kenyatta, *Facing Mount Kenya* (London, 1953), pp. 269–79.

[8] James S. Coleman, "The Role of Tribal Associations in Nigeria," Proceedings of the Second Annual Conference of the West African Institute of Social and Economic Research, Ibadan, Nigeria, April, 1952. See also *East Africa and Rhodesia*, October 5, 1951, p. 106: "Nairobi is the happy hunting ground for the organizers of tribal associations, as there are to be found in the city representatives of practically every tribe in East and Central Africa." Also K. A. Busia, *Report on a Social Survey of Takoradi-Sekondi* (Accra, Government Printer, 1950).

[9] Most advanced amongst the Yoruba, Ibo, Ibibio, Ewe, Buganda, and Kikuyu peoples.

welfare and improving the socio-economic status of the members of those groups.

2. Nationalist movements, organized and led by the Westernized elite which is activated by the Western ideas of democracy, progress, the welfare state, and national self-determination, and which aspires *either:* (a) to create modern independent African nation-states possessing an internal state apparatus and external sovereignty and all of the trappings of a recognized member state of international society (e.g., Sudan, Gold Coast, Nigeria, and possibly Sierra Leone); *or* (b) to achieve absolute social and political equality and local autonomy within a broader Eur-African grouping (e.g., French and Portuguese Africa) or within what is manifestly a plural society (e.g., except for Uganda, the territories of British East and Central Africa).[10]

3. Pan-African or trans-territorial movements, organized and led by the Westernized elite, frequently in association with or under the stimulus of American Negroes or West Indians abroad, for the purposes of creating a global *racial* consciousness and unity, or of agitating for the advancement and welfare of members of the *African* race wherever they may be, or of devising plans for future nationalist activity in specific regions.[11]

Once these very arbitrary analytical distinctions are drawn it should

---

[10] The difference between the goal orientations of the two categories of movements is partly the result of the objectives of differing colonial policies (i.e., the British policy of self-government and differentiation versus the French, Portuguese, and in a qualified sense the Belgian policies of assimilation and identity) and in part the result of the presence or absence of a settled white population. Confronted with the overwhelming obstacles to the full realization of *African self-government,* African leaders in the second category tend towards the extreme either of accommodation (Union of South Africa) or of violence (Kenya). In the territories of the Central African Federation the leaders of the African Congress have tended not to define their ultimate objectives, preferring to act empirically. The strength and persistence of the autonomic drive is reflected, however, in their reported attraction to the original Gore-Brown partition plan adopted by the European Confederate party. See David Cole, "How Strong is the African National Congress," *New Commonwealth,* Vol. 27, pp. 5–10, at p. 9 (Jan. 4, 1954).

[11] For a variety of reasons these movements have thus far apparently accomplished little more than to dramatize their existence at infrequent *ad hoc* conferences. Until recently the initiative tended to be taken by Americans or West Indians of African descent (e.g., Marcus Garvey, W. E. B. DuBois, and George Padmore), although in the early 1920's there was a National Congress of British West Africa organized by the late Casely Hayford of the Gold Coast. Also, M. Blaise Diagne, a Senegalese, was President of the first Pan-African Congress in Paris in 1919. For recent pan-African nationalist activity in British West Africa see *West Africa,* Dec. 12, 1953, p. 1165; and for British Central Africa see Cole, *op. cit.,* p. 9.

be stressed that none of the categories can be treated in isolation. Each of the movements is in one way or another a response to the challenge of alien rule, or of the intrusion of the disintegrating forces—and consequently the insecurity—of modernity. The recent so-called nationalism in Central Africa has been a mixture of "primary resistance" by the chiefs and traditionalists of Northern Rhodesia and Nyasaland and the nationalist agitation of the Westernized elite. Until the project of Federation became an active issue, African movements in this area were confined principally to religious separatist groups, tribal associations, or, in the case of Northern Rhodesia, labor unions.[12] On the West Coast, where nationalism is far more advanced, traditionalist and syncretistic movements have not been and are not absent. In some instances, kinship associations and separatist religious groups have been the antecedents of nationalist organizations; in others they have provided the principal organizational bases of the latter (e.g., the National Council of Nigeria and the Cameroons was first inaugurated as a federation mainly of kinship associations, and the African National Congress of the Rhodesias and Nyasaland as the product of fusion of several African welfare societies). In certain cases unrest or protest of a nativistic flavor has been instigated by nationalists for their modernist ends; in others nationalists have claimed such uncoordinated uprisings, as well as purely economic protest movements, to be manifestations of "nationalism," when in reality the participants were unaware of such implications.

One of the interesting differences between prewar and postwar nationalism on the West Coast of Africa is that in the former period nationalism tended to be—as Lord Lugard insisted—the esoteric pastime of the tiny educated minorities of Lagos, Accra, Freetown, and Dakar; whereas in the latter period these minorities—greatly expanded and dispersed in new urban centers throughout the interior—have made positive efforts to popularize and energize the nationalist crusade in two ways.[13] The first has been to preach education, welfare, progress, and the ideal of self-government among the masses, largely through the nationalist press, independent African schools, and kinship and tribal associations. The aim here has been, in the words of one of their leading prophets, Dr. Nnamdi Azikiwe of Nigeria, to bring

[12] See Ian Cunnison, "The Watchtower Assembly in Central Africa," *International Review of Missions*, Vol. 40, pp. 456–69 (Oct., 1951).

[13] Sir F. D. Lugard, *The Dual Mandate in British Tropical Africa* (London, 1923), pp. 83 ff.

about "mental emancipation" from a servile colonial mentality.[14] The second method has been to tap all existing nativistic and religious tensions and economic grievances among the tradition-bound masses, as well as the grievances and aspirations of the urbanized clerks and artisans, and channel the energies thus unleashed into support of the nationalist drive. The technique here has been (1) to make nationalism, and in particular its objective of self-government, an integrating symbol in which even the most disparate goals could find identification, and (2) to politicize—one would like to say nationalize—all existing thought and associations. Until recently, many observers—including colonial administrators—tended to live in the prewar climate of opinion and therefore underestimated the power which had thus been harnessed to the nationalist machine.

In the case of the Mau Mau movement in Kenya we are confronted with a complex mixture of nationalism, with a strong traditional bias on the part of the Westernized leaders, and nativism, manipulated by the leaders, on the part of the masses. Both have been generated to an especially high level of intensity as a consequence of the acute and largely unassuaged sense of frustration on the part of the Westernized elite, growing out of the very bleak outlook arising from the almost total absence, until recently, of meaningful career and prestige opportunities within either the old or the new systems, and of the masses, resulting from the land shortage and the overcrowding on the reservations. The presence of a sizable Asian "third force," which virtually monopolizes the middle-class sector, and which has been and is politically conscious, provides a new variable of no little significance in the total situation. The fact that the pattern of organization and the strategy and tactics of the Mau Mau revolt indicate a higher level of sophistication than sheer nativism would imply suggests that our analytical categories need further refinement or qualification.

A particularly striking feature of African nationalism has been the literary and cultural revival which has attended it. A renewed appreciation of and interest in "African" culture has been manifested, in most instances by the most sophisticated and acculturated Africans (e.g., Mazi Mbono Ojike's *My Africa,* Dr. J. B. Danquah's studies of the Akan peoples of the Gold Coast, Jomo Kenyatta's *Facing Mount Kenya,* Fily-Dabo Sissoko's *Les Noirs et la Culture,* Léopold Sédar Senghor's *Anthologie de la Nouvelle Poésie Nègre et Malgache,* the French African journal *Présence Africaine* edited by M. Alioune Diop, and the writings of Antoine Munongo in the Belgian Congolese journal *Jeune*

[14] *Renascent Africa* (Lagos, 1937).

Afrique).[15] In some cases this cultural renaissance has had a purely tribal emphasis; in others it has taken a "neo-African" form, such as the African dress of Dr. Nnamdi Azikiwe, nationalist leader in Nigeria. It has usually been accompanied by a quest for an African history which would in general reflect glory and dignity upon the African race and in particular instill self-confidence in the Western-educated African sensitive to the prejudiced charge that he has no history or culture. In short, there has emerged a new pride in being African. In French areas, the accent until recently has been upon French culture and literature, but there are increasing signs of a shift to African themes amongst the French African literati. The important point is that African nationalism has this cultural content, which renders more difficult any effort to separate rigidly the cultural nationalism of the urban politician from the nativism of the bush peasant.

Yet the differences are important to the student of African nationalism. Primary resistance and nativism tend to be negative and spontaneous revolts or assertions of the unacculturated masses against the disruptive and disorganizing stranger-invader. They are a reflection of a persistent desire of the masses to preserve or recreate the old by protesting against the new. Syncretism is different in that it contains an element of rationality—an urge to recapture those aspects of the old which are compatible with the new, which it recognizes as inevitable and in some respects desirable. Whereas all forms of protest are politically consequential—at least to colonial administrators—only nationalism is primarily political in that it is irrevocably committed to a positive and radical alteration of the power structure. In brief, nationalism is the terminal form of colonial protest.

Another reason for distinguishing between the various categories of assertion, which are basically differences in goal orientation, is not only to provide some basis for judging the nature of the popular support of a nationalist movement during its buildup, but also to have some means of predicting the stability and viability of the political

[15] See Rosey E. Pool, "African Renaissance," *Phylon,* Vol. 14, pp. 5–8 (First Quarter, 1953); Albert Maurice, "Union Africaine des Arts et des Lettres," *African Affairs,* Vol. 50, pp. 233–41 (July, 1951); Alioune Diop, "Niam n'goura," *Présence Africaine* (Nov.–Dec., 1947), pp. 1–3. The cultural revival is the product of four forces: (1) reflection and introspection on the part of educated Africans, frequently those confronted with the stimulating contrasts of a foreign environment while abroad; (2) the American Negro renaissance which commenced in the 1920's; (3) encouragement and sponsorship of European governments and unofficial organizations such as the International African Institute; and (4) support of missionary societies such as the United Society for Christian Literature in the United Kingdom.

order established by the nationalists once they achieve self-government. The governments of Pakistan, Burma, India, and Indonesia have each been plagued by internal tensions arising from what are fundamentally South Asian variants of traditionalism and tribalism. If a colonial nationalist movement comes to power atop a wave of mass protest which is primarily or even in part nativistic in character, this would have a direct bearing upon the capacity of the Westernized leaders of that movement, not only to maintain political unity and stability but also to carry out what is at the core of most of their programs—rapid modernization by a centralized bureaucratic machine. Any thorough study of the anatomy of a nationalist movement, therefore, must seek to determine the linkages and compatibilities between the goal orientations of the several forces from which that movement derives its élan and strength.

II. FACTORS CONTRIBUTING TO THE RISE OF NATIONALISM

It is far easier to define and describe nationalism than it is to generalize about the factors which have contributed to its manifestation. Put most briefly, it is the end product of the profound and complex transformation which has occurred in Africa since the European intrusion. It is a commonplace that the imposition of Western technology, socio-political institutions, and ideology upon African societies has been violently disruptive of the old familistic order in that they have created new values and symbols, new techniques for the acquisition of wealth, status, and prestige, and new groups for which the old system had no place. The crucial point here is not that nationalism as a matter of fact happened to appear at a certain point in time after the "Western impact," but rather that the transformation the latter brought about has been an indispensable precondition for the rise of nationalism. Nationalism, as distinguished from primary resistance or nativism, requires considerable gestation. A few of the constituent elements have been:

A. ECONOMIC [16]

1. *Change from a subsistence to a money economy.* This change, consciously encouraged by colonial governments and European en-

[16] L. P. Mair, "The Growth of Economic Individualism in African Society," *Journal of the Royal African Society*, Vol. 33, pp. 261–73 (July, 1934); Allan

terprise in order to increase the export of primary products, introduced the cash nexus and economic individualism, altered the patterns of land tenure and capital accumulation, and, in general, widened the area of both individual prosperity and insecurity.

2. *Growth of a wage-labor force.* This development has resulted in the proletarianization of substantial numbers of Africans, which has weakened communal or lineage responsibility and rendered those concerned vulnerable to economic exploitation and grievances.

3. *Rise of a new middle class.* Laissez-faire economics and African enterprise, coupled with opportunities for university and professional education, have been factors contributing to the growth of a middle class. This class is most advanced in Senegal, the Gold Coast, and Southern Nigeria, where it has developed despite successive displacement or frustration by the intrusion of Levantines and the monopolistic practices of European firms.

B. SOCIOLOGICAL [17]

1. *Urbanization.* The concentration of relatively large numbers of Africans in urban centers to meet the labor demands of European enterprise has loosened kinship ties, accelerated social communication between "detribalized" ethnic groups, and, in general, contributed to "national" integration.

2. *Social mobility.* The European-imposed *pax* coupled with the development of communications and transport has provided the framework for travel, the growth of an internal exchange economy, and socio-political reintegration

3. *Western education.* This has provided certain of the inhabitants of a given territory with a common lingua franca; with the knowledge and tools to acquire status and prestige and to fulfill aspirations within the new social structure; and with some of the ideas and values by which alien rule and colonialism could be attacked. It has been through Western education that the African has encountered the scientific method and the idea of progress with their activistic implications,

McPhee, *The Economic Revolution in British West Africa* (London, 1926); G. Wilson, *An Essay on the Economics of Detribalization in Northern Rhodesia,* Part I (Rhodes-Livingstone Institute, 1941). Cf. Karl Polanyi, *Origins of Our Time* (London, 1946); P. C. Lloyd, "New Economic Classes in Western Nigeria," *African Affairs,* Vol. 52, pp. 327–34 (Oct., 1953).

[17] J. D. Rheinallt Jones, "The Effects of Urbanization in South and Central Africa," *African Affairs,* Vol. 52, pp. 37–44 (Jan., 1953).

namely, an awareness of alternatives and the conviction that man can creatively master and shape his own destiny.

C. RELIGIOUS AND PSYCHOLOGICAL [18]

1. *Christian evangelization.* The conscious Europeanization pursued by Christian missionary societies has been a frontal assault upon traditional religious systems and moral sanctions. Moreover, the Christian doctrine of equality and human brotherhood challenged the ethical assumptions of imperialism.

2. *Neglect or frustration of Western-educated elements.* Susceptibility to psychological grievance is most acute among the more acculturated Africans. Social and economic discrimination and the stigma of inferiority and backwardness have precipitated a passionate quest for equality and modernity, and latterly self-government. Rankling memories of crude, arrogant, or insulting treatment by a European have frequently been the major wellspring of racial bitterness and uncompromising nationalism.

D. POLITICAL

1. *Eclipse of traditional authorities.* Notwithstanding the British policy of indirect rule, the European superstructure and forces of modernity have tended to weaken the traditional powers of indigenous authorities and thereby to render less meaningful pre-colonial sociopolitical units as objects of loyalty and attachment. There has been what Professor Daryll Forde calls a "status reversal"; that is, as a result of the acquisition by youth of Western education and a command over Western techniques in all fields, there has been ". . . an increasing transfer of command over wealth and authority to younger and socially more independent men at the expense of traditional heads. . . ." [19]

2. *Forging of new "national" symbols.* The "territorialization" of Africa by the European powers has been a step in the creation of new nations, not only through the erection of boundaries within which the intensity of social communication and economic interchange has become greater than across territorial borders, but also as a consequence of the imposition of a common administrative superstructure, a common

[18] William Bascom, "African Culture and the Missionary," *Civilisations*, Vol. 3, pp. 491–501 (No. 4, 1953).

[19] Daryll Forde, "The Conditions of Social Development in West Africa," *Civilisations*, Vol. 3, pp. 471–85 (No. 4, 1953).

legal system, and in some instances common political institutions which have become symbols of territorial individuality.[20]

These are a few of the principal factors in the European presence which have contributed to the rise of nationalism. As any casual observer of African developments is aware, however, there have been and are marked areal differences in the overt manifestation of nationalism. Such striking contrasts as the militant Convention People's party of the Gold Coast, the conservative Northern People's Congress of Nigeria, the pro-French orientation of the African editors of *Présence Africaine,* the cautious African editors of *La Voix du Congolais,* and the terroristic Mau Mau of Kenya are cases in point.

There are a number of explanations for these areal variations. One relates to the degree of acculturation in an area. This is a reflection of the duration and intensity of contact with European influences. The contrast between the advanced nationalism of the British West Coast and of Senegal and the nascent nationalism of British and French Central Africa is partly explicable on this basis.

A second explanation lies in the absence or presence of alien settlers. On this score the settler-free British West Coast is unique when contrasted to the rest of Africa. The possibility of a total fulfillment of nationalist objectives (i.e., *African* self-government) has been a powerful psychological factor which partly explains the confident and buoyant expectancy of West Coast nationalists. On the other hand, as previously noted, the tendencies toward accommodation or terrorism in the white-settler areas is a reflection of the absence of such moderating expectancy.

Certain African groups exposed to the same forces of acculturation and the same provocation have demonstrated radically different reactions. The Kikuyu versus the Masai peoples of Kenya, the Ibo versus the Hausa peoples of Nigeria, and the Creole and Mende of Sierra Leone are cases in point. It is suggested that the dynamism, militancy, and nationalist élan of the Ibo peoples of Nigeria are rooted partly in certain indigenous Ibo culture traits (general absence of chiefs, smallness in scale and the democratic character of indigenous political organization, emphasis upon achieved status, and individualism). Much of the same might be said for the Kikuyu peoples of Kenya.

Differing colonial policies constitute another cause of these areal differences. Nationalism is predominantly a phenomenon of British

[20] See R. J. Harrison Church, *Modern Colonization* (London, 1951), pp. 104 ff.; Robert Montagne, "The 'Modern State' in Africa and Asia," *The Cambridge Journal,* Vol. 5, pp. 583–602 (July, 1952).

Africa, and to a lesser extent of French Africa. Apart from the influence of the foregoing historical, sociological, and cultural variables, this fact, in the case of British Africa, is explained by certain unique features of British colonial policy.

It was inevitable that Britain, one of the most liberal colonial powers in Africa, should have reaped the strongest nationalist reaction. A few of the principal features of British policy which have stimulated nationalism deserve mention:

1. *Self-government as the goal of policy.* Unlike the French and Portuguese who embrace their African territories as indivisible units of the motherland, or the Belgians who until recently have been disinclined to specify the ultimate goals of policy, the British have remained indiscriminately loyal to the Durham formula.[21] In West Africa, this has enthroned the African nationalists; in Central and East Africa, the white settlers.

2. *Emphasis upon territorial individuality.* More than any other colonial power, the British have provided the institutional and conceptual framework for the emergence of nations. Decentralization of power, budgetary autonomy, the institution of territorial legislative councils and other "national" symbols—all have facilitated the conceptualization of a "nation." [22]

3. *Policy on missionaries and education.* The comparative freedom granted missionaries and the laissez-faire attitude toward education, and particularly post-primary education, has distinguished and continues to distinguish British policy sharply from non-British Africa.

[21] Regarding Belgian policy, see Pierre Wigny, "Methods of Government in the Belgian Congo," *African Affairs*, Vol. 50, pp. 310–17 (Oct., 1951). Wigny remarks (p. 311) that ". . . Belgians are reluctant to define their colonial policy. They are proud of their first realisations, and sure of the rightness of their intentions." Since this was written, there have been some very dramatic changes in Belgian policy, especially regarding the educated elite, the potential nationalists. The great debate in Belgian colonial circles on "le statut des Congolais civilisés" was terminated by four decrees of May 17, 1952 according to which educated Congolese are assimilated to Europeans in civil law. Regarding Portuguese policy, see Marcelo Caetano, *Colonizing Traditions, Principles and Methods of the Portuguese* (Lisbon, 1951). The keynote of the policy is the "spiritual assimilation" of the Africans to a "Portuguese nation dwelling in European, African, Asiatic and Indonesian Provinces." The African *civilisado* is thus a citizen of Portugal.

[22] Partly in response to nationalist pressures, the French Government has recently initiated certain measures of financial devolution to French West Africa. See G. Gayet, "Autonomies financières Française," *Civilisations*, Vol. 3, pp. 343–47 (No. 3, 1953). These measures may enhance the powers of the territorial assemblies to the point that the latter might ultimately become the foci for territorial nationalisms.

4. *Neglect, frustration, and antagonism of educated elite.* Not only have more British Africans been exposed to higher education, but the British government until recently remained relatively indifferent to the claims and aspirations of this class, which forms the core of the nationalist movements.

5. *Freedom of nationalist activity.* The *comparative* freedom of activity (speech, association, press, and travel abroad) which British Africans have enjoyed—within clearly defined limits and varying according to the presence of white settlers—has been of decisive importance. It is doubtful whether such militant nationalists as Wallace-Johnson of Sierra Leone, Prime Minister Kwame Nkrumah of the Gold Coast, Dr. Nnamdi Azikiwe of Nigeria, Jomo Kenyatta of Kenya, and Dauti Yamba of the Central African Federation, could have found the same continuous freedom of movement and activity in Belgian, Portuguese, and French Africa as has been their lot in British Africa.[23]

All of this suggests that African nationalism is not merely a peasant revolt. In fact, as already noted, nationalism where it is most advanced has been sparked and led by the so-called detribalized, Western-educated, middle-class intellectuals and professional Africans; by those who in terms of improved status and material standards of living have benefitted most from colonialism; in short, by those who have come closest to the Western World but have been denied entry on full terms of equality. From this comparatively affluent—but psychologically aggrieved—group have come the organizers of tribal associations, labor unions, cooperative groups, farmers' organizations, and—more recently —nationalist movements. They are the Africans whom British policy has done most to create and least to satiate.[24]

This brief and selective treatment of a few of the factors which have contributed to the African nationalist awakening suggests certain avenues which might be profitably explored and more fully developed

[23] The stringent police measures adopted recently in Kenya and Nyasaland, the special press laws which have long been in effect in British East and Central Africa, and the obstacles to nationalist activity which have existed in the Muslim areas of Northern Nigeria, do not necessarily invalidate this *comparative* historical generalization.

[24] The thesis here is that there are at least four ingredients in the psychology of colonial nationalism, and that British policy in Africa has come closest towards inculcating or providing them: (a) an awareness of the existence or possibility of alternatives to the status quo, a state of mind produced by Western education and particularly by study and travel abroad; (b) an intense desire to change the status quo; (c) a system within which the major alternative to the status quo—self-government—has the status of legitimacy; and (d) an area of relative freedom in which that legitimate alternative may be pursued.

by subsequent research. Specifically, what is the relationship between the nature and intensity of nationalism and the degree of urbanization, the degree of commercialization of agriculture, and the size and geographical distribution of the wage-labor force and salariat? In short, what is the causal connection between "detribalization" and nationalism? Certain aspects of such an inquiry could be subjected to statistical analysis, but the results could only be suggestive, and in some instances might be positively deceptive. In the case of urbanization, for example, the highly urbanized and acculturated Yoruba peoples of Nigeria for nearly a decade lagged far behind the Ibo peoples in nationalist vigor and élan. Ibadan, the largest urban center in tropical Africa, has been until recently one of the most politically inert towns of Nigeria. Again, in terms of the proletarianization of labor and urbanization resulting from European industrialism and commercial activity, the Belgian Congo is one of the most advanced territories, but one in which nationalism is least in evidence.[25] Freetown, Sierra Leone, one of the oldest non-traditional urban centers, became a haven of respectability and conservatism, being eclipsed by the less-developed Protectorate in the push towards nationalist objectives. Urbanization has been an important ingredient in the nationalist awakening, but it has been a certain type of urban development—mainly the impersonal and heterogeneous "new towns"—which has occurred in conjunction with other equally decisive factors.

In the case of the relationship between the degree of commercialization of land and labor and the degree of nationalism, the figures set forth for the Gold Coast in Table I suggest either a causal connection or a parallel development. Yet in turning to similar figures for other territories—especially the Belgian Congo and Nigeria—it is clear that the relationship between commercialization and nationalism, important though it may be, must be considered and interpreted in the light of other variables.

Again, the fact that the nationalist movements have been organized and led by intellectuals and the so-called middle class suggests a relationship between nationalism and the number of Africans with higher education, the size of per capita income, the degree of the individualization of land tenure, the size of middle-class and professional groups (i.e., independent traders, produce middle-men, farmers employing labor, druggists, lorry owners, lawyers, doctors, etc.), and the degree

---

[25] The Belgian policy of stabilization of labor in the urban centers of the Congo, in which 83% of the men have their families with them, is one of the several factors which may help to explain this.

of vertical mobility within the emergent socio-economic structure. In any event, the insights of an economist are indispensable for a complete anatomy of African nationalism.

The Christian missionaries have been blamed frequently for their ruthless assault upon native religious systems and the thoroughgoing Europeanization, conscious or implicit, in their evangelization. This has suggested the formula: missionaries = detribalization = nation-

TABLE I. COMMERCIALIZATION AND NATIONALISM IN CERTAIN
AFRICAN TERRITORIES

Territory	Percentage of Cultivated Land Used by Africans for Commercial Production (1947–1950) [*]	African Wage Earners as Percentage of Total African Population (1950) [†]	Degree of Overt Nationalism
Gold Coast	75%	9.0%	Advanced
Belgian Congo	42	7.6	None
Nigeria	41	1.2	Advanced
Uganda	33	3.9	Nascent
Kenya	7	7.6	Nascent

[*] E. A. Keukjian, "Commercializing Influence of the Development of Exports on Indigenous Agricultural Economics in Tropical Africa," unpub. diss. (Harvard Univ., June, 1953); United Nations, Economic and Social Council (15th session). *World Economic Situation. Aspects of Economic Development in Africa.* New York, Document E/2377, March 20, 1953.

[†] United Nations, Department of Economic Affairs. *Review of Economic Conditions in Africa (Supplement to World Economic Report, 1949–50).* New York, Document E/1910/Add.1 Rev.1-ST/ECA/9/Add.1, April, 1951, p. 76.

alism. Yet the postwar figures shown in Table II do not bear out this assumption.[26] Missionaries have been important catalytic agents in the transformation of African societies, but the causal connection between their activities and nationalist assertion cannot be established by mere quantitative analysis. The figures in Table II hint at a possible causal relationship between preponderant Protestant evangelization and advanced nationalism (viz., Gold Coast and Nigeria) and preponderant Catholic evangelization and the absence of nationalism (viz., Portuguese Angola and the Belgian Congo). Yet this connection must be examined in the light of other relevant factors, such as the degree of control and direction extended to missionary societies by colonial governments; the freedom allowed such societies to establish

[26] *World Christian Handbook* (London, 1949).

TABLE II. CHRISTIANITY AND NATIONALISM IN CERTAIN
AFRICAN TERRITORIES

Territory	Percentage of Christians to Total Population	Percentage of Protestants to All Christians	Percentage of Catholics to All Christians	Degree of Overt Nationalism
Belgian Congo	37%	29%	71%	None
Nyasaland	26	49	51	Nascent
Gold Coast	15	58	42	Advanced
Angola	15	22	78	None
Kenya	10	51	49	Nascent
Nigeria	5	67	33	Advanced

schools—particularly secondary schools—and to determine the curriculum; the tolerance accorded anti-white or anti-colonial sects (e.g., the Jehovah's Witnesses are permitted in most of British Africa but proscribed in non-British Africa); the latitude allowed African sects of a syncretistic, revivalistic, or puritanical character; the extent to which evangelical bodies have *Africanized* their church organization, the priesthood, and the propagation of the gospel; and, finally, the strength of Islam.

The corrosive influence of Western education has been a significant ingredient in the rise of nationalism. Yet the Belgian Congo claims a higher percentage of literacy than any other colonial territory in Africa.[27] In order to establish a relationship we must move beyond the superficial analysis of literacy statistics and ask the following questions:

1. *The nature of the curriculum.* Has it been and is it literary and based upon the model of a European grammar school, or is it practical and designed to train the student to be a good farmer, artisan, or clerk in European employ, and incidentally to limit his sophistication and contact with unsettling ideas? Is instruction conducted in the vernacular or in a European language?

2. *Opportunities for post-primary education.* Are secondary schools (particularly those operated by missionary societies or by enterprising and nationalist-minded Africans such as Eyo Ita in Nigeria or Jomo Kenyatta in Kenya) allowed to mushroom into existence, or are they

[27] United Nations, *Non-Self-Governing Territories.* Vol. III: *Special Study on Education.* New York, Document ST/TRI/SER.A./5/Add.2, January, 1951

carefully planned and rigidly controlled by the colonial government as to both number and curriculum? What are the opportunites for study in universities abroad? What is the latitude granted students to determine their own careers? Here we touch upon a crucial factor —in 1945, Freetown, Sierra Leone, and Lagos, Nigeria, each had more Western-type secondary schools than all of the non-British territories in Africa combined. In 1952 over 4,000 Africans from British territories were studying in universities and technical schools abroad and nearly 1,000 in territorial universities in Africa, whereas only a handful had such opportunity or inclination in Belgian and Portuguese Africa. This is in part a reflection of the existence of a larger African middle class in British Africa, but it is also the result of the unique British attitude regarding the relationship between higher education and emergent African leadership. French policy and practice, despite differing assumptions, most closely approximate those of the British.[28]

3. *Openings of careers for the talented.* The stability of any political or social order is determined by this factor. Is there any planned relationship between the output of the schools and opportunities for satisfying employment or careers? In French and Belgian Africa, colonial governments have maintained a stringent control over the supply-demand situation as between *post-primary* schools and the requirements of government and the developing economy. In British Africa there are hundreds of thousands of unemployed or underemployed "Standard VI" boys clustered in the coastal towns and urban centers of the interior.

The most potent instrument used in the propagation of nationalist ideas and racial consciousness has been the *African-owned* nationalist press. In Nigeria alone nearly 100 newspapers or periodicals have been published by Africans since the British intrusion, of which 12 dailies and 14 weeklies—all African owned—are currently in circulation. The crucial role performed in the nationalist awakening by African jour-

[28] By decree of April 16, 1950, the *Institut des Hautes Études* was established at Dakar; and on January 1, 1952, there were 1,640 scholarship holders in continental France, of whom 572 were pursuing higher education. *Civilisations,* Vol. 3, pp. 575–83 (No. 4, 1953). On British educational policy in tropical Africa see *African Education* (Oxford: The Nuffield Foundation and the Colonial Office, 1953). The Belgians within the past few years have dramatically reoriented their policy regarding higher education for the Congolese. Since 1952 Congo students have been admitted to the Albert I College at Leopoldville; the first Negro University of the Congo is scheduled for opening in 1954; and recently the Belgian press has drawn attention to the admission to Louvain University of a Negro student from the Congo. *Civilisations,* Vol. 3, pp. 599–602 (No. 4, 1953).

nalistic enterprise on the British West Coast is well known.[29] Until the publication of *Afrique Noire* (organ of the *Rassemblement Démocratique Africaine* of French West Africa) there was nothing in non-British Africa which even closely approximated this development. And even this journal is no match for the pungent criticism and racial consciousness one finds in the pages of Dr. Nnamdi Azikiwe's *West African Pilot* in Nigeria.[30] Needless to say, the nationalist press is one of our major sources of data regarding nationalist motivation, objectives, and organization. It is not the number of newspapers published which is significant, but rather the volume of circulation and areal distribution, the news and editorial content and the nature of the appeal, the types of readers, the existence of competitive papers sponsored by colonial governments, the financial stability of the paper, and other factors which would reflect its impact and influence upon the ideas, aspirations, and activities of those literate groups predisposed towards nationalism.

These are but a few of the more important factors in the rise of nationalism which require evaluation and weighting before the student of comparative colonial nationalism can go beyond the mere description of the history and anatomy of a particular nationalist movement. There is great danger in doing a disservice to scholarly research in Africa if one generalizes on the basis of observations made and data assembled in one territory. As has been suggested, there are certain general predisposing and precipitating causes of modern nationalism which are applicable to the whole continent; yet once these are mentioned, it is necessary to examine each area of nationalist activity for that special combination of factors which explains the origin, strength, and orientation of its nationalist movement.

[29] Compare with the number of *African-owned-and-edited* dailies and weeklies (combined total) in the following territories: *British Africa:* Gold Coast (17), Uganda (8), Sierra Leone (7), Gambia (3); *French West Africa* (10); and none, insofar as is known, in Belgian, Portuguese, or Spanish Africa; or in Kenya, the territories of the Central African Federation, or in the Union of South Africa.

[30] On the other hand, there appears to be no newspaper in British West Africa comparable with the European-owned-and-edited journal of French West Africa entitled *Les Echos de l'A.O.F.*, which "week after week passionately attacks the administration. . . ." See Thomas Hodgkin, "The Metropolitan Axis," *West Africa,* January 9, 1954, at p. 6.

III. FACTORS CONDITIONING
NATIONALIST DEVELOPMENT

Normally, a colonial nationalist movement directs its efforts towards the attainment of two main objectives: (1) the achievement of self-government, and (2) the creation of a cultural or political sense of nationality and unity within the boundaries of the area of the nation to be. Nationalists are obliged to adopt the second objective because imperial powers either did not or could not establish political boundaries which embraced only one self-conscious cultural unit; and certainly those powers made no conscious effort to build nations. The nationalist dilemma is that in most cases pursuit of the primary goal (self-government) lessens the likelihood of achieving the secondary goal (cultural and political unity). Put another way, the drive behind African nationalism in many instances is not the consciousness of belonging to a distinct politico-cultural unit which is seeking to protect or assert itself, but rather it is the movement of racially-conscious modernists seeking to create new political and cultural nationalities out of the heterogeneous peoples living within the artificial boundaries imposed by the European master. Their task is not only to conduct a successful political revolution and capture power, but also the painful job of national political integration. And as Professor Crane Brinton has shown, the lessons of history are that nation-building is the product of both consent and coercion, and usually the latter.[31] It is the colonial power, of course, which has had a monopoly over the means of coercion.

The major factor conditioning the development of a particular nationalist movement, therefore, is the degree of internal politico-cultural unity, tolerance, or compatibility amongst the peoples of the area moving into its national era. Disunities can exist in a given territory for a variety of reasons:

1. Traditional pre-colonial hostilities and cultural incompatibilities such as exist between the Kikuyu and Masai peoples of Kenya, or the Ibo and the Tiv peoples of Nigeria. In some instances these have been exacerbated as a result of imperial policies; in others as a consequence of the mere fact of lumping them together and endeavoring to impose territorial uniformity.

2. Tensions between groups resulting from unevenness in development, acculturation, and the acquisition of modernity. These can be the product of original cultural differences (i.e., the variations between

---

[31] Crane Brinton, *From Many One* (Cambridge, Mass., 1948).

groups in their receptivity and adaptability to modernity—e.g., the Ibo and Hausa); historical circumstances (i.e., differences in the duration and intensity of the European impact—e.g., the Creoles of Freetown vs. the Mende peoples of the Protectorate of Sierra Leone); or of constitutional reforms pointing towards African self-government. One could argue that Ibo-Yoruba hostility in Nigeria is the product of all three factors. Just as the advance towards independence precipitated a cleavage between Muslims and Hindus in India, so has the development of nationalism and the move towards self-government in Africa brought to light a multitude of disunities. Fear of domination by the more advanced and acculturated groups—European or African—is one obvious explanation.

3. Tensions between the Westernized elite—the nationalists—and the traditionalists and the masses. This nationalist disability has tended to be exaggerated in the past, usually by imperial spokesmen endeavoring to repudiate the nationalists or to isolate them from the traditionalists. The intensity of the cleavage varies widely according to circumstances. In several areas such as the Protectorate of Sierra Leone, the Northern Territories of the Gold Coast, Western and Northern Nigeria, amongst the Kikuyu in Kenya, and in Northern Rhodesia and Nyasaland the educated nationalists and some leading traditionalists have cooperated in varying degrees.

4. Differences within the ranks of the Westernized elite. These disagreements—and one is struck by their persistence, strength, and virulence—may arise from several causes, including normal competition for power and prestige or honest differences over aims, timing, or methods to be employed in the nationalist drive. Such differences as separate Messrs. Fily-Dabo Sissoko and Mamadou Konaté in the French Sudan; Lamine Gueye and Léopold Senghor in Senegal; Felix Houphouet-Boigny and Kouame Binzème in the Ivory Coast; Prime Minister Kwame Nkrumah and Dr. J. B. Danquah in the Gold Coast; the Sardauna of Sokoto, Obafemi Awolowo, and Dr. Nnamdi Azikiwe in Nigeria; Eliud Mathu and Jomo Kenyatta in Kenya; and Harry Nkumbula and Godwin Lewanika in Central Africa, have very materially affected the course and strength of nationalism in the territories concerned.

These nationalist disabilities are the product of a complex mixture of hard historical and cultural facts, of changes introduced and differentials created by the Western intrusion, as well as of the provocations of the nationalist drive itself. The success of any nationalist movement will in a large measure depend upon the extent to which these internal tensions are softened or dissipated. The latter will depend, in turn, upon the degree of repressive opposition, or unwitting or intentional cooperation, of colonial governments; upon the development of pan-territorial political associations, the membership of which is rooted in all ethnic groups and in which there is free vertical mobility into the "upper crust" which that membership constitutes; upon the emergence of pan-territorial economic-interest groups (e.g., middle-class associations or labor organizations); and upon many other sociological processes (out-group marriages, commonsality, etc.) which Professor Karl W. Deutsch has suggested are essential building blocks of any new national community.[32]

It would be naive and unhistorical to argue that a large measure of politico-cultural integration is required—as distinguished from being desirable—in order for a nationalist movement to succeed in wresting self-government from an imperial power. Most successful colonial nationalist movements have been organized and led by small minorities which have been able either to gain the support of the masses or to capitalize upon their inertia and apathy. It would be unrealistic, however, to contemplate the success of a movement which did not have at least a minimum of unity or tolerance within the "upper crust," even though it be of the sort displayed by the unstable truces negotiated from time to time between the Sardauna of Sokoto, Mr. Obafemi Awolowo, and Dr. Nnamdi Azikiwe, the regional leaders in Nigeria.

Some of these forces contributing towards integration are measurable and provide rough indices upon which the research scholar can base predictions of the development of a particular nationalist movement. In an interesting new theory regarding the growth of nations, Professor Deutsch has suggested certain criteria which might be profitably employed in seeking to determine the prospects of success of a nationalist movement in its nation-building endeavors.[33] His central thesis is that cases of successful political integration in history show a number of patterns which seem to recur. As he puts it, a nation "is the result of the transformation of people, or of several ethnic elements, in the process of social mobilization." The prospects of success are indicated by the completeness of that transformation and the intensity of social mobilization around the symbols of the new national community. A nation is not only a subjective affirmation of will of zealous nationalists; it is also the product of the operation of powerful objective forces, several of which have been mentioned.

Thus far it has been assumed that the leaders of nationalist move-

[32] "The Growth of Nations," *World Politics*, Vol. 5, pp. 168–96 (Jan., 1953).

[33] *Ibid.* See also Deutsch's *Nationalism and Social Communication* (cited in note 5), pp. 81 ff.

ments in Africa will seek to build new national communities out of the diverse human materials located within the artificial boundaries of the existing colonial territories. This was precisely what happened in Latin America (Spanish imperial provinces), in the Middle East (European and Turkish regions), and in Southeast Asia (Dutch Indonesia, Burma, and in a qualified way, British India). In the case of British Africa, where nationalism is most advanced, this same tendency for nationalism to follow boundaries established by the imperial power rather than those coincident with pre-colonial socio-political groups is in evidence (e.g., Gold Coast and Nigeria). On the other hand, in many areas the situation is still relatively fluid. Togoland nationalism has been predominantly an Ewe affair, and the Ewes are a trans-territorial group stretching from the Gold Coast to Dahomey. Separatist sentiment in Northern Nigeria is an example, *par excellence*, of incomplete social mobilization. This, when coupled with growing Yoruba and Ibo self-consciousness, suggests that earlier pan-Nigerian nationalism may be eclipsed and Nigeria may ultimately become three or more states. Until the recent decision to give the Southern Cameroons greater autonomy within the emergent Federation of Nigeria, Cameroonian nationalists were wavering between remaining an integral part of the Eastern Region of Nigeria, or seceding and joining with the nationalists in the French Cameroons in an endeavor to create a Kamerun nation based upon the artificial boundaries of the short-lived German Kamerun.[34] In Kenya, Mau Mau and all earlier proto-nationalist movements have been predominantly Kikuyu endeavors, even though the name Kenya has been employed. In Tanganyika, the Chagga Cooperative movement may be the basis for a Chagga separatism; and in Uganda, it is questionable whether pan-Uganda integrative forces can erase the "national" separatism implicit in the Buganda Kingdom. Again, in Central Africa, will the territorial separatism symbolized by the Northern Rhodesian and Nyasaland National Congresses be eclipsed by the common sentiment and institutions growing out of the new Federation?

In the case of French Africa, dissimilarities in colonial policy (i.e., assimilation and direct rule) have tended to produce a somewhat different situation. Yet since the reforms of 1946, as a result of which each of the territories of the two federations of French West Africa and French Equatorial Africa received their own representative assemblies, territorial nationalist movements have tended to eclipse the pan-French African *Rassemblement Démocratique Africain* in much

[34] *West Africa*, January 30, 1954, p. 87.

the same fashion as Nigerian, Gold Coastian, and Sierra Leonian nationalist movements have replaced the earlier National Congress of
British West Africa. Thus one finds the *Parti Républicain de Dahomey*,
Parti Progressiste Sudanaise, *Union Démocratique du Tchad*, and
similar organizations in each of the territories. The future "national"
orientation of nationalist forces in French Africa would seem to depend upon the extent to which pan-Federation forces and institutions, such as the *Grand Conseils*, or the assimilationist forces of the
French Union, such as the metropolitan parties and labor movements
projected overseas, operate to retard the growth of territorial symbols
and sentiment. One thing, however, seems certain: French Africa—
because of the French policy of assimilation and direct rule—is less
likely to encounter such movements as the *Egbe Omo Oduduwa* of
the Nigerian Yorubas, the Kikuyu Central Association in Kenya, and
the *Bataka* movement of Uganda.

In general, it would seem that where nationalism manifests itself
in considerable strength it is evidence that disintegration of the old
and social mobilization around the symbols of the new order have
occurred on a scale sufficient to weaken or destroy attachments and
loyalties of the nationalists to pre-colonial socio-political units, either
because they have been crushed and are beyond memory or because
they are unattractive or manifestly unsuitable as "nations" in a modern
world of nation-states. The European presence has done much towards
the creation of new nations, the "national" sentiment of the nationalists
being a reflection of this.

A few of the many factors which might be observed and evaluated
in order to determine the probable success, as well as the territorial
implications, of an African nationalist movement or nation-building
endeavor are as follows: [35] (1) the degree of internal social mobility,
economic interchange and interdependence, intermarriage and commonsality, and the intensity and level of social communication among
the ethnic groups comprising a given territory; (2) the location of
population clusters and "core areas," as well as of "sub-national" regions
of more intense economic interchange or of cultural focus; (3) the
powers and functions of "sub-national" political institutions (i.e., regional, tribal, etc.), and the degree of *meaningful* participation in them
by the Western-educated elements; (4) the rate at which "national"
institutions and activities are capable of attracting and absorbing new
social strata from all ethnic groups into the "national" life (e.g., the

[35] For several of the concepts used here the author is indebted to the works of
Professor Karl W. Deutsch, previously cited. See especially his *Nationalism and
Social Communication*, pp. 15–45.

ethnic composition of the central administrative and technical services); (5) the centrality and nationalness of educational institutions, particularly the professional schools and universities; (6) the degree of pan-territorial circulation of nationalist newspapers and literature and the extent to which these play up "national" events and personalities; (7) the differentials in the material development, per capita income and wealth, the acquisition of modern skills and knowledge, and the concentration and capacity for accumulation of capital amongst the different sub-national areas and ethnic groups; [36] (8) the ethnic makeup of the Western-educated categories and particularly of the active membership of nationalist or proto-nationalist groups; (9) the development and extent of usage of a trans-tribal pan-territorial language, be it English, French, Portuguese, Swahili, or Hausa; (10) the compatibility of the "detribalized" basic personality types produced by the indigenous cultures; (11) the extent to which the territory concerned embraces total cultural groups, or, put another way, the degree to which artificial colonial boundaries have bifurcated ethnic groups whose division may be the source of later irredentism; and (12) the rapport between the Western-educated nationalist elements and the traditionalists, including the existence of nativistic tensions or economic grievances which the nationalists could manipulate or exploit in their mobilization of mass support.

Results obtained from inquiries along these lines would go far to explain the present orientation of a nationalist movement, as well as possible future trends. And yet an emphatic note of caution should be sounded: objective forces of integration and disintegration are powerful determinants in the nation-building process, but so also are subjective factors.[37] By all laws of geography and economics Northern Ireland should belong to Eire, and East Pakistan to the Republic of India; but they do not. By the same laws, the Gambia should belong to Senegal, French Guinea to Sierra Leone and Liberia, Mozambique to the Central African Federation, and so forth; and yet present trends suggest that such will not be the case. The principal forces

[36] It could be argued, for example, that apart from historical and cultural factors, the difference in the per capita income of the three regions of Nigeria (£26 for the Western Region, £16 for the Northern Region, and £23 for the Eastern Region) is of no little significance in the recent and current drive for greater regional autonomy. See A. R. Prest and I. G. Stewart, *The National Income of Nigeria*, abridged ed. (Lagos: Government Printer, 1954), pp. 14–16.

[37] Given suitable conditions, including a politically favorable milieu and the proper techniques, there would seem to be no reason why subjective factors such as loyalties, attitudes, and attachments to national or "sub-national" symbols, could not to some extent be measured.

currently operating to shape Africa's emergent nations are either tribalism or a nationalism following artificial imperial boundaries; and, with few exceptions, neither of these is directed towards the creation of political units which the geographer or economist would classify as ideal. In this respect, of course, Africa is not unique.

The foregoing raises the crucial question of whether it is possible for the peoples of Africa—in their own interest—to avoid the balkanization implicit in the full application of the national principle to their continent. So long as the rest of the world is organized according to that principle, and so long as the national idea universally embodies aspirations which cannot be satisfied by other forms of human organization, the answer would seem to be in the negative. The quest for racial equality and acceptance is as important an ingredient in the African revolt as is the desire to determine one's own destiny. Rightly or wrongly, self-government within the confines of the sovereign nation-state has become the supreme symbol of the equality of peoples. The only possible alternative would be broader Eur-African political groupings or self-governing plural societies in which emergent African leaders could play what they would feel to be an equal role. In the light of the persistence of national self-determination as a symbol, and particularly in view of the growing strength and contagion of African nationalism, the future of such multi-racial experiments will depend in a large measure upon the rapidity with which European governments and leaders provide for such a role.

IV. SPECIAL PROBLEMS OF RESEARCH INTO AFRICAN NATIONALISM

There is perhaps no other type of research venture capable of evoking stronger feeling than an inquiry into colonial nationalism. The word "nationalism" in a colonial milieu has tended to be treated as the equivalent of sedition, or even treason. And this for good reason: by definition colonial nationalists are seeking to bring about a radical alteration in the power structure; namely, to evict the imperial power and to enthrone themselves. From the moment it makes its presence known, therefore, a nationalist movement is, in effect, engaged in a civil war with the colonial administration, the constitutionality of its methods varying according to the liberality of the colonial regime and the moderation of the nationalist leaders.

As regards colonial officialdom, an American undertaking a study of African nationalism is handicapped by the fact that in a large measure the African nationalist awakening is the product of American influ-

ences. Since the turn of the century, American Negro religious sects
have contributed no little to religious secessionism, particularly in
South and West Africa. The Garveyism of the early 1920's had an
influence among sophisticated Africans which has tended to be overlooked or minimized. Since 1919 a growing number of American Negro
intellectuals have taken an increasingly militant stand on African colonialism. Anti-imperialist sentiment in the United States, especially
during the Second World War, was the source of considerable inspiration and delight to budding African nationalists, as well as the
cause of no little acrimony between wartime allies. The Atlantic Char-
ter, the Four Freedoms, and public statements by Mr. Willkie and
President Roosevelt have bulked large in postwar African nationalist
literature. The most important American contribution, however, has
been the impact of our culture upon African students who have
studied in America. Many of the important pioneers in the African
awakening were profoundly affected by their American experience.
Of this group the late Dr. J. E. K. Aggrey and Prime Minister Kwame
Nkrumah from the Gold Coast, and Professor Eyo Ita and Dr. Nnamdi
Azikiwe from Nigeria are the most prominent and best known.
During the Second World War the number of African students in
America was less than 25; since 1945 it has increased to over 500. With
few exceptions these students have been and are strong nationalists,
many of them having become leaders upon their return to Africa. In
the eyes of colonial officialdom, therefore, an American inquiry into
nationalism tends to raise certain doubts.

There has been a tendency in the past for American visitors making
quick tours of Africa to rely mainly upon the white colonial administration for an appraisal of nationalist sentiment and activity. This is
unfortunate in many respects. In the first place, it is most likely that
any information bearing on nationalism is locked up in classified files.
Secondly, most colonial administrators have tended to be anti-nationalists, even though many in British West Africa have adapted themselves to working with nationalists towards a mutually agreed goal of
effective self-government. Their evaluation of nationalism is bound to
be colored by their preconceptions and vested interests or by their
honest fears regarding the welfare of the bush peasant, for whom they
tend to have a preference and a strong paternal affection. Thirdly,
circumstances have tended to place them too close to events or too
far removed from the people. Their growing preoccupation with head-
quarters administration and development schemes, the social impediments—created frequently by the presence of white wives and families
—to effective and continuous contact with the masses, and the almost

total lack of rapport or confidence between nationalists and administrators, have given the latter many blind spots. Their past miscalculations of nationalist strength and trends tend to confirm this. In short, instead of being used as informants, a role they are not anxious to perform, they should be objects of study. Their fears, their adjustments, and their efforts to suppress, retard, manipulate, or encourage nationalism are all relevant in a complete study of the many interacting factors present in a nationalist situation.

Unlike the field anthropologist, who consciously seeks to work among the traditionalists, the student of political nationalism is concerned mainly with the attitudes, activities, and status of the nationalist-minded Western-educated *elite*. Here one is in a world very different from that of officialdom or the traditionalists. It is a world of great idealism, crusading zeal, and high resolve, as well as one of suspicion, hyper-sensitivity, and exaggeration. It has its careerists and opportunists, and its chronic nonconformists; but it also has its emergent statesmen, its enterprising industrialists, and its distinguished scholars. Only here can one get a partial glimpse into the depth of nationalist feeling, the sources of inspiration and ideas, and the key elements in nationalist motivation. Yet there are distinct limitations to the interview technique, not the least important of which is the possession of a white skin. Moreover, a colonial nationalist movement must have its *arcana* as well as its propaganda.

In the quest for knowledge regarding African nationalism, the most fruitful as well as unprovocative avenues to explore are those already indicated in earlier sections. African nationalism is something more than the activities of a few disgruntled journalists and frustrated intellectuals to whom Lord Lugard referred in his *Dual Mandate*. It is the inevitable end product of the impact of Western imperialism and modernity upon African societies; it is also the inevitable assertion by the Africans of their desire to shape their own destiny. Imperial systems are disintegrating, new nation-states are emerging, and new forms of political organization transcending the national state are under experiment. These political aspects of African nationalism, however, are but the surface symptoms of a great ferment about which we know very little. The study and analysis of the many complex factors in this unfolding drama provide not only a stimulating challenge to the social sciences, but also a compelling invitation to greater interdisciplinary cooperation.

4

THE INTELLECTUALS IN
THE POLITICAL DEVELOPMENT
OF THE NEW STATES

Edward Shils

I. THE POLITICAL SIGNIFICANCE OF INTELLECTUALS
IN UNDERDEVELOPED COUNTRIES

The gestation, birth, and continuing life of the new states of Asia and Africa, through all their vicissitudes, are in large measure the work of intellectuals. In no state-formations in all of human history have intellectuals played such a role as they have in these events of the present century.

In the past, new states were founded by military conquest, by the secession of ethnic groups led by traditional tribal and warrior chiefs, by the gradual extension of the power of the prince through intermarriage, agreement, and conquest, or by separation through military rebellion. In antiquity, the demand that subjects acknowledge the divinity of the Emperor was no more than a requirement that the legitimacy of the existing order be recognized.[1] The interests of dynasty and kinship group, the lure of majesty, considerations of power, aspirations for office, and calculations of economic advantage have been

Reprinted, by permission, from *World Politics,* XII, No. 3 (April 1960), 329–368. This article is a revised version of a paper presented at a conference on political modernization held under the auspices of the Committee on Comparative Politics of the Social Science Research Council at Dobbs Ferry in June 1959.

[1] The maxim of the Peace of Augsburg: *Cuius regio, eius religio,* was the beginning of the specifically modern view that a political order must be based on articulately affirmed beliefs. It too, however, was more concerned with the protection of dynastic interests and the guarantee of public order. The substance of the religion was less important than its acceptance, and in this way it differed from the more intrinsically ideological orientation toward politics that is characteristic of the modern intellectual.

the components of political decisions and the grounds for pursuit of power in the state. It is only in modern times in the West that beliefs about man's nature, his past, and his place in the universe, and about the ethical and metaphysical rightness of particular forms of political order—the concerns of intellectuals—have played an important part in public life.

In the West in modern times, however, politics—particularly civil politics—have never been a preserve of the intellectuals. Well-established aristocrats and landed gentry with ample leisure have provided much of the personnel of politics, both oligarchical and democratic; clergymen and high ecclesiastical officials and, above all, businessmen— the former earlier, the latter more recently—have likewise added to the pool. Retired army officers, trade unionists and, of course, mere professional politicians of diverse occupational backgrounds have also been among the incumbents of or contenders for political office and the leaders in the agitation surrounding selection and decision. Intellectuals, too—professors and teachers, scientists, journalists, authors, etc.—have had a substantial share in all these activities. Radical, much more than conservative, politics have been their province, but there too they have had to share the territory with politicians and trade unionists who were not intellectuals. Modern revolutionary politics have been a domain very much reserved for intellectuals; even those who were not intellectuals by training or profession have been almost forced into becoming so by the ideological nature of modern revolutionary politics.

The prominence of intellectuals in the politics of the new states of Asia and Africa arises in part from the special affinity which exists between the modern intellectual orientation and the practice of revolutionary or unconstitutional politics, of politics which are uncivil in their nature. But even in the small space allotted to civil politics before the new states' acquisition of sovereignty and in its larger area since then, intellectuals have had a prominent position. They have not had to share their political role to the usual extent with the other participants in the building and ruling of states.

It was the intellectuals on whom, in the first instance, devolved the task of contending for their nations' right to exist, even to the extent or promulgating the very idea of the nation. The erosion of the conscience and self-confidence of the colonial powers was in considerable measure the product of agitational movements under intellectual leadership. The impregnation of their fellow-countrymen with some incipient sense of nationality and of national self-esteem was to a large extent the achievement of intellectuals, both secular and religious. The intellectuals have created the political life of the underdeveloped countries; they have been its instigators, its leaders, and its executants. Until Gandhi's emergence at the end of the First World War, they were its main followers as well, but this changed when the nationalist movement began to arouse the sentiments of the mass of the population.

One of the reasons for the political pre-eminence of the intellectuals of the underdeveloped countries is a negative one. There was practically no one else. In so many of the colonial countries, the princely dynasties were in decay, their powers and their capacities withered, even before the foreigners appeared. Chiefs and princes squirmed under foreign rule; they intrigued and schemed, and at times even resorted to arms, but they organized no political movements and they espoused no ideology. They sought only, when they protested, to retain or regain their own prerogatives. There were no great noble families producing, in generation after generation, courtiers and ministers who with the emergence of modern forms of public politics moved over into that sphere as of right, as they did in Great Britain from the seventeenth to the nineteenth century. The traditional intellectuals, the custodians of sacred texts, usually—with a few great exceptions like al-Afghani—had no political concerns. They were interested in keeping their traditional culture alive, and this traditional culture had little political content other than to recommend leaving authority to those who already had it. They were ready to adapt themselves to any ruler, native or foreign, who left them alone to carry on their scriptural studies, their traditional teaching, and their observances.[2]

Moreover, there was generally no military force either to fight against the foreign ruler once he was established or to supply the educated personnel for a modern political movement.[3] There was no military officer class except for a few subalterns in the jealously guarded army of the foreign ruler. There were many professional soldiers, but they were non-commissioned officers and other ranks and had no political interest whatsoever. The movement instigated in 1881 by the Egyptian Colonel Ahmed Orabi Pasha [4] had no counterparts until the tremors

[2] The religious reform movements like the Brahmo Samaj, Arya Samaj, the Ramakrishna Mission, and the Muslim Brotherhood which contributed so much to national consciousness were primarily movements for the purification of religious life, and for the reform of social institutions. Their political significance was either indirect or an afterthought.

[3] The practitioners of the guerrilla warfare and terrorism which have been carried on in various parts of Asia and Africa against the European rulers have always included a significant admixture of intellectuals.

[4] It was, in any case, more of a protest against unsatisfactory service conditions than a political movement.

and tribulations of independence began to be felt. There was no profession of politics which men entered early, usually from some other profession, and remained in until final and crushing defeat or the end of their lives. There were very few merchants and industrialists who out of civic and "material" interest took a part in politics on a full or part-time scale—although many of them contributed substantially to the financial support of the nationalist and even the revolutionary movements. Prudence and the narrowness of their concerns kept businessmen out of politics. The "foreignness" of many business enterprisers in underdeveloped countries has further diminished the significance of this class as a reservoir of political personnel. There was and there still is scarcely any endogenous trade union movement which produces its own leaders from within the laboring class, and there have been practically none of those self-educated workingmen who helped to give an intellectual tone to the European and American socialist and revolutionary movements in their early years. There was no citizenry, no reservoir of civility, to provide not only the audience and following of politics but the personnel of middle and higher leadership. In short, if politics were to exist at all in underdeveloped countries under colonial rule, they had to be the politics of the intellectuals.

The intellectuals did not, however, enter into the political sphere merely because other sections of the population forswore or abdicated their responsibilities. They entered because they had a special calling from within, a positive impetus from without.

II. THE INTELLECTUAL CLASS
IN UNDERDEVELOPED COUNTRIES

What is an intellectual? We deal here with the modern intellectuals of the new states—not with traditional intellectuals. Whom do we regard as modern intellectuals in the new states? The answer, in a first approximation, is: all persons with an *advanced modern education* [5] and the intellectual concerns and skills ordinarily associated with

[5] This definition is ceasing to be adequate because the extension of opportunities for higher education is changing the composition and outlook of the group of persons who have availed themselves of these opportunites. Furthermore, the increase of those with an advanced technical or scientific and specialized education is creating a body of persons whose interests are narrower than their predecessors' in their own countries, and whose contact with the humanistic and political tradition of the hitherto prevailing higher education is becoming more attenuated. They themselves will not merely be different from the conventional political intellectuals of the colonial or recently colonial countries, but will also less frequently identify themselves as "intellectuals." This will make a considerable difference. In this

it. For a variety of reasons, the present definition of the intellectuals is a less selective or discriminating one than we would use to designate the intellectuals in the more advanced countries. This is in no way condescension toward the new states. It is only an acknowledgment of the smaller degree of internal differentiation which has until now prevailed within the educated class in the new states, and the greater disjunction which marks that class off from the other sections of the society. It is also a recognition of a means of identification employed in the new states by the intellectuals themselves and by others.

In the new states, and in colonies which are shortly to achieve independence, the intellectuals are those persons who have become modern not by immersing themselves in the ways of modern commerce or administration, but by being exposed to the set course of modern intellectual culture in a college or university. Passage through this course of study is the qualification for being regarded as an intellectual, just as the possession of the diploma is regarded as a qualification for practicing a profession which is the prerogative of the intellectual. The "diplomatization" of society to which Max Weber referred, although it exists on a smaller scale than in Germany or Great Britain because there are fewer posts available, is as impressive in underdeveloped countries as in the advanced ones. It is not, however, the diploma which makes the intellectual. It is his prolonged contact with modern culture [6] which does so. The diploma is only an emblem, however valuable, of a part of his outlook which he and others regard as vitally important. The possession of a *modern intellectual culture* is vital because it carries with it a partial transformation of the self and a changed relationship to the authority of the dead and the living.

The occupational structure of the intellectuals. The professions of the intellectuals in underdeveloped countries are civil service, journalism, law, teaching (particularly college and university, but also secondary-school teaching), and medicine. These are the professions in which intellectuals are to be found and which require either intellectual certification or intellectual skill. (There are other professions with similar

respect, the underdeveloped countries will begin to approximate the more advanced countries.

This definition is not intended to deny the existence of a class of traditional intellectuals, largely religious in their concerns. Nor does it seek to obscure the influence of traditional intellectuals in political life (like the Muslim Brotherhood, the Darul Islam, etc.) or of traditional ideas on modern intellectuals.

[6] This does not mean that all intellectuals in underdeveloped countries who possess diplomas are intellectually equal, or that all intellectuals possess diplomas. There are a few who do not.

qualifications of certification and skill, such as engineering and accounting, which have usually been regarded as marginal to the circle within which the intellectuals dwell.)

The occupational structure which intellectuals enter in the underdeveloped countries is notably different from that of the more advanced countries. The occupational distribution of the intellectuals in underdeveloped countries is a function of the level of economic development and of their having only recently been colonial territories. Because they were impoverished countries, they lacked a fully differentiated middle class. They lacked and still lack a stratum of authors who could live from the sale of their literary products.[7] They have only a very meager class of technical intellectuals (electrical engineers, technologists, industrial chemists, statisticians, accountants). They have lacked the higher levels of scientific and humanistic personnel, the physicists, biologists, geneticists, historians, and philosophers who carry on the intellectual work which is the specific manifestation of the modern intellectual outlook.[8]

They lacked nearly all of these latter professions under colonial conditions, and most of the underdeveloped countries still lack most of them today under conditions of independence. In the colonial era, they lacked them because poverty and the absence of a significant development of industry prevented the emergence of demand for technical intellectuals, because illiteracy prevented the emergence of a market for literary products, and because the higher levels of modern intellectual creation and enquiry received no indigenous impulse and were too costly for poor countries to maintain. As a result, persons trained in those subjects found little opportunity for employment in their own country, and few therefore attempted to acquire these skills.[9]

Under colonial conditions, the underdeveloped countries lacked the effective demand which permits a modern intellectual class, in its full

[7] By very rough methods I estimated that there might be as many as one hundred professional literary men in India who are able to maintain themselves by their writings. The Director of the *Sahitya Akademi* thinks that there are only about fifty. Think then of the size of this stratum in Ghana, Nigeria, Egypt, or the Sudan!

[8] India is a very partial exception. It is practically alone in its possession of a large corps of intellectuals, a fair number of whom work at a very high level. This is partly a function of the much longer period that modern intellectual life has existed in India. The British stayed longer in India and exercised greater influence there than any other European power did to its colonial territory, and as a result many more modern intellectual institutions came into being.

[9] There are other important reasons, growing out of the culture of these countries, which precluded interest in these fields. We do not deal with them here since our interest lies primarily in the political sphere.

variety, to come into existence. Persons who acquired intellectual qualifications had only a few markets for their skills. The higher civil service was by all odds the most attractive of these, but opportunities were
restricted because it was small in size and the posts were mainly pre-
empted by foreigners. (In India in the last decade of the British Raj,
there were only about 1,200 such posts in the Indian Civil Service and,
of these, a little less than half were filled by Indians. In other countries,
the number of posts was smaller and the proportion held by persons
of indigenous origin was also much smaller.)

Journalism, as a result of generally widespread illiteracy, was a
stunted growth and provided only a few opportunities, which were
not at all remunerative. Journalism under colonial conditions was
much more of an unprofitable political mission than a commercially
attractive investment, and most of it was on a rather miniscule scale.

The medical profession was kept small by the costliness of the course
of study, the absence of an effective demand for medical services, and
the pre-emption of much of the senior level of the medical service by
the government and its consequent reservation for foreigners.

Teaching at its lower levels was unattractive to intellectuals because
it involved living in villages away from the lights and interests of
the larger towns, and because it was extremely unremunerative. Nor
were there many opportunities in it. On the secondary and higher
levels, opportunities were also meager. Of all the underdeveloped
countries, only India had an extensive modern college and university
system before 1920; after that date, the additions to the Indian system
of higher education came very slowly until the eve of the Second
World War and the chaos which accompanied it. Outside of India
there were at most only a few thousand posts available in institutions
of higher learning in all of colonial Asia and Africa, and some of
these were reserved for Europeans (and Americans, in the two American colleges of the Middle East). Thus opportunities for teaching
on the upper levels of an extremely lean educational system were few.
Where the authorities sought to maintain a high standard, they were
very particular about whom they chose to employ. (It should be added
that political considerations, at this time of nationalistic, anti-colonialist
effervescence, likewise restricted the chances of entry, since many able
young men disqualified themselves by the high jinks of adolescent
politics during their student days.)

The legal profession. For these reasons, many of the intellectually
gifted and interested who also had to gain their own livelihood entered
the course of legal study and then the practice of the profession of the
law. Entry to the legal profession was not restricted on ethnic grounds,

the course of study was short and inexpensive and could be easily undertaken. There was, moreover, a considerable effective demand for legal services.

The colonial powers were concerned with order and justice and, in their various ways, had attempted to establish the rule of law in the colonial territories. The wealthy landowning classes and the newer wealthy merchants were frequently engaged in litigations in which huge sums were involved and the possibility for lawyers to earn handsome fees gave an éclat to the legal profession which only the higher civil service otherwise possessed.

Furthermore, in countries like India, Egypt, or Nigeria, for example, what else could a university or college graduate do with his qualifications if he did not wish to settle for a clerkship in the government or in a foreign commercial firm? The law schools were therefore able to attract throngs of students. Once the legal qualification had been obtained, the young lawyer went into the nether regions of the bar, where he had much time for other interests. The leisure time of the young lawyer was a fertile field in which much political activity grew.

This existence of a stratum of underemployed young lawyers was made possible by their kinship connections. The aspirants to the intellectual professions in the underdeveloped countries almost always came from the more prosperous sections of society. They were the sons of chiefs, noblemen, and landowners, of ministers and officials of territories in which indirect rule existed, and of civil servants and teachers in countries under direct rule. In some countries, they occasionally came from prosperous mercantile families, though seldom in large numbers.

These social origins, against the background of the diffuse obligations accepted by members of an extended kinship system, meant that even where the income gained from a profession was inadequate to maintain a man and his immediate family, he could still continue to associate himself with the profession. The deficiencies in his earnings were made up by his kinsmen. Unlike teaching, the civil service, and most journalism, where membership in the profession is defined not merely by qualification and intermittent practice but by actual employment, a person need not earn a living by legal practice in order to be a lawyer. This is why the legal profession in nearly all the underdeveloped countries has been, before and since independence, crowded by a few very successful lawyers and a great number of very unsuccessful ones.

These are also some of the reasons why the legal profession supplied so many of the outstanding leaders of the nationalist movements during colonial times, and why the lawyer-intellectuals form such a vital part of the political elites of the new states.

Students. No consideration of the intellectual class in underdeveloped countries can disregard the university students. In advanced countries, students are not regarded as *ex officio* intellectuals; in underdeveloped countries, they are. Students in modern colleges and universities in underveloped countries have been treated as part of the intellectual class—or at least were before independence—and they have regarded themselves as such. Perhaps the mere commencement of an adult form of contact with modern intellectual traditions and the anticipation—however insecure—that acquisition of those traditions would qualify one for the *modern* intellectual professions conferred that status on university and college students and, derivatively, on secondary-school students.

The student enjoyed double favor in the eyes of his fellow-countryman. As one of the tiny minority gaining a modern education, he was becoming qualified for a respected, secure, and well-paid position close to the center of society, as a civil servant, teacher, or lawyer. As a bearer of the spirit of revolt against the foreign ruler, he gained the admiration and confidence of those of his seniors who were imbued with the national idea.

Formally, the student movements in the colonial countries began their careers only in the 1920's, but long before that the secondary schools, colleges, and universities had been a source of personnel for the more ebullient and aggressive nationalistic movements. Since the beginning of the present century, students have been in a state of turbulence. This turbulence flowed more and more into politics, until the students became vital foci of the national independence movements. The secondary schools, colleges, and universities attended by the students of underdeveloped countries became academies of national revolution. It was not the intention of the administrators and teachers that they should become such; rather, the contrary. Nonetheless they did, both in their own countries and in the metropolitan centers of London and Paris, where many of the most important architects of independence were trained, and where they found the intellectual resonance and moral support which sustained them in lean years.

The London School of Economics in particular has probably contributed much more to the excitation of nationalistic sentiment than any other educational institution in the world. At the School of Economics, the late Professor Harold Laski did more than any other single individual to hearten the colonial students and to make them feel that the great weight of liberal Western learning supported their political enthusiasm.

However, it was not only in the universities of London and Paris, but in shabby clubs and cafés, cheap hotels and restaurants, dingy rooming houses and the tiny cluttered offices of their nationalist organizations that the colonial students were educated in nationalism, acquired some degree of national consciousness, and came to feel how retrograde their own countries were and what they might be if only they became their own masters and modernized themselves. Personalities like Mr. Krishna Menon, Dr. Nkrumah, and Dr. Banda were themselves formed in these milieux, and in turn formed many of those who were to play an active part in the movement in their own countries.

The political propensities of the students have been, in part, products of adolescent rebelliousness. This has been especially pronounced in those who were brought up in a traditionally oppressive environment and were indulged with a spell of freedom from that environment—above all, freedom from the control of their elders and kinsmen. Once, however, the new tradition of rebellion was established among students, it became self-reproducing. Moreover, the vocational prospectlessness of their post-university situation has also stirred the restiveness of the student.

The unemployed intellectual. In most underdeveloped countries during the colonial period, the unemployed intellectual was always a worry to the foreign rulers and to constitutional politicians, and a grievance of the leaders of the independence movement. He still remains a problem in the underdeveloped countries which have had a higher educational system for some length of time and which are not rapidly expanding their governmental staffs. In Ghana or Nigeria, there is a shortage of intellectuals and all graduates can find posts; in Pakistan, which inherited only a very small part of the higher educational system of British India, the government has tried to restrict entrance to the universities, especially in "arts" subjects. In India and Egypt, however, despite rapid expansion of opportunities for the employment of intellectuals in government, there has been a more than proportionate expansion in the number of university graduates and the problem remains as acute as ever.

Yet the difficulty is not so much "intellectual unemployment" as under- and mal-employment. Most of the graduates, sooner or later, do find posts of one sort or another, but they are not posts which conform with expectations. They are ill-paid, unsatisfying in status and tenure, and leave their incumbents in the state of restlessness which they experienced as students.

III. THE POLITICAL OUTLOOK OF THE INTELLECTUALS

Intense politicization. The nature of the political movements which preceded independence and the indigenous traditions of the underdeveloped countries both forced political life into charismatic channels. Charismatic politics demand the utmost from their devotees.

When the intellectuals of the colonial countries were ready to engage in politics at all, they were willing to give everything to them. Politics became the be-all and end-all of their existence. Those who were not restrained by fear of the loss of their posts in government schools and colleges or by the material and psychological advantages of their jobs became highly politicized. Some of the intellectuals who graduated in the years of nationalistic fervor did not even attempt seriously to enter upon a professional career but went directly into agitational and conspiratorial politics. Their middle-class origins and the economy of the extended family system, together with the relatively few needs of charismatically sensitive intellectuals, helped to make possible this consecration to politics. For these reasons and because an autonomous intellectual life in the modern sense had scarcely taken root in any of the underdeveloped colonial countries, politics of a very intense sort had the intellectual field largely to itself.

The high degree of political involvement of the intellectual in underdeveloped countries is a complex phenomenon. It has a threefold root. The primary source is a deep preoccupation with authority. Even though he seeks and seems actually to break away from the authority of the powerful traditions in which he was brought up, the intellectual of underdeveloped countries, still more than his confrere in more advanced countries, retains the need for incorporation into some self-transcending, authoritative entity. Indeed, the greater his struggle for emancipation from the traditional collectivity, the greater his need for incorporation into a new, alternative collectivity. Intense politicization meets this need. The second source of political involvement is the scarcity of opportunities to acquire an even temporary sense of vocational achievement; there have been few counterattractions to the appeal of charismatic politics. Finally, there has been a deficient tradition of civility in the underdeveloped countries which affects the intellectuals as much as it does the non-intellectuals. Let us consider each of these aspects.

The intellectual everywhere is concerned with his relations to authority. In underdeveloped countries, where authorities have tended on the whole to be more unitary, and where alternative authorities, and the authority of alternative traditions, have not yet emerged because of the small size of the primordial community and its relatively low degree of internal differentiation, the preoccupation of the intellectual with authority is all the greater. It is difficult for him to escape from a sense of its presence and a feeling of dependence on it. Such continuous presence, and the unindulgent attitude of traditional indigenous authority, once childhood has passed, breed resentment, and antipathy which are submerged but not dissolved in the obedience required for the continuance of daily existence in the primordial community.

The external air of submission hides a deeper and unceasing enmity. Distant authority which has force at its disposal, which is impersonal, as bureaucratic authority must be, and which is not suffused with any immediately apprehensible charisma, provides an easy target for this enmity.

When one shares in authority, when one "is" authority, as a leading politician of the ruling party or as a civil servant, the antagonism toward authority is curbed by the counterbalancing need to be absorbed into it. For an intellectual in an underdeveloped country, authority is usually something into which he must be absorbed or against which he must be in opposition. It is seldom something about which he can be neutral while he goes about his business. The very structure of the underdeveloped countries, both in their primordial and in their wider aspects, both during the colonial period and during independence, is such that one can never be indifferent about authority. It cannot be overlooked, one's "business" cannot be carried on without regard to it.

Distant authority carries with it none of the compensations and urgencies of immediately present and permeative authority. Distance does not make for indifference among the politicized, among those whose passions are strong and no longer bound down by the weight of primordiality and tradition. The distance of authority renders revolt against it psychologically more practicable. Distant authority is "alien" authority. Even when it is ethnically "identical" with those over whom it rules, this "alienation" exists in those societies which are used to being ruled by visible and proximate authorities. (When distant authority is also ethnically alien, whether it be of the same general racial and cultural stock or as alien in color, cultural tradition, provenience, and physical appearance as the colonial authorities were, the impulse to revolt is all the stronger.)

The revolt against authority cannot, however, be complete and un-equivocal. The need, from which no human being can ever wholly liberate himself, to be a member of an authoritative, transcendent col-lectivity remains. The individual, striving to emancipate himself from his primordial collectivity, must feel himself a part of some other more congenial, alternative collectivity. It must, moreover, be an authorita-tive one, a charismatically authoritative one. Where, in an underde-veloped society, with its relative churchlessness, its still feeble pro-fessional and civil traditions, and in the face of persisting particularistic loyalties, both subjective and objective, can the modern intellectual find such an authoritative collectivity? It is really only the "nation" which is at hand, and that organized body which represents the "nation"—namely, the "party of national independence."

This is one reason why the intellectual immerses himself, at least for a time, in intense political activities; it is why he seeks a "cause," an encompassing ideal. It is also the reason for the oppositional char-acter of the politics of the intellectuals who themselves do not share in the authority. The belief in the efficacy of political action and in the political sources of evil and the remedies of evil also finds some of its explanation here. This is why the relatively unpolitical intellectual, or the intellectual who is indirectly connected with political affairs, the more specialized intellectual who wishes to work within his own professional intellectual tradition and to exercise his influence in the public sphere over the longer run and beyond the immediate disputes of the parties, is regarded as not being a "genuine intellectual" and even as a traitor to the ideals which the intellectual is properly called to serve.

The intense politicization of the intellectual is accentuated by the provision, through politics, of opportunities for individual effectiveness and achievement. In a society where status is traditionally determined by such primordial qualities as kinship connection, age, sex, and rank order within the family, the possibility of achievement, of making a mark on events by one's own actions, is minimal. In the larger society of the underdeveloped countries, although the narrower primordial determinants of status are to some extent transcended, the possibilities of achievement remain small. The opportunities for the satisfactory employment of an educated person under conditions of colonial rule were meager as long as the most authoritative positions in the civil service and in commerce were reserved to foreigners. They remain small under conditions of sovereignty as long as the economy is back-ward and posts integral to the modern part of the economy are rela-tively few, and as long as opportunities for specifically intellectual employment or the sale of the products of creative intellectual work are restricted.

The educated person acquires some degree of emancipation from the predominantly primordial tradition of status-determination. The content of this modern education, and its dissolution of the hold of traditional cultural standards and the traditional patterns of life, arouse in him the need to determine his status and his self-esteem by his own achievements. Where can such a person make his mark in a society which gives him little room to do so?

The political movement with its demands and challenges is almost the only arena open to him. A political movement, unlike a business firm or a university or a government department, can absorb as many people as apply to it. It can give him tasks to perform and it can thereby offer him the possibility of seeing the effects of his actions. By shooting, demonstrating, marching, agitating, threatening and bullying, fighting, destroying, obstructing, helping to organize, running errands, distributing handbills and canvassing, he can see some effects and can believe in the importance of his deeds in thwarting or coercing a distant impersonal bureaucratic authority, or in serving the will of the new charismatic authority to which he gives himself.

Especially during the period of late adolescence and youth, when the impulses of self-assertion and the striving for individuality and creativity are at their height, and before the traditional system of status has reasserted its empire over him, politics seem to be the only field in which he can act with some expectation of satisfying effectiveness.

Once independence has been attained, the need for effectiveness and achievement does not die away. Politics remain a major alternative to apathetic idiocy or regression into the acceptance of the traditional pattern of life. Politics will in fact remain a major alternative open to the intellectuals for achievement and for absorption into a wider, no longer primordial collectivity as long as the underdeveloped societies remain underdeveloped. Only when they have become more differentiated occupationally, and when they have developed a sufficiently large and self-esteeming corps of professional intellectuals, carrying on the specifically intellectual professions with their own corporate traditions and corporate forms of organization, will the passionate sentiment and energy flow into channels other than the political.

Nationalism. The nationalism of the intellectuals usually made its first appearance alone, free from the complications of socialist and populist ideas. Only in those underdeveloped countries where the nationalist movement has come more lately on the scene has it been involved in other ideological currents which are not necessarily integral to it.

The nationalism of the intellectuals of the underdeveloped countries emerged at a time when there was little sense of nationality among the peoples whose nationality the intellectuals were proclaiming. Its first impetus seems to have come from a deepening of the feeling of distance between ruler and ruled, arising from the spatial and ethnic remoteness of the foreign rulers, and the dissolution of the particularistic tie which holds ethnically homogeneous rulers and ruled together. The identification of oneself as a subject of an unloved (however feared and respected) ruler with others who shared that subjection was one phase of the process. The discovery of the glories of the past, of cultural traditions, was usually but not always an action, *ex post facto*, which legitimated the claims asserted on behalf of that newly imagined collectivity.[10]

The assimilation of modern culture, which, historically, was a foreign culture, was an essential element in this process. The first generation of constitutional politicians in most underdeveloped countries were relatively highly "Westernized." The usual antagonism toward the older generation made the next, younger generation more antagonistic toward Western culture, and encouraged their rudimentary attachment to the indigenous traditional culture to come forward a little more in their minds. This provided a matrix for the idea of a deeper national culture and, therewith, of the nation which had only to be aroused to self-awareness. It was neither a simple attachment to their indigenous culture nor a concretely experienced love of their fellow-countrymen which made the intellectuals so fervently nationalistic. These would have presupposed a prior sense of affinity, which for many reasons was lacking and often still is. In fact, however, "fellow-countrymen" became so to the modern intellectuals primarily by virtue of their common differentiation from the foreign ruler. Fierce resentment against the powerful, fear-inspiring foreign ruler was probably a much more significant factor than either a sense of affinity or a conscious appreciation of the traditional culture.

The resentment of the modern intellectual grew from several seeds: one of the most important was the derogation implied in the barrier against entry into or advancement in the civil service. The other, closely related to this, was the feeling of injury from insults, experienced or heard about, explicit or implicit, which the foreign rulers and

[10] The stirrings of religious reform and the effort to rehabilitate the dignity of the traditional religious culture became political only when there was an alliance of religious leaders with a politicized modern intelligentsia.

their businessmen fellow-nationals inflicted on the indigenous modern intellectuals. Lord Curzon's derogatory remarks about the educated Bengali in his famous Calcutta University Convocation Address were only among the more egregious of an infinite multitude of such slights, injuries, and denigrations. The belittlement extended into every sphere of life, cultural, intellectual, religious, economic, political, and personal. A sense of distress and of anticipated insult became part of the indigenous intellectuals' relationship with foreigners for a long time. Even now in independence, the alertness to insult and the readiness to perceive it persist. They were at their height in the early period of nationalism.

The situation was rendered all the more insufferable by the genuine and positive appreciation which the native intellectuals often felt for the foreign culture, and their feeling of inferiority of their own in comparison with it. Nationalism of an extremely assertive sort was an effort to find self-respect, and to overcome the inferiority of the self in the face of the superiority of the culture and power of the foreign metropolis.

It was therefore logical that prior to independence the politics of the intellectuals, once the movement for constitutional reform had waned, should have been concerned with one end above all others: national independence. It was generally assumed by most politicized intellectuals that any other desiderata would be automatically realized with the attainment of that condition. The actual attainment of independence and of a condition in which the tasks of political life have become as demanding and as diversified as they must inevitably become in a polity where the state takes unto itself so many powers and aspires to so much, has not greatly altered the situation. Nationalism still remains one of the greatest of all motive forces; [11] it underlies many policies to which it is not really germane and serves as a touchstone of nearly every action and policy.

The socialistic and the populistic elements in the politics of the intellectuals of underdeveloped countries are secondary to and derivative from their nationalistic preoccupations and aspirations. Economic policies have their legitimation in their capacity to raise the country on the scale of the nations of the world. The populace is transfigured in order to demonstrate the uniqueness of its "collective personality." The ancient culture is exhumed and renewed in order to demonstrate, especially to those who once denied it, the high value of

[11] Although it is by no means the chief reason, this nationalistic concentration is a significant factor in accounting for the poverty and uniformity of intellectual life of the underdeveloped countries.

the nation. Foreign policy is primarily a policy of "public relations" designed not, as in the advanced countries, to sustain the security of the state or enhance its power among other states, but to improve the reputation of the nation, to make others heed its voice, to make them pay attention to it and to respect it. The "world," the "imperialist world," remains very much on the minds of the intellectuals of the new states. It remains the audience and the jury of the accomplishments of the nation which the intellectuals have done so much to create.

Nonetheless, despite the pre-eminence of the nationalistic sensibility, it does not rest upon a *tabula rasa*, cleared of all other attachments. The intellectuals of underdeveloped countries are not as "uprooted," as "detribalized," as they themselves sometimes assert with so much melancholy, or as, with more spite, their foreign and domestic detractors often allege. They have remained attached in many ways to their traditional patterns of social life and culture. These deeper attachments include parochial attachments to their own tribes and ethnic and caste communities, and almost inevitably seek expression in public policies and in domestic political alignments. The presence of these attachments is a supplementary generator of nationalistic sentiment. It is against them, and in an effort to overcome them—within themselves and in their fellow-countrymen—that many intellectuals in underdeveloped countries commit themselves so fervently to intense nationalism.

By a similar process, the extensive use of a foreign language in daily intellectual life also feeds the force of nationalism. The intellectuals' very large amount of reading in French and English and their feeling of continued dependence on these cultures, their continuing and still necessary employment of French or English for their own cultural creations and even for political, administrative, and judicial purposes, and their awareness of the slow and painful course through which their nation must pass before its own language becomes adequate to the requirements of modern life cannot avoid touching their sensibilities. The constant reaffirmation of their nationalistic attachment is an effort to assuage this wound.

Socialism. The socialism of the intellectuals of the underdeveloped countries grows, fundamentally, from their feeling for charismatic authority, from their common humanity, and from the anti-chrematistic traditions of their indigenous culture. More immediately, it is a product of the conditions and substance of their education, and of their nationalistic sensibility.

The intellectuals of underdeveloped countries are, in general, devotees of authority, even though they may be inflamed against some particular authority. They regard the existing distribution of authority as the source of present economic and social inequities and they seek a new distribution of authority as the instrument to abolish them. Their critical view of the state as it exists at present in their own country is partly a manifestation of their distrust of impersonal authority and of their faith in a more charismatic alternative.[12] They do not believe in the capacities of businessmen to increase the well-being of the nation. They have little sympathy, conscious or unconscious, with the man who is engaged in the pursuit of wealth.

None of the great traditional cultures gives a high rank to the merchant; even when they revolt against the traditional culture, or slip away from it unwittingly, the intellectuals usually retain that part of it which allots no high place to the businessman. In their mind, the life of the businessman is unheroic; it is untouched by sacredness and they will have none of it. Intellectuals very seldom seek careers in private business; when necessity forces them into it, they are ill at ease and restless. The intellectual who works for a private business firm lays himself open to the charge of having deserted his calling, even though he has deserted it no more than a civil servant or a lawyer. The notion of an economic system ruled by the decisions of businessmen, out to make a profit for themselves, is repugnant to the intellectuals of underdeveloped countries—even more than it is in advanced countries, where the businessman does not fare very well either at the hands of the intellectuals.

As long as the intellectuals of underdeveloped countries pursued the paths of constitutional reform and confined their attention to administration and representation, these deeper dispositions whose source was the traditional indigenous culture did not enter into their politics. They accepted most of the existing regime. When, however, they began to direct their attention to the society and the nation, when they ceased being politically "superficial" and began to touch on politically "sacred" things, the socialist potentiality of their fundamental orientation became more manifest.

These inner developments within the intelligentsia of underdeveloped countries coincided with the upsurge of socialist thought among the European intellectuals. To these, the intelligentsia of the underdeveloped countries felt drawn. The attractive power of the metropolis was enhanced by the congeniality of intellectual socialism. From the 1920's to the 1940's, the example of the late Professor Harold Laski elicited and fortified the socialistic disposition of many young in-

---

[12] *Vide* the Gandhian socialists and the Bhoodan movement in India.

tellectuals of the English-speaking underdeveloped countries; Jean-Paul Sartre has played a parallel role among the French-speaking intellectuals from 1945 onward.

The spread of socialistic ideas was aided by the large-scale migration of Asian and African intellectuals to Europe for further study and professional training. The great stream of Asians to European educational centers began in the 1890's; their intensive politicization, in the 1920's. The stream of the African students began in the 1920's and became much wider after 1945. From the end of the First World War and the Russian Revolution, the young Asians and Africans, impelled by events in the world and at home, found themselves in an atmosphere which gave the encouragement of a nearly universal assent to their socialist aspirations.

The association between socialism as a domestic policy and hostility toward an imperialistic foreign policy—a connection which is inherent in the postulates of socialist thought and its Leninist variant, although not all socialists have at all times shared it—made European, and especially British and French, socialism even more acceptable to the Asian and African students who came to the intellectual capitals of the European metropolis.

To these factors which made socialism appear such a bright ideal should be joined the nature of large-scale business enterprise in their own countries. In practically all instances, large-scale business enterprise in the underdeveloped countries was owned and controlled by foreign capitalists. Not just the Europeans, and latterly the Americans, owned large firms in Africa and Asia, but Chinese, Syrians, Lebanese, Parsees, Armenians, Greeks, and Italians, away from their own countries, showed exceptional enterprise. Encountering few indigenous competitors, they built up extensive organizations and ample fortunes in underdeveloped countries. The ethnic diversity and separateness of the peoples, even within large, centrally governed countries, often brought about a situation in which private businessmen who were of the same "nationality" as those in the midst of whom they lived and conducted their affairs, but who were of a different "community," were regarded as outsiders who had no moral claims on the loyalty of the intellectuals. Businessmen, by the nature of their calling, could never be part of the "people"; their ethnic distinctness was a further justification for treating them as alien to the "people."

On the other side, a socialistic economic system conducted in accordance with principles which are of intellectual origin, guided by persons who are imbued with these "principles," seems to be the only conceivable alternative to a privately operated economy. The intellectuals who dare to differ from such obvious conclusions constitute a small fraction of the intellectual classes in most of the underdeveloped countries, both colonial and sovereign.

The socialism of the intellectuals of underdeveloped countries, it should also be stressed, is a product of their pained awareness of the poverty of their own countries. The heightening of national sensibility led perforce to the discovery of the "people." Agitational activities brought them into contact with the "people"; the vague doctrine of nationalism, even in its liberal form, brought the idea of the "people" into the consciousness of the intellectuals. Often, too, on return from a period of foreign study where they had encountered socialist ideas and experienced a heightened national consciousness, the sight of their impoverished fellow-countrymen had a traumatic force. Confrontation with the poverty of their country evoked anguish and desperation in many intellectuals. They have been humiliated by their sense of the backwardness of their country. They have learned how gradually the advancement of the Western countries has moved, and they have heard of the speedy progress of the Soviet Union from a backward country to the status of one of the most powerful industrial nations in the world. What could be more harmonious with their present perceptions, their aspirations, and their background than to espouse a socialist solution to their unhappy problem? And if to this is added the fact that their countries have been held in subjection by capitalistic countries and the socialist countries proclaim their hostility to imperialism, the disposition toward socialism receives another impulsion.

Populism. The populism of intellectual politics in underdeveloped countries has a familial affinity to the populism of the intellectuals of more advanced countries during the past century and a half. It is a part of a universal process consequent on the emergence of an incipient and fragmentary world-wide intellectual community. It is a phenomenon of the tension between metropolis and province which arises from the trend toward that world-wide intellectual community.

The populism of the intellectuals is German in origin. It was a critique of the pretensions of a worldly, urban, and urbane authority. It was a critique of the feebleness of the petty elites of the system of *Kleinstaaterei*, alongside the grandeur of the Holy Roman Empire, and of the Germany which could emerge if the regime of the princelings could be abolished and all of Germany unified. It was a critique of the central institutional system, and particularly of the claims of the state, of the universities, and of the ecclesiastical authorities to embody what was essential in their society and of their insistence, on that basis, on their right to rule over it. It was a rejection of the urban bourgeoisie. It was a denial that the "nation" could be found in existing authoritative institutions and an assertion that the root of the future lay in the "folk."

In Russia, populism was a product of a similar situation, aggravated by resentment against a prevailing enchantment by the West, which was more pronounced than the Francophilia of the princely courts against which the first generations of romantic German populism had been a reaction. In Russia, the intellectuals had carried on a passionate love affair with Western Europe and many had been disappointed and had even come to feel guilty for deserting their "own" for foreign idols. Alienated from their own authorities of state, church, and university, hostile to their own mercantile bourgeoisie, disillusioned with Western European socialism after its failures in the revolutions of 1848, it had nowhere to turn except to the "people," whom it glorified as a repository of wisdom and as the source of Russia's salvation.

American populism was not very different in its general origins. It, too, was the product of a reaction against the Anglophile intellectual elite of the Eastern seaboard and the political and industrial elites who ruled the country from the Eastern cities. In America, too, therefore, it was an effort to find a firm foundation for intellectuals who were alienated from the authorities of their society and from their xenophilic fellow-intellectuals. In America also it was a phase of the struggle of province against metropolis.

In the underdeveloped countries, the process has been essentially the same. Alienated from the indigenous authorities of their own traditional society—chiefs, sultans, princes, landlords, and priests—and from the rulers of their modern society—the foreign rulers and the "Westernized" constitutional politicians (and since independence, politicians of the governing party)—the intellectuals have had only the "people," the "African personality," the "Indian peasant," etc., as supports in the search for the salvation of their own souls and their own society.

The "people" are a model and a standard; contact with them is a good. Esteem and disesteem are meted out on the basis of "closeness to the people" or distance from them. It is a common worry of and an accusation against the intellectuals of the underdeveloped countries that they are "out of touch with the people," uprooted, déraciné, "brown" or "black" (as the case may be) "Englishmen" or "Frenchmen," etc. Many make the accusation against themselves, most make it against their fellow-intellectuals.

Factually it is usually quite untruthful. Most intellectuals in underdeveloped countries are not as "cut off" from their own culture as they and their detractors suggest. They live in the middle of it, their wives and mothers are its constant representatives in their midst, they retain close contact with their families, which are normally steeped in traditional beliefs and practices. The possession of a modern intellectual culture does remove them, to some extent, from the culture of their ancestors, but much of the latter remains and lives on in them.[13]

The experience to which the allegation of being "cut off" from the "people" refers is not to any serious extent a real result of the intellectuals' acceptance of the "foreign," modern culture. It rests rather on their own feeling of distance from the rest of their fellow-nationals, which is a product of the ethnic, tribal, kinship, and caste particularism of these underdeveloped societies and of the consequent lack of a true sense of civil affinity with the rest of their fellow-countrymen. It is the resultant of the superimposition of a nationalistic ideology, which demands fellow-feeling, on a narrower particularism, inharmonious with it and psychologically contradictory to it. There is a genuine feeling of strain; all the burden of this strain is put upon the fact that they possess some elements of an exogenous culture.

The frequent reiteration of the charge testifies to an awareness of this tension, and the choice of the foreign culture as its focus is a manifestation of a desire to find a way out which will conform to the requirements of ideological nationalism. Because the intellectuals assert it and, to some extent, believe it, they often try to make amends for it by some form of nativism, which extols the traditional ways of the people and juxtaposes them with modern and thus "foreign" ways.

This nativistic reaction accentuates demagogic political tendencies, and fosters a race among contenders for the distinction of being more "for" the "people" or more "akin" to them. It accentuates prejudice against the educated and a hostility against the modern education which the intellectuals of the new states need if they are to perform intellectual functions in a productive way, and without which they would not be intellectuals and their countries would flounder and sink.

Nonetheless, despite this preoccupation with the "people," the populism of the intellectuals of underdeveloped countries does not necessarily bring with it either intimacy with the ordinary people, a concrete attachment to them, or even a democratic attitude. It is compatible with them but it does not require them. It is equally compatible with a

[13] Much of the intellectuals' self-accusation rests on the populistic assumption that the "people," not being distracted or corrupted by modern culture, are the bearers of the traditional culture in its fullness and its glory. This assumption is probably an error; the "people" are quite unlikely to be in more than fragmentary possession of the corpus of traditional culture.

dictatorial regime which treats the people as instruments to be employed in the transformation of the social and economic order, and their culture and outlook as a hindrance to progress.

Populism can be the legitimating principle of oligarchical regimes, as well as of democratic regimes and of all the intermediate types. The "people" constitute the prospective good to be served by government policy, and they serve as the emblem of the traditional culture which is thus glorified even while it is being eroded and its traditional custodians disregarded or disparaged.

Oppositionalism. The populism of the intellectual is a product of opposition to the authorities who rule at home and to the foreign culture which fascinates him and his fellow-intellectuals in his own country. It is one facet of an oppositional syndrome.

The origins of this inclination to oppose constituted authority seem, at first glance, easy to locate. Practically all politics in the colonial period, once the constitutional phase had passed, consisted and still consist of root and branch opposition. Whether they took the form of conspiracy, sabotage, riots, assassination, clandestine or open journalism, public meetings, boycotts, demonstrations and processions, civil disobedience or unco-operative participation in representative institutions, opposition and obstruction of the foreign ruler were the main aims. Where it was impossible to share in the responsible exercise of authority, opposition was in fact the only alternative.

The degree of alienation from the constituted authority varied but it was almost always deeper and more drastic than the opposition which exists in advanced pluralistic societies.[14] It was the opposition of politicians excluded or withdrawn from the constitutional order, who accepted neither the rules nor the ends of the prevailing system. It was, therefore, the opposition of politicians who refused in principle to consider the problems of the government as real tasks needing resolution. It was an opposition which was convinced by situation, temperament, and principle that it would never share authority with the foreign ruler. The only authority to which it aspired was complete and exclusive control of the entire machinery of state. Until that point was reached, its only policy was opposition.

The oppositional attitude of the intellectuals has another point of origin far removed from the political experience of a colonial situation.

[14] Its only parallel in the West is the conduct of the Irish members in the House of Commons in the latter part of the last century and of Communistic members of European parliaments when they were a small minority and did not seek a popular front. The "Irish members" had considerable resonance in India and their influence still survives, even where its origin has been forgotten.

In most underdeveloped countries the traditional character of the culture sustains diffuseness in the exercise of authority. Diffuse authority, omnicompetent in the tasks facing the society, at least according to legendary beliefs, derives its legitimacy in part from its comprehensive effectiveness. Even though the substantive actions performed by such diffuse traditional authorities are no longer respected by intellectuals, the older pattern of expectation persists. Specific, delimited, impersonal, constitutional authority gives the appearance of being a weak authority, an unloving one which possesses no inner relationship with the ruled. The diffuseness of a charismatic authority is desired, and the bureaucratic rule of the foreign power or of its sovereign indigenous successor arouses little enthusiasm or even willing acknowledgment of any deeper legitimacy. The intellectuals of underdeveloped countries, despite their immersion in modern culture and their overt acceptance of modern political principles, are at bottom averse to a relatively weak, self-limiting government, even when that government is their own, bound to them by common ethnic ties, a common culture, and comradeship in the struggle for independence.

This is one of the underlying grounds for the widespread disillusionment which overcomes so many intellectuals in underdeveloped countries after independence. It must be remembered that, whatever has happened since, practically every new state of the postwar world began as a modern constitutional regime of representative institutions and public liberties. They have all had to employ modern bureaucratic methods of administration, even when they lacked the requisite personnel. They have tried to operate the rule of law. They all began as remote impersonal machines, exercising authority without the diffuseness of charisma or tradition. Their equilibrium has depended on a great charismatic personality who, at the peak of the governmental mountain, offset the distaste for bureaucratic-legal rule.

Thus, the establishment of a tradition of opposition in political life has, as has happened so often in almost every sphere of life in underdeveloped countries, coincided with a fundamental disposition resting on an indigenous cultural tradition.

It would be wrong perhaps to claim a universal validity for a generalization which could be drawn from Max Weber's criticism of Bismarck and the paralyzing influence which his autocracy in the Reichstag exerted on the opposition parties of that body. It was Max Weber's view that the irresponsible opposition which the Bismarckian regime and its Wilhelmine successor evoked would make the opposition parties incapable of responsible, efficient rule when they were given the opportunity to govern. He also asserted—and this is more important for our present discussion—that they would become incapable of conducting themselves as a responsible opposition, working within the rules of the parliamentary game. In certain of the underdeveloped countries, this generalization does not seem to be applicable. In India, for example, certain of the intellectual politicians, and above all the Prime Minister, have shown great adaptability in turning from a condition of complete and irreconcilable opposition to a responsible hard-headed exercise of authority, and some of the socialists and independents conduct their opposition in a most intelligent and responsible manner. The same obtains in varying degrees in Ghana and in Tunisia. Certain intellectual politicians have shown considerable capacity to rule, even though they have not been as democratic or liberal as they once aspired to be or as Mr. Nehru has succeeded in being. Not a few firebrands of the days of the independence movement have turned out to be responsible parliamentarians of the highest order.

Nonetheless, much truth remains in Max Weber's proposition. The intellectuals of the underdeveloped countries since they acquired independence, insofar as they are not in authority, do incline toward an anti-political, oppositional attitude. They are disgruntled. The form of the constitution does not please them and they are reluctant to play the constitutional game. Many of them desire to obstruct the government or give up the game of politics altogether, retiring into a negative state of mind about all institutional politics or at least about any political regime which does not promise a "clean sweep" of the inherited order.

Incivility. Although the intellectuals of the underdeveloped countries have created the idea of the nation within their own countries, they have not been able to create a nation. They are themselves the victim of that condition, since nationalism does not necessarily become citizenship. Membership in a nation which is sovereign entails a sense of affinity with the other human beings who make up the nation. It entails a sense of "partness" in a whole, a sense of sharing a common substance. This feeling of being part of the whole is the basis of a sense of concern for its well-being, and a sense of responsibility to it and for it. It transcends ineluctable divisions, softening them and rendering them tolerable to civil order, regarding them as less significant than the underlying community of those who form the nation. In political life, these dispositions form the virtue of civility.

Civility has hitherto not been one of the major features of the politicized intelligentsia of the underdeveloped countries. An intense politicization is difficult to bring into harmony with civility. Intense politicization is accompanied by the conviction that only those who share one's principles and positions are wholly legitimate members of the polity and that those who do not share them are separated by a steep barrier. The governing party in many sovereign underdeveloped states, and those intellectuals who make it up or are associated with it, tend to believe that those who are in opposition are separated from them by fundamental and irreconcilable differences. They feel that they *are* the state and the nation, and that those who do not go along with them are not just political rivals but *total* enemies. The sentiments of the opposition are, *mutatis mutandis*, scarcely different. These are the fruits of intense politicization.

The incivility of the politicized intellectuals has a history which precedes their birth. Traditional societies, based on kinship and hierarchy, are not civil societies. They do now know the phenomenon of citizenship, since rights and obligations are not functions of membership in a polity determined by territorial boundaries. The primordial qualities of traditional societies—kinship, age, sex, locality, etc.—are not qualities which define the citizen. In a pluralistic society they are not by any means incompatible with citizenship. In the more unitary, traditional society, they suffocate incipient civility.

The moral structure of the independence movement has enabled this uncivil tradition to persist. The independence movement conceived of itself as the embodiment of the nation, and after its victory it became and conceived of itself as identical with the state. Given the oppositional dispositions which come to the surface in parliamentary and journalistic circles not attached to the government party, there often appears to be a semblance of justification for the belief of an impatient and hypersensitive government that the opposition is subversive of the state and cannot be reconciled to it.

This does not imply that there are not civil intellectuals in every underdeveloped country, some of them in the government, some of them in opposition, and some in journalism, the universities, and the other liberal professions. They are, however, in a marked minority. The traditions by which they are sustained, although they do exist in some of the states, are frail.

IV. THREE STAGES IN THE POLITICS
OF THE INTELLECTUALS
IN UNDERDEVELOPED COUNTRIES

The first stage—(a) *Constitutional liberalism.* The first efflorescence of the modern intellectual in the underdeveloped countries occurred roughly between the years when India was recovering from the trauma of the Mutiny and its repression and the First World War. In the few countries where there was anything of a class with a modern education and a certain amount of political stirring, these were the years of constitutional liberalism, eloquently and courteously argued. This first stage came considerably later to Black Africa and lasted a shorter time than it did in British India and the Middle East. In Southeast Asia, too, the course of development was greatly telescoped. The backwardness of Southeast Asia and Black Africa in the construction of modern cultural and legal institutions, and the smaller numbers of persons who went abroad for higher studies, resulted in a much smaller intellectual class than in India, and a later, briefer, and feebler life of constitutional liberalism. Where the intellectual class scarcely existed, politics could only be embryonic.

This was the stage of the politics of lawyers and journalists. Their politics were the politics of *honoratiores*. They were well-educated men, many of whom had studied in the metropolitan countries; they had absorbed and appreciated something of the metropolitan culture and the liberal constitutional political outlook, which, in the circles in which they moved in the France and Great Britain of that period, appeared to be almost unchallenged.

They were not revolutionaries and they did not always aspire to independence, at least, not in the immediate future. One of their main grievances in this earliest phase was the restriction of the right of entry of their fellow-countrymen into the civil service which ruled their country on behalf of the foreign sovereign. They also desired that legislative institutions should be a little more representative of persons like themselves. These two concerns could be interpreted crudely as a manifestation of a narrow class interest, but they were actually broader and better than that.[15] There were serious grounds, in their own self-image, for their claim to share in the administration of the country and for a vote in the determination of the budget.

[15] Nor were these their only interests. They proposed the liberalization of the legal system, greater equity in its administration, and certain liberal social reforms such as the improvement of the legal position of women, the provision of more ample educational facilities, etc.

Obviously, there was some element of "class" and "self-interest" in some of their demands, such as the insistence that imported foreign manufacturers should not be allowed to enjoy any advantages over indigenously produced industrial goods. The interest of the whole society, the interest of a class and of an individual might all coincide on particular issues. This is probably the most that can be credited to the charge against the first generation made by the actors who came on the political stage a little later.

They had been brought up in a hierarchical tradition in which the landowning classes and the learned, in their own view and that of others, were the possessors of a "stake in the country." Insofar as it was a country, they felt it to be "theirs," and "theirs" almost exclusively. Many came from families which had in the past exercised great influence and which, in the countryside, still continued to do so. It was therefore part of their conception of the right order of things that they should share in the ruling of their own country, under a sovereign whom they were not in the main inclined to challenge in principle.

The liberal constitutional ideas which they acquired in the course of their mainly legal studies fitted in with their conceptions. Europe was boiling with democratic agitation—the labor and socialist movements were in process of formation. In the main, however, the very small trickle of Africans and the larger numbers of Asians who before the First World War went to the metropolis for advanced studies did not, on the whole, come into contact with these circles. They wanted a liberal governmental and legal order in the administration of which they could share.

Since they were largely lawyers, they developed the rhetorical skills and the self-confidence in dealing with authority which are an indispensible part of the equipment of the modern politician.[16] The structure of legal practice also gave them the time and the resources to absent themselves from their professional activities. As the occasion demanded, they were able, while still continuing to practice their professions, to devote themselves to public agitation, to attend and address meetings, to write books, pamphlets, and articles for the press, to meet representatives of their rulers from time to time in order to argue their claims, and to participate in consultative and representative bodies.

Side by side with this form of lawyers' politics, a daily and periodical press struggled to come into existence, largely in the metropolitan language but also in the indigenous languages. The journalists were not professionals. They were often political lawyers who had either left their profession or practiced it alongside of journalism; there were also among them men who had been teachers, or who had aspired to join the government service, or had actually been in governmental employ. They were usually well-educated men, with the gravity of the Victorian and Continental bourgeois liberals whom they admired. All this gave dignity and decorum to the political life of that stage of political development.

[16] It seems to me not accidental that even now the highest flights of Indo-Anglican prose have the rhetorical quality of high-grade lawyers addressing a court or a parliamentary body.

As journalists, they were not following a career in the material sense of the word. They were not trying to become rich. They were not interested in being purveyors of news and diversion. They were not seeking a livelihood in journalism. Where they could not gain their livelihood from journalism or from their auxiliary professions, they unquestioningly relied on the support of their kinsmen and patrons. They were journalists because there was a small literate public which could be reached and rendered coherent and articulate on behalf of the ideal of constitutional government in which the best-qualified of the ruled would have some hand.

These journalists and lawyer-politicians had few followers other than themselves, i.e., like-minded men in similar stations of life, such as liberal businessmen or princes, chiefs, and landowners. Leaders and followers together constituted no more than a small group. Only in India were the absolute numbers fairly large. In the Middle East they were fewer, and in the rest of Africa and in Southeast Asia their numbers were negligible. Nonetheless they created, by their activity, the foundations of a still surviving tradition of the modern intellectuals in politics.

They did not have the field to themselves, even at the time of their greatest pre-eminence. They were being challenged by a more aggressive group, less complaisant toward their Western rulers and toward Western culture. These new rivals claimed that constitutional tactics led nowhere. They were the forerunners of the political type which came to the center of the political arena in the second stage. During the first stage, however, there was also another trend of intellectual activity which profoundly affected subsequent political developments, though it was not in itself primarily political or even political at all.

(b) *Moral renewal.* An impassioned effort of religious and moral self-renewal accompanied the development of political life of the underdeveloped countries during their colonial period. It was at first a feature of the countries which possessed conspicuous evidence of great indigenous achievements in the past—i.e., of the countries with a literary and architectural inheritance which in the midst of present degradation could remind contemporaries that their country had once been great. It was therefore also a characteristic of countries with an indigenous traditional intelligentsia made up of the custodians of sacred writings. Thus it was that in India and in the Middle East, through much of the nineteenth century, protagonists of the traditional cultures, and particularly of the religions of Hinduism and Islam, sought to purify their inheritance, to restore it to its pristine greatness or to fuse it with modern elements. Both in India and in the Middle

East, the aim was to reinstate the dignity of the traditional religious culture, and the society which was based on it, and thereby to establish its worth in the face of the encroachment of Western culture and religion.[17]

This movement to evoke a national self-consciousness, through the renewal of cultural traditions which had been allowed to decay, was not directly political. There was not much contact between the modern men who represented constitutional liberalism, and the energetic, pious traditionalists.[18] The two movements seemed to run almost independently of each other; there was no antagonism between them, often little mutual awareness.

The agents of moral renewal were not secular social reformers. They were not modern intellectuals in the sense of the word used here. They were men of the traditional culture who were sufficiently sensitive to the impact of modern culture to feel the need to reaffirm their own.[19] Their task was the cleansing of the cultural—and this meant largely religious—inheritance of their society from what they claimed were historically accidental accretions which had brought it into disrepute among modern men and allowed their country to sink in the world's esteem and in its own and, particularly, to appear enfeebled and unworthy in comparison with Western achievements. They claimed that what was essential in their religious traditions could—by restoration and cleansing or by syncretism—be reformulated in an idiom more appropriate to the modern situation, and that if this were done, it would recommend itself to their fellow-countrymen who were needlessly and even perniciously enamored of Western culture. They were not unqualifiedly fanatical enemies of Western culture. They claimed that much of what it had to offer—particularly science, technology, and forms of organization—were necessary for the improvement of their countries and the re-establishment of their greatness among the nations. They insisted, however, that their countrymen must not lose their own souls to the West. They must instead rediscover their own essential being by the acceptance of a new and purer version of their own cultural tradition.

The older generation of modern "Victorian" intellectuals did not

[17] Movements to "re-establish" the glory of African civilization are a much later product.

[18] There were of course exceptions like al-Afghani, Mohammed Abdou, and M. G. Ranade.

[19] Their influence made itself felt, however, in both India and the Middle East, primarily among modern intellectuals. They exerted little effect on their fellow traditional intellectuals, who persisted in their torpor.

pay much heed to these preachments, although they were not hostile. In the next stage of political development, this effort of moral redis- covery and self-renewal had very profound repercussions. When, in the second stage, constitutional liberalism seemed to disappear or to be confined in a very narrow space, the movement of moral and religious reform was taken up and developed into a passionate nationalism. Now, even where the religious element in the traditional culture is passed over, praise of the essence of the traditional culture has be- come a plank in the platform of every movement for independence and of every new state.

The second stage. From constitutional liberalism and religious-moral renewal, the intellectuals of the colonial countries passed to a fervently politicized nationalism. With this shift, there also occurred a shift in the mode of political action and its audience.

India was the first of all the underdeveloped colonial countries to execute this movement; it was the one in which the traditional in- digenous culture was richest and most elaborate and in which that culture had developed most systematically and comprehensively. It was also the country where the foreign rulers had been longest es- tablished in a thoroughgoing way and where the contact of the in- digenous intellectuals with a metropolitan Western culture had given birth to a longer and richer modern tradition than was possessed by any other country of Asia or Africa. It was the country with the largest and most differentiated modern intelligentsia. The first long phase of fascination with the West had already begun, in the India of the 1880's, to produce from within itself a reaction in favor of more purely Indian things.

This was also the time of growing strength in the socialist move- ment in Europe and of the growth of anarchism. Terrorism was in the ascendancy in Russia and Ireland. Tales of the Russian underground spread in Asia, together with the repute and glory of the deeds of the "Nihilists" in Russia, the Sinn Fein in Ireland, and the Carbonari in Italy. Mazzini, Stepnyak, and Kropotkin were names well known among the younger generation of Indian intellectuals. Yeats was be- coming a figure of weight among the literary intelligentsia and along with this went a feeling for the Irish Renaissance and a belief in the possibilities of a comparable Indian Renaissance. The writings of these *rishis* became known in India, imported from England; some of them appeared in Bengali translations.

The new generation which came to the surface of public life around the turn of the century was no longer content with constitutional agitation, or with such limited goals as more places in the Indian Civil

Service and more consultative and deliberative institutions in which
Indians would be amply represented. Indian traditional culture was
being revived through the Ramakrishna Mission and the Arya Samaj,
and a new Indian self-consciousness took hold of young men who,
while not deeming themselves religious, were possessed by a profound
resonance toward traditional Indian symbols. The Maharashtrian and
Bengali terrorists gave no thought to the kind of social or political
order which they wished to see established. They wished only to have
India free of foreign rule, free to be itself, in its own Indian way.

Parallel developments a third of a century later could be seen in
areas as far apart as the Gold Coast and Egypt. A half-century later,
they began to appear in East Africa. The same pattern was visible in
more foreshortened form in Syria and Iraq. The proportions and the
tone of the movements in these smaller countries, with much smaller
intelligentsias, have been roughly what they were in India.

In these smaller countries, too, there was a tendency to regard the
older generation of liberal constitutionalists and piecemeal reformers
as excessively subservient to the foreign rulers and as excessively be-
mused by their foreign culture and their foreign forms of government.
The later, populistic phase of intellectual politics, which in a variety
of forms continues into the present, only intensified and made more
complex and luminous an already established pattern. The generally
socialistic orientation of the politics of the Asian and African intellectuals, which took form after the First World War and became preponderant after the Second World War, in a similar fashion only
elaborated the inherent potentiality of intense nationalism.

The intensification of political concerns was the outgrowth of the
earlier political interest, in fusion with the more acute sense of nationality which the heightened awareness of the traditional indigenous
culture had helped to arouse. The politics of the "second generation"
touched a very much deeper chord than that which the earlier generation had reached; it is a chord which still vibrates. The greater depth
of the new political movement meant also that it was more passionate,
more in the complete possession of politics. The fundamental politicization of the intelligentsia of Asia and Africa led to the discrediting of
the first liberal generation. The politics of cultured and urbane gentle-
men, speaking French or English to perfection, interested in much else
besides politics, was not for this generation.

The politics of the second generation received a further powerful
impetus from its participation in a cosmopolitan movement, in which
foreign, Western countries were involved. The intellectuals of the
second generation, like those who preceded and those who have fol-

lowed, were also held by their attachment to Western culture. The extremist nationalist movements in Asia and subsequently in Africa had a Western legitimation for their strivings. They drew inspiration and comfort from abroad, they felt that their actions were one with a mighty surge all over the world, a surge toward a new order of freedom, with possibilities unknown and unregarded.[20] This sense of being a part of the larger world infused into the politics of the second generation the permanently bedeviling tension between province and metropolis, and added, as it always does, the heat which arises from conflicting loyalties.

When the second generation was still in its youth in India, and only in conception in other Asian and African colonial countries, the Russian Revolution took place. Only a little while thereafter M. K. Gandhi established his ascendancy over the political scene in India.[21] These two events precipitated the populistic consciousness, which had been only latent in the exacerbated nationalism which had preceded them.

The early leaders of the second generation had been deferential to "ancient traditions," in contrast to the liberal, moderate, and progressive attitude of the earlier constitutional politicians, who had not given political significance to indigenous cultural traditions. The "people" had, however, not yet acquired the eminence which was later to be their due in the political outlook of the intellectuals. Now, under the guidance of Gandhi and an attenuated Leninism, they ascended to a central position.

Socialism was no further away than a step of the imagination. The

[20] The role of exiles and expatriates living in the metropolitan centers of Great Britain, France, Germany, and Switzerland helped to maintain a continuous link between the revolutionary and radical tendencies in the metropolis and those in the underdeveloped countries. These exiles and expatriates provided a sort of training school for young Asians and Africans who had gone abroad to study, and they constituted a continuous representation of the interests of their countries before the public opinion of the ruling metropolis.

Like exiles and expatriates everywhere, they also were more "uprooted" than their countrymen who either stayed at home or returned home after a few years. This "uprootedness" did not, however, diminish the intensity of their politics. Rather, the contrary.

[21] And with it, he began his march toward ascendancy over the Western colonialist conscience. A skeptical attitude about the rightfulness of imperialism had already existed in the West for a long time, but it was Gandhi more than anyone else outside the European Socialist and the Communist movements who impressed it on the consciousness of the Western educated classes. As a result, a body of Western allies was formed and its existence was a reassurance and a stimulus to the politicized intellectuals who continued to stand in need of a sustaining tie with modern "Western" culture.

preceding generation had been neither socialist nor anti-socialist. The
issue had never arisen, as long as civil-service personnel policies, the
extension of representative institutions, and criticism of the "drain"
had been the main objects of political debate.[22] Politics now became
"total politics" and its claims on those who gave themselves to it became all-embracing. Politics in colonial countries became a vocation,
without becoming professionalized. Many came to live "for" politics,
but few lived "from" politics in the way in which professional politicians live from it. The politics of the colonial intelligentsia became in
a sense more profound; that is, they came into contact with the deeper
layers of the intelligentsia's existence. The politics of the intellectuals
became charismatic politics.

As one might expect from charismatic politics, a tremendous pull
was exerted on the youth. Leadership still lay with the lawyers and
a few who had once served the government as officials and clerks [23]
or had been tempted sufficiently to prepare themselves to do so. A large
and important part of the following, however, consisted of students—
college and university students in countries with colleges and universities and high school students where these were absent. A great deal of
the clamor and volatility of the politics of the second generation of the
intellectuals came from the students.

The third stage. The third stage of intellectual politics sees the
intellectuals in power in a sovereign state, ruled by an indigenous elite.

With this stage the intellectuals who have reaped the fruits of the
struggle become dissociated from the intellectual class. A schism occurs
in the corps of intellectual-politicians. One sector comes into power
and takes to it like a fish to water. The exercise of authority—which is
not identical with the efficient exercise of authority—seems to be almost as natural as breathing to those intellectuals who are in power.
To an increasing extent, they see themselves as different from the
intellectuals who do not share their power, and whom they chide as
naggers, unreasonable critics, backsliders from the great national cause.
The intellectuals in power feel themselves less continuous with the
intellectual class than they did during the struggle for independence.
As the burdens and challenges of office preoccupy them, and as they

---

[22] In Africa after the Second World War, nationalism, intense politics, socialism,
and populism came into life almost simultaneously, as if they were inseparably involved with each other.

[23] Where there were few indigenous lawyers or others with higher education,
leadership was exercised by clerks with secondary or elementary education. The
educated, the *évolues*—intellectuals—have kept the lead, the highly educated when
they have been available, the less well-educated where the former were lacking.

spend so much of their time with party bosses and machine-men who have never been or who long since ceased to be intellectuals, their own image of themselves as intellectuals wanes and they become more sensitive to the anti-political dispositions of their old companions.

This drift toward schism is aggravated by the fact that the opposition becomes the magnet which draws the intellectuals. Although within the political elite, at the peak of government there are many who were once intellectuals by education, vocation, or disposition and who have now become hardened politicians, no longer paying any attention to things of intellectual interest. Those who remain intellectuals in vocation and disposition seem to find their natural habitat on the opposite benches. There—and in common rooms and cafés—gather the intellectuals who in their outlook, in their studies and their self-identification, remain intellectuals.

The transformation of the intellectuals in power discloses the duality of the oppositional mentality. The hatred of authority is often no more than a facet of the fascination and love that it evokes. When they come to power, intellectuals who have hated it quickly allow the identification with it, against which they struggled previously, to come into full bloom. They attach to themselves the regalia of authority and feel that they and the state are now identical. Whereas during the struggle for independence, they felt that they represented the nation and that all who disagreed with them were outside the national community and had allowed their souls to be possessed by the foreigner, now when they are in power, they regard themselves and the state as identical and all those who disagree with them as enemies of the state.[24]

On the other side of the floor, where it is allowed to exist, the oppositional mentality retains all of its old forms. Bureaucratic administration is criticized as too remote and too impersonal. The government is charged with corruption; it is alleged to be "too distant" from the people, and to be the betrayer of the national idea. It is accused of damaging the reputation of the country in the world, or of turning the country over to a new form of foreign control.

The oppositional mentality of the third stage, however, possesses one feature which the second did not possess—i.e., disillusionment. Whereas the opposition of the second generation imagined an amorphously happy condition once their antagonists were removed, the oppositional

[24] Mr. Nehru is something of an exception, although he too regards the opposition as an unavoidable pestilence, as an inconvenient part of the community which remains, notwithstanding, as much a part of the community as he himself is. At the other extreme is that other intellectual in politics, Dr. Nkrumah, who regards any criticism or disagreement as *staatsfeindlich*.

mentality of the post-colonial period has no such utopian euphoria to assuage its present melancholy.

Oppositionalism, which was so involved in an intense politicization, tends among some of those who are out of power to shrivel into an anti-political passivity. It is not that politics no longer engages the attention. It still does, but among many intellectuals it has become a source of despondent inaction.

Among others, a quite substantial bloc, it flows into a more rigid form of activistic extremism. In some instances, this extremist alternative to passivity takes on a traditionalistic guise; in others, it assumes a Leninist visage. Both of these foster the intense and total rejection of the muddled, compromising, and often compromised, incumbent government, in the name of a higher ideal.

V. THE PROSPECTS OF THE INTELLECTUALS IN THE POLITICAL LIFE OF THE NEW STATES

Practically every new state has begun its career with a commitment to a regime of representative government and public liberties. Whatever might be the democratic and consultative elements in the indigenous tradition of government, the particular constitution which was actually chosen to give form to self-government is evidence of the role of intellectuals in the establishment of the new states. It was only through the influence of the intellectuals in contact with the modern political ideas which circulated in the larger world that this decision could have been made. This alone would be sufficient to testify to the still living inheritance of the notables who peopled the first stage of modern political life in the then colonial countries.

The fate of the new states, whether they persist and flourish as democracies, or whether they regress into more oligarchical forms of government, is as undeterminable as anything which lies in the future. As long, however, as they do not disintegrate into tribal and local territorial sovereignties, and as long as they at least aspire to be "modern," the intellectuals will go on playing a large role in the fulfillment of whatever possibilities fortune allots to their societies.

In most of the new states, the intellectuals still constitute a notable part of the ruling political elite, although their position is no longer as preponderant as when politics were a charismatic movement. Politics, as the new states were consolidated, became a profession and ceased to be a calling or a mission. The emerging professional politician, military or civilian in origin, is forced to be less of an intellectual in his outlook. The inevitability of the formation of a political machine has meant, and will continue even more to mean, that organizers with little intellectual disposition, interest, or sympathy will move into a more prominent position in the political elite. Back-benchers and party functionaries will include a very considerable proportion of place-holders, and the tasks they will have to perform will not be very attractive to intellectuals, living in the traditions of modern intellectuals.

Nonetheless, even on the government benches, if the regime continues to be more or less democratic there will remain some readiness of the professional party leaders to receive and sponsor intellectuals. The prestige of modern education will continue to be high and any political party and government will therefore wish to draw on its beneficiaries. Furthermore, the reservoir of persons available for political leadership will continue to be limited in the forseeable future; this will force the party leaders to look in the intellectuals' direction, however reluctantly. At the same time, however, the oppositional tendencies of intellectuals and the hypersensitivity to criticism on the part of politicians of any sort—and of the politicians of new states in particular—will add to this reluctance.

Opposition parties, insofar as they are allowed to exist, will certainly draw on intellectuals for their critical ideas concerning the government and for leadership and following. Such parties are their natural home.

If the underdeveloped countries become completely oligarchical and are ruled by a military junta or a one-party state, the role of intellectuals in political life in the narrower sense will certainly decline. The diminution of public political life will tend to narrow the area permitted to intellectuals. Even then, single-party regimes are likely, because of their ideological nature, to find a place for some intellectuals within their leading circles.[25]

Regardless of the fate of democracy in underdeveloped countries, intellectuals will undoubtedly continue to be called upon for the civil service and for higher education. There will be increasing scope for intellectuals as the governments expand the range of their activities

[25] The professional army officer in the new states is to a certain extent an intellectual since he, especially in the technical branches, is the recipient of a modern education. In fact, the intrusion of the military into politics in the Middle East, at least, may be partly attributed to their attachment to modern ideas about order, efficiency, and probity in government, ideas which are not part of the indigenous tradition of government and which come to them through their modern training. The military *coups d'état* which have occurred in many of the new states may be interpreted as, at least in part, revolutions of the technological intelligentsia, acting on behalf of modern ideas of efficiency and progress.

and as the demand grows for highly qualified persons for engineering, teaching, publicity and propaganda, health and social services, and research in social and natural sciences.

If the new states avoid the fate of the Latin American countries in the first century of their independence, and progress economically and socially, then indifferently of the political regime which rules them, the intellectual classes will become larger and more differentiated, and more fully incorporated into their own cultural institutional system in a variety of technological, administrative, educational, and therapeutic capacities.

This incorporation of the intellectuals into their own societies will depend to a large extent on the establishment of an equilibrium between the demand for and the supply of intellectuals. If there always is such a surplus of university and college graduates that their salaries are low and many of them have to take posts which they regard as unsuitable, the process of incorporation will be obstructed. Instead the oppositional mentality will go on reproducing itself. Where a public political life is permitted, there they will be a perpetual source of unsettledness.[26]

Let us imagine that the economies of the new states develop toward greater productivity and that a measure of liberal political life survives the burdens under which the new states now labor. The intellectual classes will become more diversified than they are at present, as they find employment in applied science and technology, in governmental, industrial, and commercial administration, in scientific and scholarly research, and in the profession of letters. With this diversification, there will be less unity of sentiment, less sense of a common identity among them. The "intellectuals" will become only one part of the educated class and a situation which already exists in the advanced countries will emerge.

[26] This, in turn, would increase the demand for an ideological oligarchy, from outside the government, and would also impel the government itself to adopt oligarchical measures.

There is also the opposite danger of a disequilibrium in the relations between the intellectuals and the central institutional system arising from an excessive demand for intellectuals in technological and administrative roles. In countries which entered upon independence with an insufficient supply of qualified intellectuals and a very scanty complement of intellectual institutions, it is definitely possible to draw practically all of the best intellectuals into executive and technological roles, leaving too few for civil and intellectual functions. The rapid growth of the public services and the general trend toward the governmental pre-emption of so many diverse functions might well result in too small a proportion of the intellectual classes being left free for independent creative work and for vital activity in that publicistic borderland between the intellectual and the political.

There will be more specialization, more philistinism, and a less general cultural sympathy in the new intelligentsia than in the old. The new intelligentsia will also be much less political in its outlook and more practical and professional. Each intellectual profession will, as it has long since done in the advanced countries, nurture its own traditions and ways of working. As in the past, these traditions will draw on the more differentiated and more elaborate intellectual traditions of the advanced countries. Creativity will come to be more appreciated and one necessary condition for its realization will thus be provided. The intellectuals of the underdeveloped countries will cease in the course of this process to be as dependent and provincial as they are now. They will become, as some already are, full citizens, with completely equal status, in the intellectual community of the world.

The opportunities for fruitful and satisfying employment of the skills of the intellectuals in the various spheres of civil and economic life and the establishment of absorbing and guiding traditions of an autonomous creativity in intellectual life proper will foster an attenuation of ideological dispositions. It can never eradicate them but it can reduce the commonness of their occurrence and mollify their asperity. Many with political interests will no longer feel the urgent obligation to participate directly in day-to-day political life. More of them will be content to play an equally vital but less immediate part in the formation of the life of their countries. They will concern themselves less than they do now with the issues of the here and now, and will deal with problems which are of longer-run significance, more remote from the immediate issues of party politics and of the prospects and favors of the incumbent political elite. The indirect influence on politics which comes from the cultivation of the matrix of opinion, and from the provision of the personnel and the institutional conditions of long-term development, will bring satisfaction to a larger proportion than it now does, and politicians will perhaps learn to appreciate the equal and perhaps even greater value to the community of this kind of activity on the part of intellectuals.

Their direct participation in politics will probably continue to have a radical bent. The traditions of the modern intellectual are too deeply rooted and the tendency is too intrinsic to the exercise of intellectual powers for this to be avoided—even if it were ever desirable. The radicalism of the intellectual's politics need not however be revolutionary or ideological; it can also work within the civil order. In the espousal of this standpoint at the center of political decision, in party councils, in parliaments and in cabinets, the intellectual will continue to have a unique and indispensable role, the abdication of which cannot be compensated by purely intellectual creativity or the efficient performance of executive, technological, and educational functions. In order, however, for this possibility to exist, the political society—the civil order itself—must first come into existence.

This brings us to one of the prototypical paradoxes of political development. For the intellectuals to inherit their true estate, they must live in a political society. But this civil order cannot be achieved unless the intellectuals, who would be among its greatest beneficiaries, help, against the greatest difficulties, to bring it about. Some of these difficulties reside within the intellectuals themselves, within the political and cultural traditions which enter into their constitution. The outcome then depends on whether those intellectuals who speak for civility in a modern society will by their talents, virtue, and good fortune be able to outweigh their own inhibitions, the dense incivility of their fellow-intellectuals, and the rocky obduracy of the traditional order.

5

NON-WESTERN
INTELLIGENTSIAS
AS POLITICAL ELITES

Harry J. Benda

In the course of the past century, the non-western world has experienced a series of revolutionary changes, most, if not all, of them caused by the impact of western civilization on the traditional societies of Asia, Africa and the Middle East (and to some lesser extent also of Latin America). Since 1914, political evolution has proceeded at an accelerated rate, leading in recent times to the creation of new political, national entities, either by internal revolution or by the voluntary or forced withdrawal of western political control. In these states new political élites have come to power in many parts of the non-western world, and a pattern is emerging which allows some preliminary classifications of the new ruling groups.

I

Non-western societies can broadly be divided into two categories, those that have so far remained outside the orbit of westernization or have, at best, barely or only superficially embarked upon it; and those that have travelled along the road of westernization to a more or less marked and significant degree. The first group is fairly rapidly dwindling; its hallmarks are a continuation of the old socio-political moulds and *mores*, with political authority continuing to be vested in traditional élite groups. Some Arab sheikdoms, including (for the time being at least) Saudi Arabia, and the tribal societies in many parts of Negro Africa are the prototypes of this group.

Within the other category, that of westernizing non-western coun-

Reprinted from *The Australian Journal of Politics and History*, VI, No. 2 (November 1960), 205–218, by permission of the Editorial Board and the author.

tries, two main types can be discerned. There are, first, those countries in which westernization—to whatever degree it has been or is
being achieved—has actually been accomplished by traditional ruling
classes, so that the revolutionary changes that have taken place in
the process of adaptation have left the pre-revolutionary power pattern more or less intact. One of the outstanding examples of this type
was, of course, nineteenth century Japan, which achieved the fullest
degree of westernization attained anywhere in the non-western world
through the guidance of the *samurai,* a military-feudal class that
adapted itself, and directed the adaptation of the rest of the country, to
a modern economic and political order without abdicating its intrinsic
control, even though in time it came to share power with other classes,
notably a new economic middle class.[1]

Other examples of this type can be found in more and more isolated instances in the Middle East, as *e.g.* Iran and (until recently)
also Iraq. But the most numerous instances occur in the areas of the
erstwhile Spanish and Portuguese empires in Latin America and Asia
(mainly the Philippines). Spanish and Portuguese colonialism, an overseas extension of a feudal, pre-industrial west, through Christianiza-
tion and cultural assimilation, called into existence a distinct social
pattern whose main beneficiary was a class of either Spanish or *mestizo*
landowners. It was they who either won independence from the
mother countries (as in Latin America), or who at any rate gained
social and economic prominence (as the *cacique* in the Phillippines),
where they only assumed political control under American aegis, after
Spain had forfeited political control. By origin and education westernized, they naturally proceeded to lead in the further—but, compared to Japan, very slow—process of modernization while retaining
political power in most parts of the former Spanish and Portuguese
realms. The Mexican revolution of 1910 marked the first successful
challenge to this socio-political *status quo,* to be followed by incidental
upheavals in other parts of the area, notably Uruguay, Peru, and quite
recently, in Cuba. As yet, however, the old pattern predominates. The
fact that military dictatorships are such a common political institution
in Latin America should not obscure the fact that in most cases (including Juan Perón until 1945) these military *juntas* are an offshoot of,
and tend to govern in the interest of, the traditional ruling classes of
hacienderos.

In contrast to this prototype, political power in the second category

---

[1] In spite of the fact that the Meiji Restoration of 1868 marked a break with the
preceding political order, in terms of élite structure it signified a change within the
samurai class rather than a social revolution.

is exercised by essentially new ruling groups. These new élites are the products of revolutionary changes of more profound significance, of social as well as of political revolutions. This second category consists of western-trained intellectuals and military leaders; for reasons which will presently be discussed, they can be subsumed under the more general, generic term of "intelligentsia." It is with these élites that the present paper is primarily concerned.

What distinguishes such non-western intelligentsias from most intellectuals in western societies is that they wield political power as it were independently, *i.e.*, they wield it in their own right, *as* intelligentsias, rather than as spokesmen for entrenched social forces. In other words, these intelligentsias are a *ruling class*, or rather *the* ruling class *par excellence*, whereas elsewhere intellectuals do not as a rule constitute a socio-political class of their own so much as an adjunct to other classes or groups in society. Representatives of this group can be easily identified throughout the non-western world. Among intellectuals as rulers are men like Nehru, Bourguiba, Kwame Nkrumah in Ghana and Francisco Madero in Mexico; among the "military intelligentsia," men like Nasser, al-Kassem in Iraq, Ne Win in Burma and also Argentina's Perón in his later years. In several non-western areas there has, moreover, been a tendency—recently demonstrated in Pakistan, Burma, and the Sudan—for the military to take over from civilian leaders within this intelligentsia.

A third category should, perhaps, be added to this list, *viz.* the communist élites in the Soviet Union, China and other non-western countries. To some extent they, in fact, historically fall within the categories listed above, for Lenin and several, if not most, of the early bolshevik leaders belonged to the intellectual prototype. While in the Soviet Union intellectuals as wielders of political power are now an anachronism,[2] the Chinese communist élite and its Asian variants (North Korea and North Viet Nam) are still largely recruited from among the intelligentsia of the early twentieth century; but the Chinese élite (as, for that matter, that of Yugoslavia) is, even by early Soviet standards, a unique intelligentsia in that it combines within itself "ideological" with "military" qualities that, among non-communist élites, tend to be divided into two, often competing, branches of the new non-western ruling classes. In this essay, communist élites will only receive peripheral consideration.

[2] See for example "L," "The Soviet Intelligentsia," *Foreign Affairs*, vol. 36, 1957, pp. 122–30.

II

To avoid confusion, we should distinguish between two kinds of non-western intellectuals, *viz.* the "old" and the "new" intellectual. The first bears a distinct resemblance to the intellectual of the pre-industrial west, especially—though neither invariably nor exclusively—to the "sacral" intellectual of mediaeval times.[3] For purposes of our present analysis, this group is of relatively minor importance, since it does not furnish the new political élites of contemporary non-western nation states. This is not to deny that it has played, and in some significant ways continues to play, important political roles. But for one thing, the "old" intellectuals' role, like that of their western counterparts, has almost invariably been limited to an ancillary function, a political task delegated to them, so to speak, by more or less powerful classes in their societies. Not infrequently these intellectuals (in west and non-west) were actually members of the ruling classes themselves and did not exercise independent political power *qua* intellectuals (priests, scholars, etc.) as such.[4] Admittedly there were at all times also members of this "old" intelligentsia—such as Buddhist monks and Muslim *ulama*—who here and there allied themselves with the "outs" rather than the "ins," and who thus attained political significance by resisting the indigenous *status quo* and, in modern times, western colonialism. On the whole, however, the "old" intellectuals of the non-western world have suffered, and are suffering, a decline in their prestige, great as it may still be in areas hitherto untouched by modernization, especially the countryside, where the "new" intelligentsia's influence is only slowly penetrating.[5]

These "new" intellectuals are a recent phenomenon, for they are for the greater part the product of western education during the past few decades. But though western-trained and therefore in several respects kin of their western counterparts, they also differ from the

[3] On "sacral" and "secular" intellectuals see Edward Shils, "The Intellectuals and the Powers: Some Perspectives for Comparative Analysis," *Comparative Studies in Society and History*, vol. 1, 1958–9, pp. 5–22.

[4] This is basically true also of the Chinese scholar-gentry, in spite of the fact that entry into that élite group was—in theory and partly also in practice—open to all. To some extent, the scholar-gentry, by representing the state cult of Confucianism, also fulfilled some of the functions of the sacral intellectual, in competition with the Buddhist priesthood.

[5] For a fuller discussion, see the present writer's essay, "Revolution and Nationalism in the Non-Western World," in Warren S. Hunsberger (ed.), *New Era in the Non-Western World*, Ithaca, New York, Cornell University Press, 1957, pp. 17–51.

western intellectuals in some very significant respects. In the first place it is not literacy *per se* but westernization that stamps the non-westerner as the "new" intellectual. To the traditional tasks of manipulating the tools of communication have now been added the tasks of what Toynbee has aptly called the "human transformer." He, so Toynbee says, has "learned the tricks of the intrusive civilization . . . so far as may be necessary to enable their own community, through [his] agency, just to hold its own in a social environment in which life is ceasing to be lived in accordance with the local tradition." [6] Since, then, the criteria of westernization and "transforming" are their hallmarks, non-western intelligentsias will tend to include wider categories than has been the case of western intelligentsias. Westernization—thinking and acting in western, rather than traditionally indigenous ways—can extend to types of social activity that in the west have not, as a rule, formed part of intellectual activity as such.

The most common, and historically also most significant, representative of this category is the new military group, the "Young Turks" so to speak, of the non-western world.[7] Nor is this at all surprising, since one of the prime contacts between west and non-west during the past century-and-a-half has been military in nature. As a result, the desire to attain equality with the west has often found expression in terms of military equality, and officers were often the first social group to receive western training. Thus very frequently military westernizers, or westernized officers, have played a leading—at times a preponderant—role as independent political leaders in non-western countries. What distinguishes them as prototypes from traditional military rulers or dictators is, first, the fact that they are consciously using the means of coercive, military power for the attainment of essentially non-military, ideologically conceived social ends. And, second, unlike *e.g.* the military *juntas* of Latin America, the twentieth century military leaders in Asia and the Middle East are almost invariably social revolutionaries whose coming to power signals the end of the *status quo* and the eclipse of the traditional ruling classes. In some isolated instances of the twentieth century, non-western military leaders can be found who combine these ideological ends with the qualities of charismatic leadership. The Peróns, the Nassers, and the Castros are thus yet another phenomenon of the "new" non-western intelligentsia.

Second, to a degree unparalleled in the west, non-western intellec-

[6] Arnold J. Toynbee, *A Study of History*, Abridgement of Volumes I–VI by D. C. Somervell, New York, 1947, p. 394.

[7] Toynbee, *ibid.*, p. 395, specifically includes the military leaders in the category of the intelligentsia.

tuals are very frequently an isolated social group in indigenous society. This is largely due to the fact that this "new" intelligentsia is not, as in the west, a product of organic social growth, but rather a product of alien education more or less precariously grafted on indigenous non-western societies.[8] Unlike the "old," predominantly sacral, intellectuals most of whom represented or spoke for the powers-that-were, and who thus performed the ancillary political roles usually assigned to intellectuals throughout the world, non-western intelligentsias do not, sociologically speaking, as a rule represent anyone but themselves. It is the exception rather than the rule that the young aristocrat, the landowner's son or for that matter even the scion of a newly-established bourgeois class, once he has acquired a western education of any kind, becomes the defender and spokesman of the class of his social origin. In turn, it is equally the exception rather than the rule that these "new" intellectuals will be supported by traditional social classes with a vested socio-economic interest in non-western societies.

In short, non-western intelligentsias, insofar as they are politically active—and, as will be seen, most of them are so to a far higher degree than in the west—tend to be social revolutionaries whose ideological aims as often as not militate against the *status quo*. Since, by definition, most of these aims are western-derived and transplanted to a social environment inherently still far more conservative than is true of the more advanced industrial societies of the west, the task of social engineering becomes far more radical, and its proponents, the only group with a vested ideological interest in change, may find themselves driven to the use of radical reforms in order to hasten the approximation between reality and ideal.

There is, third, an additional reason for the relatively high incidence of radicalism among non-western intelligentsias, and it is connected both with their numbers and employability. As for size, it is on the whole relatively smaller than in industrialized western societies, for the number of persons able to afford western education, at home but particularly abroad, is more limited, and democratization of education has—with the exception of Japan—not yet paralleled that in the west. Yet, in spite of the smallness of non-western intelligentsias, the supply by far exceeds social demand. This unhappy phenomenon of the over-production and underemployment of intellectuals is in part doubtless conditioned by the social, psychological and ideological traditions of most non-western societies.

[8] cf. E. Shils, "The Culture of the Indian Intellectual," *Sewanee Review*, 1959, pp. 3–46. Shils seeks to minimize the extent of the Indian intellectuals' "alienation."

Since education, in these predominantly pre-industrial communities, still enjoys great traditional prestige, western education has automatically attracted large numbers of non-westerners; but in spite of the fact that the process of modernization and industrialization would indicate the need for technical, vocational and scientific training, the aristocratic or gentry bias common to pre-industrial societies has, in fact, led non-western students to bypass these fields in favour of humanistic and legal studies. Thus, while a crying shortage exists almost everywhere in Asia, the Middle East, Africa and even Latin America for physicians, engineers and scientists, the bulk of non-western intellectuals can be found in the humanities and the law, both of which appear to promise status satisfaction in traditional terms. In fact, it is predominantly graduates in these fields that compose the present-day political élites of so many non-western states.

The absorptive capacity for this kind of intellectual is, however, severely limited in non-western societies. As a result, intellectual unemployment—a phenomenon by no means unknown in some western countries—has social and political consequences of great importance, for non-western intelligentsias are by and large politicized to a degree unknown in the west. Particularly in areas recently freed from western colonial control, where national liberation has invariably led to a rapid expansion of western-style education, the steady growth of a largely unemployable "intellectual proletariat" presents a very real political threat to stability and social peace.[9] There, the "new" intellectual-rulers are thus, paradoxically enough, threatened by their own kind.

Finally, there is a fourth factor of great importance, that of ideological causation. In opposing the *status quo* of traditional non-western societies, most of the "new" intellectuals also tend to oppose the *status quo* of a world which either directly or indirectly can be held responsible for the internal social and political conditions that form the prime target of the intelligentsia's attack. Thus "feudalism" as well as colonialism—rule by entrenched native classes or rule by foreigners—can be blamed on the political, military and economic preponderance of the western world. It is, therefore, not surprising that socialist and communist teachings have found far more fertile soil among non-western intellectuals than among their western counterparts. If it is symptomatic that the first statues ever erected for Marx and Engels stand on Russian soil, it would be equally fitting to find statues, say of Harold Laski gracing the main squares of New Delhi, Colombo, Rangoon, Accra, and even Baghdad.

[9] *cf.* Justus M. van de Kroef, "The Educated Unemployed in Southeast Asia," *Journal of Higher Education*, vol. XXXI, 1960, pp. 177–184.

Indeed, it is not too surprising that modern socialism has so profoundly attracted intellectuals all over the world. In the most highly
industrialized countries of the west, it is, in fact, among intellectuals,
rather than among the proletariat itself, that this social philosophy
has found its most numerous adherents. This is very likely due to the
fact that socialism, especially Marxism, is the most recent, and perhaps
also the most coherent and intellectually most respectable version of
the philosopher king, the social engineer ruling in the interest of abstract social justice *par excellence*. An intelligentsia thus not only
has a vested intellectual interest in socialism, it also has a vested social
and political interest in it. In spite of the Marxian theory of the class
struggle as the major social determinant of history, in spite even of the
quasi-humility at times exhibited by Marx and his later followers in
terms of their willingness to be "guided by," and "learn from," the
proletariat, programmatic, "scientific" socialism has always, as Lenin
himself bluntly stated, been the product of a bourgeois intelligentsia.[10]
It is the "vanguard" of the proletariat, not the proletariat itself, that
is cast for the crucial role of governing, and for quite obvious reasons:
in proclaiming the rule of social justice, the socialist intellectual is
proclaiming rule by his own kind.

But whereas in the west the Marxist intellectual's political aspirations have as a rule encountered great difficulties, at least in working-
class movements dominated by, or at least highly dependent upon,
union leaders,[11] the non-western socialist intellectual can in the absence of a sizable proletariat (as well as of other organized socio-
economic forces) actually become ruler in his own right. Socialism,
in addition to providing the desired combination of anti-western—
i.e., anti-capitalistic—westernization also provides the non-western
intellectual with a justification for rule by the intelligentsia. In embracing it, he feels *ipso facto* justified in looking askance at political

[10] The fact that the intelligentsia is the actual ruling group in the early stages
of communism has never been admitted in Marxist analysis. For a recent re-state-
ment, *cf.* Oscar Lange, *Some Problems Relating to the Polish Road to Socialism*,
Warsaw, 1957, p. 28: "Wherein lies the specific character of the intelligentsia? In
the fact that it is not really a class. Its position comes from the superstructure and
not from production relations. . . . Its very essence prevents it from being an
independent force; it can only express the opinions and wishes of the working
class. . . . It can help, but it is not the social force which by itself can bring about
social change. . . ."

[11] Lenin encountered such opposition and crushed it after the Kronstadt revolt,
thereby subjugating the workers to the control of the party intelligentsia. By contrast, Harold Laski was never able to play a truly decisive role in the British Labour
Party.

competition from other segments of society, such as "old" intellectuals, aristocracies, and landowners, but also nascent capitalistic middle classes.[12] Planning in the name of socialism means planning with the intelligentsia as planners, irrespective of whether they be the military intellectuals of Nasser's stamp or the "pure" intellectuals of the Nehru variety.

III

Up to this point we have drawn no distinction between the military and the civilian, or "pure," intellectual, yet this distinction is of great analytic significance. It is by no means a matter of historic accident whether a non-western country, insofar as it has become westernized and undergone change, is ruled by either one or the other prototype. The existence of a military group of young officers in itself depends on the political status of a country; it depends, that is to say, on the fact of political (though not necessarily economic) independence. It is, therefore, only in non-colonial countries that westernization has been primarily channelled through military leaders. Kemal Ataturk, Yüan Shih-k'ai and the Satsuma and Choshu *samurai* are good examples, as are the many military régimes in Latin America and the newly emerging élite groups in the Middle East.

Wherever, then, the impact of the west did not lead to outright political domination, wherever a non-western society was given a chance of adjusting to the demands of the modern era by internal adaptation without suffering direct political control from the outside, there the officer has almost invariably emerged as the modern political non-western leader. Since he as a rule possesses a monopoly of physical power, he can fairly easily grasp control in a society where he represents the most powerful—even if numerically weak—social group with a vested interest in modernization and change.[13]

[12] *cf.* the following comment connected with the governing intellectual élite group in Indonesia: "Speaking to the Constituent Assembly on November 10, 1956 [Sukarno] expressed his fears at the recent emergence of a great many prospective Indonesian capitalists. . . . [He] believed that the development on the Indian model would mean, as Sukarno sees it, permitting the growth of a group of capitalists; in other words the *oligarchy of the educated* who now control the society would have to share power with a private entrepreneurial group . . . with different interests. To have economic development on either the Russian or the Chinese model would obviate the need to surrender power." (Italics added.) Leslie H. Palmier, "Sukarno, the Nationalist," *Pacific Affairs,* vol. 30, 1957, pp. 117–18.

[13] See *e.g.* Dankwart A. Rustow, *Politics and Westernization in the Near East,* Princeton, N.J., 1956, pp. 26–33.

Westernization as well as the *status quo* prevailing in these countries, have, as we said, combined to stamp many, if not most of these younger military leaders with an ideological orientation not usually found among the professional soldiers in the west, or for that matter among the older generation of officers in independent non-western states. While this orientation is at times fairly close to the socialism so prevalent among non-western intelligentsias in general, while as a rule little love is lost between them and either the aristocracies, clergies or the nascent capitalist classes in their lands, their political goals tend to centre around the creation of strong, "socially just" régimes rather than around the creation of parliamentary régimes. In their distrust of the professional politician, including the "civilian" intelligentsia, non-western military leaders like the Japanese *samurai* of the nineteenth century and Colonel Nasser of today bear a recognizable similarity to the military prototype of modern societies in the west. Under a military régime "pure" intellectuals play a subordinate role as political leaders, if indeed they are at all tolerated by their military colleagues. In some of the contemporary non-western military dictatorships the intellectual as an independent political actor is politically as ineffectual as he was in, say, Meiji Japan. He has the choice between playing auxiliary to the new powers-that-be and being doomed to political impotence.

If the military intelligentsia has emerged as the most universal revolutionary phenomenon in the non-colonial countries of the non-western world, the "pure" intellectual has made his appearance as political ruler in many areas recently freed from western colonialism. This is an interesting phenomenon, for, unlike the military, the "pure" intellectual does not *a priori* command the means of physical coercion that have, throughout history, made military power so significant a factor. It is, indeed, a phenomenon rooted in modern western colonialism itself. The absence of an indigenous military élite proper is one of the most significant sociological aspects of colonialism of all times. Since military power rests with the alien ruling class, this occupation is closed to the indigenous population.[14] Nineteenth century colonialism had other stultifying effects on social growth as well, particularly in preventing or retarding the development of a sizable bourgeoisie within the populations of many areas. This is particularly true of the plural societies of South-East Asia and parts of Africa, in which

[14] This does not mean that the western colonial powers did not recruit soldiers among the native population. But, for one thing, colonial armies were almost invariably officered by westerners, and, for another, in many instances the soldiers were purposely recruited from among ethnic and/or religious minority groups in the colony.

the introduction of capitalist economies has tended to benefit foreign rather than indigenous entrepreneurs.

It is this stunted social growth that turned the western-trained intellectuals—the doctors, the lawyers, the engineers, the professors and the students—into the only sizable group with a vested interest in political change. Unlike their military counterparts in non-colonial areas, however, the intellectuals of colonial Asia and Africa remained politically impotent as long as colonialism lasted, *i.e.*, they had no instruments for physically seizing power, and had to content themselves with the weapons of ideological warfare, political organization and nationalist protest within the limits set by their alien overlords. As the westernized leaders of nationalism and anti-colonialism, these non-western intelligentsias formed a numerically very small, and in most cases also very weak, élite group. In some few areas, like British India, where indigenous entrepreneurs had gained a measure of economic strength, they have supported the intelligentsia in order to bolster their position *vis-à-vis* foreign competition. In most cases, however, the nationalist leadership did not have such support at its disposal. Smarting under the constant vigilance of colonial masters, it was vociferous rather than politically entrenched. It is doubtless true that these intellectuals—as westernized intelligentsias throughout the non-western world—have sought identification with the rural mass of the population and the "nation" at large, but this identification rests, as we will presently discuss, on slender roots. Partly this is due to the very westernization of these urban élite groups and partly to the fact that in virtually all colonies access to the peasantry was rendered extremely difficult, if not impossible, by the colonial authorities. Only in British India again did the urban intelligentsia—largely through Gandhi—succeed in forging a link with the peasantry.

Thus, whereas military leaders were able to grasp political control in non-colonial areas whenever the opportunity arose from the internal power constellation—as *e.g.* in China after 1911, in Japan after 1867, in Turkey in 1918, in Thailand in 1931, etc.—the "pure" intellectuals had to wait for external liberation from colonial rule to step into the political arena as actual rulers in their own right. It is not coincidental that the Japanese occupation of South-East Asia performed this act of liberation for the intellectuals of Burma and Indonesia,[15]

[15] In Thailand (a non-colonial country) and the Philippines (where Spanish rule had created a quasi-feudal social system), the Japanese did not vitally affect the pre-war socio-political structure. In the former country the military oligarchy retained power, in the latter the landowning class. Only among the anti-Japanese Filipino underground did potential new leaders, like Ramon Magsaysay and

and that the train of post-war liquidations of colonial possessions has paved the way for the intelligentsia elsewhere, as in India, Ghana, Tunisia and to some extent also in Malaya. In the social and political vacuum created by modern colonialism, the western-trained intellectual was, at the crucial hour, the only politically and ideologically trained élite group on whom political power could devolve.

But if there is historic logic in the emergence of "civilian" intellectuals as rulers in post-colonial non-western areas today, continuation of this fairly unique phenomenon is fairly problematical. The demise of colonialism itself has brought with it the breaking down of the artificial barriers to social growth that were, as we said, one of its most significant sociological aspects. In the newly independent countries of Asia and Africa the "pure" intellectual is now free to search for non-intellectual avenues to social status and prestige, and some of them—Aung San of Burma is an excellent example—have rapidly turned towards a military career. In this sense, colonial countries are socially "coming of age," and are demonstrating the adaptability of non-western intelligentsias to new social conditions, an adaptability previously exhibited by Leon Trotsky and some members of the Chinese communist intelligentsia in a non-colonial setting.

Second, quite apart from this incidental transformation of individual "pure" intellectuals, independence, and in particular the revolutionary struggle against colonialism—in South-East Asia, conscious Japanese policies [16]—has given rise to a distinct group of military leaders, who socially, educationally and often also ideologically stand apart from the western-trained academic intellectuals of the colonial era. Having played a significant role in the liberation of their countries and having gained access to military power, they have also created a political following, both among their subordinates and, quite often, among the public at large. The military, in short, have become a competing élite which has increasingly come to challenge the "civilian" intelligentsia's monopoly of political power in formerly colonial non-western countries.

As the struggle between Sun Yat-sen and Yüan Shih-k'ai symbolically showed, the contest between "pure" intellectuals and military leaders

Huk leader Luis Taruc, come to the fore. Magsaysay's presidency in the 1950s constituted the first major breach in the Philippine political scene, in that it temporarily brought to power an intelligentsia, partly military in character, and based on widespread peasant support centred on the charismatic leadership of the president. Since Magsaysay's sudden death, the pre-war *status quo* seems to have been more or less restored.

[16] For Indonesia, see the present writer's *The Crescent and the Rising Sun; Indonesian Islam during the Japanese Occupation*, 1942–1945, The Hague/Bandung/New York, 1958, pp. 138–41, 172–3, 203.

is, because of the latter's physical superiority, fraught with grave dangers to the civilian leadership. But the new military élites, it must be remembered, are for the greater part not simply war lords or "strong men" only.

To a large extent, they, too, make ideological appeals—if nothing else, appealing for national unity in the face of disunited civilian leadership—that render them truly formidable political opponents.[17] In recent times, military leaders have taken over from civilian intelligentsias in the Sudan, in Burma and in Pakistan,[18] while in Indonesia army leaders appear to be gaining increasing political influence.[19]

The apparent ease with which civilian régimes are being replaced by military ones points to the inherent weakness and instability of rule by "pure" intellectuals. The causes of these are not far to seek. In the first place, the "pure" intellectual, however well versed he may have been in the politics of opposition to colonialism, very rarely possesses actual administrative experience that could make him an effective and efficient statesman. Second, the democratic or parliamentary institutions imported by western-trained intellectuals are as a rule operating in a social and political vacuum, with no organizational framework connecting the new edifice at the centre with the country at large. It is true that many non-western intellectuals are stressing the intrinsically democratic nature of traditional village government in their countries; but it may be doubted whether this "village democracy"—whatever its merits—can serve the purpose of providing an adequate underpinning for a modern, viable constitutional state.

Finally, the political parties functioning under most non-western parliamentary systems do not as a rule represent organized social forces so much as factions centred around personalities. The temporary unity

[17] As we said earlier, it is so far only among Asian communist élites that a more or less complete merger has apparently been effected between "pure" and military intelligentsias. It was, in fact, Russian advice and aid that had helped to produce a similar merger within the Kuomintang leadership in the 1920s. In the measure that the Kuomintang in later years de-emphasized ideology and political organization it dug, so to speak, its own political grave by yielding supremacy to the Chinese communists who excelled in combining military striking power with organizational and ideological strength.

[18] Burma and Pakistan are not, strictly speaking, identical cases. The civilian régime displaced in Pakistan was not a régime of intellectuals so much as of landowners. Schematically, Pakistan's case is thus comparable to that of Iraq rather than that of Burma.

[19] cf. Guy J. Pauker, "The Role of Political Organizations in Indonesia," *Far Eastern Survey*, vol. 27, 1958, pp. 141–2.

exhibited before the attainment of independence thus tends to wane
once nationhood has been achieved, and to give way to fierce factional
struggles.[20] It is these struggles, accompanied by lack of central purpose and achievement, that leave the intellectual in a precarious
position, and thus render the appeal of the military so forceful.

The substitution of a military for a civilian régime does not necessarily involve more than a change within the intelligentsia, and thus
a structural change in the façade of government. The short-cut solution
of the military *coup* does no more than eradicate the often anaemic
institutional forms of a western-style political system; it does not
substitute more viable forms in their stead. If the "pure" intellectuals
encounter almost insuperable obstacles in realizing their goals, the
military leadership, moving into the *terra incognita* of politics, may
find it at least equally difficult to translate their long-term aspirations
into reality.

If the difficulties besetting non-western intelligentsias as ruling
classes of both types appear formidable, they are in many areas partly
offset, or at least obscured, by the "countervailing" power of *charisma*
embodied in individual members of both the civilian and the military,
such as Nehru, Nasser, Nkrumah, Sukarno and Castro, to mention but
a few outstanding examples.[21] The simultaneous appearance of charismatic leadership in Asia, Africa, the Middle East and Latin America
is perhaps one of the most important phenomena accompanying the
political readjustments in the contemporary non-western world.[22] It
is the charismatic leader who by force of sheer personality can apparently bridge the gap between the westernized élites and the rural
population, and who can serve as the symbolic link between the ruler
and the ruled.

It is a moot point whether the presence of such leadership alone
can suffice to guarantee a measure of political stability or to extract the
co-operation required to set sustained modernization and economic

[20] *cf.* Richard L. Park, "Problems of Political Development," in Philip W.
Thayer (ed.), *Nationalism and Prospects in Free Asia,* Baltimore, Md., 1956,
pp. 103–104, and Vera M. Dean and others, *The Nature of the Non-Western
World,* New York, 1958, pp. 212–13.

[21] On charismatic leadership see also George McT. Kahin, Guy J. Pauker, and
Lucian W. Pye, "Comparative Politics in Non-Western Countries," *American
Political Science Review,* vol. 49, 1955, p. 1025, and Gabriel L. Almond, "Com-
parative Political Systems," *Journal of Politics,* vol. 18, 1956, p. 401.

[22] Charismatic leadership is, nonetheless, not a *sine qua non* of political modernization as witness its absence in Meiji Japan, republican China and in communist countries. Stalin's "cult of the individual" or Mao's all-pervading presence
are by no means synonymous with *charisma.*

improvement in motion. It is similarly a moot point whether an intellegentsia, bereft of its charismatic leader, will produce adequate cohesion to continue in power.[23] At any rate, there can be little doubt that the charismatic leader is already a deviant from the standard pattern of the western-educated intelligentsia, whether civilian or military: insofar as the charismatic appeal is politically important in the non-western world it is so not because of these leaders' western training and ideological orientation, but perhaps in spite of them. In the eyes of the general population, the charismatic leader may well be *malgré lui,* the reincarnation of the "old," sacral intellectual rather than the modernizer and westernizer he claims to be.

IV

An intelligentsia ruling in its own right as a ruling class or group is, strictly speaking, not necessarily a specific non-western phenomenon only. In the course of western history, there have been brief episodes when intellectuals—sacral, secular and military—have performed similar functions, as for example Calvin, Cromwell, the Jacobins, or the Puritan founders of Massachusetts. This random list indicates that rule by intelligentsias has almost invariably been the hallmark of revolutionary eras in the west. It may thus be suggested that the differences between western and non-western history—leaving aside the specific characteristics of the new non-western élites discussed in the preceding pages—are quantitative rather than qualitative. In other words, since the non-western social and political revolution of the twentieth century is a virtually global phenomenon following the wake of historically well-nigh simultaneous dissolutions of traditional social moulds, what in the west have been chronologically and geographically disparate, local and sporadic incidents, have now assumed the proportions of a world-wide socio-political phenomenon. If, then, western history is to serve as a measuring rod, it could be further argued that rule by contemporary intelligentsias in parts of Asia, Africa, the Middle East and Latin America may represent an interim stage in the political evolution of the non-western world, and that sooner or later it will be superseded by other élites and new forms of political organization.

Suggestive as such a hypothesis may be, it needs to be qualified. The brevity of revolutionary régimes led by intellectuals in western

[23] The assassination of Aung San in Burma was followed by gradual dissolution of the party headed by him, until the civilian intelligentsia surrendered power voluntarily to the military.

history was intimately connected with the presence of powerful social and economic classes bent on eliminating the "dictatorship of the intellectuals" imposed on their societies. These opponents may have belonged to entrenched social interests (as *e.g.* the Genevan bourgeoisie or the much-discussed English gentry of the 1640s), or, more paradoxically, to groups born of, or vastly strengthened by, the very changes inaugurated by the intelligentsia (as *e.g.* the French bourgeoisie or the *nouveaux riches* landowners and businessmen in Massachusetts). *Mutatis mutandis,* a very similar process led to the elimination of the original core of bolshevik intellectuals by a new generation of party bureaucrats and managers in the 1930s, a process anticipated by Trotsky, and later described by both Milovan Djilas and Arthur Koestler. In the west, intellectuals have only been able to rule in the intervals between the breakdown of an old social and political order and the establishment of a new one (or, as in the *terra nova* of Massachusetts, between the birth of a new order and its normalization, so to speak). Their régimes have usually been ended by "counter-revolutionary" movements instigated by social classes who, in the proper Marxian sense, have commanded wealth and power, as a rule based on control over important sectors of the economy, and who were thus able, sooner rather than later, to displace the intellectual as wielder of independent political power. This done, the intelligentsia invariably found itself reduced to its more "normal" and ancillary role in politics, *i.e.*, it reverted to the task of verbalizing or ideologizing the political interests of other classes or groups, either those in power or those opposing them.

It is not unlikely that intelligentsias represent a similar intermediate stage in the non-western political evolution. But it is probable that their displacement is not a matter of the immediate future, even though, as we have seen, there exists an apparently growing trend for power to devolve upon the military within these non-western intelligentsias. Members of older social groups, such as landowners [24] or sacral intellectuals—as *e.g.* the Muslim Brotherhood in Egypt, the Hindu Mahasabha in India, or the Darul Islam in Indonesia—though they may here and there exert significant political influence, seem as a rule to be lacking in strength or social dynamism to constitute a real threat to the new order. The urban bourgeoisie is numerically and often also economically too weak to challenge the new intelligentsia-

---

[24] Their political influence appears to be stronger in formerly Hispanic lands than elsewhere. Moreover, it is very likely that in Latin America they have been able to obtain aid from abroad, as witness the short-lived régime of Col. Arbenz in Guatemala.

rulers. And, finally, the revolutions are of too recent date to have laid the groundwork for the growth of other social groups able and willing to form a viable opposition, in terms of economic strength at least.

For quite some time to come, non-western intelligentsias may therefore be expected to retain their virtual monopoly of political power. To a large extent this continuity seems to be assured by the fact that the national polities over which they rule are of recent date, and, indeed, of the intelligentsias' own making. Essentially, these are modern governmental edifices superimposed on societies which, as yet, do not nourish them by established channels of political communication. The political process in non-western societies is thus, to a far greater extent than is true of most western societies, a superstructure without viable underpinning.[25] This state of affairs, for sure, cannot but be transitional. But as long as it lasts, intelligentsias are very likely to remain the prime political actors in many non-western countries. Political changes are likely to take place within these élites rather than to affect their predominance as ruling classes.*

[25] See also the illuminating essay by Lucian L. Pye, "The Non-Western Political Process," *Journal of Politics*, vol. 20, 1958, pp. 469–86.

* A companion article by Harry J. Benda, "Intellectuals and Politics in Western History," appeared in the *Bucknell Review*, X, No. 1 (May 1961), 1–14.

6

IDEOLOGIES OF DELAYED INDUSTRIALIZATION: SOME TENSIONS AND AMBIGUITIES

MARY MATOSSIAN

History and value are worlds apart, but men are drawn to both, with an emotional commitment to the first and an intellectual commitment to the second; they need to ask the two incompatible questions, and they yearn to be able to answer "Mine" and "True." [1]

—J. R. Levenson

It is difficult to discern, at first glance, any important common characteristics in ideologies such as Gandhism and Marxism-Leninism, Kemalism, and Shintoism. If they have anything in common, it seems to be a strong infusion of self-contradiction. But on second glance the diverse characteristics and geographic origins of these ideologies fade into the background. In their very self-contradictions one may detect recurrent patterns.

The recurrent patterns can, I think, be accounted for by the similarity of context in which these ideologies have emerged. This context is the industrially backward country which has the following characteristics: (1) it has been in contact with the industrial West for at least fifty years; (2) in it there has emerged a native intelligentsia composed of individuals with at least some Western education; and (3) large-scale industrialization is currently being contemplated or has

Reprinted from *Economic Development and Cultural Change*, VI, No. 3 (April 1958), 217–228, by permission of The University of Chicago Press. Copyright 1958 by The University of Chicago Press.

[1] J. R. Levenson, " 'History' and 'Value': Tensions of Intellectual Choice in Modern China," *Studies in Chinese Thought*, Arthur Wright, ed., Chicago, 1953, p. 150.

been in progress for no more than twenty-five years. The ideologies which have emerged in such conditions would include Marxism-Leninism, Shintoism, Italian Fascism, Kemalism, Gandhism, the current Egyptian Philosophy of the Revolution, Sun Yat-sen's Three Principles of the People, the Indonesian Pantjasila, and many others.[2]

Industrially backward countries have two common problems: the destruction of traditional institutions and values, sometimes even before the impact of industrialism is felt; and the challenge of the modern West.[3] The "assaulted" individual must reorient himself in at least three directions: (1) in his relationship to the West, (2) in his relationship to his people's past, and (3) in his relationship to the masses of his own people. It is the "assaulted" intellectual, and his relationship to the uneducated masses, which will be considered here in particular: for although everyone has ideas and wishes, only intellectuals devise ideologies.

Ideology may be defined as a pattern of ideas which simultaneously provides for its adherents: (1) a self-definition, (2) a description of the current situation, its background, and what is likely to follow, and (3) various imperatives which are "deduced" from the foregoing. In ideology there is a strong tendency to merge fact and value, to superimpose upon "things as they are" the things that are desired.[4] Sjahrir, the Indonesian socialist, said that the weaker the intellect, the greater the element of wish in the formulation of a man's thought. He has held that the element of wish is strongest among "backward" persons.[5]

[2] Perhaps Nazism should be included, even though it emerged on the German scene about sixty years after industrialization began. In any case, Nazism has many characteristics of ideologies of delayed industrialization.

[3] These are the two important situational factors with which Rupert Emerson accounts for Asian nationalism. See "Paradoxes of Asian Nationalism," *Far Eastern Quarterly,* Vol. XIII, No. 2 (February 1954), pp. 131–142.

John K. Fairbank has pointed out that as contact with the West increases, the response increases but is less discernible because Western culture has been incorporated in indigenous culture. He says, " 'Westernization' gives way to 'modernization,' the demand for defense is followed by the demand for reform, and by the time when a reform accelerates into a revolution, the entire society has become involved in a process of change which is too cataclysmic and far-reaching, too autonomous, to be called any longer a mere 'response.' " See "China's Response to the West: Problems and Suggestions," *Journal of World History,* Vol. III, No. 2, pp. 404–405.

[4] In a moment of unusual insight Gamal Abdul Nasser wrote: "Our souls are the vessels in which everything we are is contained; and everything we are, everything placed in these vessels, must take their shape, even truth. I try as much as humanly possible to prevent my soul from altering the shape of truth very much, but how far can I succeed? That is the question." *Egypt's Liberation: The Philosophy of the Revolution,* Washington, D.C., 1955, p. 29.

[5] Soetan Sjahrir, *Out of Exile,* New York, 1949, pp. 89–90.

Perhaps it would be more accurate to say that the intellectual in an industrially backward country cleaves to contradictory propositions because of the situation in which he finds himself. His experience and his present problems tend to direct his reasoning into certain channels. His ego needs protection which science and logic cannot provide. This seems to be true of all men to some extent. If the intellectual is to lead the masses of an industrially backward country in the undertaking of great endeavors, he must provide them with incitement balanced by comfort, with self-criticism balanced by self-justification.

To seek a "morphology" and "natural history" of ideologies of delayed industrialization seems premature, given the present state of Western knowledge. The following analysis is not intended to provide neat answers to big questions, but to indicate some areas where further probing might be productive.

The impact of the modern industrial West is the initial challenge in the industrially backward country. The various ways in which the West has disrupted traditional societies are beyond the scope of this analysis. The point to note here is that irreversible processes are set in motion. The contemporary scene is littered with fallen idols, desecrated by unsanctioned violence, an uncomfortable place in which to live. Thus, all ideologies of delayed industrialization are essentially revolutionary —in Mannheim's usage, utopian.[6] They direct activity toward changing a social order which is already changing. Even the superficially conservative ideologies turn out to be pseudo-conservative in the sense that they advocate a change in the status quo. Pseudo-conservative or radical, these ideologies advocate the manipulation of the disagreeable Present. In this sense, Les extremes se touchent.[7]

The first problem of the "assaulted" intellectual is to assume a satisfactory posture vis-a-vis the West. The position taken is frequently ambiguous, embracing the polar extremes of xenophobia and xenophilia. The intellectual may resent the West, but since he is already at least partly Westernized, to reject the West completely would be to deny part of himself.

The intellectual is appalled by discrepancies between the standard of living and "culture" of his own country, and those of modern Western nations.[8] He feels that something must be done, and done

---

[6] See Karl Mannheim, Ideology and Utopia, London, 1936.

[7] See Samuel P. Huntington, "Conservatism as an Ideology," American Political Science Review, Vol. LI, No. 2, p. 460. Levenson (loc. cit., p. 149), holds that the very existence of traditionalism belies its ultimate doctrine.

[8] The usage of the word "culture" depends on the extent to which the ideologist is Westernized. It may mean ideals, values, or simply habits. Sun Yat-sen,

fast. He is a man on the defensive, searching for new defensive weapons. As Gamal Abdul Nasser wrote to a friend in 1935:

Allah said, "Oppose them with whatever forces you can muster!" But what are these forces we are supposed to have in readiness for them? [9]

Another characteristic of the "assaulted" intellectual is his uneasy attitude toward himself and his own kind—the intelligentsia and middle classes. Often he scorns his kind (and by implication, himself) as "pseudo," "mongrel," neither truly native nor truly Western. In order to find self-respect, he goes in search of his "true self"; he tries to "discover India"; he revisits the West. For example, Gandhi wrote in 1908:

"You, English, who have come to India are not good specimens of the English nation, nor can we, almost half-Anglicized Indians, be considered as good specimens of the real Indian nation. . . ." [10]

Speaking of the lack of good Indonesian literature, Sjahrir wrote in 1934:

In reality, our cultural level is still too low for a real renaissance. There is no thought, no form, no sound, and what is worse, there is not yet enough earnestness and integrity among us. There is still only unsavory counterfeit, which is published with great fuss, but which still has little merit. [11]

Nehru, while in prison in 1944, recalled:

The present for me, and for many others like me, was an odd mixture of medievalism, appalling poverty and misery and a somewhat superficial modernism of the middle classes. I was not an admirer of my own class or kind, and yet inevitably I looked to it for leadership in the struggle for India's salvation; that middle class felt caged and circumscribed and wanted to grow and develop itself. [12]

Nehru leans toward xenophilia, but his close associate Gandhi took an emphatic xenophobic posture. He asserted that Indians, to be successful in dealing with the British, must "consciously believe that Indian civilization is the best and that the European is a nine days' wonder." Of course, Indian civilization has some defects, he admits,

a trained physician, deplored such Chinese habits as spitting, letting gas loudly, and never brushing the teeth, as "uncultured." He said that foreigners "can see that we are very much lacking in personal culture. Every word and act of a Chinese shows absence of refinement: one contact with the Chinese people is enough to reveal this." *San Min Chu I*, Shanghai, 1927, pp. 135–138.

[9] Nasser, *op. cit.*, p. 27. See also Jawaharlal Nehru, *The Discovery of India*, London, 1946, p. 34.

[10] Mohandas K. Gandhi, *Hind Swaraj*, Ahmedabad, 1946, p. 73.

[11] Soetan Sjahrir, *op. cit.*, p. 5.

[12] Nehru, *op. cit.*, p. 36.

such as child marriage and religious prostitution. But, "the tendency of Indian civilization is to elevate the moral being, that of the Western civilization is to propagate immorality." [13]

The "assaulted" intellectual works hard to make invidious comparisons between his own nation and the West. He may simply claim that his people are superior, as did Gandhi: "We consider our civilization to be far superior to yours." [14] Or he may hold that his ancestors had already rejected Western culture as inferior.[15] But these assertions can elicit conviction only among a few and for a short while. More often the intellectual says, "We are equal to Westerners," or "You are *no better* than I am." Around this theme lies a wealth of propositions: (1) "In the past you were no better (or worse) than we are now." [16] (2) "We once had your good qualities, but we were corrupted by alien oppressors." [17] (3) "We have high spiritual qualities despite our poverty, but you are soulless materialists." [18] (4) "Everything worthwhile in your tradition is present or incipient in ours." [19] The slogan, "trade, not aid," when used metaphorically, is another variation on this theme. The nationalist claims to seek a blend of the "best" in East and West. But why must both East and West inspire the new culture?

[13] Gandhi, *op. cit.*, pp. 45–46 and 74.

[14] *Ibid.*, p. 72.

[15] *Ibid.*, p. 46, and Levenson, *loc. cit.*, p. 158.

[16] For example, see Sun Yat-sen, *op. cit.*, p. 140. This is a common assertion of Arab ideologists. Of course, there is truth in it, but how does it serve to solve the problem at hand, except to bolster the ego of the "assaulted"?

[17] Levenson, *loc. cit.*, p. 167, reports that the Chinese used the Manchus as their scapegoat. The Arabs blame the later Ottoman sultans, and the Russians blame the Mongols. There is some truth in these assertions—but it remains to be seen why the native subject peoples failed to get rid of their "alien oppressors."

[18] For example, "European superiority to China is not in political philosophy, but altogether in the field of material civilization." Sun Yat-sen, *op. cit.*, p. 98. See Herman Finer, *Mussolini's Italy*, New York, 1935, p. 170 for the Fascist case. See Masaki Kosaka, "Modern Japanese Thought," *Journal of World History*, Vol. III, No. 3, p. 610 for the Japanese case. The Indonesian socialist, Sjahrir, however, rejects this notion:

"Here there has been no spiritual or cultural life, and no intellectual progress for centuries . . . Most of us search unconsciously for a synthesis that will leave us internally tranquil. We want to have both Western science and Eastern philosophy, the Eastern 'spirit' in the culture. But what is this Eastern spirit? It is, they say, the sense of the higher, of spirituality, of the eternal and religious, as opposed to the materialism of the West. I have heard this countless times, but it has never convinced me." *Op. cit.*, pp. 66–67.

[19] See Levenson, *loc. cit.*, pp. 160–161, for a Chinese case; or Mohammed Naguib, *op. cit.*, p. 134: "There is nothing in the Koran that calls for theocratic government; on the contrary, the Prophet was in favor of parliamentary rule."

Behind this there is perhaps the implicit wish to see the "East" a genuine partner, an equal, of the West.[20]

The foregoing postures vis-a-vis the West may be comforting to the intellectual, but they will not stimulate action unless certain imperatives are "deduced" from them. For example, "We must purge our national culture of alien corruptions and realize our true character which has been lying dormant within us." But doses of self-criticism are equally important incentives to action, because they make it impossible to relax in complacency. In 1931, Joseph Stalin, leader of one of the most spectacular cultural transformations in human history, told Soviet industrial managers,

One feature of the history of old Russia was the continual beatings she suffered for falling behind, for her backwardness. She was beaten by the Mongol khans. She was beaten by the Turkish beys. She was beaten by the Swedish feudal lords. She was beaten by the Polish and Lithuanian gentry. She was beaten by the Japanese barons. All beat her—for her backwardness: for military backwardness, for cultural backwardness, for political backwardness, for industrial backwardness, for agricultural backwardness. She was beaten because to do so was profitable and could be done with impunity . . .

That is why we must no longer lag behind . . . We are fifty or a hundred years behind the advanced countries. We must make good this distance in ten years. Either we do it, or they crush us.[21]

[20] Levenson, *loc. cit.*, p. 174. The "assaulted" intellectual is sometimes comforted by the thought that Westerners have borrowed some element from his own culture. K. M. Panikkar, in *Asia and Western Dominance*, London, 1953, devotes two chapters to the subject of the impact of Asia on the West. However, the element that Westerners borrow may be one which the native intellectual has already rejected as "backward." For example, Americans in Arab countries who adopt the bedouin headdress on occasion are a source of amusement or irritation to the educated city Arab. He looks down on the bedouin, and he does not want the American to identify Arabs with bedouins. Speaking of such British adventurers as Doughty, Lawrence, and Glubb, an Egyptian intellectual remarked, "We're sick to death of Britishers who can recite the Koran." (As quoted by Roland Pucetti, "Three British Bedouins," *Middle East Forum*, Vol. XXXII, No. 4, p. 34.)

Sjahrir thinks that Westerners who are seeking "Light from Asia" are wasting their time. He says: "I know only too well what the Eastern attributes, so admired by the Westerner, really are. I know that those attributes are molded and nourished only by the hierarchical relationship of a feudal society—a society in which a small group possess all the material and intellectual wealth, and the vast majority live in squalor, and are made acquiescent by religion and philosophy in place of sufficient food.

"That longing of Westerners for the East, in effect, amounts to the same thing as longing for the lost land of the Middle Ages, and the greater goodness and universality that presumably characterized it." *Op. cit.*, p. 160.

[21] J. v. Stalin, *Problems of Leninism*, Moscow, 1947, p. 356.

Another man who administered blunt criticism was Mustafa Kemal Ataturk, who told the Turkish Grand National Assembly in 1920,

We have accepted the principle that we do not, and will not, give up our national independence. Although we always respect this basic condition, when we take into consideration the level of prosperity of the country, the wealth of the nation, and the general mental level, and when we compare it with the progress of the world in general, we must admit that we are not a little, but very backward.[22]

Ataturk praised the Turkish nation, however, for high moral qualities and great past achievements. Although he was probably a xenophile by conviction, he succeeded to a remarkable degree in overcoming the xenophobia of his people by means of his ideological rhetoric. When it was suggested that to borrow from the West "all that Turkey needs" might conflict with the national ideal, Ataturk retorted that the national principle itself had become *internationally* accepted; and also,

Countries are many, but civilization is one and for the progress of a nation it is necessary to participate in this one civilization.[23]

Ataturk justified the importation of specific alien inventions, such as terms from non-Turkish languages, with the assertion that the so-called import was actually indigenous: according to the Sun Language Theory, Turkish was the mother of all the languages of the world, so that "borrowed" words were actually prodigal sons come home.[24] This technique of encouraging an import by calling it indigenous was complemented by the technique of eradicating the indigenous by calling it imported. For example, Ataturk pointed out that the fez was a headgear imported from Europe a hundred years before.

When the intellectual in an industrially backward country surveys modern Western civilization, he is confronted with five hundred years of scientific, artistic, social, economic, political, and religious developments. He sees a flood of heterogeneous Western cultural elements, from jazz to steel mills, pouring into his country. Then, fearing that he will be "swamped" by the deluge, and lose his own identity, he tries to control cultural imports. In order to do this, he must find a standard to determine exactly what should be borrowed. The standard used by the nationalist is that the element to be imported should be in "conformity" with his own national culture and should serve to strengthen his nation. This formula is very elastic, and can be used to

[22] Mustafa Kemal Ataturk, *Atatürk'ün Söylev ve Demeçleri*, I, Istanbul, 1945, p. 29.

[23] Ataturk, *op. cit.*, III, Ankara, 1954, pp. 67–68 and 87.

[24] Uriel Heyd, *Language Reform in Modern Turkey*, Jerusalem, 1954, pp. 33–34.

justify the borrowing or rejection of practically anything. But the Marxist-Leninist holds that the element to be imported should be one that is "progressive" in terms of the Marxist-Leninist pattern of social evolution. According to this pattern, the "bourgeois" West is decaying; it is the "toilers" of both East and West who ride the wave of the future.[25] Imperialism is the highest and the last stage of capitalism. However, Western industrialism and science are the great hope for the non-Western peoples; and the Soviet Union is represented as a model of rapid industrialization and scientific development. If the industrially backward nation borrows from the West only what is most "progressive," it can skip a part, or a stage, of the long and difficult social development of the West. Then, as the West decays, the former backward nations will surpass the best that the West has ever achieved.

The tension between archaism and futurism is another ambiguity in ideologies of delayed industrialization. It is closely related to the xenophobia-xenophilia tension, because the West is "the new" and the native culture is "the old" at the onset of contact.

Archaism is an attempt to resurrect a supposed "golden age," or some part of it. This "golden age" is usually not in the disagreeable recent past, but in a more remote period, and it can only be recovered by historical research and interpretation. For example, Mussolini gloried in imperial Rome and the medieval "corporate state"; the Slavophiles glorified the peasant *mir* and the indigenous Christian Orthodox practices in Russia; the Shintoists revived an ancient mythology that deified the Emperor; Sun Yat-sen and Chiang Kai-shek exhorted the Chinese to revive Confucian ethics; Gandhi urged that India return to the age of "Rama Raj"; and Ataturk exulted in the barbaric virtues of the Osmanli nomads. According to Gandhi,

It was not that we did not know how to invent machinery, but our forefathers knew that, if we set our hearts after such things, we would become slaves and lose our moral fibre. They, therefore, after due deliberation, decided that we should only do what we could with our hands and feet. They further reasoned that large cities were a snare and a useless encumbrance and that people would not be happy in them, that there would be gangs of thieves and robbers, prostitution and vice flourishing in them, and that poor men would be robbed by rich men. They were, therefore, satisfied with small villages.[26]

[25] Marxism-Leninism is of course not the only ideology that contains this proposition. Western ideologists who talk of "the Decline of the West" and "the Awakening of the East" have contributed to, and reinforced, such sentiments.

[26] *Hind Swaraj*, p. 46. Gandhi's archaism went to incredible lengths. In the same work (pp. 42–43) he indicted Western medicine:

According to Mussolini,

Rome is our point of departure and of reference; it is our symbol, or if you like, it is our Myth. We dream of a Roman Italy, that is to say wise and strong, disciplined and imperial. Much of that which was the immortal spirit of Rome resurges in Fascism.[27]

According to Sun Yat-sen,

So, coming to the root of the matter, if we want to restore our race's standing, besides uniting all into a great national body, we must first recover our ancient morality—then, and only then can we plan how to attain again to the national position we once held.[28]

But Nehru condemns archaism:

We have to come to grips with the present, this life, this world, this nature which surrounds us with its infinite variety. Some Hindus talk of going back to the Vedas; some Moslems dream of an Islamic theocracy. Idle fancies, for there is no going back, there is no turning back even if this was thought desirable. There is only one-way traffic in Time.[29]

Archaism may slip into a futuristic ideology, such as Marxism, and create an ambiguity. Adam Ulam has suggested that Marxism has its greatest appeal for semi-proletarianized or uprooted peasants who are nostalgic for the "good old days" when their actions were governed by nature, the village elders, the family patriarch, and the religious authorities—instead of the less congenial factory boss and the State. To the uprooted peasant Marxism offers a comforting strain of archaism: that is, it envisions a utopia in which state and factory, as coercive institutions, have "withered away." [30]

Whenever a resurrection of the past is contemplated, the question arises, "What part of the past?" or "Which age was our golden age, and

"I have indulged in vice, I contract a disease, a doctor cures me, the odds are that I shall repeat the vice. Had the doctor not intervened, nature would have done its work and I would have acquired mastery over myself, would have been freed from vice and would have been happy.

"Hospitals are institutions for propagating sin. Men take less care of their bodies and immorality increases."

These opinions might be dismissed as unimportant since they were expressed so early in Gandhi's career. However, in a preface to a new edition of *Hind Swaraj* which Gandhi wrote in 1938, he said:

"The booklet is a severe condemnation of 'modern civilization.' It was written in 1908. My conviction is deeper today than ever. I feel that, if India will discard 'modern civilization,' she can only gain by doing so." (P. 11).

[27] As quoted by Finer, *op. cit.*, p. 191.

[28] Sun Yat-sen, *op. cit.*, pp. 125–126.

[29] Nehru, *op. cit.*, p. 447.

[30] Adam Ulam, "The Historical Role of Marxism and the Soviet System," *World Politics*, Vol. VIII, No. 1, pp. 20–45.

why?" Sometimes the age selected is an imperial age, when the people in question enjoyed their greatest authority over others. Sometimes a period of "pristine simplicity" is admired. But new imperial conquests are incompatible with the weak political and economic position of industrially backward countries, and a return to the "simple life" is incompatible with industrialization. In such cases archaism is not a solution to the problem at hand, but an escape from it.

However, there are more constructive uses of the past. The intellectual may discover that in the remote past his people possessed the very virtues which are supposed to make a modern nation great. For example, the Kemalists glorify their ancestors as brave, tolerant, realistic, generous, peaceful, and respectful of women; in short, "spiritual" exemplars of the well-bred Western European gentleman. These "genuine" Turks were temporarily "corrupted" by Arab-Persian-Byzantine culture, but they are now due to take their rightful place among "civilized" nations.[31] The manifest content of such an ideological position may be archaistic, but its latent content is futuristic.

The Communists also use the past in this way. But they have characteristic standards for determining what elements of the past are desirable. The Chinese Communists have cultivated peasant literature and art because they are "progressive," being products of a "progressive" class; whereas gentry culture is rejected as "feudal."[32] In the Soviet Union the pre-revolutionary leaders most cherished by the Communist regime are those it considers "progressive" for their time (such as Peter the Great), whereas "reactionaries" (such as Dostoyevsky, until recently) have been under a cloud.

Nationalists, when selecting elements from their past, ask, "What will tend to strengthen the nation?" But tradition has lost its natural charm, and traditionalism is something the nationalist must "work at." He uses the shared traditions of his people as raw material with which to build national morale; but tradition is a means, existing only for the sake of national strength, and not as an axiomatic, self-justified good.[33] For example, Sun Yat-sen said in 1924:

Our position now is extremely perilous; if we do not earnestly promote nationalism and weld together our four hundred millions into a strong nation, we face a tragedy—the loss of our country and the destruction of our race. To ward off this danger, we must espouse Nationalism and employ the national spirit to save the country.[34]

[31] See Halide Edib Adivar, *Turkey Faces West*, New Haven, 1930, pp. 1–9.
[32] Levenson, *loc. cit.*, p. 184.
[33] Levenson, *loc. cit.*, pp. 172–173. See also Emerson, *loc. cit.*, pp. 136–142.
[34] Sun Yat-sen, *op. cit.*, p. 12.

There are other uses of the past besides escapism, the sanctioning of innovations, the glorification of "progressive" individuals and groups, and national self-strengthening. The past may be used to eradicate what the intellectual feels to be undesirable in the present and for the future. By publicizing the results of historical research, showing that a supposedly indigenous cultural element (like the fez) is of foreign origin, he may thereby stigmatize it. He may use other grounds to stigmatize the Ottoman and Chinese literary languages; they are the languages of reactionary and oppressive ruling classes who have cared only for their own welfare, rather than the welfare of the people.

The concern of both nationalists and Communists for vernacular languages and peasant arts is closely related to a third problem of the "assaulted" intellectual: his relationship with the uneducated masses. Some intellectuals have a sentimental, patronizing, or contemptuous attitude toward the masses.[35] Sun Yat-sen said,

The Ming veterans spread the idea of nationalism through the lower classes; but, on account of their childish understanding, the lower classes did not know how to take advantage of the ideas, but were, on the contrary, made tools of by others.[36]

Mohammed Naguib of Egypt wrote in 1955:

Given the deplorable conditions in Egyptian villages, however, the distinction between compulsion and cooperation is irrelevant. The average *fellah* has fallen too low to be able to help himself without a great deal of compulsory assistance from the government.[37]

Other intellectuals, like Nehru, wonder if the peasants are the "true" Indians, while they (the intellectuals) are only "pseudos." The Russian Narodniki went "back to the people" to learn from them and to teach them; and so have Turkish intellectuals in our own century. Undeniably, many intellectuals have felt sincere compassion for the sufferings of the peasants and sincere respect for the folk arts. But it is unlikely that the attitude of an intellectual toward the uneducated masses in an industrially backward country (or in any country) is free from ambiguity: he looks up to "the people" and down on "the masses."

However he may feel about the majority of his compatriots, the intellectual must face the practical problems of industrialization and modernization. The intellectual knows that a government which really

[35] See the statement of an Arab, al-Kawakebi, in Hazim Z. Nuseibeh's *The Ideas of Arab Nationalism*, Ithaca, 1956, p. 132. See also D. P. Mukerji, "The Intellectual in India," *Confluence*, Vol. IV, No. 4, p. 446, and James Mysbergh, "The Indonesian Elite," *Far Eastern Survey*, Vol. XXVI, No. 3, p. 39.

[36] Sun Yat-sen, *op. cit.*, pp. 61–62.

[37] Naguib, *op. cit.*, p. 149.

represents the thinking of the uneducated masses will not attack these problems boldly and comprehensively. The peasant may long for riches, but he is not eager to give up his traditional ways. To attain its ends, the intelligentsia must arouse the masses to strenuous effort, or, as Alexander Gerschenkron puts it, give them an emotional "New Deal." [38]

The intelligentsia must provide just the right amount of criticism, and just the right amount of comfort necessary to make the masses follow its lead into the "battle" of industrialization. That is why ideologies of delayed industrialization condemn the peasant for his backwardness, and then praise him for being a *real* representative of the indigenous culture. Such ideologies may stand for class equality and simultaneously exhort the masses to follow orders and to accept unequal rewards, both as individuals and as occupational groups. This does not mean that "assaulted" intellectuals are necessarily cynical and manipulative; they may be sincerely attached to contradictory premises.

In most cases, when an ideology of delayed industrialization emerges, the traditional rulers (king, sultan, tsar, etc.) have been overthrown, or are on the verge of being overthrown. But when traditional rulers remain in power, as in Japan, they are supported by new social groups and assume new social functions. They must now mobilize the masses to meet the challenge of the modern industrial West. Whether there has been a massive social revolution or a "circulation of elites," the cultural revolution is inevitable.

Rupert Emerson has suggested that if reform and revolution in industrially backward countries are led by Westernized intellectuals drawn from various social strata rather than by traditional elites, the prevalent ideology tends to include a stronger egalitarian element. The intelligentsia, having no solid power base of its own, is especially in need of mass support. This is particularly true, he believes, in areas which have been longest under Western domination, such as India, where the traditional native elite lost most of its power and indoctrination in Western political values went deep. But in countries like Japan, where the traditional elite took command of social and economic reform, the prevalent ideology tends to put a premium on hierarchical values: loyalty, obedience, respect. [39] This theory may be useful in explaining differences between developments in India and Japan, but its applicability elsewhere is dubious. It is important here to distinguish

---

[38] Alexander Gerschenkron, "Economic Backwardness in Historical Perspective," in *The Progress of Underdeveloped Areas*, Bert Hoselitz, ed., Chicago, 1952, pp. 22–25.

[39] Emerson, *loc. cit.*, p. 140.

between symbolic values, which may be egalitarian, and their accompanying operational values, which may be hierarchical. It is also important to define "equality": is it legal, economic, spiritual, or does it refer to the possession of a common culture?

The tension between egalitarian and hierarchical values is sometimes resolved theoretically by the doctrine of "tutelage." According to this doctrine democracy must be introduced into a country in two stages. In the first stage, a single, "all-people's" party of the most "enlightened" and "progressive" elements of the nation takes over the government and acts as a faculty for educating the masses in democratic ways. At some time in the indefinite future the masses will be ready for direct self-government and the "all-people's" party will "wither away." This doctrine, with various modifications, has appeared in Turkey, India, and China; but when the doctrine has been applied, it has led to a variety of unexpected results.

In order to understand an ideology it is important to determine what problems its initiators are trying to solve. In the case of intellectuals in industrially backward countries, the three main problems are: (1) What is to be borrowed from the West? (2) What is to be retained from the nation's past? (3) What characteristics, habits, and products of the masses are to be encouraged? It is remarkable that intellectuals in widely separate parts of the world have reacted similarly to these problems.

7

THE POLITICS OF
TRADE UNION LEADERSHIP
IN SOUTHERN ASIA

George E. Lichtblau

Labor movements in areas of South Asia which are, or were until recently, under the control of British, French, or Dutch administrations have assumed considerable political, social, and economic importance despite the fact that industrialization and wage employment affect only a small segment of the popluation. As adjuncts of national movements they played a significant role in the struggle for independence; they have served the interests of the Communists and other dissident revolutionary groups; and they have participated in the tasks of economic reconstruction. In some areas, moreover, these labor organizations have exceeded in size not only existing political parties, but also other movements built on common occupational interests, such as peasant organizations. As a result, they have become a focal point for extra-parliamentary political activities.[1] Their importance in most South Asian countries is all the more surprising, considering that they are purely Western institutions characteristic of highly industrialized and occupationally stratified societies. Yet in South Asia these move-

Reprinted, by permission, from *World Politics*, VII, No. 1 (October 1954), 84–101.

---

[1] The Indian National Trade Union Congress (INTUC) and the Congress Party; the All-India Trade Union Congress and the Communist Party of India; the Hind Mazdoor Sabha and the Praja Socialist Party; the Trade Union Congress of Burma and the Anti-Fascist People's Freedom League (AFPFL); the Central Trade Union Federation of Indonesia (SOBSI) and the Partai Kommunis Indonesia; the Islamic Trade Union Federation of Indonesia (SBII) and the Masjumi Party; the General Confederation of Labor of Viet Nam (Tong Lau Doan) and the Lien Viet movement and the Lau Dong, or Workers' Party; the All-Pakistan Confederation of Labor and the Muslim League, etc.

ments are thriving in predominantly agricultural societies, with an occupational stratification bearing little resemblance to that of industrialized countries.

Two questions are of particular interest for the student of international relations in connection with this phenomenon. First, what factors account for the rise of such a movement in these areas? Secondly, what political roles are the trade union leaders in the countries of South Asia tending to play?

In what follows, it is worth remembering that these countries have in common not only their struggle for independence from colonial rule, but also a leadership remarkably similar in outlook on future political and economic developments. They all face serious Communist opposition. They are preoccupied with the problem of trying to reconcile their predominantly urban outlook and desire for centralized political power and economic initiative with traditionalist regional, tribal, and rural-feudal elements which are trying to extricate themselves as much as possible from centralized control. However, because of differences in the relative size of their wage labor forces, in the status of their industrial development, in the intensity of their struggles for independence, the applicability of generalizations will vary with each country. And, because of the preoccupation of South Asian trade union leadership with political matters, general political attitudes and the emergence of national as well as trade union leadership in this area will be discussed in order to provide an understanding of the special role of organized labor.

I. LABOR'S ROLE IN THE ACHIEVEMENT
OF INDEPENDENCE

Chief among the factors favoring the growth of mass trade union movements in South Asia was the creation of a rapidly growing but still small urban proletariat, dependent for its livelihood on wage employment, and led by a highly volatile and intensely nationalistic educated group. This new intellectual class, which counted among its members many uprooted and often property-less university and high school students, felt that the policies of the colonial powers frustrated its aspirations to assume political responsibility and leadership. Thus a sharp dilemma presented itself to the colonial powers: on the one hand, they sought to promote the growth of the educated classes by providing the native peoples with Western academic training; on the other hand, they felt their control over the colonial areas increasingly threatened by the very people they had trained. As a measure of self-protection, they excluded most of this group from positions of leadership and trust and in this way promoted among these native intellectuals a kind of proletarian consciousness [2] which led them to seek revolutionary solutions to their problems. Consequently, when the colonial powers took sharp repressive measures, they often forced the anti-colonial nationalist leaders either into clandestine operations or into activities politically less objectionable to the colonial administrations, such as the organization of labor.[3]

Ideological influences, particularly that of Marxism on the nationalist movements, also helped colonial labor to gain increasing organizational importance. Control of organized labor not only gave the nationalist leaders the power to paralyze the economic life of the country, thereby weakening the hold of the colonial power (whose primary motive was considered to be economic exploitation); it also provided them with a disciplined following around which production could be reorganized and rapid industrialization started, once independence had been achieved. Thus trade unionism attracted to its leadership an important segment of the Western-educated native nationalists, who expected to attain through their new positions an upward social and political mobility otherwise denied them.

The workers, in turn, followed these intellectuals because they needed leaders who were articulate and sufficiently militant to voice their grievances and to impress both the government and their employers. Lack of education, inexperience in negotiation, and an apathy often born of poverty and malnutrition, which prevented the workers from acquiring the necessary skills, had made the rise of a leadership

[2] This proletarian consciousness was produced by wide unemployment among the intellectuals, their exclusion from legitimate political activities, and their conception of the role of the working class in the future industrial development of their countries.

[3] A clear example of this policy is the attitude of the Dutch East Indies administration to political parties and trade unions during the 1930's. Organization of nationalist trade unions was far less hazardous than other forms of political activity.

Labor legislation in both Burma and India not only provided trade union leaders with certain organizational advantages, but actually gave them political representation. In Burma, sharp repressive measures against the Thakin Party in 1939 led to the immediate outbreak of a series of strikes and the founding of the All-Burma Trade Union Congress. In India, this selective policy of favoring politically pliable trade unions and trade union leaders backfired after World War II. When the Congress Party started its "quit India" campaign in 1942, most Congress Party political and trade union leaders were arrested, while the Communists, who cooperated with the British in the war effort, were actually encouraged to capture the leadership of the All-India Trade Union Congress.

from the rank and file well-nigh impossible. Thus, in return for their advocacy of the workers' interests, the leaders gained effective political support. Ordinarily, relations between the rank and file and the leadership were rather loose. However, when grievances mounted and tension increased, solidarity between the followers and the leaders became quite strong. The interests of both sides converged, and they identified their diverse grievances with the suppressed cause of nationalism.

Trade union activities were thus ideally suited to the purposes of the nationalists. Since trade unions had already been accepted as part and parcel of the economic structure of Western society, the metropolitan governments were restrained by their liberal economic outlook, as well as by socialist and trade union pressure at home, from permitting their colonial administrations to suppress organizations which were ostensibly economic in their objectives, provided these did not seriously threaten trade policies.[4]

Even when these nationalist trade unions resorted to political strikes and demonstrations, the colonial governments preferred to regulate and curtail their activities rather than to ban them outright, although they had no compunction about suppressing political groups which challenged their rule. The primary reasons for this tolerance of trade unions were the expectations that they would follow the development of Western labor movements, that this process could be speeded up by official guidance and encouragement, and that such native unions would through voluntary means instill orderly working habits in the colonial workers. Wage incentives were insufficient to keep workers on the job and the old paternalistic relation between employers and workers was being undermined by rising nationalist sentiment. Accordingly, colonial administrations frequently resorted to such coercive means of controlling workers as punitive labor legislation, special police, contract labor, etc., in order to maintain an orderly flow of production.[5] By the same token, however, this indifference to wage

---

[4] The major exception was France, which prevented the formation of native trade unions in its colonial empire until after World War II. In the Philippines, the concept of national liberation from colonial powers did not develop to the same extent as in other South Asian countries because of the unique relation between the United States and the Philippines. No revolutionary liberation movement developed which required special organizational tools (other than the relatively small Huk movement). Thus the Philippine trade unions did not play a significant role in the nationalist movement.

[5] In this connection, it is significant that while wage increases provide little incentive to work harder, payments in kind and employer-furnished welfare services provide a paternalistic tie between employer and worker. When the bulk of wage remunerations is paid in cash, serious problems of economic choice present

incentives and the high "disutility of labor" among native workers provided trade union leaders with a potent weapon in the struggle for independence, by making it relatively simple for them to disrupt the extractive economic process of the colony. For that matter, even today anything from a genuine grievance to a native holiday, such as the Muslim fasts during Ramadan, can still provide occasion for a strike. Therefore, in addition to enforcement measures directed at individuals, labor legislation offering both political and economic privileges to compliant trade unions, as well as strict governmental supervision of the activities of such unions, was considered an effective means of counteracting the resistance to industrial discipline among the native workers.

After World War II, which brought liberation from the Japanese as well as independence from colonial rule to most countries of the area, economic incentives were further weakened by strong inflationary trends,[6] while the means of physical coercion were lacking. Often nationalist and ideological appeals were the only inducements sufficiently strong to restore a semblance of working order to their economies. Accordingly, both colonial administrators and nationalist governments tried to use the trade unions to persuade the workers to accept a system of industrial working discipline.[7]

Even before the war, the colonial policy of permitting the formation of trade unions appears to have been based, at least in part, on some expectation that through them native oppositionist activities could be diverted from the government to the smaller target of private employers. Such conflicts were expected to be more easily resolved by *ad hoc*

themselves to the inexperienced workers, thereby adding to their discontent with wage employment, which in most Oriental societies is stigmatized as a social status bordering on slavery.

Communist labor leaders are fully aware of the importance of this economic phenomenon. The stress which they place upon money wages in preference to full or partial wage payments in kind is intended to weaken further the workers' ties with their jobs and their employers, thereby facilitating the disruptive activities of Communist labor agitators. Although the primary emphasis on monetary incentives is intended to prepare the workers for the coming industrialization under socialism, it has backfired on several occasions in India, Indonesia, and Malaya, turning the discontent of the rank and file against the unions.

[6] See Ragnar Nurkse, *Problems of Capital Formation in Underdeveloped Countries*, Oxford, 1953, p. 17.

[7] Royal Commission on Labour in India, *Report of the Royal Commission on Labour in India, June 1931*, London, 1931, pp. 317–32. For Congress Party policy, see P. S. Narasimhan, "Labour Reforms in Contemporary India," *Pacific Affairs*, xxvi (March 1953), p. 46. For the attitude of the Indonesian nationalist movement toward labor in 1945, see Virginia Thompson, *Labor Problems in Southeast Asia*, New Haven, Conn., 1947, p. 255.

solutions, and thus reduce the over-all threat to both colonial and business interests. In fact, large national trade union federations were much more closely under the surveillance of the colonial police and intelligence services than were the smaller local independent organizations.[8]

As a result of governmental policies favoring the growth of trade unions, nationalist leaders were able to use them as valuable political and administrative training grounds. Such men, for instance, as Gandhi, Nehru, and even Patel in India,[9] Sjahrir and Salijm [10] in Indonesia, Thakin Mya and U Ba Swe [11] in Burma, and a large segment of the South Asian Communist leadership had been active in the labor movements of their countries. Following independence, nationalist leaders put the development of the trade union movement into the forefront of their activities because of its strategic importance.

II. COMMUNIST LEADERSHIP

It is precisely the appeal of Communism in underdeveloped areas that it assigns to the educated, but uprooted, *avant-garde* a key role in the transformation of a "colonial" agrarian society into an industrial one. Furthermore, Communism proposes to substitute drastic technical and organizational methods for the slow and often seemingly inefficient system of political checks and balances which was inherited from the colonial powers with the institution of parliamentary government. The promise of rapid industrialization and of a quick alteration of the social structure into an efficient, productive machine appears to ensure attainment of all the elements of Western superiority, i.e., Western technical proficiency. Finally, Communist belief in the inevitability of a proletarian victory seems to have a strong attraction for the Eastern mentality, which because of religious belief and temperament is intensely preoccupied with the concept of "fate."

Communism appears to offer means for the effective utilization of

[8] Willard Galbraith, *Organized Labor in the Netherlands Indies: A Basic Labor Report*, U.S. Consulate, Batavia, December 15, 1941; also Thompson, *op. cit.*, p. 8.

[9] Richard L. Park, "Labor and Politics in India," *Far Eastern Survey*, xviii (August 10, 1949), pp. 181 ff.

[10] The Socialist Sutan Sjahrir was leader of the Central Labor Federation of Indonesia (Pusat Perserikatan Buruh Indonesia) from 1932 to 1934. For Haji Agus Salijm, see Anonymous, "Trade Unions in Indonesia," *Indonesian Review*, Djakarta, No. 7 (December 1950), pp. 6–10.

[11] Virginia Thompson and Richard Adloff, *The Left Wing in Southeast Asia*, New York, 1950, p. 250. For U Ba Swe, see *New Times of Burma*, Rangoon, December 17, 1950.

overabundant and hitherto wasted human resources in underdeveloped areas and claims the ability to create a modern industrial society without outside help. Russia and China are cited as examples of such promises come true. Claiming that conventional (i.e., Western) political and economic techniques are slow and inefficient, Communists seek to substitute for them the iron-clad political discipline of a small elite, through which they can eventually achieve power. Once power is seized, they can maintain control through the refined terrorist methods of the police state.

Nevertheless, despite the existence of revolutionary situations in most South Asian countries, the Communists have been unable to gain control in any area except Indochina, where their task was facilitated by special circumstances, such as acquisition of arms from the surrendering Japanese army, and military and political aid from the Kuomintang and later from the Chinese Communists. Moreover, in Indochina they had the psychological advantage of being the *de facto* native government, challenged by an outside "imperialist" force that was trying to make a comeback. In all other areas, the Communists have failed to achieve control of the government, and their attempted revolutions have degenerated into disruptive raiding tactics, strikes, political opposition, and encouragement of other dissident elements.[12]

However, by representing the existing native governments as camouflaged continuations of the old colonial system, the Communists have appealed to those who are inclined to distrust the centralist policies of the nationalist governments, as well as to those who feel that social reforms have been far too slow. They claim that the colonial powers went through the pretense of surrendering sovereignty to the new governments in return for guarantees that their economic interests would be fully protected. Thus the newly independent countries are alleged to be, in effect, still subject to colonial exploitation.

By means of this rationale, Communist-controlled political and labor movements have also attracted a militant, politically disruptive element which, under the momentum of newly won independence and

---

[12] Communist failure to gain mass support is particularly conspicuous among the peasants of Southern Asia, notwithstanding Mao Tze-tung's efforts to make a political appeal to rural elements. Attempts to gain large-scale rural support through peasant movements have never enjoyed more than temporary successes, despite Communist efforts to infiltrate traditional leadership positions in the villages and religious institutions, and to gain rural confidence by opposing—as, for instance, in Sumatra—the introduction of modern agricultural equipment and techniques in a government-operated resettlement project. The Communists have also attempted to bolster their cause by advocating land reforms and by aiding and encouraging tribal or regional irredentist movements.

the process of industrialization, will challenge any constituted authority of either colonial or incumbent nationalist governments. This element feels that the government leaders are blatant opportunists who do not enjoy the support of the people but merely came to power by historical accident. They thus consider their own disruptive and oppositionist activities not only politically expedient but morally right. Furthermore, acquiescence to a social or economic *status quo* would necessarily curtail their political maneuverability and might permanently relegate them to secondary roles. This they consider hardly an acceptable alternative to imperialist oppression. Therefore, they prefer a climate of political and economic instability in which they can exploit widespread insecurity and dissatisfaction. Such leaders, although very useful to the Communists, are in the long run questionable allies.[13]

Mao Tze-tung, aware of this danger, has made an effort to forestall the purely negative disruptive aspects of the various Communist revolutions by directing the party's appeal not only to the workers and peasants, but also to the managerial and proprietary classes. Without the cooperation and the managerial skill of the formerly despised bourgeoisie, an industrialized "socialist" society would be difficult to achieve, and despite immediate tactical successes, a revolution would bog down. Mao, therefore, has assigned to the middle class (i.e., the "national" and "petty" bourgeoisie) not merely transitory roles, but an important long-range function in the Communist scheme of things. In countries not under Communist control, where members of the middle class might be reluctant to associate themselves with the Communist movement, they are to be enlisted in national front organizations that are not as closely associated in popular opinion with the interests of Soviet imperialism as in the Communist Party. Among these front organizations, labor unions are of strategic importance in that they give Communist activities the appearance of democratic respectability.

Both from a tactical and from an ideological point of view, Communists have found the trade unions very useful tools in challenging first the colonial powers, later the Japanese occupation authorities, and now the new and still shaky nationalist governments. They anticipate that strikes, militant demonstrations, the undermining of traditional paternalistic relations between employers and workers, and the exploitation

---

[13] In this connection, it must be pointed out that disruptive and opportunistic elements are by no means exclusively characteristic of the Communist movement. They pervade other radical nationalist movements, particularly xenophobic splinter groups organized on a religious basis, such as the Muslim Brotherhood, Ahrar-e-Islam in Pakistan, Darul Islam in Indonesia, and Mahasabha and RSSS in India.

of discontent and grievances will promote class consciousness among the workers and thus make possible a Communist mass uprising at some future date.

Experience has shown that while the instigation of strikes and demonstrations meets with considerable success, largely because an industrial pattern of life still works considerable hardship on people not accustomed to the rigorous discipline imposed by factory jobs, Communist (as well as non-Communist) unions, despite their impressive size, fail to retain the loyalty of their members. When Communist unions rigorously follow unpopular dictates of the party line,[14] as from time to time they do, they tend to fall apart, leaving little feeling of workers' solidarity behind. Instead, other loyalties—to the family, the village, the tribe, the church, and the nation—prevail. Nevertheless, it is the appeal of direct action as such, with its apparent solution to the largely insoluble problem of misery and poverty among the workers and its promise of ultimate stability, that drives people to rebel and accounts for the elusive attraction of Communist unions.[15] In the face of great hardships and the absence of other protective devices, the workers often tend to follow the most militant

[14] For a recent example, see *New York Times,* April 26, 1953, "Reds in Indonesia Start Wage Drive"; also *ibid.,* October 11, 1953, "Indonesia Reds' Rift Breaks out in Open." This rift appears to have broken out over a no-strike pledge given by the Communist-dominated SOBSI trade union federation in October 1952 at a National Congress in connection with Communist support of the government. Recently this pledge was rescinded by the Indonesian Communists because it had led to severe losses in trade union membership.

[15] Except for the select small cadres that make up the Communist trade union leadership, there is little disciplined rank-and-file participation in union affairs. Also lacking is the coherence of Western trade unions, in which, even when the members are inactive, there is at least a strong vested interest in union membership as such. In this connection, it may be of some interest to note that the Communist unions of India and Indonesia—and presumably elsewhere in South Asia—do not stress in their programs literacy campaigns or general workers' education, two prerequisites for the creation of a planned society, and two extremely important factors in promoting both national and trade union consciousness. This may be due to a lack of funds and teachers, which forces the Communists to concentrate on leadership. On the other hand, this neglect of workers' education is not in evidence in the Viet Minh area or in Communist China, where there must be an even greater shortage of teachers and leaders. In these areas, the trade unions are very actively engaged in such literacy campaigns. In areas where the Communists have failed to gain control, their unions concentrate on the creation of professional trade union cadres, which provide the Communists with additional power to disrupt their country's economy. In view of the traditional role that labor education plays in the programs of Western labor and socialist movements, which are often the prototypes of colonial trade unions, this omission would appear to be deliberate, pointing up more clearly the disruptive aspect of Communist union activities.

leadership in the hope that its daring tactics will effectively impress both the employers and the authorities. Furthermore, Communist militancy affords the workers an occasion to inflict punishment and injury with a large degree of impunity on the most apparent source of their misery, while the leaders eagerly assume responsibility for the consequences of the actions of the workers.

III. NON-COMMUNIST LEADERSHIP

Political and trade union development in South Asian countries has given rise to two groups of non-Communist leaders who can maintain through their personal influence a precarious balance of law and order. One of these groups consists of leaders whose authority is local and based on native traditions; the other is the democratic leadership which seeks to maintain to a certain degree the political, administrative, and even the ideological framework left by the Western colonial powers.

The influence of the traditional leaders is strongest among the peasants, native handicraft artisans, and agricultural workers. These leaders come from the feudal, aristocratic landholders, the village headmen, tribal chieftains, and heads of guilds. They include a type of foremen, such as the *cays* in Indochina, the *sardars* in India, or the stevedore bosses in Far Eastern ports, who hire out not only their own services, but also those of a gang of workers whom they control. They seldom assume the role of trade union leaders, as this term is understood in the West, because they are little concerned with the protection of the workers and even participate in their exploitation. Nevertheless, they constitute a native labor leadership which facilitates the supply of labor and imposes upon the people whom they control a social stability that is highly effective (although perhaps excessively harsh). Under special circumstances, new labor legislation or the political situation of the country has made it profitable for these traditional leaders to establish formal trade unions—as, for instance, the Bangkok *Samlor* (Pedicab) Drivers' Union, which was organized among ex-soldiers by former army generals who control all *samlors* in the city and prevent all non-veterans from operating such conveyances. In Malaya a union of fishermen, under the leadership of a tribal chieftain, exercises sweeping controls over fishermen, fishing boats, and fishing rights. On occasion—as, for instance, in Sumatra—a member of the aristocracy has used the influence of his name to organize a union of estate laborers [16]

[16] Persatuan Buruh Perkebunan Republik Indonesia, or Association of Estate Workers of the Republic of Indonesia.

in competition with Communist plantation workers' unions. Such a leader, however, appears to be motivated as much by local political considerations as by his interests in trade unionism.

Despite the frequent ruthlessness of these traditional leaders, their hold on the workers is quite strong, based as it is on the importance attached to rank and hierarchy in most Oriental societies.[17] The workers under their control have predominantly rural backgrounds and are accustomed to a society closely regulated by tradition. In the new environment of factory or plantation, they find themselves overwhelmed by the need to plan their own life and livelihood and become only too eager to delegate responsibility, even of the most personal nature, to their leaders. Sometimes this relationship, complicated by the political situation, becomes so burdensome to the workers as to lead to disturbances, usually localized, which seriously threaten the position of the leaders. However, in the absence of interference from the national authorities, the prestige and influence of the traditional leaders tend to reassert themselves. Despite its abuses, local traditional authority is preferred by the workers to the unknown and untried authority of the national government, making the traditional leader an important stabilizing element not only in South Asia, but throughout the Far and Middle East.[18]

The second and perhaps more important group is composed of the Western-oriented democratic leaders.[19] They represent the urban population, which dominates the political and economic life of these newly independent states of South Asia. Furthermore, they are the leaders with whom foreign nations, Western employers, and international trade union leaders have to deal. These leaders usually received a Western education and were prominent in the revolutionary nationalist independence movements until the end of the colonial administration. Unlike the Communists, however, this group of leaders dropped

[17] In order to reinforce their control over the workers, the traditional leaders often resort to such means as indebtedness, control of the supply of widely used narcotics, and threats of physical violence. See Bruno Lasker, *Human Bondage in Southeast Asia*, Chapel Hill, N.C., 1950, pp. 102–4.

[18] Recognition that in Oriental society the concepts of humanism and of individual welfare are almost completely lacking tends to shock Western sensibilities. This factor is important, however, because it explains why many Asians are not repelled by the cruelties of the Communist system. Furthermore, it should be remembered that the methods applied in Europe in creating an industrial labor force and an urban proletariat were probably more cruel and ruthless, because they were used on a more extensive scale than those applied in the Orient. For a discussion of the conflict between Marxism and traditionalism, see Paul Mus, *Viet Nam, Sociologie d'une Guerre*, Paris, 1952, pp. 248–67.

[19] This term does not refer to the leaders' position in the East-West struggle.

its revolutionary attitude after independence and showed itself willing to operate within the framework of the new nationalist governments, whether it was directly associated with them or not.

Many of these leaders actively engaged in underground activities during the Japanese occupation, while some gained their first major political and administrative experience by collaborating with the Japanese. Others, although opposed to colonialism, were willing to accept limited cooperation with the colonial administrations. They saw that the social and economic ills of their countries were not exclusively the fault of the imperialist nations, and that independence *per se* would not rectify all of them. They also knew that any solution of these problems would depend on retaining the continued interest of the former colonial powers and of the industrial West in general, as well as on making aid and investment from these sources palatable to their own people. They regarded nationalism as a vital constructive force which could be used not only to maintain law and order, but also to overcome the difficult problems of labor discipline; yet they also recognized the threat implicit in its more extreme manifestations.

This, however, does not mean that these Western-oriented leaders are free from prejudices against the former colonial countries under whose administrations many of them suffered jail sentences, enforced exile, and other personal humiliations. They are interested in finding their own way toward a planned economy which, according to their expectations, would avoid both the oppression of totalitarian Communism and the insecurity born of fluctuations in the world market. They are reluctant to make exclusive political commitments to the West, because this would upset the precarious political balance in their countries at large. In some areas—as, for instance, in Indonesia—such involvement would undermine their control of the non-Communist labor movement, inflame anti-imperialist hotheads, and thereby encourage the pro-Communist elements. Involvement of their countries in a war, these leaders feel, would not only increase the possibility of intense civil strife, but would in the end—whether by conquest or indebtedness—bring their countries under the subjugation of either the Eastern or the Western power bloc. This would mean the end of all national hopes and aspirations.

Despite their cautious neutrality, however, they prefer Western democratic institutions, and a continuation of the political and administrative system set up by the former colonial powers, to a "peoples' democratic system." While they are ardent nationalists themselves, they are aware of the danger of extreme nationalism, which easily passes from constructive collectivism to lawlessness and destruction.[20] Despite their policy of neutrality, they know that continuity with the West offers the only chance of stabilizing the political and economic situation of their countries.

It is this group of Western-oriented leaders which started the trade union movement in most South Asian countries. Some of these labor movements were quickly taken over by Communists prior to or during World War II and rival non-Communist unions were relegated to secondary positions. However, with the achievement of independence, the non-Communist leaders by and large were more successful in attracting followers among the workers, because they were closely associated with the new source of political power and thus could exercise their influence on both the government and the employers. The power relations between trade union leadership and the rank and file, in turn, followed closely the traditional pattern of patronage, even in the modern forms of labor organizations, and was closely related to the labor policy of the new regimes.[21]

After independence, the democratic leaders started to transform their non-Communist unions from political instruments intended for use against the colonial powers into somewhat more pliable movements which could be used to build up the economy of their countries. On occasion these democratic union leaders have encouraged their organizations to resort to acts of violence, partly because of their own past political experience, partly because of rank-and-file pressure for such tactics, and not least because of Communist competition. Nevertheless, in India, Pakistan, and to a lesser extent in Indonesia, Burma, Ceylon, and the Philippines, they have succeeded in building up a moderate

[20] L. N. Palar, "Nationalism—Friend or Foe of Democracy?", *Indonesian Affairs*, II, No. 3 (June–July 1952), pp. 24–28.

[21] Both INTUC and the Trade Union Congress of Burma enjoy considerable advantages over rival unions because of their close link with the Congress Party and AFPFL respectively. In this connection, it is of interest to note that the success of the largest Communist trade union of the area, i.e., SOBSI in Indonesia, can be explained at least in part by the fact that the government's Ministry of Labor is continually favoring that organization, even when the government has elsewhere cracked down on Communists. Since attainment of independence in 1949, the government has used SOBSI for the realization of its labor policies and has constantly favored it in labor legislation and arbitration decisions. Only for a brief time in 1951 did the government proceed against Communist strikes and labor agitation.

The rise of the one other major Communist union of the area, the All-India Trade Union Congress, was also linked with the favored treatment it received from the British India government during the war. Since India's achievement of independence, it has steadily lost influence and membership.

and by and large politically responsible labor movement, even in the face of severe Communist rivalry.

Because of the usefulness of such trade union movements, the parties in power, as well as other moderate democratic parties of most South Asian countries, have undertaken to ensure support for themselves from these movements by furnishing them with leadership and financial aid, and by favoritism in wage decisions and social legislation. In this way they hope to facilitate the realization of their economic plans and to speed up industrial development. Such tactics, however, engender several political problems affecting both the future development of the labor organizations and relations between the leadership and the rank and file.

The adjustments required by the shift from traditional, feudal, hierarchical relations in the village to the discipline of industrial employment are quite drastic. The passive attitude of the workers to such changes often tempts the leaders to take short cuts toward their objectives without reference to the interests of the workers, as, for instance, in the setting of wage rates in government-operated enterprises. The propensity of the Oriental workers to delegate even the most personal responsibilities to leaders who have assumed their positions from above rather than by any democratic process is an invitation to these leaders to direct the workers either by autocratic-paternalistic means or by force, often in conjunction with law enforcement agencies or with the connivance of the labor inspectorate.[22] Both methods are convenient and get immediate results; and even the most idealistic leaders tend to become impatient and yield to the temptation of their efficacy. The danger lies in the habit-forming nature of such tactics. Furthermore, the anti-democratic forces are much more ruthless in the application of such methods and may in the end have the advantage over the democratic forces.

There is also a tendency for the democratic leadership, which looks upon itself as a new elite, to resort to autocratic measures, making it hardly distinguishable from traditional forms of leadership, except perhaps in its professed ultimate objectives. This tendency has already manifested itself, particularly in the new nationalist civil services of several South Asian countries. Even such men as Nehru, Sukarno, Hatta, and U Nu, prototypes of Asian democratic leadership, have on occasion resorted to strong autocratic methods in order to quiet the opposition.

[22] Government aid is most often invoked in the elimination of rival unions, but also in the acceptance of working conditions or sending workers back to work when this entailed a political advantage to the leaders.

Further problems derive from the political ambitions of this type of trade union leadership. In all too many cases, these leaders consider trade union leadership as a steppingstone to national politics. Even after World War II, the trade union movement remained attractive to the lower echelon of political leaders as a means of gaining political support for their parties, of providing leadership training to promising young men, and of satisfying the political ambitions of men outside the major parties.

While it would seem neither possible nor practical for trade unions in South Asia to be independent of or inactive in politics, their role as a training ground for political leaders and their frequent domination by political parties may make their future development unduly hazardous in view of the fluctuations of political fortunes in the area. Moreover, the development of trade unions as organizations primarily intended to protect the workers' interests may be obscured by the eagerness of zealous young reformers to bring about a developed industrial society which would quickly react to economic incentives provided by governmental planners. A large proportion of the labor leadership already occupies management and high civil service positions.[23] Such leaders may become impatient with the resistance of that large segment of the labor force with strong rural traditions to the disruptions caused by the process of industrialization and the difficulties created by the co-existence of money and barter economies. This impatience of the Western-oriented urban nationalist leaders with rural traditionalism [24] is not restricted to trade unionism; it is a serious problem affecting all nationalist movements. There is, therefore, a distinct possibility that even Western-oriented labor leaders, particularly in view of their strong political ambitions, may be tempted to subvert the purposes of trade unions in order to achieve centralized direction and control over the industrial working force in the interest of more rapid economic development.

This possibility is further strengthened by legal provisions—as, for instance, in Malaya and Viet Nam [25]—which require trade union leaders to have had from three to five years of working experience in their specific industry. Such legislation may further speed up the trend among non-Communist labor movements toward either govern-

[23] U.S. Department of Labor, *Point Four Training Project for the Indonesian Labor Group, September 1952 to March 1953*, Washington, D.C., n.d., pp. 2–6.

[24] This attitude has its counterpart in Western society, where the urban population holds the farmer in contempt. See J. H. Boeke, *The Interests of the Voiceless Far East*, Leiden, University of Leiden, 1948.

[25] Federation of Malaya, *Annual Report of the Labor Department for the Year 1948*, p. 34; and *Journal Officiel du Viet-Nam*, November 1952, p. 1,686.

ment-controlled or company unions, since leadership developed from the rank and file is lacking and unlikely to arise in the near future, leaving the field open to management and civil servants. Thus the Western-oriented democratic leadership manifests an ambivalence in which its professed attachment to the political and social principles of parliamentary democracy and constitutional government may yet be sacrificed to an intense drive for industrialization.

IV. CONCLUSIONS

Because of the control of the trade union rank and file from above, whether by government officials, political leaders, or employers, the governments of South Asia exhibit a tendency to protect the workers through extensive social legislation (which is often difficult to enforce) rather than to permit them to develop independently their own protective devices. The leaders continue to use the trade unions for the furtherance of their own economic and political aims. So long as workers fail to develop a real class or group consciousness under a bona-fide labor leadership which can articulate their enlightened self-interest, the South Asian labor movement will thus remain a political tool inadequate to protect the workers against the social and political hazards of rapid industrialization in economically underdeveloped areas.

It is questionable whether the promotion of such independence among the organized workers can be expected from even the most enlightened and progressive government. This absence of an enterprising spirit which could give the trade unions an independent existence and enable them to create their own protective devices opens up a problem far beyond the limited field of trade union development in Southern Asia—i.e., the general inclination to rely on governmental or other leadership to provide political, economic, and social initiative in the absence of well-formed public opinion and of effective two-way communication between the leadership and the people.

In Western industrial development, the trade union movement has provided both an effective defensive weapon for the workers and a safety-valve for the release of social and political tensions. In South Asia, however, trade unions, organized primarily as political weapons by political leadership from above, have largely failed to develop the necessary protective devices for workers. Strike calls, while providing temporary emotional release, seldom lead to solutions of the workers' problems, which require not only economic but also social changes of greater magnitude than any single employer could provide. Thus the dependence of the workers on intellectual spokesmen whose political outlook transcends the limited field of the defense of labor interests poses a serious problem. The only possibility for the development of a strong labor movement in South Asia lies in the hope that it will assume more solid institutional forms, and that a permanent trade union bureaucracy will then develop which will identify its own interests not so much with any political party as with the strength and advancement of its own movement.

8

CURRENT COMMUNIST
STRATEGY
IN NONINDUSTRIALIZED
COUNTRIES

BERNARD S. MORRIS AND MORRIS WATNICK

As a program for the organization of society, communism confronts the world with a twofold challenge. In advanced "capitalist" countries, it offers the vision of a planned social order based on an industrialization already achieved; to the underdeveloped areas, it promises an accelerated industrialization-to-come, telescoping the protracted period of development through which the advanced Western countries reached their present height of wealth and power under capitalism.

By and large, the Communist appeal in the advanced countries has reached its limit; here the predictions of sharpening class conflict, impoverishment of the masses, and widening discrepanies in wealth have been belied by the trend toward the welfare state, achieved within a framework of political democracy. Forecasts of industrial crisis and mass unemployment have fared no better. In this respect, communism ironically has turned out to be something of a self-negating prophecy; as long as it stands as a political and military threat to the West it perpetuates a defense economy and full employment. There is every reason to suppose, however, that democratic institutions can be used to stabilize employment at a high level in a full-time peace economy.

By contrast, the Communist appeal in underdeveloped areas is still formidable. In particular, it holds an attraction for those groups of the population who prefer drastic industrialization "from above" to the gradualist, evolutionary tradition of the West—notably for the various layers of intellectuals who cannot find accommodation in a slower process of change. For these groups, it is the USSR and China, not the

Reprinted, by permission, from *Problems of Communism*, IV, No. 5 (September–October 1955), 1–6.

Western industrial countries, which—to borrow a phrase from Marx—present to other underdeveloped areas an image of their own future.[1]

That the industrialization of the USSR was accomplished at a much greater social and human cost than in the West is a point frequently minimized by those in other areas who put more store by the West's technology than by its humanistic tradition. Moreover, the basic social and political conditions in the underdeveloped areas of today are such that comparisons with Western development are not very pertinent. (In this respect, the use of such terms as "democracy" and "nationalism" to describe what is happening can be misleading, for they imply a degree of mass participation and response which simply does not exist at this stage.) Finally, the international political situation is one that forces a development in these areas totally different from that experienced by the West over the last 300 years. The very existence of two opposing power centers, the US and the USSR each bidding for the support of the underdeveloped countries, tends to increase the pressure on them for centrally planned and very rapid social change.

Whether these countries can hold their own under such circumstances without succumbing to the totalitarian impulse of communism is, of course, one of the major questions of our day. Real as are the tendencies which favor communism in some of the underdeveloped countries of Asia, there is no grim finality about them. We are not confronted by a "wave of the future," nor do the Communists assume it in their activities; they recognize in their doctrine the simple political truism that power is not the automatic result of the working of "social forces," that it must be won before it can be exercised. It is the purpose of the following survey to outline, in more or less schematic terms, the type of political strategy Communists are following today to eradicate Western influence from underdeveloped areas and to win a mass following for an eventual seizure of power.

How much Communist strategy owes to classical Marxism as distinct from power politics has been the subject of extensive discussion and study, and is too complex a question to be considered in a brief paper. Undeniably, certain elements of Marxian doctrine exercised some influence on Communist strategy in the early period of Bolshevik expansion, perhaps as much because of their emotive symbolism as for their analytical substance. But Marxism as a doctrine soon found a strong competitor in the power interests of the USSR and, with the

[1] See Eduard Heimann, "Marxism and Underdeveloped Countries," *Social Research*, September 1952, pp. 322–345; and G. F. Achminov, *Die Macht im Hintergrund* (The Unseen Force), Grenchen/Ulm, Spatenverlag, 1950, Chapters 3–9.

passage of time, it became increasingly difficult to disentangle the respective influence each had in determining the strategy of Communist parties all over the world. Fortunately, however, it is possible to analyze a Communist strategy in simple operational terms without settling the theoretical question of its derivation.

Like any other group aspiring to power, Communists must try to identify their probable friends and foes in the population at large and work out a relation to each which will maximize their mass following, maneuverability and the like. In trying to do this, Communists—particularly in underdeveloped areas—have run afoul of two problems peculiar to their own movements: how to reconcile their own political needs with the power interests of the Soviet Union and how to translate their own version of Marxism into specific political policies. The root of these problems and the key to Communist political strategy is the type of "alliance" the Communists choose to make with various "classes" in a given situation.

THE BASIC CHINESE COMMUNIST PATTERN

Communist strategy in underdeveloped areas today may be described as Chinese in origin, Russian by adoption, and with the possible exception of parts of Africa, worldwide in application. Its basic ingredients are borrowed from Mao Tse-tung's strategy as it evolved after 1940 in response to conditions in China. Despite vast differences in the historical development, cultural traditions and social structure of the countries of Asia and Latin America, this strategy governs the policies of all the local Communist movements; it is based on a standardized reading of the problems of these areas and is applied with startling uniformity though, of course, with tactical diversity.

In summary terms, its underlying purpose is to weld into a political bloc under the direction of the Communist Party a following of urban workers, peasants, the "petty bourgeoisie" and those sections of the "national bourgeoisie" whose business interests bring them into conflict either with the national government or with foreign influence, or both, as the case may be. What distinguishes it from past strategies followed under Comintern direction is the attempt to widen communism's appeal; the type of bloc which is to be led by a Communist Party is virtually all-inclusive, even to the extent of counting within its ranks the "national bourgeoisie," which was formerly rejected for the most part as a domestic agent of foreign imperialism. Moreover, in attempting to form such a bloc, Communists appeal to *classes as classes,* not to different political parties which in the traditional Marxian reading are supposed to represent class interests. The present Communist strategy thus goes far beyond anything generally ventured in the "united front" period of the thirties. It is not so much an attempt to conclude working arrangements with the leadership of other parties (the so-called "united front from above") or even to win away merely the worker following of Socialist parties, as it is an appeal to the aspirations of all classes.

It is the penultimate form of a strategy which Communists, even of the less doctrinaire stripe, formerly denounced as "class collaboration." [2] By an extension of Communist terminology of the 1930's, the strategy might be described as a *national popular front "from below."* Yet while its obvious purpose is to enable the Communists ultimately to displace the leadership of all other parties, the strategy does not preclude *"united front from above"* arrangements with more powerful parties where expedient.

In line with the Communists' bid for a broad national base, the present strategy is neutral with regard to the employment of armed force—a widespread notion to the contrary notwithstanding. In fact, the employment of armed force has always been a tactical matter in Communist policies, never basic. The present strategy is no exception to the rule. A Communist-led bloc can employ military force (the Chinese Communist and Vietminh revolutions, for example) or dispense with it (the Communists of India after 1950), depending on the prevailing tactical situation. At present the Soviet diplomacy of "accommodation" places a premium on nonviolent action as the most likely to eliminate or neutralize American influence in these areas.

The broad outlines of this strategy first appeared in Mao Tse-tung's writings of the late "united front" period, notably in "The Chinese Revolution and the Chinese Communist Party" (1939) and in "On New Democracy" (1940).[3] The all-inclusive national appeal outlined in these tracts is abundantly in evidence. What Mao proposed was a

[2] For all his denunciation of sectarianism in Communist strategy, Lenin never envisioned such a watering-down of the Communist appeal. In his remarks before the second Congress of the Comintern, dealing specifically with Communist strategy in underdeveloped areas, he made it unmistakably clear that while Communists in the "colonies and semicolonies" might collaborate with organized "bourgeois-democratic" parties, they should always preserve "the independence of the proletarian movement even in its most embryonic form." (See Lenin's *Selected Works,* International Publishers, New York, Vol. X, pp. 239–44.)

[3] *Selected Works of Mao Tse-tung,* Vol. 3, Lawrence & Wishart, Ltd., London, 1954, pp. 72–101 and 106–56, respectively. The text of "On New Democracy," also has been printed by the US 81st Cong., 1st sess., H. Doc. 154, Pt. 3, "Communism in China," Washington, 1949, Appendix B, pp. 67–91.

multiclass alliance of workers, peasants, the "petty bourgeoisie" and "national bourgeoisie," directed by the Communist Party to the overthrow of "foreign imperialist rule in China and domestic feudalism." The "national bourgeoisie"—formerly accepted skittishly, if at all, only as a temporary ally in Comintern strategy—was now granted a place within the political bloc; the Communists were to hold the real levers of power but were to postpone the Communist aspects of their own program in favor of an initial period of "bourgeois democratic revolution," following seizure of the government.

This new Maoist strategy emerged from and ran parallel to the peasant-based armed struggle with which Chinese communism is usually identified. When the strategy was generalized for all other underdeveloped areas, however, it was divested of its peculiar Chinese form and could be applied with or without "armed struggle" as circumstances required.

It is easy enough to dismiss Mao's "bloc" thesis as an attempt to beguile China and the world into a grand misreading of what the Chinese Communists intended to do, once they came to power. Five years of Communist rule in China has given ample evidence that the role assigned in Mao's works to the bourgeoisie—and for that matter to every other class in the bloc—is pure fiction if taken at face value. The Communist regime in China is a government by a party elite which manipulates *all* classes to achieve its own goals. Yet these early statements contain a grain of truth which bulks large in the wider application of the strategy in other underdeveloped areas. In the 5 years during which the Communists have governed China, its business classes have been effectively pulverized as classes and deprived of any real control over their properties. But, in contrast to the pattern of obliteration followed by the Commmunists when they seized power in Russia, the Chinese Communists have managed to transform the role of certain sections of the Chinese business community, absorbing them by degrees into the managerial bureaucracy. In Asia, where business groups frequently owe their existence to governmental policies, and are intimately dependent upon the state apparatus, the bureaucratization of a portion of the Chinese "national bourgeoisie" may be regarded with far less concern than is generally imagined. What use Communist propaganda elsewhere in Asia makes of the Chinese experience is illustrated in the following passage from a propaganda tract published in India:

Supposing, therefore, communism of the Chinese type comes to India: the majority of our capitalists and particularly the industrialists would not only survive but receive every possible encouragement from the Government in the interest of production. In fact, the national bourgeoisie, or patriotic capitalists who have not tied themselves with Anglo-American cartels, would have every reason to welcome such a changeover. The ax of the new regime would fall only upon half a dozen of the bigger cartel kings of India—the compradors with powerful foreign alliances, the zemindars, the black-marketeers, speculators and moneylenders. These would probably be sent to reformatories. The rest of our bourgeoisie would be allowed to coexist, cooperate, and coprosper together with the people.[4]

GENERALIZATION OF THE CHINESE COMMUNIST STRATEGY

The substance of the four-class bloc strategy was incorporated in the programs of a number of Communist parties—notably those of Japan, Indochina, and Brazil—in the early postwar period. But not until the victory of the Chinese Communist Party was it prescribed as mandatory for most parties in underdeveloped areas. The official endorsement came at a trade union conference of Asian and Australasian countries, held under the auspices of the World Federation of Trade Unions in Peiping, November 16–December 1, 1949. Liu Shao-chi, the acknowledged ideologue of the Chinese Communist Party, sounded the keynote in his opening speech at the conference:

The course followed by the Chinese people in defeating imperialism and its lackeys and in founding the People's Republic of China is the course that should be followed by the peoples of the various colonial and semi-colonial countries in their fight for national independence and people's democracy.

The steps which led the Chinese people to victory may be demonstrated by the following formula:

1. The working class must unite with all the other classes, political parties and groups, organizations and individuals, who are willing to oppose the oppression of imperialism and its lackeys, in order to form a broad and nationwide united front and wage a resolute fight against imperialism and its stooges.

2. This nationwide united front must be led by the working class and its party, the Communist Party, which oppose imperialism most resolutely, most courageously and most unselfishly, and must be built around the working class and the Communist Party as its center. It must not be led by the wavering and compromising national bourgeoisie or petty bourgeoisie and their parties.

3. In order to enable the working class and its party, the Communist Party, to become the center for uniting all the forces throughout the nation against imperialism, and competently to lead the national united front to victory, it is necessary to build up through long struggles a Communist Party, which is armed with the theory of Marxism-Leninism, understands

[4] R. K. Karanjia, *China Stands Up*, Bombay, 1952, p. 160.

strategy and tactics, practices self-criticism and strict discipline and is closely linked with the masses.

4. It is necessary to set up *wherever and whenever possible* a national liberation army led by the Communist Party, powerful and skillful in fighting the enemy, as well as the bases on which it relies for its activities, and to coordinate the mass struggles in the enemy-controlled areas and the armed struggles. Armed struggle is the main form of the fight for national liberation in many colonies and semicolonies.

This is the basic way followed and practiced in China by the Chinese people in winning their victory. This way is the way of Mao Tse-tung, and it may also be the basic way for winning emancipation by the people of other colonial and semicolonial countries *where similar conditions prevail.*

At the close of its sessions the conference resolved:

In the colonial and semicolonial countries of Asia, *to take into account local conditions and national characteristics and use the appropriate methods* to achieve people's unity in the fight for genuine national independence, for democracy and peace, and against the imperialists and their agents. For the correct assessment of these methods, valuable lessons may be drawn from the experience of the Chinese people, who under the leadership of their working class, have created a united national front, and who, with the support of all strata of the population, in the first place with the support of the peasantry, have waged a great struggle for national liberation, finally routing the combined forces of domestic reaction and international imperialism. [Italics added.] [5]

It is clear, then, that the Communist parties of Asia were called upon to adopt the Chinese model of the multiclass bloc and to couple it with armed action only where and when feasible. That suitable conditions for successful military action were not to be taken for granted in all cases has been made clear in numerous Communist pronouncements. A statement by Ye. M. Zhukov, a leading Soviet commentator on Communist movements in "colonies" and "semicolonies," is typical:

. . . It would be risky to regard the Chinese revolution as some kind of "stereotype" for people's democratic revolution in other countries of Asia. In particular, it is difficult to presuppose that other countries of the Orient following the path of a people's democracy could necessarily calculate on acquiring the vitally important advantage of the Chinese revolution—a revolutionary army such as there is in China. [6]

If there were any doubt about the endorsement of Chinese Communist strategy—not as a prescription for "armed struggle" but in its political dimension as a model for the Communist parties of other

[5] *World Trade Union Movement,* published by WFTU, Paris, No. 8, December 1949, pp. 14 and 40, respectively.

[6] *The Current Digest of the Soviet Press,* published by the Joint Committee on Slavic Studies, New York, June 28, 1952, p. 3.

areas in Asia—it ought to be dispelled by the following statement of R. Palme Dutt, a leading British Communist of Indian descent, who has often served as spokesman for the international Communist movement on "colonial" matters:

The Chinese people's revolution and the achievements of the Chinese People's Republic, won under the leadership of the Chinese Communist Party, have shown the way to build the united national front of the working class, the peasantry, the intellectuals and urban petty bourgeoisie, and the national bourgeoisie, for the victory of the democratic, anti-feudal, anti-imperialist revolution, and for the establishment of the new type of state of people's democracy. . . .[7]

THE FOUR-CLASS BLOC APPEAL

Today the strategy of the four-class bloc is *de rigueur* for all Communist parties in underdeveloped areas. It was explicitly invoked in January 1950 when Moscow intervened in Indian Communist Party affairs to force out the "left" leadership of B. T. Ranadive and bring the party into line with the Maoist strategy. Omitting India from the list of countries where armed struggle was sanctioned, the Moscow-inspired statement in the Cominform journal of January 27, 1950, stated:

In these conditions the task of the Indian Communists, drawing on the experience of the national-liberation movement in China and other countries, is, naturally, to strengthen the alliance of the working class with all the peasantry, to fight for the introduction of the urgently needed agrarian reform and—on the basis of the common struggle for freedom and national independence of their country against the Anglo-American imperialists oppressing it, and against the reactionary big bourgeoisie and feudal princes collaborating with them—to unite all classes, parties, groups, and organizations willing to defend the national independence and freedom of India.

How far the Indian and other Communist parties are prepared to go in catering to different classes is illustrated in party programs adopted after 1950. The Communist Party of India, suddenly turning "protectionist," declared: "The working class must come out for the protection of national industries against the competition of the imperialists."[8] The draft program of the Indonesian Communist Party, adopted in March 1954, provided for seizure without compensation

[7] "New Features in National Liberation Struggle of Colonial and Dependent Peoples," *For a Lasting Peace, For a People's Democracy!*, Bucharest, October 8, 1954, p. 6.

[8] Third Congress of the Communist Party of India, Madurai, December 27, 1953 to January 4, 1954, *Political Resolution*, Communist Party of India, New Delhi, February 1954, pp. 28–29.

of all foreign and native-owned large estates but stipulated that the land and other properties of "rich peasants" would not be seized and that the land and other properties of middle peasants would be protected by the government. Similarly, the Indonesian Communist-dominated trade union federation (SOBSI) at its 1952 conference went so far as to delete from its constitution all reference to the terms "socialism" and "people's democracy" to allay any suspicion of its program.[9]

To take another case, the Israeli Communist Party, describing Israel as a "semicolonial" country because of its dependence on American and foreign capital, set itself the task of replacing the present government with a coalition representing all anti-imperialist forces including the "working class, the working *fellahin* [peasants], professional people, educated workers, middle groups and part of the industrial bourgeoisie." Although the program defines the party's aim as the establishment of a socialist regime, it rejects this goal in the present period. The problem at the present stage is envisioned, not as one of putting an end to capitalism in Israel and setting up a "socialist" regime, but as one of eliminating the hold of foreign capital on the Israeli economy.[10]

The strategy also has been taken over in the programs of Communist parties in Latin America, of which the Brazilian may serve as an example. Luiz Carlos Prestes, general secretary of the Communist Party of Brazil, stated in a recent report to the party central committee:

This position of Brazil as a semicolonial and semifeudal country is becoming even more pronounced as a result of the growing domination of the North American imperialists. . . . The US imperialists and the feudal remnants are the chief enemies of progress and of the life and security of the overwhelming majority of the population.
Thus the Brazilian revolution at the present stage can be characterized as a people's democratic revolution, an anti-imperialist, antifeudal and agrarian revolution.[11]

Calling for the "broadest possible Democratic Front of National Liberation" under the control of the Communist Party, Prestes not only

[9] The Indonesian Communist Party has not gone as far as SOBSI, but in its recent election manifesto the party stated that its program for a national coalition government would not be that of a "people's democracy." (Peiping NCNA broadcast to Southeast Asia, June 28, 1955.)

[10] Program of the Israeli Communist Party adopted by its Twelfth Congress held in Tel Aviv, June 1, 1952. For a summary, see *Ost-Probleme*, Bonn, Jahrg. 4, #28, July 12, 1952, pp. 890–891.

[11] *For a Lasting Peace*, January 21, 1955, p. 5.

made a place in the bloc for the "national bourgeoisie" but also set up the Communist Party as the defender of its interest:

The party program not only does not threaten the interests of the national bourgeoisie, but upholds those of its demands which are progressive in character, in particular, the demand for developing the national industry. It would be a mistake—one which could weaken the anti-imperialist, anti-feudal forces—to confuse the national bourgeoisie with the forces of the feudal and imperialist camp and to underrate the significance of this bourgeoisie, particularly in the present stage of the revolutionary movement in Brazil, owing to its influence on the petty bourgeoisie, the peasant masses and even on part of the workers.[12]

It should be noted parenthetically that these Communist programs are not promulgated as statements of strategy in the strict sense of the term. What they purport to do is to analyze the contemporary political scene in terms of the Marxist class schema and from such an analysis to derive the political and economic policies the Communists would put into effect were they to achieve power. Obviously, however, the programs are and are intended to be crucial strategic weapons in the sense that they attempt to influence mass behavior by exploiting prevailing popular discontent and the hope for a better future.

THE PRESENT TACTICAL SITUATION

It seems clear from the above that the Communist parties in the underdeveloped areas share a uniform strategy sanctioned alike by Moscow and Peiping. In it, the United States has become the main target of attack, and any demand for a Communist revolution, properly so-called, has been subordinated to a program more palatable to influential groups of the populations.

How is this to be achieved? On the positive side, Communist programs have been redrawn as indicated, in an attempt to make them more acceptable to propertied groups. On the other hand, since the use of armed force would alienate precisely those groups which the Communists are trying to attract, there has been a tendency to abandon military action or violence except when a Communist-sponsored politi-

[12] For a Lasting Peace, January 21, 1955, p. 5. The Brazilian Communist Party draft program is reprinted in For a Lasting Peace, February 26, 1954, pp. 3–4. See also statement of Diogenes Arruda, secretary of the Central Committee of the Brazilian Communist Party, in Imprensa Popular (Rio de Janeiro) December 5, 1954, and a shortened version in For a Lasting Peace, February 25, 1955, p. 3. See also the statements by the Argentine Communist Party and the People's Socialist Party (Communist) of Cuba in For a Lasting Peace, January 15, 1954, p. 5, and June 18, 1954, p. 5, respectively.

cal coalition feels it is strong enough to be certain of victory.[13]

Soviet strategy and diplomacy also have been such as to deflect Communist action, in most cases, from violence to political warfare and propaganda. In his last full-dress discussion of the subject, Stalin took the view that war is more likely to occur between "capitalist" states than between the capitalist world and the Soviet bloc. He drew the strategic inference from this assumption that the first task of Communist parties throughout the world was to isolate the United States and thereby to improve the relative power position of the Communist bloc.[14] In support of this position, the USSR has set in motion a worldwide peace campaign geared not to revolution, but to weakening American defense arrangements by creating distrust of US policies, encouraging neutralism and winning new allies.

Under these circumstances, it makes sense for Communists in Asia to terminate their rebellions and to emphasize political activity of a legal type, designed to promote "unity of action" and "peace." By capitalizing on the anti-Western animus of many of the peoples of the underdeveloped areas, as well as on their desire for peace and for neutrality, and by holding out the promise of rapid social improvement to all groups in a "people's democracy," the present Communist strategy may, in the long run, prove to be a far greater obstacle to orderly economic progress and the evolution of stable political institutions than the abortive recourse to armed struggle in the late 1940's.

[13] The only exception has been the Japanese Communist Party, which at the behest of Moscow and Peiping jeopardized its political future by incorporating (in 1950–51) an element of illegal "direct action" into its strategy. The party has since discarded illegal action in an attempt to recoup some of its political losses.

[14] *Economic Problems of Socialism in the USSR*, Supplement to *New Times*, No. 44, October 29, 1952, pp. 14–16.

9

RECENT SHIFTS IN
COMMUNIST STRATEGY:
INDIA AND
SOUTH-EAST ASIA

Bernard S. Morris

No great perspicacity is needed to note that a marked shift has taken place during the last two years in the direction of Soviet post-war diplomacy—a shift that has diverted the main strategic interest of the Soviet Union from Western Europe to Asia and the Near East. What is not so generally appreciated is that the geographic shift has been accompanied by a drastic revision in Soviet estimates of the political 'correlation of forces' in underdeveloped areas.

In 1949, the Soviet expectation was that revolutionary upheavals would bring much of Eastern Asia into the Communist fold. Today, the Soviet leaders have come to terms with the non-Communist regimes in these regions, hoping to win them over with the more traditional techniques of diplomacy and trade, even if such a policy means a further eclipse in the fortunes of local Communist parties. The new dispensation was summed up at the 20th C.P.S.U. Congress by Krushchev when he declared that:

'The forces of peace have been considerably augmented by the emergence in the world arena of a group of peace-loving European and Asian states which have proclaimed non-participation in blocs as the principle of their foreign policy. The leading political circles of these states rightly hold that to participate in restricted military imperialist alignments would merely increase the danger of their countries being involved in the military gambles of the aggressive forces and draw them into the maelstrom of the arms drive.

'As a result, a vast Zone of Peace, embracing peace-loving states, both socialist and non-socialist, of Europe and Asia, has emerged in the world.' [1]

Reprinted, by permission, from *Soviet Survey*, No. 16/17 (June–July 1957), 40–44.

[1] *For a Lasting Peace, For a People's Democracy!*, February 17, 1956, p. 2.

The shift raises a number of arresting questions: Is the new policy toward Asia merely a reflection of the U.S.S.R.'s European policy? How has the Communist movement as a whole accommodated itself to the shifting scene and what has been the effect on the internal condition of the various parties? And finally, what do the Soviet leaders hope to accomplish with their new strategy towards the underdeveloped areas? What follows is an attempt to throw into relief the major post-war turns of Communist strategy and tactics, and the conflict, where it occurred, between Soviet and local Communist interest.

I. TWO-CAMPS DOCTRINE

The point of departure for the shift in the international line of the Communist movement from the war-born 'united front' was the 'two-camps' doctrine, promulgated at the founding meeting of the Cominform in September, 1947, according to which the Soviet Union and the people's democracies were locked in global conflict with the U.S. and its allies. The area chosen as the contesting ground was Europe, where the U.S.S.R. had twin and complementary objectives: the consolidation of its newly-acquired hold over Eastern Europe and the paralysis of Western Europe. In all this, the non-European world was of secondary concern to the Soviet leaders.

Standing thus outside the main scheme of things, deprived of any real guidance from the Kremlin, and even temporarily confused by the emerging strategy which they (and all Communist parties in underdeveloped areas) were eventually to adopt, the Asian Communist parties provided only rear-guard support for Soviet policy in Europe. The new strategy, outlined as early as 1940 in Mao Tse-tung's *New Democracy*, called for the 'four friendly classes'—the working class, the peasantry, the petty bourgeoisie *and the national bourgeoisie*—to join together under the leadership of the Communist party for the seizure of power and the industrialisation that was to follow. For Communists, accustomed to dealing with political parties *qua* parties on a strictly tactical level (when they were not cutting away at these parties 'from below'), the novelty of appealing directly to landed and urban propertied groups to join in an alliance that was supposed to endure long after the revolution, must have been disconcerting. Furthermore, Communist failure to distinguish between the tactical aspect of the Maoist programme—armed struggle—and its strategic essence, compounded their difficulties. As a result of international Communist pressure, local imperatives, and misreadings of strategy—and the precise genesis of each of the rebellions in Southeast Asia is still far from clear—the Communist parties paid a costly political price for their military adventures in 1948–50.

During the first phase of the cold war (1947–50), then, Western Europe was the principal concern of the Soviet Union's diplomacy, with the Communist parties offering their local support; in eastern Asia, on the other hand, the Soviet government relied mainly on post-war political instability and social discontent to bring the Communist parties to power and accordingly left these parties largely to shift for themselves in their choice of strategies. By 1950–51, if not sooner, it had become clear that this phase of Soviet policy had been played out. Tito had escaped from the mesh of controls imposed on the Eastern European Communist countries. Western Europe was on the road to economic recovery and drawing together more closely in political and military agreements. The Communist parties had failed to undermine the governments of Europe and, in their attempts to do so, had suffered losses in prestige, membership, electoral support, and vitality (even, to some degree, in France and Italy). Although the French and Italian Communist Parties remained formidable organisations capable of exerting considerable pressure on the centre political parties, their power was not great enough directly to affect major governmental decisions during this period.

In Asia, with the exception of Vietnam, the Communists fared no better in the direct bid for power. The revolts in Indonesia, the Philippines, Burma, and Malaya were either crushed or contained. In India, the limited guerrilla warfare kindled by the Indian Communist Party under Ranadive, led to suppression and the falling off of its following. The Japanese Communist Party, revived and steadily increasing its post-war influence on the basis of the Maoist prescription, had its fortunes reversed in 1950 when it was forced into a course of violent action, undoubtedly imposed on it to hamper logistical support for the American forces on the Korean front. By 1951 Communist uprisings, even where they were not fully suppressed, could no longer be reckoned as military threats to the new independent states of Asia.

The years 1950–52 marked a transitional stage in Communist strategy and tactics, the main 'line' being indicated at the 19th Congress of the C.P.S.U. held in October, 1952. The keynote for the Communist parties out of power was Stalin's brief farewell address in which he urged them to adopt a 'national' position within their respective countries, uniting all classes on the basis of specific grievances against the ruling groups. By recalling the Leninist concept of the inevitability of inter-capitalist wars (*Economic Problems of Socialism*, 1952)—he singled out the possibility of conflict between Britain and the U.S. as well—

Stalin loosened somewhat the rigid bipolarity formula, and permitted the Communist parties broader tactical flexibility. But Europe still remained the chief geographical target of Soviet diplomacy, and the local Communist parties of Western Europe still hewed to a line that left them isolated from the mainstream of political life. They responded to Stalin's dictum by calling for a 'united national front' which crudely aped the Maoist formula of the 'national liberation front.' Directing specific appeals (wages, social security, trade, taxes) to specific groups, and more general symbols to gain the support of the population at large (rearmament, fear of Germany, foreign tutelage, fear of general war), the Communist parties attempted to reach hitherto inaccessible groups in the population. Their strategy did not, however, contemplate the revival of the 'popular front' of vintage 1935; joint action offered to political parties or trade unions, even if accepted, which it usually was not, did not imply subordination of a Communist party's role as it would have in an insitutionalised front agreement. In short, it was still a strategy of the 'united front from below' variety, based on appeals designed to emasculate N.A.T.O. and drive American troops from the European continent; in the process, the Communist party might build up a 'national movement' with which the other political parties would have to reckon.

II. TOWARDS A 'NATIONAL' STRATEGY

For the Communist parties of Asia, the problem was to reintegrate themselves into the normal political life of their respective countries. The Philippine, Burmese, and Malayan parties (the latter as early as 1951) began to send out peace feelers, offering to end their guerrilla activities in return for an amnesty and permission to engage in political activities. The governments, for their part, though anxious to liquidate the hostilities, were notably reluctant to make peace on rebel terms and, particularly, to allow the Communists to become part of the 'legitimate' opposition.[2] A statement issued by the Central Committee of the Malayan Communist Party on December 22, 1955, illustrates both the political aim of the Communists and the obstacles in the way of coming to terms with the governmental authorities. Relegating the aim of a 'People's Democracy' or 'Socialism' to the future, the party proposed a 'common programme for all nationalities, classes, and strata in their struggle for independence, democracy,

[2] See, for example, the statement of the Malayan government in rejecting the Communist offer to negotiate the end of the war, *New York Times*, June 24, 1955, p. 1.

and peace . . .' in accordance with the 'actual conditions in Malaya today.' It declared that it had stood all along for cessation of the war by negotiation.

In the Philippines, the Communist forces, crippled by the government, began in late 1952 to bring their strategy in line with the international trend. Refusing to surrender, and demanding amnesty and guarantee of their right to re-enter politics—in time for the 1953 elections—the Communists proposed a 'New Democratic' programme on the Maoist model directed against the American 'imperialists.' Their attempts to negotiate with the government failed because the gap was too great between the government's demands for surrender, trial of suspected criminals, etc., and the Communist demand for amnesty and legalisation of their political activities. However, Luis Taruc, the personification of armed rebellion, personally entered in discussions with the Magsaysay government in 1954. The circumstances surrounding the Taruc mission are far from clear, e.g., the pre-conditions agreed upon by him and the government for the talks, but his expulsion from the party is indication enough that he was prepared to accept terms which the other Communist leaders rejected.

In Burma, the pattern was similar. Contained and isolated by government action, the Communists adjusted their programme from a peasant-worker orientation to the Maoist formula, later offering to enter cease-fire negotiations with the government. The attempts to come to terms with the government have continued over the years, though the party has been politically active through its front organisations. Through the National United Front, a Communist-dominated coalition, they polled one-third of the popular vote and won 50 of 250 seats in the April, 1956, elections for the Chamber of Deputies (lower house), compared with the ten seats they held in the last parliament.

The post-war history of the Communist Party of Indonesia differs in many ways from that of other Communist parties of Asia, but its strategy after the unsuccessful Madiun revolt in 1948 has been essentially Maoist. Operating along constitutional lines, it has built up a substantial base of public support for its policies, emerging as the fourth of more than 40 parties represented in the Indonesian Parliament.

In India, the transition from the Zhdanov-oriented policies of Ranadive to the 'national' strategy of Ajoy Ghosh was a slow and painful process consummated with Soviet support over the bitter opposition of the left faction. The key issue at the Party's third congress, held in Madurai (December 27, 1953–January 4, 1954), was the position to be adopted towards the Nehru government. In a compromise not quite satisfactory to any of the factions, the congress agreed to back the government on selected issues, but not to give it all-out support. In any case, it reiterated the Party's position that it was premature to fight for 'socialism,' and the decision to devote its efforts to the building of a national front that was to include the national bourgeoisie and intellectuals was reaffirmed.[3] The Party's fourth congress, held in Palghat, April 19–26, 1956, was no more successful in resolving the positions of the major factions. In a 'political resolution' reflecting a slight shift towards the right-wing faction's views, it agreed to support Nehru's foreign policy and attempted in general terms to draw the line between those domestic policies it will support and those it will oppose. The Communist party's search for respectability—the 'responsible parliamentary opposition'—was most vividly underscored in the recent state elections where the Communists with 60 seats emerged as the largest party in the southern state of Kerala.

Together with the five seats captured by the Independents (Communist-supported), they won an absolute majority in the 126-member legislature and on April 5 formed the first provincial Communist government in the history of India. The Communists have since reassured the population that they intend to abide by the country's laws. Although there has been a good deal of talk about nationalization of British-owned plantations, any Communist move in this direction would be restricted by the constitutional stipulation providing for compensation and the assent of the President of India. Nationalization and expropriation would also conflict with the Communists' attempts to attract industrial capital into Kerala in order to alleviate unemployment and reduce the pressure on the land.

III. THE NEW PHASE

In sum, it is reasonably clear that the Asian parties, during this transitional period after the disastrous upshot of their armed action, brought their programmes into line with Maoist strategy, and resumed, where they could, the constitutional road to political recovery. This transitional phase ended when Stalin's successors came to terms with the implications of nuclear parity between the U.S.S.R. and the U.S.

With the nuclear stalemate as a datum, the Soviet leaders proceeded to liquidate some marginal interests in Europe (the Austrian occupation, Finland) and, by what then appeared to be a master stroke of diplomacy, Khrushchev paved the way for what he hoped

[3] John H. Kautsky, *Moscow and the Communist Party of India*, New York, 1956.

would be Tito's return to the fold by securing his partial support on issues of foreign policy. At the Geneva 'summit' conference in 1955, the Russians not only achieved the recognition, if tacit, of the existence of a nuclear stalemate, but managed to give the impression that the Austrian state treaty, Geneva, etc., were merely stepping stones to a more inclusive and lasting settlement. What the Soviet leaders had accomplished, however, was to reassure their people and the world that there would be no nuclear war; to stalemate Europe politically—the line on the crucial problem of Germany being now drawn tight—and to set the scene for a shift in interest to the East.

In positing a substantial change in Soviet perspectives and a major shift eastward in Soviet strategy, I do not mean to suggest that Europe has become less important. On the contrary, there is no reason to believe that Europe has been displaced as the major target of the century. It is, after all, to Europe and the West—and not to Asia or the Near East—that the U.S.S.R. looks when it boasts of its faster rate of production growth. The U.S.S.R.'s sensitivity about its cultural inferiority stems from comparisons not with Asia but with Europe; and militarily, it is Europe, not Asia and the Near East, that gives the Kremlin something to worry about. What is here suggested is rather that a combination of scientific, military, and political developments, coupled with the containment of the U.S.S.R. in Europe, have deprived the Soviet Union of the chance for further encroachment in the West, while at the same time opening an arena in Asia singularly suited to the kind of political game the U.S.S.R. is capable of playing.

The 20th Congress of the Communist Party of the Soviet Union (February, 1956) clarified and formulated the new position. War between capitalist and Communist states—if not inter-capitalist wars— was officially proclaimed to be avoidable (not 'fatalistically inevitable'). Military action and violence as part of the Communist party arsenal were ruled out for the present period. 'Different roads to socialism' were officially validated in deference to the Chinese and Yugoslav Communists, and for the sake of tactical flexibility as well, and the capture of state power by peaceful means was said to be quite possible. The denigration of Stalin, for purposes of external policy, reinforced the impression the Congress was trying to encourage of autonomous, peacefully-inclined, and more sophisticated Communist parties. Geographically speaking, Asia replaced Western Europe as the scene of the U.S.S.R.'s active diplomacy; the Communists' 'forward' strategy in early post-war Europe was transferred to the East.

Saddled with the responsibility for carrying on the burden of political action in the wake of the Soviet diplomatic reorientation to the East, the Western European Communist parties dropped their appeal to all 'patriotic' groups in favour of Socialists and trade unions, in order to extract the most from the 20th C.P.S.U. Congress pronouncements on national roads to Socialism, and from Khrushchev's and Bulganin's personal bid for socialist co-operation.

But the more interesting aspect of the shift in Soviet policy came to the fore in Asia. For one thing, the rigid two-camps position enshrined in the protocols of the 1947 Cominform conference was relaxed to allow for the third group of Asian states. The political—if not the economic—independence of the Asian countries, with the exception of Malaya and certain island territories, was finally conceded and their national interests were identified with the objectives of the U.S.S.R.'s international policy.[4] Starting from a position in the 40's and early 50's, when it was held that the independence of such states as India was a sham, a new cover for Western exploitation, the U.S.S.R. was now prepared not only to concede their independence but also to award them a special place in the global political spectrum. Moscow had been moving in this direction before the Bandung Conference (April, 1955), but that occasion, which challenged the world to meet the colonial and former colonial peoples on a new basis, may well have crystallised the idea in the Soviet mind. With the common bond of anti-Westernism, the Soviet Union proceeded to develop a case of ideological affinity—though not identity—in the desire of these countries to assure their independence.

IV. THE SEIZURE OF POWER

At the 20th C.P.S.U. Congress Khrushchev, having posited a 'vast zone of peace' including the Asian countries which, by implication, leaned towards the U.S.S.R., applied the doctrine of different roads to socialism to the underdeveloped areas where, of course, the parliamentary tradition is largely absent. If this is subterfuge, it is a more realistic strategy in its implications than its application to Western countries. The possibility of peaceful transition to socialism, it was pointed out at the Congress, depends on the strength of the ruling groups. In the West there is no question that the governments dispose of sufficient strength to overcome any Communist-led uprising. Since no Soviet leader could conceive of the ruling groups voluntarily re-

---

[4] For example, V. Mikheev, 'New Asia,' in *Kommunist*, No. 12, 1955, pp. 80–94. See also 'The Collapse of the Colonial System of Imperialism and Questions of International Relations,' *Kommunist*, No. 18, 1956, pp. 97–114.

linquishing their power, there is no alternative to the use of violence in the attainment of power. Hence, the doctrine of peaceful transition as applied to the West was merely tactical in nature. As applied to Asia and most of the underdeveloped countries, however, the doctrine carries some weight because of the fluid nature of these societies and the relative weakness of the ruling groups. It is not 'parliamentary transition' that the Communists are interested in, it is the possibility of manipulating groups with the intention of taking power 'from within.' Put differently, local Communists, if they have any chance at all of seizing power, can do so not on the basis of a mass movement primed for revolution, but rather as a small group using traditional means to seize the reins of authority in a *coup d'état* which would be bloodless enough to be called a 'peaceful' take-over. The seizure of power in Czechoslovakia, which at the 20th Congress was cited as an outstanding example of 'peaceful transition,' is more relevant to the underdeveloped countries than to the West.

Be that as it may, the endorsement of a peaceful road to socialism serves Soviet diplomacy well. For the present period the Soviet Union is not relying on the Communist parties of the underdeveloped areas to promote its interests, let alone seize power. These parties are small and, as Mikheev put it, their strength lies in their 'consciousness, organisation, and . . . firm international ties.' The accent is on 'firm international ties,' i.e., on the Soviet-led Communist movement as a whole, for the accretion of power depends, by and large, on the Soviet Union's fortunes, not on the weak Communist movements. This position is both the hope of the Communist leaders out of power and the bane of those who see—or think they see—the possibilities of revolution within the national framework.

The best example of what is involved for these parties is afforded by the case of the Indian Communists who, having finally extricated themselves from their left-sectarianism, were pushed by Moscow right through the political spectrum to a 'united front from above' strategy. In practical terms, this position means that in Moscow's interest, the Indian Communist Party is forced to support Nehru on all essential aspects not only of his foreign policy, but his domestic policy as well. No single incident set off Moscow's position as sharply as the *Pravda* article praising Nehru's foreign *and* domestic policy published before the Andhra elections.[5] Soviet demands have thus placed the Indian

[5] See Marshall Windmiller, 'Indian Communism and the New Soviet Line,' in *Pacific Affairs*, December, 1956, pp. 347–366 for an excellent description of the Indian Communists' dilemma since their Third Congress, December, 1953–January, 1954.

Communists in a fundamental dilemma: either they drop their opposition to the Nehru government, in which case they lose all reason for existence, or they defy the Moscow line with all the dangers of internal splitting and the like. Cajoled into support of Nehru's policies, the Indian Communist Party feels nonetheless that its existence depends on challenging them. Confronted by a government that is 'socialistically'-oriented, the Communists, quite apart from their doctrinal guidelines, are constrained to follow a leftward course to make their appeal felt, to acquire new members and to increase their numbers at the polls. Furthermore, if the Party is not permitted to make the necessary accommodation to national and local conditions, it will inevitably become weaker, thereby losing its value even as a purely Soviet instrument. Moscow's indifference to the problem underscores its complete lack of interest in the domestic fortunes of the Indian Communist Party which is, after all, one of the very few parties of any size in the entire underdeveloped area, and demonstrates the Kremlin's concentration on the primary consideration: the diplomatic wooing of Nehru. If the Soviet leaders do at all reflect on the Indian Communists' local problems, they are probably consoled by the conviction that in the long run, the Congress Party will be unable to solve India's basic problems, thus providing the Indian Communists with their main chance.

The Indonesian Communist Party (P.K.I.) has also modified its Maoist position to follow a partial 'united front from above.' Supporting the nationalist-led government coalition, the party had to curb the more aggressive and outspoken of its members. Disciplinary measures were taken in 1953 against the veteran party leader, Alimin, and Tan Ling Djie, a party functionary and General Secretary of the largest S.O.B.S.I.[6] affiliated trade union, the Plantation Workers' Union (S.A. R.B.U.P.R.I.), was expelled for his opposition to the no-strike pledge given by S.O.B.S.I in October, 1953, as a gesture to the government. Before the 1955 elections the P.K.I. Politburo, in a draft resolution of June 24, stated that it '. . . will not oppose a new government headed by a non-Communist Prime Minister if the government is progressive. . . . Co-operation between the Communist, Nationalist, and Moslem parties . . . is not limited only to the election period. . . . We will continue to co-operate even after the elections no matter which party wins. . . . The P.K.I. does not propose that the government after the elections be a People's Democracy.'[7] After the elections, the Indonesian Communists bided their time, supporting Sukarno and the Nationalist Party (P.N.I.) and waiting for an opening such as Sukar-

[6] General Central Trade Union Organization of Indonesia.

[7] *Harian Rakjat*, Djakarta, June 25, 1955.

no's proposal in early 1957 to include them in his proposed new super-cabinet. Their position differs remarkably from that of the Indian Communists who have to contend with a responsible government on the Western order. The Indian Communists have no chance of coming to power and have been sacrificed to immediate Soviet foreign policy interests. In Indonesia, the stakes are higher and the political situation is more fluid. The Indonesian Communists can afford to neglect their mass support if, in going along with the dominant groups, they will be rewarded by a share in the government, a precondition for establishing socialism 'from within.'

V. CONCLUSION

In sum, the present Communist challenge in Asia and the under-developed areas is largely external, and where it threatens the social system, the threat is 'from above' and not from the mass action of the Communist parties. With few exceptions the Communist movements are weak and uninfluential. They did not cause the present crisis and they are largely being ignored by the Soviet leaders. For the Soviet leaders do not think of these parties as mass movements capable of revolutionary action; rather they view them as elite groups which, in conjunction with the U.S.S.R. and at the propitious time—and the Communists have time—will move, they hope, into power.

The U.S.S.R. is admirably equipped to wage the kind of political and psychological warfare called for at the moment. In its competition with the West for the loyalties of these areas, it has a distinct advantage because it is not burdened by the desire for achieving 'settlements' and abating tension. Militarily protected and ideologically outward-looking, Soviet policy is not geared to the traditional politics of compromise and relaxation, especially in an area where it takes no serious risks. Representing its institutions as an advance over those of the West and as the only modern model for lifting erstwhile colonial areas out of their backwardness, the U.S.S.R. does hold out an attraction to groups who are confronted with what might be called a purposeless independence. The measure of the Soviet Union's success will be found in its ability to come to terms with the politically articulate and ambitious groups in these areas.

10

THE NATIONALIST-
COMMUNIST
SYMBIOSIS
IN THE MIDDLE EAST

Joel Carmichael

During the past few years a new constellation has been taking shape
in world politics. It may be referred to as the seeming convergence or
coordination of activities between the Soviet bloc and the present
leadership of the Arabic-speaking countries. This constellation, which
first became a visible political prospect with the Czech-Egyptian arms
agreement of 1955, has had its ups and downs. Since it was merely one
element in the complex interaction of all the world powers, any
particular event in its formation was understandably bound to be a
variable ricochet. Nevertheless, one can safely say that for a number
of reasons the Soviet Union, or the Soviet bloc as a whole, has now
become a dynamic factor in the socio-economic evolution of the Middle
East.

Understanding of this has been hampered somewhat by the tendency—perhaps inevitable—to think of events of great inner significance in terms of their most superficial aspects. Thus, what has arrested
world attention most of all in respect to the Middle East during the
past year or two has been specifically the relationships or attitudes of
the Arab national leaders toward the local Communist Parties. Since
these relationships or attitudes have varied substantially, it has been a
perplexing business to assess the net impact on the region of the Soviet
regime as such. Moreover, even knowledgeable students—to say nothing of the world press—have been inclined to concentrate their emphasis on publicly recognizable parties, official announcements,
diplomatic statements, etc., a practice which has sometimes made it

Reprinted, by permission, from *Problems of Communism*, VIII, No. 3 (May–
June 1959), 35–41.

difficult to grasp what, for instance, the repression of the Communist Party in some Middle Eastern country means in terms of the more comprehensive relationship of that country to the Soviet Union as a great power.

More broadly, there has been a widespread, essentially doctrinaire misunderstanding of the historic cultural factors involved in the interaction between Arab nationalism as a political movement and communism as a theoretical system. This misunderstanding has revolved around an abstract view both of Islam—the religion of the great majority of Arabic-speaking peoples—and of communism. Since Islam is not well understood outside the Moslem-inhabited countries, and since Arabic is a difficult language, most Western observers have been at the mercy of scholars, who until very recently—that is, until they were outstripped by actual events—maintained that Islam was somehow inherently resistant to the influence of Communist doctrine. At the same time, it has been claimed that this same Marxist-Leninist doctrine determines the whole thinking of the Soviet leadership and hence its policies, both internal and international.

Obviously, if these interpretations were correct, the great impact of the Soviet Union on the Middle East in recent years would be well-nigh inexplicable. However, it can be shown that neither the shifting relations between the local Communist Parties and the various national regimes of the area, nor the interaction between Islam and communism on the purely ideological plane, were particularly relevant to the historic process which has culminated in the implantation of the Soviet regime as a basic element in the political life of the Middle East.

If instead we approach the problem in the light of the concrete situation which faced the new rulers of the emergent Middle Eastern regimes, it becomes apparent that a factor of much greater relevancy was the attractiveness of a number of Communist institutions because of their underlying suitability to that situation. For what were the new rulers confronted by? Translated into practical terms, the "backwardness" of the underdeveloped countries boils down to the existence of a sharp disproportion between the capital resources available for investment and the need for capital entailed by the popular insistence upon comprehensive economic renovation. Nowadays economic renovation in the underdeveloped countries means industrialization. The intelligentsia there has been swept into power by the force of the new political movements generated by the diffusion of Western technology, and the leaderships in these countries are now uniformly committed to doing *something* to "catch up with the West."

In all the underdeveloped countries, accordingly, the newly arrived political leaders have found themselves compelled to embark upon a comprehensive overhauling of the national economies. The overhauling amounts, in practical terms, to an attempt to achieve maximum national self-sufficiency within the organizational framework of the new groups in power. Essentially, these groups are drawn from the white-collar intelligentsia, which throughout the underdeveloped world has been multiplying in disproportionate ratio to the socio-economic opportunities available. The political environment in which they operate is characterized by their command of the volatile, feverish support of the other strata of the population touched by the diffusion of "modern" political thought since the end of World War II.

In essence, then, the situation common to the newly emergent nations is one which combines the need for vast capital investments with the channelization of that need through a political leadership propped up by an immature but insistent mass following. Once this is understood, the nature of the problem that has confronted the new national leaderships emerges more clearly. Where were they to look for the needed capital funds? The indigenous entrepreneurial, middle-class elements were manifestly far too small to be able to supply these funds on the scale demanded by the new economic goals, quite apart from the fact that their traditional characteristics inherited from the backward economic system of the past stood in the way of their absorption into any large-scale program of centrally directed economic expansion.

But all new leaderships feel the ground burning beneath their feet: they must do something, or at least seem to be trying. It is this simple, indeed glaring, fact that lies at the root of the convergence between the ferment of Arab nationalism and the structural dynamics of the Soviet bloc. The youngish men making up the juntas which took power in Egypt, Syria and (most recently) Iraq have had to cope with the insistent demand for huge capital outlays while playing—for their followers—the role of dynamic executives on a national scale. In these circumstances, whatever may have been their personal opinions concerning the validity of communism or Marxism as *theory*, they could not help but view the Soviet system—with its foreign trade monopoly, state economic planning, and breakneck industrialization program, all within the framework of a huge mass movement inspired by a certain mystique or "ideology"—as remarkably fitted to their own situation. In fact, the Soviet regime may be said to offer the only institutional complex which enables the youthful leaders in underdeveloped countries to make a show of instituting ambitious programs of "reform" (*i.e.*, economic construction) on the one hand, and on the other to hold the reins of power while paying lip-service to the collective mystique which justifies their enterprise of renovation.

The tendency toward a sort of institutional osmosis between the Soviet bloc and the new Middle Eastern regimes is evidently a factor of far greater and more immediate potency than any imagined doctrinal irreconcilability between Islam and communism. Even from the scholarly viewpoint, for that matter, the institutions which formed the foundations of the historical structure of Islam are not at all repugnant to those of modern Communist society. Islam, after all, was based from its very inception upon the triangle of the theocratic state (a centralized sovereign authority having divine sanction), the army (which engendered the actual organization of Islam in the primitive period and later), and the intelligentsia (the ancient scribal bureaucracy inherited from the defunct Persian Empire and Byzantium, plus the clergy). Thus, apart from the element of divine sanction, the actual organizational pattern of Islamic society was entirely capable of institutional adaptation to the Soviet system once the right ideological key was found and appropriate tactical accommodations made.

But more important than these broad historical and philosophical considerations is the fact that the problems of a new regime in *any* country are bound to be of a functional nature, not matters of doctrinal analysis. The prime example of this is the Soviet state itself—the very regime whose ideology is so often pictured as the antithesis of Islamic thought, thus guaranteeing the invulnerability of the Middle Eastern countries to the charms of communism.

When the Bolshevik Party seized power in 1917, it was almost exclusively a party of intellectuals. Its very assumption of power in the name of "socialist revolution" flew in the teeth of Marxist dogma as hitherto interpreted by all Socialist parties, which held that even if it were possible for a proletarian party to take power in a backward, agrarian, and unindustrialized society, it could not institute socialism at this stage. Be that as it may, once the Bolsheviks proceeded to build a socialist society in defiance of previously accepted Marxist tenets, something happened that no one—not even the sharpest critics of the regime—had foreseen: the Bolsheviks were transformed from a party of intellectuals into a corps of administrators.

The transformation of the party—of its composition, its mentality and aims—resulted automatically from the basic requirements of governing a vast country with a huge population, compounded by the gigantic problems involved in carrying out a comprehensive industrialization program directed by central planning boards. But while we can readily see now that this process was inevitable, the protagonists themselves were unaware of it—or perhaps subconsciously reluctant to admit its inevitability.

It is not difficult to understand how psychological inhibitions could well have deterred recognition of this obvious fact among even the most acute internal critics of the regime, *i.e.*, the Left and Right Oppositions from Trotsky to Rykov. Once the Bolsheviks had taken power on the assumption that the revolution in Russia would immediately be backed—and rescued—by revolution in industrial Europe, culminating ultimately in world revolution, any thinking as to what might happen if these assumptions were to prove incorrect entailed the necessity of acknowledging that the seizure of power by the Bolshevik minority in defiance of all other political groups would then be proven, in fact, what the Mensheviks had said it was—a piece of adventurism. Critics of the Stalin faction naturally were reluctant to point out that the "moral" degeneration of the Bolshevik *esprit de corps* into the ethos of a self-enriching and self-multiplying bureaucracy was, in this sense, inevitable; consequently, during the period of the most virulent internecine strife within the Bolshevik Party, culminating in the blood purges of 1935–38, there simply were no clearly defined, practical alternatives. Having failed to offer any, Stalin's critics seemed to the masses to be hanging in the air of theory and hence were highly vulnerable to the counterattacks of the Stalinist faction.

But if one can find in the psychological inhibitions just described a plausible explanation for the limited insight of Stalin's fellow Bolshevik critics in the earlier years, these cannot explain why even today, a generation after the Russian Revolution, it is still very widely assumed that the Communist Party remains made up of the same kind of men as before. Yet the reason for this "idealization" of the Soviet regime, for the supposition that present-day Communists still are doctrinaire fanatics steeped in Marx, is also not hard to find. In large part it may be traced to the fact that the regime is bound to think of itself in terms of its own mythology; ideology, after all, is little more than a vast rationalization accepted by its subscribers as truth. Doctrinal reasons for doing anything at all on the highest state level are invariably sought, and of course found, in the voluminous literature of Marxism-Leninism—and, for that matter, are often believed in. (The regime's bitterest opponents have themselves drawn upon the same doctrinal arsenal for their weapons, for these are easily come by.) Thus, the Soviet regime explains itself to both friends and foes in terms of the current official version of its ideology, which after all is what ideology is for.

Perhaps the most striking development in Soviet political evolution was the emergence of the Stalin cult and the concomitant reduction of the party apparatus to a symbolic and ceremonial role. The complete suppression, under Stalin, of democratic centralism, which had been at least an ideal of the Bolshevik Party before its transformation into a body of administrators, was the inevitable socio-intellectual by-product of the party's coalescence with the bureaucracy which had to be created to cope with the problems of the new order. The bureaucracy grew rapidly and in almost geometric proportion to the expanding programs of collectivization and industrialization; and its sanctification was reflected in the mores and beliefs of the new society. The party and bureaucracy, placed at the summit of this society, have established its intellectual norms. In this sense, the theory of communism has of course remained—serving as the ideological arm, philosophical arsenal, social mask and icon of worship of a bureaucracy which, in its actual day-to-day functioning, is altogether engrossed in practical tasks. But the preoccupation with theory for its own sake, which characterized the early Bolshevik Party, as well as all other socialist parties before the Russian Revolution, naturally receded into the background as the bureaucracy, parallel with the growth of its administrative and diplomatic functions, evolved into its present form.

The touchstone of Soviet policy has accordingly become the practical self-interest of the Soviet state and bureaucracy, rather than any real dedication to the theoretical principles of Marxism. A by-product of this subordination of theory to material self-interest has been transformation of the foreign Communist Parties into instruments of Soviet *Realpolitik* rather than of Marxist world revolution *per se*. This has meant the suppression of free and uncommitted discussion in all the foreign parties, and their incorporation into an international Communist apparatus under the direct and exclusive control of the Kremlin.

The question of how the interests of the Soviet state are to be interpreted is another matter. Indeed, it is precisely in the varying interpretations of Soviet material interests that the functional dynamics of Soviet policy as distinct from Communist doctrine may most clearly be perceived. However, the important point is that, whatever the specific policy decision in question, the regime's material interests that inspired it are invariably set forth—as a matter of course—in a language, or jargon, that sums up the mythological hangover from the past, however genuinely it still may be reflected in the faith of individuals.

It is the failure to grasp this vital point which is responsible for the bafflement of so many students who undertake to assess the motivations of the Soviet regime. There is an inherent tendency—among scholars it may become an occupational disease—to accept rationalizations at their face value, even when specific rationalizing statements are denied: many students, that is, take the *point of departure* for granted, even though they may disagree with the conclusions drawn by Soviet strategists from their theoretical premises. Thus, the doctrinal explanations of Soviet policy are often over-emphasized at the expense of a more functional or materialist explanation based on practical interests which may or may not also be discerned.

What all this boils down to on the practical plane is that the Soviet Union may, for instance, conclude alliances with other powers on what may well seem to outsiders an "unprincipled" basis. For in the pursuit of tactical goals, the Soviet regime—despite its ostensible doctrinal rigidity—has invariably proved flexible enough to accommodate itself to any aspect whatever of the non-Soviet world. This was true, in fact, even in the earliest days when the Bolshevik Party was still dominated by men of predominantly theoretical intellect. In signing the Treaty of Brest-Litovsk with the German armies, the Soviet regime —experiencing its first tussle with the realities of power politics— showed itself capable of giving way to *force majeure* while simultaneously finding an ideological cover for the operation, a process to which the Soviet leaders have grown more and more accustomed ever since.

Thus, despite the extraordinary reluctance of Western opinion to make a realistic estimate of the possibilities of cooperation between the Soviet bloc and the Arab nationalist movement, the stage actually had been set for such cooperation for some time. Viewed from the standpoint of the new regimes in the underdeveloped Middle Eastern countries, as already pointed out, the institutional complex underlying the Soviet system appeared to correspond precisely with their most pressing requirements, which were of course quite independent of abstract doctrine. On the other hand, the Soviet view of ideology had become more and more plastic as Moscow's interest in theory *per se* yielded to the quest for practical solutions: in other words, the "theory" governing Soviet practice became supple enough to justify any tactical enterprise in terms of some principle or other.

Consequently, it is not surprising to see the same flexibility which permitted the Soviet leadership to conclude the 1939 pact with the Nazis again being displayed in Soviet relations with the Middle East. The most characteristic illustration of the shift in Soviet tactics may be found in the difference between the present Moscow attitude toward the new regimes in Arabic-speaking countries and the attempt made more than ten years ago to transform Iran into a "People's Democracy" from within.

In 1945–46 the Russians tried to utilize a more or less *bona-fide* mass movement, the Tudeh Party, to institute a Soviet satellite regime in Iran. The Soviet Union at the time was profoundly enfeebled by the war and utterly outclassed on the military and economic plane by the United States, which then held the exclusive nuclear advantage in addition to a still impressive conventional military apparatus. The situation of Iran itself, moreover, differed radically from that of the East European countries where Soviet satellization efforts were already proceeding successfully. In these countries Soviet or quasi-Soviet regimes could be established on the groundwork of a disaffected proletariat, pliable segments of the intelligentsia, and to some extent of the peasantry, whereas such a base was lacking in the primitive agrarian background of Iran. Above all, the decisive factor in the satellization of Eastern Europe was the actual presence of the Red Army. Iran was not in this position and, though obviously incapable of resisting Soviet armed intervention across the Soviet-Iranian border, was protected against this eventuality by the world balance of power. Nevertheless, in spite of these vast differences, the postwar Soviet leadership sought to apply essentially the same tactics in Iran as in Eastern Europe and finally had to retreat in the face of explicit American intransigence.

Since then the Soviet Union has acquired an infinitely more powerful position in the international arena, and has discovered as a result that, in its efforts to penetrate other countries, it no longer even needs the legitimate façade provided by the existence of a genuinely pro-Soviet indigenous regime. Not only can it now deal with the underdeveloped countries on the plane of normal power politics, but it can also take advantage of two things peculiar to itself—*i.e.*, the mystique inspired in these countries by the success of the Soviet Union in transforming itself in one generation from a backward agrarian country into a front-rank world power; and, far more important, the attractiveness of the Soviet institutional complex from the standpoint of what it seems to offer not merely to the "impoverished masses" of the Middle East yearning for a better life (a rather empty cliché), but more especially to the restive young intelligentsia who have come to the fore throughout the former colonial and semi-colonial world.

The officers, students, and white-collar intellectuals who constitute the effective centers of political agitation throughout Africa and Asia occupy a far more important position in these countries than do their counterparts in the industrial West. And it is precisely these groups which have been most sensitive to the shift in the balance of power between the West and the Soviet bloc—a phenomenon which they view against the background of their own countries' limitless need for socio-economic renovation.

The whole problem of the Soviet impact on former colonial countries must accordingly be considered from the standpoint of the functional temptations held out by the Soviet regime to the new national leaderships. The Soviet institutional complex mentioned above offers them practical administrative techniques for coping with the renovation demanded by their own followings, while simultaneously enabling them to manipulate these followings through the creation of party propaganda apparatuses which provide them with both an operational structure and an ideological disguise.

It must be emphasized further that none of this implies the existence of a cynical or deeply-rooted contradiction between the political ideas of the youthful national leaders and Communist theory, even in its ideal form. In the West there is a tendency to forget that although the political doctrines and institutions developed in Europe have spread throughout the world and indeed may be said to dominate it completely, the French Revolution itself—from which they all stem, basically even though unconsciously—does not form part of any non-European tradition. The absence outside Europe of such a point of reference makes for a certain diffuseness of reaction and lack of sense of proportion among non-Europeans with respect to Western political and sociological concepts.

It is this absence of a historical lodestone, so to speak, that has placed the Arabic-speaking and other excolonial intelligentsias on such slippery ground. These somewhat patchily educated intelligentsias find themselves confronted by a bewildering jumble of ideas, doctrines, institutions, and organizational conventions. Whereas young intellectuals in the West, brought up in a specific sociological milieu for which certain ideas are modern and others are outdated, react more or less instinctively to what lies at hand, their Asian and African counterparts, receiving, so to speak, simultaneous translations of a host of different Western political ideas, must in effect choose between them.

This implies a certain equalizing effect upon the presentation of these ideas to the rising Afro-Asian intelligentsias. The latter must necessarily react to them from within the matrix of their own cultures, and also make the appropriate adaptation to each emergent idea considered primarily as an exotic but compelling importation.

In this sense, communism is no more startling an importation than what Westerners regard as old-fashioned democracy: since both are more or less alien notions for the Afro-Asian intellectuals, it is inevitable that the reaction to them arises out of the local background. In this context, the earlier mentioned flexibility even of theory (including traditional Moslem theory) in terms of accommodation with the Soviet regime assumes decisive importance for the approach of the new Middle Eastern regimes to the solution of their various national dilemmas. Stated more concretely, this means that any discussion of an alleged inherent irreconcilability between Islam and communism is beside the point since societies in flux will ruthlessly select the elements they need for social reconstruction and find a justification for them either during the process or afterward.

This is a far cry from the assumption that the political development of the Middle Eastern region as a whole is to be understood in terms of the theoretical allegiances or interests of specific leaders. It would be misleading to imagine that any of these leaders have had the time—or even the inclination—during the past ten years to indulge in abstract political thinking. The development of the Middle East, though staccato, has been proceeding with a certain momentum, and if a specific leader were to begin operating on a doctrinaire basis that seemed likely to interfere with this broad institutional development, other individuals would leap to the task of eliminating him as a "traitor" to whatever the new pseudo-ideological formulation might be.

The new momentum of events in the Middle East, in fact, merely facilitates the conventional rivalries between cliques and the struggle for power among individuals. For no matter how prominently any given leader seems to be in the limelight, it must not be forgotten that many others are waiting in the wings. Once the limelight shines upon them, they in turn will take on the aspect of "great" and "revolutionary" leaders.

The real question, then, is not the attitudes of individual leaders toward such theoretical abstractions as communism, but the degree to which the present-day Arab nationalist movement *as a whole* is accessible to the influence of the Soviet bloc. And here the verdict seems unmistakable. Whatever frictions may exist between various Arab leaders, and whatever may be the attitude of any one Arab leader toward the Kremlin, the fact is that the absence of any concrete, functional program in the Arab nationalist movement has made it highly vulnerable to Soviet machination.

Essentially, after all, Arab nationalism revolves around the mere assertion that the Arabs—that is to say, the Arabic-speaking peoples —are one; bafflement begins the moment it becomes a question of what to do about it. Given this situation, the Russians have found in Arab nationalism a sort of built-in Trojan horse. For by furnishing the Arab leaders with an institutional model for the internal development of their new states on the one hand, and by being able to offer them limitless bounty (subsidies, arms, technical personnel, etc.) without any apparent strings attached, on the other, the Russians are in a position to accommodate themselves to any likely combination of local political personalities.

In conclusion, it is abundantly clear that the surface byplay in the Middle East involving attitudes either toward Communist theory abstractly, or toward the local Communist Parties concretely, is fundamentally irrelevant to the larger development which has led the new national regimes of the region, hemmed in by the political tug-of-war between the great powers, to lean over to the side representing the combination of state economic control and a party-bureaucratic apparatus. The compulsion to favor this combination is doubtless inevitable at present for any underdeveloped country in quest of national self-sufficiency, however chimerical the quest may be. To drive home this point, a strong case could legitimately be made for the paradox that such a combination would be realized even if the new Arab states were to align themselves with the West. It is in this profound sense that the Soviet bloc has already laid its imprint upon the colonial and semi-colonial countries, regardless of surface alliances.

But basic tendencies are nonetheless easily reinforced by surface alliances, and these, too, will be easily come by in the atmosphere of worldwide tension which will be with us for some time to come. Nor need these alliances necessarily be merely superficial. If one recalls that, in addition to the "cultural" influences mentioned above, the Soviet government—despite all the recent frictions with the Arabs played up so conspicuously by the world press—has undertaken to supply the armies of both the UAR and Iraq with weapons, has assumed exclusive administration of the Aswan High Dam project (including furnishing technical personnel and financing for the entire first phase, with provision for further renewal), and has stationed huge consular and pseudo-consular staffs throughout the Arab states, it is quite plain that alliances present no problem, indeed that the most important ones are those just beneath the surface.

In sum, by virtue of its enormously increased capacity to wage power politics on a worldwide scale, of its demonstrated flexibility in making theory fit the needs of practice, and above all of the functional suitability of Soviet institutions to the internal situation and needs of the underdeveloped nations, the Soviet Union has gained a strong foothold at the classic crossroads of history. Communism's practical compatibility with Arab nationalism is thus unquestioned. Whether or not the Kremlin will be able to continue exploiting it is a crucial question for the future.

11

THE APPEAL OF
COMMUNISM TO THE
UNDERDEVELOPED PEOPLES

Morris Watnick

If time is a power dimension in any political strategy, the odds facing the West in the underdeveloped areas of the world today are heavily weighted against it. The effort to capture the imagination and loyalties of the populations of these areas did not begin with the West in President Truman's plea for a "bold new program" of technical aid to backward areas. It began more than a generation earlier when the Communist International at its second world congress in 1920 flung out the challenge of revolution to the peoples of colonial and dependent countries and proceeded to chart a course of action calculated to hasten the end of Western overlordship. We thus start with an initial time handicap, and it is a moot question whether we can overcome the disadvantage unless we acquire the radically new appreciation of the human stakes involved necessary to meet the challenge of the Communist appeal to the peoples of these areas.

Fortunately, there is no need to trace out the tortuous course of the careers of the various Communist parties in the backward areas of the world in order to gain some appreciation of the extent and intensity of their indigenous appeal. For purposes of this discussion we can confine ourselves to China, India, and the area of southeast Asia, where they have had their greatest successes to date. Despite the blunders and ineptitudes which marked their initial grand play in China in 1924–27, ending in almost complete disaster for their most promising single party organization in these areas, they have emerged today as a politi-

Reprinted from *Economic Development and Cultural Change*, I, No. 1 (March 1952), 22–36, by permission of The University of Chicago Press. Copyright 1952 by The University of Chicago Press.

cal magnitude of the first order, boasting a seasoned leadership, a core of trained cadres, and a mass following recruited mainly from the peasant masses of the region. It is the purpose of the remarks which follow to indicate the nature of the Communist appeal to the peoples of these areas and to suggest some of the sociological factors which have made that appeal so effective.

It was once the wont of certain continental writers, preoccupied with the problem of imperialism, to refer to the peoples who form the subject of our deliberations as the "history-less" peoples. Better than the Europacentric term, "underdeveloped peoples," it delineates in bold relief all the distinctive features which went to make up the scheme of their social existence: their parochial isolation, the fixity of their social structure, their tradition-bound resistance to change, their static subsistence economies, and the essential repetitiveness and uneventfulness of their self-contained cycle of collective activities. With a prescience which has not always received its due, these theorists of imperialism also called the right tune in predicting that the isolated careers of these archaic societies would rapidly draw to a close under the impact of economic and social forces set in motion by industrial capitalism and that these history-less peoples would before long be thrust onto the arena of world politics, impelled by a nascent nationalism born of contact with the West and nurtured by a swelling resentment against the exactions of its imperialism.[1]

The final result of this process is unfolding today with a disconcerting force and speed in almost all the backward regions of the world. We can see its culmination most clearly among the classic exemplaries of history-less peoples in China, India, and the regions of southeast Asia where the political and economic predominance of western Europe is being successfully challenged by forces unmistakably traceable to the forced absorption of these societies into the stream of world history. Their internal cohesiveness, largely centered on self-sufficient village economies, has been disrupted by enforced contact with the West, giving way to a network of commercialized money transactions in which the strategic incidence of economic activity has shifted from subsistence agriculture to plantation production of raw materials and foodstuffs for the world market. Their economies thus took on a distorted character which rendered the material well-being of the native populations peculiarly subject to the cyclical fluctuations of the world market. All this, coupled with rapid population increases which the

[1] For typical discussions see Otto Bauer, *Die Nationalitätenfrage und die Sozialdemokratie* (Vienna, 1907), pp. 494–97 *et passim;* Rudolf Hilferding, *Das Finanzkapital* (Vienna, 1910; Berlin, 1947), p. 441.

existing state of primitive technique, available area of cultivation, and customary allocation of soil could not adjust to the requirements of maximum output, has conspired to create widespread rural indebtedness, abuses of plantation and tenant labor, and other excrescences traditionally associated with the prevalence of a raw commercial and financial capitalism superimposed on a predominantly agricultural economy.[2]

Given the fact that the new economic dispensation in these regions was fashioned under the aegis if not active encouragement of the Western imperialisms, it should occasion no surprise that these regions, particularly southeast Asia, have seen the efflorescence of a distinctive type of nationalism, especially after the debacle of Western rule during the second World War, differing in many crucial respects from the historical evolution of nationalism as experienced by western Europe. Indeed, the employment of a term like "nationalism" with all its peculiarly Western connotations to describe what is going on in southeast Asia today is in a sense deceptive precisely because it diverts our attention from some of the distinctive attributes of native sentiment which set it apart from the nineteenth-century manifestations of nationalism in Europe. It is, moreover, a particularly inappropriate characterization because it inhibits a full appreciation of the potency of the Communist appeal among the populations of these regions. Historically, nationalism in western Europe has flourished with the burgeoning of an industrial technology, the urbanization of the population, the growth of a self-conscious middle class and an industrial proletariat, the spread of literacy, and the multiplication of media of mass communication. Now it is one of the distinctive features of the movements of revolt in southeast Asia today that they lack any of these marks of Western nationalism. The indigenous "nationalism" of southeast Asia today, lacking any of these props, nevertheless derives its peculiar potency from a universal reaction of personalized resentment against the economic exploitation of foreign powers. Whether all the economic and social dislocations of this region are directly attributable in refined analytic terms to Western rule is quite beside the point. The simple and crucial datum which we must take as the point of orientation in all our thinking is that to the mind of the masses of indigenous peoples they do stem from this common source. The Indochinese peasant victimized by usurers, the plantation worker in Malaya periodically deprived of his income by a drop in world price of rubber, the Indonesian intellectual debarred from a higher post in the gov-

---

[2] For an excellent analysis of the economic impact of the West on the rural economies of southeast Asia, where the results are most clearly apparent today, see Erich Jacoby, *Agrarian Unrest in Southeast Asia* (New York, 1949).

ernment service, the Burmese stevedore underpaid by the *maistry* system of contract labor—all tend to attribute the source of their grievances to the systems of government and economy imposed on them from without. The distinctive and novel aspect of the native movements of southeast Asia, then, is that they represent a mass collective gesture of rejection of a system of imposed economic and social controls which is compelled by historic circumstances to take the form of a nationalist movement of liberation from foreign rule.[3]

It is this distinctive coalescence of two sources of resentment which offers the Communist parties the opportunities they lack elsewhere to any comparable degree. The two-dimensional direction of native resentment lends itself ideally to Communist appeal and manipulation for the simple reason that Communists can successfully portray Soviet Russia both as a symbol of resistance to political imperialism imposed from without as well as a model of self-directed and rapid industrialization undertaken from within.[4] This twin appeal gains added strength from the multinational composition of the U.S.S.R., which enables indigenous Communists of southeast Asia to confront their audience with the glaring disparity between the possibilities of ethnic equality and the actualities of Western arrogance and discrimination. Communist propaganda has accordingly exploited this theme in almost all important policy pronouncements directed to the people of Asia.[5]

With the victory of the Chinese Communists, the incidence of these appeals has perceptibly shifted the symbolism of successful resistance and internal reconstruction from Russia to China, which is now being held up as a model for emulation by the other areas of southeast Asia.[6] The shift is not without its tactical and propaganda value, since

[3] Bauer (*op. cit.*, pp. 262–63) has given the classic formulation of this relationship in his analysis of the problem of national conflicts in the old Austro-Hungarian Empire which showed some formal resemblance to the situation in the backward regions today. The resemblance was superficial, however, since the lines of conflict were far less clearly drawn in Austria-Hungary, especially as regards professional and intellectual groups.

[4] It is noteworthy that variations of both types of Communist propaganda have also been attempted in western Europe in the last three years. The Marshall Plan, for example, has been presented to Europeans as an attempt on the part of the United States to impose its political rule over the Continent and to throttle its industries, without, however, carrying the conviction it enjoys in Asia.

[5] See the report of L. Soloviev at the Congress of Asian and Australasian Trade Unions at Peking, November 19, 1949, in *World Trade Union Movement* (organ of the WFTU), No. 8 (December, 1949), pp. 25–27. Also cf. "Manifesto to All Working People of Asia and Australasia," *ibid.*, pp. 43–46.

[6] "Mighty Advance of National Liberation Movements in Colonial and Dependent Countries," *For a Lasting Peace, for a People's Democracy!* (organ of the Cominform), January 27, 1950; cf. speech by Liu Shao-chi at the Trade Union

the adjacent region of southeast Asia is now regarded as the "main battle-front of the world democratic camp against the forces of reaction and imperialism." [7] Success in this case carries its own rewards beyond the frontiers of China itself, for it is altogether probable that Mao Tse-tung will take his place alongside Lenin and Stalin as a font of revolutionary sagacity for these movements in India and southeast Asia.[8]

Unfortunately, recent discussions of the Communist movement in Asia have done more to obscure than to clarify the nature and direction of its appeal to the indigenous populations. All too frequently, the tendency has been to fall back on the blanket formula that Communists have sought to identify themselves with local nationalism and demands for agrarian reform. We have already seen that their identification with nascent nationalism, if such it must be called, derives its peculiar strength from certain of its unique qualities. It is no less important to an appreciation of the problem to recognize that the Communist appeal does not by mere virtue of this process of identification acquire the same uniform access to all sectors of the population. Indeed, the most striking and disconcerting feature of much of the propaganda appeal emanating both from Moscow, Peking, and other centers is that it is not, and in the nature of the case cannot be, designed for peasant or worker consumption. The appeal of communism as such in these areas is first and foremost an appeal which finds lodgment with indigenous professional and intellectual groups. Its identification with native nationalism and demands for land reform turns out to be, when carefully scrutinized, not so much a direct appeal to specific peasant grievances, powerful though its actual results may be, as it is an identification with the more generalized, highly conscious, and sharply oriented outlook of the native intelligentsia.[9]

Conference of Asian and Australasian countries, Peking, 1949, *World Trade Union Movement,* No. 8 (December, 1949), pp. 12–15.

[7] R. Palme Dutt, "Right Wing Social Democrats in the Service of Imperialism," *For a Lasting Peace, for a People's Democracy!* November 1, 1948, p. 6.

[8] See statement of Ho Chi-minh's newly constituted Laodong party, which "pledges itself to follow the heroic example of the Communist party of China, to learn the Mao Tse-tung concept which has been leading the peoples of China and Asia on the road to independence and democracy" (Viet-Nam News Agency, English Morse to Southeast Asia, March 21, 1951). Likewise, the ruling body of the Indian Communist party fell into line with the general trend by declaring its adherence to Mao's strategy (*Crossroads* [Bombay], March 10, 1950).

[9] Failure to appreciate the true direction of the Communist appeal in these areas frequently causes some observers to commit the mistake of minimizing its effectiveness. Thus, Mr. Richard Deverall, the AF of L representative in these

Given the entire range of sociological and economic forces at work in these areas, the very logic and terms of the Communist appeal must of necessity filter through to the peasant masses by first becoming the stock in trade of the intellectual and professional groups. To revert to the terminology suggested at the outset of this paper, we may say that, by and large, it is the old history-less style of social existence which still claims the loyalty and outlook of the bulk of the indigenous populations. It is still the old village community which serves as the center of peasant and worker aspirations, and, if they have taken to arms, it is because European rule has destroyed the old securities and values without replacing them by new ones.[10] Without leadership and organization, their unrest would be without direction and certainly without much chance for success, quickly dissipating itself in spontaneous outbursts against individual landowners and achieving no lasting goals. Whatever else it may be that we are facing in southeast Asia today, it certainly does not resemble the classic uprisings of peasant *jacquerie* but a highly organized and well-integrated movement, with a leadership that has transcended the immediate urgencies of its mass following and can plan ahead in terms of long-range perspectives.

That leadership is supplied by the new indigenous intelligentsia. It is from this group that native Communist and non-Communist movements alike recruit their top leadership as well as the intermediate layers of cadres, for, of all the groups which make up the populations of these areas, it is the intelligentsia alone (taking the term in its broadest sense) that boasts an ideological horizon which transcends the history-less values of the bulk of the population and makes it the

areas and an otherwise very perceptive student of the subject, ventures the opinion that Communist propaganda in these areas is mere "rubbish" because it is for the most part couched in terms which hold no interest for the masses, having meaning only for intellectuals (see his "Helping Asia's Workers," *American Federationist*, September, 1951, p. 16). Mr. Deverall's account of the nature of Communist propaganda is quite accurate, but, if the thesis presented above is a valid estimate of the current situation in Asia, he has not drawn the conclusion which follows from the evidence.

[10] In most backward areas the tie to the countryside is still apparent in the tendency of laborers engaged in industry and mining periodically to drift back to the village (W. E. Moore, "Primitives and Peasants in Industry," *Social Research*, XV, No. 1 [March, 1948], 49–63). See also the observations of Soetan Sjahrir in his *Out of Exile*, trans. C. Wolf (New York, 1949), pp. 74–75, concerning the mental outlook of the masses in these regions. This fact was not lost on the leaders of the Communist movement. In the 1928 resolution on colonial strategy the Sixth Comintern Congress noted that the proletariat "still have one foot in the village," a fact which it recognized as a barrier to the development of proletarian class consciousness (see *International Press Correspondence* [Vienna], VIII, No. 88 [December 12, 1928], 1670).

logical recruiting ground for the leadership of political movements. For this, it can thank the formal schooling and intellectual stimulus provided by the West, which not only brought such a group into existence but also—and this is crucial—condemned large sections of that intelligentsia to a form of *déclassé* existence from the very beginnings of its career. The new intelligentsia was in large measure consigned by the imperial system to hover uneasily between a native social base which could not find accommodation for its skills and ambitions and the superimposed imperial structure which reserved the best places for aliens. There were, of course, considerable variations and differences in the various areas of southeast Asia—India, for example, did succeed in absorbing a good many of its professionally trained native sons—but, by and large, the picture is one of a rootless intellectual proletariat possessing no real economic base in an independent native middle class. The tendency in all these areas, moreover, has been to train technicians, lawyers, and other groups of professional workers in numbers far out of proportion to the absorptive capacity of the social structures of the home areas, even if more of the higher posts in industry and administration were thrown open to native talent. In any case, those who did find such employment were frozen in minor posts, the most coveted positions going to Europeans.[11]

But if these groups could not be integrated into the social structure of these dependent areas, the same does not hold true of their acclimatization to the cross-currents of political doctrine. Western education exposed many of them to the various schools of social thought contending for influence in Europe, and from these they distilled the lessons which seemed to offer the best hope for their native communities. Western capitalism was necessarily excluded from their range of choices if for no other reason than that its linkage with imperialist rule over their own societies debarred it from their hierarchy of values. The anticapitalist animus is common to the intellectual spokesmen of these areas, whatever their specific political allegiance or orientation may be.[12] Nor does it appear that any populist variety of Gandhiism, with its strong attachment to the values of a static sub-

[11] Some interesting data on this score for Indonesia are offered by J. M. van der Kroef's "Economic Origins of Indonesian Nationalism," in *South Asia in the World Today*, ed. Phillips Talbot (Chicago, 1950), pp. 188–93, and his "Social Conflicts and Minority Aspirations in Indonesia," *American Journal of Sociology*, March, 1950, pp. 453–56. Cf. L. Mills (ed.), *New World of Southeast Asia* (Minneapolis, 1949), pp. 293–95.

[12] For a typical rejection of the capitalist solution coming from anti-Communist sources see D. R. Gadgil, "Economic Prospect for India," *Pacific Affairs*, XXII (June, 1949), 115–29; Sjahrir, *op. cit.*, pp. 161–62; and the remarks of H. Shastri,

sistence economy, has won any considerable following among these intellectual groups. Soetan Sjahrir voiced a common sentiment when he wrote:

> We intellectuals here are much closer to Europe or America than we are to the Boroboedoer or Mahabrata or to the primitive Islamic culture of Java or Sumatra. . . . For me, the West signifies forceful, dynamic and active life. I admire, and am convinced that only by a utilization of this dynamism of the West can the East be released from its slavery and subjugation.[13]

The sole possibility, then, which appeared acceptable to them was one or another of the forms of state-sponsored reconstruction and industrialization, for which liberation from the rule of European states was naturally considered to be a prerequisite. Liberation and internal reconstruction thus came to be two inseparable operations, intimately tied together as they seldom have been before.

We can now appreciate the enormous initial advantage which was thus offered the Communist movements in these backward areas. The Russian Revolution of 1917 and the subsequent course of planned industrialization could not but fail to impress native intellectuals as offering a model pattern of action by which they could retrieve their communities from precapitalist isolation and backwardness without paying the price of continued foreign exploitation. There is doubtless a large measure of self-revelation in Mao's reaction to the Russian experience in his statement:

> There is much in common or similar between the situation in China and prerevolutionary Russia. Feudal oppression was the same. Economic and cultural backwardness was common to both countries. Both were backward. China more so than Russia. The progressives waged a bitter struggle in search of revolutionary truth so as to attain national rehabilitation; this was common to both countries. . . . The October Revolution helped the progressive elements of the world, and of China as well, to apply the proletarian world outlook in determining the fate of the country. . . . The conclusion was reached that we must advance along the path taken by the Russians.[14]

of the Indian Trade Union Congress at the Asian Regional Conference of the International Labor Office, Ceylon, January 16–27, 1950, *Record of Proceedings* (Geneva, 1951), p. 112. Cf. van der Kroef's article, "Social Conflicts and Minority Aspirations in Indonesia," *op. cit.*, pp. 455–56, and J. F. Normano, *Asia between Two World Wars* (New York, 1944), pp. 83–87.

[13] Sjahrir, *op. cit.*, pp. 67 and 144.

[14] Mao Tse-tung, *On People's Democratic Rule* (New York: New Century Publishers, 1950), pp. 2–4. For the same reaction of M. N. Roy, one of the earlier leaders of the Indian Communists who later broke with the Comintern, see his *Revolution and Counter-revolution in China* (Calcutta, 1946), p. 522.

It should also be noted, in passing, that the Comintern lost no time in launching a large number of international front organizations such as the Red International of Trade Unions, International League against Imperialism, International of Seamen and Dockers, International Red Aid, etc.—all of which furnished the necessary organizational scaffolding and support for facilitating the dissemination of propaganda. Finally, as will be noted presently, the Comintern provided a rallying point for their aspirations by outlining a program of revolutionary action in the colonies and dependent areas which was ideally calculated to provide them with a mass peasant following.

The result, though viewed with some misgivings by the leadership of the Comintern, was merely what might have been expected under the circumstances. The Communist parties of these underdeveloped areas of Asia were from their very beginnings initiated, led by, and predominantly recruited from (prior to their conversion into mass organizations as has been the case in China after 1949) native intellectual groups. Though this vital sociological clue to the nature of the Communist appeal in the colonial areas has not received the recognition it deserves, amid the general preoccupation with the theme of Communist appeals to the peasantry, its implication was perfectly plain to the leaders of the Comintern. One of the most revealing (and to date largely unnoticed) admissions on this score is contained in the Sixth Comintern Congress in 1928 in its resolution on strategic policy in the colonies and semicolonies in which the point is very clearly made that

experience has shown that, in the majority of colonial and semi-colonial countries, an important if not a predominant part of the Party ranks in the first stage of the movement is recruited from the petty bourgeoisie, and in particular, from the revolutionary inclined intelligentsia, very frequently students. It not uncommonly happens that these elements enter the Party because they see in it the most decisive enemy of imperialism, at the same time not sufficiently understanding that the Communist Party is not only the Party of struggle against imperialist exploitation . . . but stuggle against all kinds of exploitation and expropriation. Many of these adherents of the Party, in the course of the revolutionary struggle will reach a proletarian class point of view; another part will find it more difficult to free themselves to the end, from the moods, waverings and half-hearted ideology of the petty bourgeoisie.[15]

The fact that this did not accord with the *idée fixe* of this and all other Comintern pronouncements that leadership of colonial revolu-

[15] "The Revolutionary Movement in the Colonies and Semi-colonies; Resolution of the Sixth World Congress of the Communist International" (adopted September 1, 1928), *International Press Correspondence*, VIII, No. 88 (December 12, 1928), 1670.

tionary movements is properly a function of the industrial urban workers should in no way blind us to the fact which Comintern leadership was realistic enough to acknowledge, namely, that membership of these Communist parties is heavily weighted in favor of the intelligentsia. On may, in fact, go one step further and say that, in accepting the predominance of the "colonial" intelligentsia, the Comintern was closer to the genus of Leninist doctrine than were any of its indorsements of the leadership role of the urban proletariat. No other group in these areas but the intelligentsia could be expected to undertake the transformation of the social structure under forced draft and in a predetermined direction and thus fulfil the main self-assigned historical mission of Leninism.[16]

If we bear this key factor in mind, it throws a new light on the nature of the grip which Communists exercise on the political movements of these areas. The usual formulation of the character of these movements is that they stem from mass discontent with the prevailing system of land distribution, with the labor practices in force, with the overt or indirect political control of these areas by foreign governments, etc. These are perfectly valid empirical descriptions of the necessary conditions for the rise of liberation movements in these areas. But they obviously fail to take notice of the specific social groups that give these movements their *élan*, direction, and whatever measure of success they have had thus far. As matters stand today, the intellectuals are the sole group in these areas which can infuse these raw social materials of agrarian discontent, etc., with the organization and leadership necessary for their success. And it is largely this group which has acted as the marriage broker between the international Communist movement and the manifestations of indigenous revolt.

Enough empirical material exists to warrant the conclusion that the "colonial" Communist parties of Asia today, as in the 1920's, are the handiwork of native intellectuals. Since 1940, they have, of course, greatly expanded their mass following and membership, but their leadership is still drawn overwhelmingly from the intelligentsia. As regards China, this elite character of Communist party leadership was

---

[16] Though cognizant of the role of the intellectuals in the Chinese party, Benjamin Schwartz's illuminating study, *Chinese Communism and the Rise of Mao* (Cambridge, 1951), falls short of an appreciation of its significance by focusing attention on a purely strategic problem—Mao's peasant-oriented movement—and concluding from this that Mao's ideology represents a radical break with classical Leninism.

326

MORRIS WATNICK

expressly recognized by Mao Tse-tung in 1939,[17] and the entire history of the party from its founding by Li Ta-chao and Ch'en Tu-hsu to Mao Tse-tung and Liu Shao-chi is virtually an unbroken record of a party controlled by intellectuals.[18] India illustrates the same trend. Its earliest Communist leadership is exemplified in M. N. Roy (who later broke with the movement), a high-caste Brahmin of considerable intellectual attainments. Also indicative of the predominance of intellectuals in the leadership of the Indian Communist party is the fact that, at its first All-Indian Congress in 1943, 86 of a total attendance of 139 delegates were members of professional and intellectual groups.[19] And in the postwar period the leading position of this social group in the affairs of the Indian Communist party finds expression in men like Joshi, Ranadive, and Dange.[20] The same pattern also holds good for the Communist parties of Indochina, Thailand, Burma, Malaya, and Indonesia, all of which show a heavy preponderance of journalists, lawyers, and teachers among the top leadership.[21] The Burmese Communists afford an especially pointed illustration in this respect, since the parent-organization, the Thakens, originated in the early 1930's among university students who today comprise the leadership of both rival Communist factions.[22] If any doubt exists as to the extent to which the leadership of these movements is dominated by intellectual groups, it is quickly dispelled by an examination of the top echelons of trade-unions, as instanced, for example, by the names of those attending the WFTU-sponsored Congress of Asian and Australasian Unions in Peking in 1949. Here, at least, we can appreciate the full impact of the trend by noting that, while European trade-union leadership (in contrast to the leadership of parties) has been largely recruited from within membership ranks, the reverse is true in southeast Asia. The trade-union movement in that region is largely a newborn postwar phenomenon, and the various bodies (whether Commu-

[17] Mao Tse-tung, *The Chinese Revolution and the Communist Party of China* (New York: Committee for a Democratic Far Eastern Policy, n.d.), pp. 13–14.

[18] Mao Tse-tung's excursion into an instrumentalist approach to Marxian philosophy is one manifestation (see his "On Practice," *Political Affairs* [organ of the United States Communist party], April, 1951, pp. 28–42).

[19] *People's War* (organ of the CPI) (Bombay), June 13, 1943.

[20] See a review of Dange's *India, from Primitive Communism to Slavery* (Bombay, 1949), in *The Communist* (organ of the CPI) (Bombay), III, No. 4 (October–November, 1950), 78–91. Cf. M. R. Masani, "The Communist Party in India," *Pacific Affairs*, March, 1951, pp. 31–33.

[21] See, e.g., biographic data in V. Thompson and R. Adloff, *The Left Wing in South East Asia* (New York, 1950), pp. 231–86.

[22] *Ibid.*, pp. 80–82.

nist-dominated or controlled by other political groups) have been
fashioned and directed by professionals with no direct experience in
the occupations concerned.[23]

This, in its larger perspectives, is the structure of leadership for
both the Communist and the non-Communist groups in the entire
region. More detailed research might serve to throw some light on the
sociological factors which determine the distribution of these professional groups among Communist and anti-Communist movements. But,
even if a completely detailed analysis is still lacking, enough is already
known of the larger trends to indicate that these sections of the native
populations constitute the key operational factor in the Communist
appeal. It is they who spearhead the propaganda drive, organize the
unions, youth groups, and other organizations, plan the tactics of their
parties, etc.

As matters stand, then, the organization and leadership of Communist parties in colonial areas do not accord with their accepted doctrinal precepts. For over a generation now it has been a standard item
of doctrine, reiterated again and again, that the leadership of these
parties must rest with the industrial working class.[24] The realities of
the situation in these areas have not been very obliging to this formula,
though it still occupies its customary niche in all their pronouncements.
From the standpoint of their own strategic imperatives and long-term
objective, however, the Communist parties of these areas have not
hesitated to draw the necessary practical conclusions. They have ac-
quiesced in the primacy of the intellectuals in the movement because
the acceptance of any alternative leadership coming from the ranks
of the peasantry or the industrial workers (assuming the possibility of
such leadership) would entail the sacrifice of the prime objectives of
the party—viz., the seizure of power and the launching of a long-range
plan for internal planning and reconstruction. Gradual and piecemeal
reforms and certainly basic reforms designed to bring immediate economic relief to the masses (for instance, in the credit structure of an
area) undertaken by non-Communist regimes would be welcomed by

[23] *New York Times,* May 21, 1950; see also Institute of Pacific Relations,
Problems of Labor and Social Welfare in South and Southeast Asia ("Secretariat
Paper No. 1 Prepared by Members of the ILO" [New York, 1950]), p. 20. Cf.
statements of delegates from India and Ceylon to Asian Regional Conference of
the ILO, Ceylon, January 16–27, 1950, *Record of Proceedings,* pp. 98, 113.

[24] See, e.g., "The Revolutionary Movement in Colonies and Semi-colonies;
Resolution of the Sixth Congress of the Communist International" (adopted September 1, 1928), *International Press Correspondence,* VIII (1928), 1670–72 *et
passim;* and Mao's pamphlet, *The Chinese Revolution and the Communist Party of
China,* pp. 15–16.

the mass of the peasantry because they are in accord with their immediate and most pressing interests.[25] A program of seizing political power followed by prolonged industrialization, economic planning, recasting of the social structure, realignment of a country's international position in favor of the U.S.S.R.—these are considerations of the type which can attract intellectuals only.[26]

Accordingly, if the main appeal of Communism per se, in underdeveloped areas, has been to the native intelligentsia, a transgression has apparently been committed against an expendable item of party dogma, but the fundamental spirit of the Leninist position with regard to the relation between leadership and the masses has actually been preserved in its pristine form. There is no need to labor this point, since there is enough evidence to indicate that the leadership of Communist parties in underdeveloped areas is acutely aware of the conflict between its own long-range objectives and the "interests" of its mass following, as well as of the conclusions to be drawn for the practical guidance of their parties' activites. Thus a recent party document issued by the Malaya Communist party to cope with internal criticism of its leadership and policies contains this cogent passage:

Regarding these masses, our responsibility is not to lower the Party's policy and to accede to the selfish demands of small sections of the backward elements, but to bring out a proper plan to unite and direct them courageously to carry out the various forms of struggle against the British. If this course is not followed we will retard the progress of the national revolutionary war, and will lose the support of the masses. The proper masses route is not only to mix up with them [mingle with them(?)—M.W.] but to resolutely and systematically lead them to march forward to execute the Party's policy and programme. By overlooking the latter point, we will not be able to discharge the historical duty of a revolutionary Party.[27]

[25] This is all the more true of large sections of southeast Asia, where the land problem is not identical with the structure of ownership distribution and where no direct correlation prevails between tenancy and poverty. In large sections of this region the problem arises largely from the primitive credit and marketing facilities rather than from concentration of land titles.

[26] Communist leaders are not loath to recognize that this cleavage exists between the immediate interests of the masses and the party's long range perspectives (see Liu Shao-chi, "On the Party," Political Affairs, October, 1950, p. 88).

[27] The document from which this passage is taken is contained in a Malaya Communist party publication titled How To Look After the Interests of the Masses ("Emancipation Series," No. 5), published secretly by the Freedom Press in Malaya, December 15, 1949, and made public after its seizure by the local authorities. Another document titled "Resolution To Strengthen Party Character" reaffirms the doctrine of democratic centralism against the more "extremist democratic" demands of some of the members. For an expression of the same standpoint

If we discern the central driving force of communism in the under-developed areas to be its appeal to a considerable number of the indigenous intelligentsia, we are also in a position to reassess the meaning and changes of its mass appeal, most notably its program of land redistribution. To no inconsiderable extent, much of the confusion which attends thinking and discourse on the subject in this country can be traced to a widespread impression still current that the Communist movement in underdeveloped areas owes its success to the fact that it is finely attuned to the most urgent and insistent "land hunger" of millions of the poorest peasants living on a submarginal level of existence. There is just enough historical truth in this impression to make it a plausible explanation of Communist strength. It is unquestionably true that the mass base of the Communist parties in southeast Asia can be accounted for by the almost universal prevalence of local agrarian unrest which thus constitutes the necessary precondition for the activities of the Communists. But if—as is not infrequently done—this is offered as the crucially strategic element in the complex of circumstances which have served the cause of the Communist parties, we are once again confronted with the old confusion of necessary with sufficient causes.[28] For there is no intrinsic reason which compels the ground swell of agrarian discontent to favor the fortunes of the Communist parties—unless that discontent can be channeled and directed in predetermined fashion by the intervention of a native social group capable of giving organized shape to its various amorphous and diffused manifestations. If the foregoing analysis has any merit, the balance of the sociological picture in these areas will have to be redressed in our thinking to give greater weight to the Communist-oriented intelligentsia and to its role as the prime mover of the native Communist movements.

A more balanced picture of the sociological roots of the Communist movement in the underdeveloped areas would also serve to throw some light on the shift which has recently taken place in their agrarian reform program and therefore, too, in the direction of their appeal.

In its original form the agrarian program of the Comintern was an outright bid for the support of the poorest and therefore the numerically preponderant sections of the peasantry. At the Second Congress of the Comintern in 1920, Lenin placed the question of agrarian re-

regarding the relation between the party and the masses from a Chinese source see Liu Shao-chi, "On the Party," *op. cit.*, p. 78.

[28] An otherwise excellent discussion by Miss Barbara Ward verges on this error, especially in its opening remarks. See her article in the *New York Times Magazine*, March 25, 1951.

form at the very center of the Communist appeal and dismissed as utopian any notion that a Communist movement in these areas was even conceivable without an appeal to the masses of peasantry.[29] The resolution adopted by that congress repudiated any attempt to solve the agrarian problem along Communist lines and instead accepted the inevitable fact that, in its initial stages, the agrarian revolution in these areas would have to be achieved by a "petty bourgeois" program of land distribution, directed "against the landlords, against large landownership, against all survivals of feudalism."[30] Eight years later the Sixth Congress of the Comintern was more specific. Its resolution on the strategy of the Communist movement in colonial areas called attention to the presence of a "hierarchy of many stages, consisting of landlords and sublandlords, parasitic intermediate links between the laboring cultivator and the big landowner or the state" who were destroying the basis of the peasant's livelihood. More particularly, "the peasantry . . . no longer represents a homogeneous mass. In the villages of China and India . . . it is already possible to find exploiting elements derived from the peasantry who exploit the peasants and village laborers through usury, trade, employment of hired labor, the sale or letting out of land." While the Comintern was willing to collaborate with the entire peasantry during the first period of the liberation movement, the upper strata of the peasantry were expected to turn counterrevolutionary as the movement gained momentum. When the chips were down, therefore, the program would have to shift to "a revolutionary settlement of the agrarian question."[31]

The "revolutionary settlement of the agrarian question" was never accomplished, save in the case of Korea. Wherever the Communists have achieved power in these areas, the program of agrarian revolution, stipulated in the resolution of the Sixth Comintern Congress, soon became a dead letter.[32] Except for North Korea, where its application was dictated by the previous expropriation of native lands in favor of the Japanese, its place was taken by a series of moderate

[29] For the text of Lenin's remarks see *Selected Works*, X, 239–40.

[30] "Theses on National and Colonial Questions," *ibid.*, pp. 231–38. See also the speech of Zinoviev at the Congress of Eastern Peoples held in Baku, 1920 (*I. S'zed Narodov Vostoka September 1–8, 1920, Baku, Stenograficheskii Otchety* [Petrograd, 1920]).

[31] "The Revolutionary Movement in the Colonies and Semi-colonies; Resolution of the Sixth Congress of the Communist International" (adopted September 1, 1928), *International Press Correspondence*, VIII (1928), 1663–67.

[32] Except in Kiangsi and Fukien in the late 1920's and later discontinued. Similarly, the radical confiscatory program of 1946–49 was abandoned with the Communists' final accession to power.

reforms designed to mollify the poorer sections of the peasantry without alienating the "parasitic intermediate links" or impairing the productive capacity of agriculture. During the period when the Chinese Communists held sway in the border regions, for example, steps were taken to alleviate the lot of the poorer peasantry in such matters as rentals and interest rates; but wholesale confiscation and redistribution were not attempted to any great extent. Similarly, under the present regime in China, the revolutionary formula has been virtually dismissed as a propaganda appeal, once useful for enlisting the support of the poorer peasantry in the period before the Communist accession to power, but having no relevance to the problems of agriculture today. In fact, the propaganda appeal is now designed to reconcile the middle and wealthier sections of the Chinese peasantry to the new regime in political terms and to promote increased output and land improvements as prerequisites to a program of industrialization.[33] Without the active intervention of a Communist-oriented intelligentsia, a large-scale peasant movement in China as well as in the region of southeast Asia, if successful, would not go beyond agrarian reform pure and simple. The end goal would be Sun Yat-sen's and Stambulisky's rather than Lenin's, given the essentially static and conservative temper of the bulk of the peasant populations. As matters stand now, however, the schedule of agrarian reform under Communist sponsorship has definitely been subordinated to the long-range perspectives of industrialization with a program of collectivization in store for the future when conditions are more favorable to its success.[34] Accordingly, the imperatives of the "New Democracy" require a shift in the main incidence of Communist appeal to secure for the regime a base of support more in accord with its long-range plans.

The shift is equally apparent in the industrial field, where attempts are being made to enlist the support of the "national burgeoisie" during an indefinite transition period pending the introduction of "genuine" socialism. The present program envisions a form of limited state-sponsored and state-regulated capitalist enterprise to promote

[33] Liu Shao-chi, "On Agrarian Reform in China," *For a Lasting Peace, for a People's Democracy!* July 21, 1950, pp. 3–4; see also Teh Kao, "Peasants in the New China," *For a Lasting Peace, for a People's Democracy!* October 13, 1950, p. 2. For a summary of the history of the Communist agrarian program see F. C. Lee, "Land Redistribution in Communist China," *Pacific Affairs,* March, 1948, pp. 20–32.

[34] Mao Tse-tung, *On the Present Situation and Our Tasks* (East China Liberation Publishers, 1946); see also remarks of Liu Shao-chi in *People's China,* July 16, 1950.

the process of industrialization,[35] and the attractions now being employed to enlist entrepreneurial co-operation are strangely reminiscent of the "infant-industry" argument so familiar in "imperialist" countries.[36]

An identical transposition of appeal may also be detected in the program of Ho Chi-minh's newly organized Laodong (Workers') party in Viet-Nam.[37] Its program proclaims it the leader of a national united front comprising *all* classes, parties, and races, and its leading motif is the need to oust the French oppressors who are charged not only with exploiting Viet-Namese workers but also native landlords and capitalists who must pay a tribute to the French in the form of high prices for imports and the sale of their own products at depressed prices.[38] The socialist regime is indefinitely postponed until such time as the country is ready for it, and in the meantime

the national bourgeoisie must be encouraged, assisted and guided in their undertakings, so as to contribute to the development of the national economy. The right of the patriotic landlords to collect rent in accordance with the law must be guaranteed.

Our agrarian policy mainly aims at present in carrying out the reduction of land rent and interest . . . regulation of the leasehold system, provisional allocation of land formerly owned by imperialists to poorer peasants, redistribution of communal lands, rational use of land belonging to absentee landlords.[39]

To say, then, that the Communist program in the underdeveloped areas of Asia is designed purely and simply as an appeal to the poorest and landless sections of the peasant population is to indulge in an oversimplification of the facts. The Communist appeal is rather a complicated function of the total interplay of political forces in these areas and has therefore tended to shift both in direction and in content with the degree of influence and political power exercised by the Communist parties. The only constant element among all these changes

[35] See, e.g., Mao Tse-tung, *On People's Democratic Rule*, p. 12, and the text of the "Common Program of the People's Political Consultative Conference of 1949" included as an appendix to Mao's speech, esp. p. 19.

[36] Wu Min, "Industry of People's China Grows," *For a Lasting Peace, for a People's Democracy!* November 17, 1950, p. 4. This outright nationalistic appeal to the interests of domestic business groups is also plainly apparent in the latest draft program of the Indian Communist party (see *For a Lasting Peace, for a People's Democracy!* May 11, 1951, p. 3).

[37] Actually a revival of the Communist party dissolved in 1945.

[38] Viet-Nam News Agency in English Morse to Southeast Asia, April 12, 1951.

[39] Viet-Nam News Agency in English Morse to Southeast Asia, March 18 and April 10, 1951.

has been the abiding appeal of the Communist system to certain sections of the intelligentsia. Whether the new dispensation of the appeal can be expected to evoke the same degree of sympathetic response from the "national bourgeoisie" and the more prosperous peasantry as the discarded slogan of outright land confiscation had for the impoverished peasants is open to considerable doubt. The avowed transitional character of the program of the "People's Democracy" is alone sufficient to rob these appeals of any sustained response. It does not require any high degree of political sophistication on the part of the "national bourgeoisie," for example, to realize that a full measure of co-operation with a Communist-controlled regime would only serve to hasten its own extinction. How seriously such a withdrawal of support would affect the fortunes of a Communist regime would depend to a crucial extent on the speed with which it could find a substitute support in newly evolved social groups with a vested stake in its continued existence. Some indication of how the problem is visualized by the leaders of the Communist regime in China may be gleaned from the following remarks made by Liu Shao-chi in a speech to Chinese businessmen last year:

As Communists we consider that you are exploiting your workers; but we realize that, at the present stage of China's economic development, such exploitation is unavoidable and even socially useful. What we want is for you to go ahead and develop production as fast as possible and we will do what we can to help you. You may be afraid of what will happen to you and your families when we develop from New Democracy to Socialism. But you need not really be afraid. If you do a really good job in developing your business, and train your children to be first-class technical experts, you will be the obvious people to put in charge of the nationalized enterprise and you may find that you earn more as managers of a socialized enterprise than as owners.[40]

For the time being the challenge which confronts the West in its efforts to deny the underdeveloped areas of southeast Asia to the Communist appeal is therefore compounded of two distinct elements. The more obvious of these is, of course, the problem of depriving the Communists of their actual and potential "mass base" by an adequate program of technical aid and economic reform designed to remove the blight of poverty and exploitation from the scheme of things heretofore in force in these areas. The other and more imponderable aspect of this twofold challenge requires the development of an

[40] Quoted by M. Lindsay in *New China*, ed. O. van der Sprenkel (London, 1950), p. 139.

ethos and system of values which can compete successfully with the attraction exercised by communism for those sections of the native intelligentsia which have been the source and mainstay of its leadership. To date, there is little evidence that the West is prepared to meet either of these challenges on terms commensurate with its gravity.

12

THE POINTS OF THE COMPASS

Richard Lowenthal

Our thinking about world affairs has come more and more to revolve around the relation between the familiar East-West conflict and that other complex of problems which somebody has termed the "North-South struggle": the pressure of the underdeveloped have-not nations, with their new pride of independence and their rapidly growing populations, to obtain both more material aid for their own development and more influence on the world stage.

In both cases, we are dealing with the impact of revolutionary social changes and ideologies on the balance of forces in the world and the prospects of peace or war; yet the two movements concerned—totalitarian Communism on one side and revolutionary nationalism on the other—remain distinct in their nature and effect.

Monistic minds, of course, are forever trying to "simplify" the issue by telling us that the one set of conflicts "really" is a part of the other, or at any rate ought to be. To the Communist doctrinaire, the rise of the new nations is just part of the world-wide struggle against capitalist imperialism, and must naturally be carried on under the guidance of the "socialist camp" headed by the Soviet Union. Just so, to some last-ditch defenders of colonial rule and "white supremacy," all movements for national independence and racial equality among the peoples of Asia and Africa appear as the result of "Communist machinations"—at least when they first manifest themselves. Conversely, we may be told by well-meaning Leftists that all our troubles with Communist Russia and China are just due to the natural desire of these late-comer nations for "a place in the sun," which is not basically different from the equivalent desire of, say, India; while hopeful conservatives (reported to include President de Gaulle) see the tensions between advanced, increasingly comfortable, Russia and lean and hungry China

Reprinted from *Encounter*, XV, No. 3 (September 1960), 22-28, by permission of the Editors and the author.

as part of the world-wide "North-South" pattern, and look to a re-alignment of Russia with the old industrial nations of the West in a common effort to control and civilise the have-not upsurge.

The common error of all these attempts to reduce all the world's troubles to a single formula, to group all the conflicts along a single East-West or North-South axis, is that they underestimate the effectiveness and persistence of human beliefs fanatically held, and hence the crucial importance of the presence or absence of totalitarian Communist ideology for the nature of any particular conflict. But besides the error, there is in all these simplified ideas of the contemporary world also the perception—now dim, now more distinct—of an important truth: that the Communist and Nationalist revolutions of our time, however different in their nature and impact, originate from broadly similar historical and social situations—that they are, in a sense, alternative responses to these situations.

In fact, all those Communist movements which have conquered power wholly or chiefly by their own efforts—those of Russia, Yugoslavia, China, and Vietnam—have done so in societies which were faced with unsolved development problems in various stages. All of them have conceived Communism not merely as a means to achieve an earthly paradise of social justice, but to catch up with the advanced industrial countries and overtake them; and it is now generally recognised that their methods have proved remarkably successful in approaching the latter, though not the former objective. It is, above all, as an engine for the forced modernisation of an underdeveloped society that Communism is to-day admired by large sections of the intelligentsia of the new nations, while it is the peculiar price of using that engine—in ideology, in institutions of permanent totalitarian rule, and in subjection to Soviet imperialism—which repels many of them.

The real link between the future course of the East-West conflict and the rise of the new nations, the key to the influence they are bound to exert on each other, thus lies in the choice of a road of development confronting the Nationalist movements and the intelligentsia as their leading stratum. The crucial questions are: (1) Which are the factors in the situation of an underdeveloped country that favour a totalitarian solution to its problems? (2) What are the practicable alternatives? And (3) What influence is one or the other choice likely to have both on the country's internal evolution and on its relations with the outside world?

These questions form the underlying theme of Professor Hugh Seton-Watson's study of the post-war world. Contrary to its somewhat misleading title,* this is not just another survey of the Cold War, but a thoughtful and original discussion of the totalitarian and Nationalist revolutionary forces which in the author's view now form much of the stuff of world politics. Its reader will not find, e.g., any systematic account of the course and motivations of American foreign policy since the last war, but a wealth of information on the world's crisis areas and the history of revolutionary movements in Asia, Africa, and Latin America as well as on the Soviet Empire.

It would be futile as well as presumptuous for me to attempt to summarise the contents of this storehouse of historical and social facts, or to try to give an idea of the sober independence of judgment and massive good sense which Professor Seton-Watson brings to bear on many concrete and critical issues. I prefer to be unfair to his work, and to concentrate on the argument of those central chapters, dealing with the forces of revolution and the nature of totalitarianism, which have a direct and general bearing on the problem of the crucial choice facing the underdeveloped countries.

This argument centres on the role of the "intelligentsia" in these countries—the group which has been torn from its traditional moorings by a secular, "Westernised" education, but cannot merge its identity, as did their Western predecessors at a corresponding stage of development, in a rising, individualist middle class, because the other elements of that middle class—private entrepreneurs and a modern civil service—are largely lacking. On the contrary, in some of the under-developed countries many of the younger, professionally trained officers are by social origin and outlook an extension of this new group, an "intelligentsia in uniform." It is this group which first becomes aware of the backwardness of its country and the poverty of its people, having learned to measure both by the standards of the advanced countries, and which, acting both from a "populist" sense of obligation to the people and from frustrated individual and collective ambition, becomes the leader of revolutionary movements for modernization.

Professor Seton-Watson points out that such a development is not inevitable. Where the ruling group of a country succeeds in com-bining thoroughgoing modernising reform from above with the pres-ervation of traditional authority, as in the Japan of the *Meiji* era after 1868, the new intelligentsia may be integrated in the new state and come to form part of a new upper stratum with its bureaucrats and state-licensed capitalists. At the same time, a thoughtful educational

* H. R. Seton-Watson: *Neither War nor Peace. The struggle for power in the post-war world.* London: Methuen, New York: Praeger, 1960.

policy that takes care to develop elementary village schools at the same pace as the training of the intellectual élite may avoid the yawning gap between the latter and the common people characteristic of so many underdeveloped countries. But such favourable conditions have only exceptionally been realised under a régime that retained some continuity with the past. In general, the intelligentsia is kept out in the cold as long as possible and correspondingly radicalised, be it by an independent autocracy of the traditional type or by foreign "imperialist" rulers. Hence when it comes to power, it does so at the head of a popular movement directed against the former régime—either after a direct revolutionary clash, or where this is avoided by timely withdrawal of the colonial suzerain, at least with a revolutionary ideology.

In most cases, then, a revolutionary-minded intelligentsia will sooner or later take charge of the modernisation of an underdeveloped country, whether ex-colonial or not. Professor Seton-Watson points out that resentment of traditional Western influence and real or alleged exploitation, impatience to catch up and get powerful quickly, and lack of understanding for the importance of limiting the exercise of power by objective legal standards and for the value of tolerance for divergent opinions are likely to exert great influence on the mentality of such a group, and to make it incline towards uncritical admiration of the totalitarian Communist recipe for rapid modernisation which has proved so strikingly successful in terms of power. He is, of course, well aware of such non-totalitarian Nationalist revolutions as that which created Kemalist Turkey, and of the fact that the final orientation of the revolutionary régimes created by the "intelligentsia in uniform" in the Middle East, or of the Nationalist movements that have lately taken over some of the former African colonies, is still open. But he offers no general reasons why a modernistic, "populist" intelligentsia, once it has embarked on the road of revolution, should be likely to reject totalitarianism.

Yet as so much of the future is seen to hinge on this question, it seems worth while to enquire whether another approach might not yield a more definite answer. Instead of starting from the intellectual and psychological profile of the Nationalist intelligentsia, let us have a look at the task confronting them—the problem of "development" itself.

An underdeveloped country is not one whose people suffer from an innate, biological lack of aptitude for industry and modern organisation; nor is it one, as the opposite legend maintains, whose people have been forcibly prevented from developing these aptitudes by foreign imperialist rule. An underdeveloped country is one whose traditional society did not allow the growth of sufficiently strong independent middle classes—the classes which in the West were the main promoters of the accumulation of capital, the creation of industrial enterprise, and the growth of a spirit of rational industrial discipline.

If such a country is exposed to the impact of Western capitalism from without, as almost all of them were successively in the past two centuries, its traditional social order is disrupted, but no functioning modern industrial society is automatically created in its place. Foreign enterprise may develop some extractive industries or export crops, but there will be no all-round growth of industry or improvement of agriculture. The subsistence economy of the countryside with its cottage industries may be ruined by the need for money payments and the import of cheap industrial goods, but no corresponding employment opportunities arise automatically for the rural overpopulation. Traditional beliefs are undermined by the impact of events rather than by missionary activity, but the ideas imported by Western missionaries or secular educators have no obvious relation to either the traditions of the country or its actual problems. Before, life may have been stagnant and poor if viewed from the outside, but it had a meaning that was understandable in terms of home-grown culture. Now this meaning, the assured role in society, is lost for millions at the same time as their material security. As a result, some may be richer, some poorer than before; most will have a longer life, if a colonial régime introduces modern medical methods; but nearly all will feel more miserable.

These effects are generally worse in countries which are open to the disruptive foreign impact without being colonised, than in countries where the "imperialists" take governmental responsibility: China and India are the classical examples. After the breakdown of the traditional order, the colonial power may ensure public security, health, a measure of education, the training of a civil service. But no colonial power in the age of *laissez-faire* ever dreamt of creating a new social order; none tackled the problem of all-round economic development.

The task of solving that problem, then, devolved on the Nationalist movements. It could, in the circumstances, only be attacked by public action—above all, public action of three kinds:

(1) a policy of forced saving to raise funds for development which might in favourable circumstances be combined with foreign loans or aid;

(2) a policy of state-directed investment, to ensure placing of these limited funds in such a way that all-round development would result, in-

cluding such tasks as road-building or canalisation as well as immediately profitable tasks, power as well as consumer goods, agricultural improvement as well as technical and administrative training; and

(3) the promotion of a cultural revolution to make people work-minded and development-minded, to tap human reserves by the emancipation of women, to overcome the countless obstacles to disciplined rational effort resulting from traditional superstition—in short, to achieve what reformation, counter-reformation, and enlightenment combined achieved over centuries in the West, and to do so in the atmosphere of a demoralising breakdown of tradition.

The achievement of these tasks is impossible with the methods of a liberal economy: if conditions were such that a liberal economy could work, the country would not have remained underdeveloped in the first place. It is extremely difficult in a liberal democracy, because it requires the concentration of a great deal of economic and social power in the state, and the constant taking of decisions which impose sacrifices and hurt many interests: the less the foreign aid and the greater the need for forced savings, the less likely is democracy to succeed. Finally, it requires the predominant role of an officially-favoured ideology, which in the circumstances can only be a secular ideology, to bring about the cultural revolution.

Consider now, in the light of the foregoing, the attractions of Communist totalitarianism for an underdeveloped country. In its Stalinist form, the Communist ideology has been specifically adjusted to deal with the problem of forced modernisation. If justifies a ruthless policy of forced savings in the name of "socialist industrialisation." It proclaims the superiority of planned investment by the state over *laissez-faire*. Finally, it furnishes the militant faith needed for the cultural revolution, with its materialist attack on traditional superstition, its glorification of dedicated, disciplined work for the community, its emphasis on production as the highroad to national power and individual liberation from misery. It invests the uprooting of traditional life, the frightening impact of social and technical change, the bitterness of years of sacrifice with a meaning. And, last not least, it justifies all the privileges a self-appointed but dedicated élite may require.

Thus, Communist totalitarianism does not only appeal to some of the prejudices and *ressentiments* of the Nationalist intelligentsia: it points a precise path for their modernising ambitions and offers a ready-made secular faith for enlisting the obedience of the masses. Yet there are also obvious drawbacks: they spring in part from the doctrinaire rigidity inherent in any totalitarian ideology, and in part from its links with Soviet imperialism.

An underdeveloped country that wants to plan for rapid development may need nationalising *powers* against recalcitrant domestic and foreign capitalists; it will not necessarily *wish* to drive out the few native industrialists it has. It may find the expropriation of absentee landowners vital to its purposes; it will hardly find the experience of collectivisation attractive. It may be both proud to get a heavy industry of its own and convinced of its genuine economic necessity; yet it may think twice before giving its development absolute priority over the need to improve agricultural yields or textile supplies for a rapidly growing population. A commitment to Communism would deprive its leaders of much, if not all, of their freedom of choice in these matters.

Again, a "populist" revolutionary intelligentsia about to take power in an underdeveloped country, however sincere in its desire to serve its people and raise their standard of living, may not be anxious to pledge itself to achieve a "classless society." Depending on the background of its national culture, it may find it unnecessary to prepare future trouble for itself by preaching a utopian doctrine. Yet without such a doctrine with its implied need for permanent revolution, it may find it possible to constitute itself openly as a bureaucratic élite while avoiding the specific form of totalitarian party rule, and to conduct the propaganda of the cultural revolution by other means.

Finally, while the Nationalist élites frequently start with a background of anti-Western emotions, nothing in their records suggest that they have an unconquerable aversion to Western economic aid, or even to Western private investments if offered in accordance with their laws and in the framework of their plans. Their natural preference is for taking aid from both sides while rejecting political interference from either. But the Communist dogma, with its basic assumption of irreconcilable conflict with the non-Communist world, justifies modernisation by the road of maximum sacrifice—the road of absolute priority for heavy industry—precisely on the ground that every other procedure would entail prolonged dependence on "the enemy." Even now, the Russians accuse the West of trying to keep the new nations backward and dependent by offering them help for agricultural improvement and consumer goods industries. With greater truth, we might suggest that they are seeking to create dependence on their empire, as well as on internal dictatorship, by seeking to commit these countries to lop-sided concentration on slowly-maturing goods, and to preempt their exports for years ahead as repayment for their loans.

Altogether, the advantages of an undoctrinaire approach to development planning, of an avoidance of egalitarian promises of a utopian type, and of keeping a new nation uncommitted in a divided world, are so striking that they go far to explain why, in most of the new nations, the initial attitude of the majority of the intelligentsia at any rate is *not* a truly totalitarian one—why their admiration for Communist achievements is in fact as eclectic as it is widespread.

It is precisely this eclecticism—the conscious, critical imitation of some features of the Communist model of modernisation, coupled with the equally conscious rejection of others—that constitutes the only practicable alternative to full-scale, ideological totalitarianism in many of these countries. Neither traditionalism nor imitation of Western institutions on a different stage of development offer such alternatives.

Traditionalist régimes are in many cases either unwilling or unable to embark on a serious programme of economic development; hence they become more vulnerable to revolutionary movements as the disruptive impact of the modern world makes itself felt from outside. Even where such a régime makes a determined effort at economic development with a reasonable degree of efficiency, it may find itself decisively handicapped by inability or unwillingness to enlist the loyal and responsible co-operation of the intelligentsia. And in the exceptional case where the intelligentsia is for a time successfully integrated in a régime combining traditional authority with modernistic policy, the alliance is apt to prove unstable because the roots of authority itself are being eaten away by the growth of a modern, secular society, until they can no longer withstand any serious shock. The vulnerability of social stagnation is illustrated to-day by the case of Iran, that of modernisation without co-operation of the intelligentsia by the fate of Nuri's Iraq and the present difficulties of South Vietnam, while the instability of intelligentsia integration under traditional authority is shown by the contrast between the remarkable achievement of the first sixty years of modern Japan (used as an example for successful non-revolutionary modernisation by Professor Seton-Watson) and the pre-war and post-war sequel.

As for the attempt to imitate Western liberal democratic institutions under different conditions, it may have a measure of success in the special case where a strong tradition of respect for law and individual rights coincides with the stabilising force of a virtually uncontested forward-looking national leadership, as in Nehru's India. Even there it is at least an open question whether the use made of these institutions by vested interests to slow down urgent economic and social reform measures will not undermine them to a dangerous degree.

Elsewhere, the sincere defenders of Western democratic ideals are apt to suffer the fate of the Mensheviks, like Dr. Sjahrir in Indonesia; while the more power-conscious imitators of Western parliamentary forms tend to create a caricature which is unable either to cope with the problems of modernisation or to win and hold the allegiance of the intelligentsia and the masses, as may be seen in South Korea and the Philippines.

Given the magnitude of the problem of modernisation, and the obvious weaknesses of most traditional or pseudo-liberal régimes, the remarkable phenomenon is not so much the prevalence of revolutionary ferment in so many underdeveloped countries, but the fact that so comparatively few of the revolutionary movements have been captured by totalitarian ideology. So far from being the "natural" outlook of any revolutionary intelligentsia, totalitarian dogma seems to be adopted by most of its members only as a last resort, when all efforts to gain power with a more independent or eclectric programme of modernisation have proved obviously futile, and when the rising despair of both the intelligentsia and the masses cries out for a vision of secular salvation.

Indeed, the original attitude with which the Nationalist revolutionary intelligentsia first becomes conscious of its mission, and which we have described as "eclectic" from the viewpoint of the practical tasks of modernisation, is based on an ideological outlook of its own—an outlook which Professor Seton-Watson, in a happy analogy with the familiar history of the Russian revolutionary movement of the 19th century, has described as "populist." The common characteristic of all populist ideologies and movements is the search for a synthesis between the basic values on which the traditional culture of the society in question was founded and the need for modernisation. In contrast to the traditionalist régimes and movements, the populist intelligentsia is aware that these values can only be preserved by a radical reinterpretation and in a transformed institutional framework. In contrast to the bearers of alien, totalitarian ideas or to spiritually uprooted "Westernisers," it feels that those specific values must be preserved if the cultural revolution is not to lead to a nihilistic destruction of the common culture of their society, but is to have the invigorating effect of a true Reformation.

This populist formula covers such diverse attempts at ideological synthesis and practical eclecticism as are represented by the Buddhist-Marxist régime in Burma, the Indonesian Nationalists, or the Egyptian Council of the Revolution. They all correspond to the deeply-felt need to adopt Western rational techniques of production and power while preserving what is viable in the traditional culture—they are attempts to react to the "schism in the soul" brought about by the impact of modern conditions from outside. There is nothing inherently unrealistic in such an attempt, as the example of Russian populism might suggest at a superficial glance; for it may well be argued that the Russian Bolsheviks ultimately succeeded only by accepting the same task and transforming their Western Marxism in accordance with certain specifically Russian traditions. But particular attempts may well fail either because their exponents prove naïve and unrealistic in the execution of their programme, or because they are successfully kept from power by the defenders of the old régime until disruption and despair have so far advanced that the totalitarians appear to offer the only solution.

In fact, the earlier the stage in the disintegration of the traditional order in which the revolutionary intelligentsia comes to power, and the smoother its path has been made by the previous régime, the less likely does it seem to embrace totalitarian dogma. Moreover, experience suggests that the Communist type of totalitarian movement can only win power if circumstances permit it successfully to appropriate the nationalist element in the populist tradition, and if its leaders have gained a degree of tactical independence from Soviet "advice" which has hitherto been exceptional. The only true Communist revolutions which have so far gained power outside Russia's sphere of military domination—those of Yugoslavia, China, and North Vietnam—have all been led by men who, thanks to unusual circumstances, had succeeded in emancipating themselves from Russian leading strings in the actual conduct of their struggle, and who had used this freedom of movement to capture the leadership of a national uprising against invading or colonial powers. The record hardly suggests that such a course is typical, let alone inevitable for the revolutionary movements of underdeveloped countries, or for the intelligentsia as their leading stratum.

This is not to say that the non-totalitarian régimes of the revolutionary intelligentsia, whether civilian or military, whether semi-democratic or dictatorial, will not commit many costly blunders due to emotionalism and inexperience, or will be models of stability. The Kemalist régime in Turkey committed some appalling acts of cruelty, and by the time it handed over power in a genuinely free election it still had not created a stable foundation for democracy (as we have recently had occasion to note). The régime of the Thakins in Burma—perhaps the most tolerant and democratic of the intelligentsia régimes —at first nearly foundered in civil war, and later had to be rescued from its internal intrigues by a period of military rule. We may yet see similar crises in some of the newly-independent states of Africa. Yet looking back, the remarkable thing about both the Turkish and the Burmese cases is that they have succeeded in creating a sense of growing national unity and legitimacy which has outlasted the crises, and in the process seem to have largely immunised their peoples against totalitarian ideas.

The reason for that success seems to be that these régimes have convinced their peoples that a genuine and independent effort was being made, in however blundering a fashion, to solve their problems of survival in a rapidly changing world by planned modernisation. It is in that sense that those régimes are a practicable alternative to totalitarianism. It follows that I warmly agree with Professor Seton-Watson's conclusion that the Western powers should not worry too much whether a particular régime in such a country is democratic in the sense of Western liberal democracy, but be content if it is non-totalitarian, and above all not tied to the Soviet bloc. Yet I should go farther than he does in saying that we have a positive interest in fostering modernising régimes committed to planned development rather than régimes of tradition stagnation, and régimes working with the nationalist intelligentsia rather than those working against it, even if the former do not stick to the forms of parliamentary democracy and the latter do. And I should base this recommendation not on the Left-wing ideological grounds that economic planning is "socialism" and socialism is more important than democracy (I happen to think that there can be no socialism without democracy, and that there is none in Communist countries), but on the pragmatic grounds that such planning is urgent for freeing the people of these countries from abysmal poverty and at the same time keeping them out of the clutches of the Soviet bloc. Democracy and socialism may come later.

But, the reader may well ask, if you are prepared to compromise and co-operate with "development dictatorships," what then is your objection to totalitarianism? This question of the difference between totalitarian and other dictatorships has been treated in masterly fashion in Professor Seton-Watson's book. Here I can only pick out a few salient points.

The first is that totalitarian dictatorship recognises no private sphere outside its grasp—that it aspires to total power as a means to achieve a total transformation of man and society. Every dictatorship ignores constitutional limitations of state power; totalitarianism ignores *all* limitations. Every dictatorship suppresses organised opposition and public criticism; totalitarian dictatorship suppresses all forms of autonomous organisation and all independent sources of information, permitting only those that directly and positively serve the purposes of the ruling party. This follows from the need to make people not only submit to the government's policies, but to compel their active and enthusiastic participation in the changes planned for their lives: not only the economic and social, but the cultural revolution is to be enforced by the ruthless use of political power.

In the second place, the totalitarian dictatorship seeks to perpetuate itself indefinitely, because its ideological aim can never be fully achieved. It does not justify itself by the transitory need to overcome an acute crisis or to solve a definite task of modernisation, but by the mission to usher in "the end of pre-history"—heaven on earth. It is based not simply on the downfall of traditional authority under the impact of secularisation, but on its replacement by a secular religion, a political messianism that is to end all evil among men by institutional means. There is, of course, no guarantee that dictatorships that proclaim a transitory purpose will abdicate when this purpose has been fulfilled, but it is no accident that a number of them have done so after longer or shorter periods. Yet as the example of Russia and now China shows, a dictatorship that sets itself chiliastic aims can always find a new task to justify its continuation—it tends to make the revolution permanent.

Lastly, the claims of totalitarian ideology are in its nature worldwide; hence totalitarian dictatorships live in irreconcilable conflict with any state that does not recognise that claim. While that conflict need not in every phase be fought out by violent means, and need not lead to world war in any phase, it does produce a state of permanent tension with the non-totalitarian world in which all means may be used according to expediency—whether at any particular moment that state of tension may be labelled "peaceful coexistence" or "cold war." Since at present the Soviet bloc is the only totalitarian power bloc in the world, we are forced to live in such a state of permanent, worldwide conflict with the Soviet bloc—whether we like it or not.

But we are not forced to live in a similar state of permanent conflict with every national revolution or nationalist dictatorship in an underdeveloped country, even if its rulers begin their work of independent modernisation with a strong traditional distrust of the "imperialist" West. On the contrary, it is our interest to help those countries to achieve their goals of economic development as quickly and with as little sacrifice as possible, so as to provide no cause for the distrust to harden into permanent ideological hostility.

The tension between "North and South" is bound to diminish as the underdeveloped countries catch up, and "South" automatically comes to resemble "North" economically. The conflict between East and West can only disappear if the totalitarian, ideologically dominated régimes disappear, for only then will "East" come to resemble "West" politically.

That is the difference between the points of the compass.